Merchant,
Soldier,
Sage

THE PENGUIN PRESS
New York
2013

Merchant,
Soldier,
Sage

A HISTORY OF THE WORLD

IN THREE CASTES

DAVID PRIESTLAND

THE PENGUIN PRESS
Published by the Penguin Group
Penguin Group (USA) Inc., 375 Hudson Street,
New York, New York 10014, U.S.A.

USA • Canada • UK • Ireland • Australia
New Zealand • India • South Africa • China

Penguin Books Ltd, Registered Offices:
80 Strand, London WC2R 0RL, England
For more information about the Penguin Group visit penguin.com

First American edition
Published in 2013 by The Penguin Press,
a member of Penguin Group (USA) Inc.

Library of Congress Cataloging-in-Publication Data

Priestland, David.
Merchant, soldier, sage : a history of the world in three castes /
David Priestland.
p.   cm.
Originally published: London : Allen Lane, 2012.
Includes bibliographical references and index.
ISBN 978-1-59420-310-7
1. History, Modern.   2. Economic history.   3. Power (Social sciences)—
History.   4. Elite (Social sciences)—History.   5. Social structure—Economic
aspects—History.   6. Social values—History.   I. Title.
D210.P935   2013
305.09—dc23
20120468111

Printed in the United States of America
1   3   5   7   9   10   8   6   4   2

DESIGNED BY MEIGHAN CAVANAUGH

For Maria

CONTENTS

═══════════

Introduction

Future generations will see 2008 as a year of tectonic shifts—a year to be classed alongside 1917, 1929, 1945, 1968, and 1989.

Three seemingly unrelated crises in rapid succession in the summer of 2008 showed that the world had reached a turning point: in July, oil prices hit $147 a barrel, forcing us to recognize the environmental limits of economic growth; in August, we witnessed a major challenge to America's sixty-year global hegemony when it looked on powerless while Russia invaded its ally and client Georgia; and in September, the collapse of a major American investment bank, Lehman Brothers, finally destroyed the credibility of the ultra-free-market capitalism that had reigned virtually unchallenged for three decades.

For a few months it really seemed that a fundamental change in the world order was in the offing; even the conservative French president, Nicolas Sarkozy, took to reading Marx's *Das Kapital*. Yet the drama of that autumn has produced not cathartic crisis and renewal but a sense of powerlessness, confusion, and unease.

Political leaders tell us that after a quick dose of virtuous austerity (in Europe) or can-do optimism (in the United States) we will soon return to the sunny uplands of the pre-2008 world. But these assurances convince few. Most anticipate several years of crippling debt, falling living standards, and rising inequality. And in the long run, we have no real sense of how, in this global free market, the West can ever match the dynamism of rising Asian powers without driving wages and living standards down to far lower levels—with all the personal suffering, social disruption, and political conflict that would ensue. Nor can we see how any of this might allow for improved living standards for the mass of the world's population that still lives in poverty.

But while we are skeptical of narratives promising a phoenix-like rebirth from the embers of hard times, few see any real alternative. Some economists and public intellectuals have identified a "crisis of capitalism," but they have generally been reluctant to engage with the enormity of what has happened.[1]

This book does not pretend to offer a blueprint for world recovery and enduring human happiness. Rather, it seeks to lay the foundation for solutions by urging that we rethink our history; for we can start to solve our present problems only if we have a clear-eyed view of the past. Before we can go forward, we have to go back—to understand how we got to where we are, what has gone wrong, and why.

A New Narrative

Unfortunately, the most influential current view of our history in the West—a retread of the nineteenth-century "Whiggish" belief in inevitable liberal progress—has made it very difficult for us to think our way through this crisis. According to one popular reading, the crisis was caused by greed and folly, similar events have happened before, and, while the effects will be unpleasant, they are of little long-term historical significance.[2] With a better moral framework and a little regulation, it is assumed, capitalist globalization and liberal democracy remain the inevitable destination points of history.[3]

There is another, Marxist view: that we are witnessing a fundamental crisis of capitalism, brought about by overproduction and a collapse in profits.[4] But this is implausible, for consumer capitalism seems to offer prospects for economic growth in many parts of the world outside the West—something that did not seem likely in the 1930s. And though environmental limits pose many more problems for current economic models, it is still difficult to believe that capitalism will collapse in the foreseeable future and a new society, free of markets, will emerge.

Yet while the crisis does not mark the end of capitalism as a system, it is more serious than the liberal optimists believe; rather, it is a change on the scale of 1929 or the 1970s: it signals the crisis of a particular form of capitalism—what I call a "merchant" social, economic, political, and ideological order that rose to preeminence some thirty years ago. This book will show how this system became so powerful in the twentieth century and why it has failed to achieve economic stability and to meet modern expectations of equality and social justice. But it will begin by going back to the origins of the merchant order, as human societies entered the modern world. For neither Whiggish nor Marxist histories help us to diagnose our problems. We need an alternative history, and this book will suggest a new approach.

Although it has become academically fashionable to deny the validity of any "grand narrative" of history, on the grounds that they all collapse into naive fables of progress, it is still possible to seek the forces of historical change without suggesting inevitable movement toward a particular end point. There is now, moreover, a great deal of excellent historical research on the broader trends of global history that can help us in that quest. This, then, is a book on the roots of the current crisis for a general readership, not an academic study. But it seeks to build on a rich research literature that avoids simplistic assumptions about the nature of change, without denying our ability to see the broad sweep of historical development.

Introducing the "Castes"

To begin with, we need to think anew about the forces that impel historical change. For Marx, it was *economic* interest groups, or "classes," that were always the motors of history; more fashionable today, though, is the view that the conflict between *ideologies* was the real story of the modern era.[5] So, while it has become common to believe that we, as individuals, are motivated by personal economic interests, when it comes to groups, societies, and nations, we are more likely to concede that ideas and values matter—hence our tendency to think about world politics as a series of ideological clashes: "democracy" *versus* "totalitarianism" or "liberalism" *versus* "Islamofascism." A fashionable alternative has been to emphasize culture rather than ideology; thus, for the American academic Samuel Huntington, world history has been a series of "clashes of civilizations" among, for example, Anglo-Saxons, Muslims, Hindus, and Confucians,[6] while for the journalist Thomas Friedman, the era since the 1990s has pitted tolerant, cosmopolitan Lexus drivers against more rooted and parochial olive-tree tenders.[7]

But we are motivated by both values and economic interests, and one of the crucial ways in which they are connected is through what we do at work—our occupations. Of course, our views and values are shaped by many other things; family, gender, and ethnic identity have an influence, as does—importantly—our generational experience. There is, therefore, no simple and inevitable relationship between occupation and worldview, but occupation plays a major role in forming our attitudes. So, for example, sociological research has shown that we are more likely to have egalitarian views on economics if we work for the public sector than if we are in the private sector;[8] and we are more likely to be culturally liberal if we have an occupation that grants us some autonomy than if we work in a highly micromanaged job.[9] This is partly because we tend to find work that suits our values and education, and partly because our work experience molds those values. It is as difficult to be a free marketeer in a local social-work department as it is to be a socialist in an investment bank. It follows that if we are to get on with our colleagues, win promotions, or achieve status, we have to accept the fundamental values of the work-place—its customs and forms of behavior, or "*habitus,*" as the French thinker Pierre Bourdieu has called them; we can fake them, of course, but only the most Machiavellian can keep up the pretense for very long. And it is often those who begin as phonies who end up as the most con-vinced of true believers.

This has been the case in many societies throughout history, and it is something the ancients understood. They saw society not as an aggrega-tion of atomized individuals, nor as Marx's economic classes (where peo-ple are categorized according to their property),[10] nor as ideological parties, but as occupational groups, each of which, they believed, had its own ethos. In the medieval West they were called "orders," after Roman military contingents (*ordines*); and in India they are still called "castes" (from the Portuguese word for "pure"—though Indians themselves used the Sanskrit term *varna,* or "color," because they assigned a color to each group).[11] According to ancient Hindu ideas, each *varna* has its own *dharma,* or morality and way of life—concepts that have some parallels with Bourdieu's *habitus.* "Caste," then, is the term that I shall use in this book, for it allows us to see social groups not only as self-interested bodies seeking economic advantage but also as embodiments of ideas and life-styles, which they often seek to impose on others.

This is not to say that modern societies are similar to ancient India or that a "caste system" of social discrimination exists in most countries today—though its legacy survives in parts of India. In true caste systems, people are born into occupational groups, which are organized into rigid hierarchies, often harshly enforced. Modern societies, in contrast, are much more mobile and egalitarian, as they are less dominated by aristo-cratic values of hierarchy and deference. They are also more integrated: occupational groups no longer have their own separate rules of marriage,

mores, or morality, and many people subscribe to universal, Enlightenment values of human equality and freedom—at least in theory. National
and other identities bind different social groups together, and in the past
century many societies have become more culturally democratic. But
even so, the division of labor, so necessary for economic productivity, inevitably creates differences of outlook and culture, and I use the term
"caste" to capture those differences. The word is also helpful because it
points to the continuing presence of social hierarchies today. As I shall
argue, the dominance of one particular caste—the merchant—in the last
thirty years may have helped to dissolve older hierarchies based on aristocratic status and newer ones founded on technocratic expertise. However,
it has at the same time increased economic inequalities, while entrench-
ing hierarchies of power, especially in the workplace—an issue that I
shall return to in the epilogue.

So what are the principal castes? Thinkers in many premodern, agrarian societies identified four: sages/priests, rulers/warriors, merchants, and
peasants. Sometimes they found more, sometimes fewer. In the Christian
West, it was common to list only three: those who pray (*oratores*), those
who fight (*bellatores*), and those who work (*laboratores*). And because most
people followed the professions of their fathers and forefathers, occupations were often closed to outsiders; people were born into their occupational group and raised in its customs and ethos. Much, of course, has
changed in the past three centuries: work has become more specialized,
occupations have multiplied, and people are no longer expected to inherit
their work and their outlook from kith and kin (though they often do).
Meanwhile, some occupational groups have waxed and others waned. (In
parts of the world, aristocracies and peasantries have all but disappeared.)
But the values of the old groups persist in very broad outline to this day.
This is clearest in present-day India, where many people still assume that
somebody of a Brahmin (sagely) family background will have a different
outlook than somebody from a Kshatriya (warrior/ruler) caste or a member of a merchant subcaste, like the *banias*;[12] many also make discrimina-

tory judgments against those from the Shudra (worker) caste. India is unusual, but I shall argue that we can best understand our recent history if we appreciate the role of these "castes" and their values, with their distant roots in the ancient four occupational-cultural groups: the aristocrat and soldier, the sage or priest, the merchant, and the worker or peasant.

In most premodern societies, the warrior aristocracy was the dominant caste. Rulers were expected to combine two closely connected roles: the heroic, fame-seeking warrior and the paternalistic "father of the people," and this caste created intensely hierarchical societies at home and empires abroad. While this group has declined in the West, we can still see its remnants in a cluster of values associated with strongman rulers, from Russia's Vladimir Putin to Iraq's Saddam Hussein. It even survives in a very reduced form in the British royal family: the Queen is supposedly the nation's matriarch, while her male descendants go about in military gear upon their modern warhorses (helicopters) in far-flung outposts (the Falklands). But often the warrior ethos has been separated from the paternalistic one: Genghis Khan's Mongol hordes, modern military units, and Los Angeles drug gangs all have mimicked patterns of brotherhood within the group while being anything but familial in their dealings with "outsiders."[13] And as the aristocrat, together with his values of paternalism and inherited status, declined in the course of the nineteenth and twentieth centuries, this "democratized" warrior became increasingly common.

Sages—the literate manipulators of ideas—also originally had two functions: as "clerics," or religious figures, and as "clerks," or officials. The sage-priest's role as ideological defender or reformer of the prevailing order has been adopted by a range of modern types, from speechwriters, journalists, and academics to latter-day "holy men"—with their culture of inspiration, passion, and spontaneity, seen, for example, in the Shelleys of the Romantic era or figures such as Mahatma Gandhi, Martin Luther King Jr., and Bob Dylan in the twentieth century.[14] But it is the other form of sage-priest—the clerk, or expert "sage-technocrat"—who is more dominant, and in much of the world his culture of both expert professionalism and bureaucracy has increasingly eclipsed aristocratic forms of rule.

The third ethos—the merchant's—has penetrated most areas of life today, but, unsurprisingly, it can be seen in its purest form in trade and finance. The merchant is often Janus-faced: with his flexibility, love of networking, and willingness to trade with all, regardless of class, ethnicity, or religion, he shows his "soft," tolerant, and cosmopolitan face. He has, at times in history, played a significant role in undermining old hierarchies. But he also has a much "harder," more moralistic, hierarchical, and authoritarian aspect that can become apparent when in conflict with others. The switch from soft to hard can occur when the merchant is faced with international competition. But it has happened most frequently in the merchant's struggles with peasants, artisans, and workers. For while his love of efficiency and innovation has undoubtedly helped to promote higher living standards for many, his tendency to pursue the highest profit in the quickest time is often difficult to align with the interests of particular communities—for instance, when he refuses to invest for the long term, in case he misses out on better opportunities, or seeks as much profit as possible from the exploitation of labor. That compulsion inevitably creates tensions, and historically the hard merchant has often allied with warrior elites to defend his interests. Debt is a particularly common cause of conflict, for while the merchant favors credit to keep the wheels of the economy turning, he tends to demand repayment and harsh austerity in downturns.

These three castes have been dominant throughout much of world history—hence their presence in the title of this book. But this does not mean that the fourth caste, the "workers"—peasants, artisans, and proletarians—should be neglected. With the rise of industrial capitalism, they developed a powerful culture of community solidarity to defend their interests. They have also tended to favor economic equality—understandably, given that they have little power in market economies—

and in the course of the twentieth century they successfully fought for welfare states and higher wages, especially in the West.

This "caste" vision of society is an unusual one, and some will reasonably ask how this archaic view of the world, with its cast of Tolkienian types, can be serious history. Surely modern societies have changed too much for these ancient ideas to be relevant? Is it really likely that there should be such strong continuities between the medieval and modern worlds, or that categories of medieval analysis—founded as they were on observations of agrarian societies—should have any power today?

In fact, however, there are very good reasons for the castes, with their associated cultures and values, to persist over long periods of time. Human beings have many different objectives, but if they are to achieve them, they need to exercise power, by mastering the environment and establishing some form of social cooperation. They form a wide variety of social networks and institutions to help them achieve their goals, from extended families to professional armies, each with different forms of organization. But some types of networks—such as militaries, commercial companies, and bureaucracies—are more effective at exercising power and gaining social acceptance than others, and it is these that tend to survive across societies and history, even as particular occupations and economic structures change.[15] It is also likely that these groups will develop their own cultures, though the sharpness of the differences between them varies enormously among societies.

In modern societies castes are very rarely found in pure form; they mutate and merge with one another over time. Nor are they always to be found in the occupations one might expect. Today the merchant is powerful in some areas of business—such as banking and commerce—but less so in complex industrial firms, where the sage-technocrat has greater influence, in the form of managers. This is why the term "capitalism" is not always a helpful one, for capitalism takes many forms, some more dominated by merchant institutions, such as investment banks, others by sage-technocratic organizations, such as large corporations, and others by paternalistic, boss-led cultures, as in the "patrimonial capitalism" of Russian business today.[16] Similarly, modern states in developed societies are usually dominated by technocratic bureaucracies, but before the nineteenth century they were controlled by military aristocracies, and in the past thirty years they have been increasingly influenced by merchants and their values.

The Locomotives of History

It is my argument, then, that the conflicts and alliances among these castes and their values as they adapt to the changing environment—economic, technological, geopolitical, and ideological—are some of the main locomotives of history. Societies are transformed when an alliance of groups, embodying particular caste values, is able to impose itself more successfully than its rivals. It then achieves "hegemony," penetrating other areas of society, replicating itself in other occupations and organizations, through either force or persuasion.[17] In premodern societies, for instance, aristocracy not only dominated politics and landholding; its paternalistic habits shaped all realms of life. Businesses were often run like aristocratic families, with a "master" controlling the lives of apprentices and journeymen as if they were his children. But today, it is merchant values that are increasingly dominant in most areas of life, even in such apparently alien spheres as the aristocracy. To take a trivial but telling example, the heir to the British throne has established a multimillion-pound business using his Duke of Cornwall crest to market organic biscuits and other luxury food as "Duchy Originals." We might think this is perfectly normal behavior, but our ancestors would have been profoundly shocked by such an extraordinary violation of caste norms.

So why do caste alliances rise and fall? To answer the question, we need to look at both economic and social structures, on the one hand, and ideas, on the other: to flourish, castes have to be able to adapt to social and economic change and also to justify themselves according to the values prevalent at the time.[18] Paternalistic aristocrats did well on both counts in agrarian societies. Differences in power between peasant producers and military rulers were enormous, aristocrats plausibly offered protection at times of insecurity, and their dominance was justified by religious worldviews. But as societies became more urban, commercial, and mobile, and more egalitarian ways of looking at the world took hold, not only did aristocrats lose economic power, but their acute sense of hierarchy and status alienated their "inferiors." Their arrogance then united their caste opponents, in some cases triggering classic revolutions—whether the French Revolution of 1789 or its Russian successor in 1917.

The new rising castes of the nineteenth and twentieth centuries all claimed to meet the two major demands of the post-aristocratic world—economic prosperity and greater social equality—but in different ways. Sage-technocrats provided long-term planning and expertise, which were invaluable as industries and states became more complex. They also challenged rigid aristocratic rankings in the name of a meritocracy based on education. Merchants were equally opposed to aristocratic hierarchies, but they offered different economic solutions, based on flexible trade. However, both castes found it much more difficult to forge alliances with workers, who demanded a more radical, economic equality. It was only after serious conflicts between merchants and sages, on one side, and workers, on the other, that a postwar compromise was reached in the West, based on a Social Democratic sage/worker alliance. However, its dominion was not to last. The growth of welfare states and mass higher education after the Second World War contributed to the rise of a new type of sage, a "creative" caste of "people-centered" professionals—teachers, social workers, and doctors—who prized post-1960s values of autonomy and equality of gender, race, and sexuality.[19] Together with their counterparts in a more flexible, consumer-oriented business world, they rebelled against old technocratic hierarchies and cultural illiberalism—opening the way for the dominance of the merchant.

For the past thirty years, the merchant and his ethos have been preeminent in much of the developed world: his love of efficiency and productivity has fueled a cornucopia of consumption; his tolerant cosmopolitanism has held up the promise of a world bound together by trade and commerce, in which war is unthinkable. Meanwhile, his view of the world as a vast market—a democracy of consumers—has helped to dissolve the ethnic hierarchies of previous orders and forge a greater cultural equality. With all of these advantages, it is hardly surprising that the problems of rule by the merchant have often been less obvious than those brought by the other castes.

The disadvantages of all of these caste orders become clear, sometimes rather suddenly, after a major failure—defeat in war, economic crisis, social revolution, or all three together—and a collapse of this kind can clear the way for a previously marginalized caste competitor. Marx emphasized the role of class revolutions—or economic struggles; these were the "locomotives of history," and they certainly can be important. However, the failures of the ruling castes, and the ideological crises that accompany them, also bring change, and elite implosions can be more important than revolutionary explosions. Social orders can crumble when their rulers believe that they are failing. The classic example is Mikhail Gorbachev's loss of faith in Marxist-Leninist solutions in the 1980s, his efforts to reform the system, and the sudden, unexpected collapse of the Soviet Communist system between 1989 and 1991.

Caste orders are at their most vulnerable when they are least balanced and inclusive: sage-technocrats can bring bureaucratic ossification or expert conceit; workers and artisans ruling alone can find it difficult to promote broader economic prosperity; warriors fuel endless wars of honor and revenge; and when the merchant rules without constraint, his influence can be equally catastrophic, inflicting roller-coaster economic instability and vertiginous inequality. In the twentieth century, merchant-dominated orders were vulnerable to collapse beneath mountains of debt and ensuing slumps, ultimately bringing social conflict and even war.

But if caste orders can collapse with remarkable speed, rebuilding them is a much more protracted affair. This is partly because ruling castes use their wealth or political power to entrench themselves. Just as the old Soviet managers used their control over factories to resist market reforms after the collapse of the USSR, so American financiers since the 2008 crisis have protected their interests by funding politicians.[20] But dominant castes have also been remarkably successful in colonizing our minds, making it difficult for us to conceive of alternatives. It is often only generational change that produces a new consensus, as different castes learn contrasting lessons from the failure of the old order—for people who have come of age during a crisis often have a rather clearer view of its lessons. Unfortunately, it takes twenty or thirty years for the new generation to rise to positions of influence.

It is this pattern of caste struggles and shifting alliances that helps us to understand the crisis the developed world faces today. The merchant's rise to global political and cultural power began in seventeenth-century Holland and England and reached a feverish high point in Jazz Age America, before spectacularly imploding in the 1930s. But it was only in the 1980s that the merchant began to dominate the world order.

History, then, strongly suggests that no caste should ever rule alone, but the merchant is especially ill suited to sole dominion. The problem does not lie in the very existence of markets; after the failures of Communist regimes, we know how self-defeating it is to outlaw the merchant entirely. But neither is the ultra-free-market model—especially dominant in America and Britain and influential in international organizations—sustainable. We need to learn new lessons from our recent history. Only by recognizing the dangers of merchant rule and limiting its excesses can we avoid a repeat of the breakdowns suffered in 1929 and so narrowly averted in 2008.

In the past thirty-five years, Britain, where I live, and Russia, where I have studied, have been ideal places from which to observe the rise and fall of caste orders. My earliest political memories are of the bitter conflict between a new merchant vision of society and a Social Democratic order in which the technocratic sage and, to a lesser extent, the worker had more power. Margaret Thatcher was elected prime minister in 1979, promising to promote merchant values—which she claimed she had inherited from her shopkeeper father. In doing so, she fought not only labor unions and the public sector but also the survivals of "aristocratic" paternalism among elites within her own Conservative Party. She had enormous success in propagating her ideas—partly because they seemed to be in tune with broader historical developments. And despite a backlash against her hard, warriorish style, governments of both the left and the right have presided over the penetration of merchant values into every area of life.

Britain's course has been followed by many developed societies since the 1980s. Aristocratic values have continued to wither; elites now tend to be split between the professional and the mercantile, manifested in the tension between public and private sectors; commercial values have become dominant within both; and as working-class organizations and their egalitarian values have become weaker, economic inequality has increased.

If I saw the steady advance of the merchant in Britain, I saw how rapidly he could both rise and fall in Russia, where I was studying the history of economic and political ideas in Stalin's Soviet Union. When I was a graduate student in the late 1980s, the merchant was gaining ground, as he was elsewhere throughout the world. The old Soviet alliance of technocrat, paternalistic official, priestly ideologue, and collectivist worker was under attack. None of my Russian friends could understand why I was interested in this antiquated system. Surely I should be studying that new panacea for the world's ills, free-market economics? But the market enthusiasm did not last long. The Russian financial crisis of 1998 brought a sharp backlash against the merchant, and a new elite has now emerged that owes much to the traditional castes of Russian and Soviet politics.

Putin, with his macho love of martial arts and his claims of no-nonsense efficiency, has re-created a merger of warrior and sage-technocrat for a more populist age.

I have therefore observed the rise of the merchant where he has struggled to gain influence over powerful rivals, and I have also studied a civilization—Marxist-Leninist Communism—that tried to outlaw him and failed. So, while I am rather typical of academics in my skepticism of merchant values, I am also well aware of the drawbacks of sole rule by other castes: the sage-technocrat can bring the dominion of arrogant experts and bureaucratic sclerosis, and Communism showed that prosperity is very difficult to achieve in the absence of the merchant. But I am also convinced that the history of the modern world is not one of the merchant's inevitable and inexorable rise. His world is inherently unstable; it has imploded before, and could do so again.

The Story in Brief

The book presents two intertwined narratives. One is an account of the long-drawn-out decline of the warrior aristocracy and the demise of the social structure and values it embodied: hierarchy and caste division at home, and empire abroad. The second tells how the other castes— first the merchant and the sage-technocrat, then the worker and the creative, competed to supplant the aristocrat and bring the economic dynamism and social justice that aristocratic rule had so signally failed to deliver. This second story, however, is not one of gradual change but of zigzags, reversals, and returns as caste alliances were forged, challenged, and reforged. And at its center lies the dramatic rise, fall, and rise of the merchant.

The book takes the shape of a five-act drama. The first chapter briefly surveys the dominant castes in ancient and medieval agrarian societies.

It then shows how the merchant, for centuries constrained by warrior-aristocrats, sage-priests, and peasants, broke out of his confinement. However, this occurred only in a few commercial societies where the merchant could achieve some political power—most significantly in the Netherlands and England. Elsewhere, the old "agrarian" castes were still more dominant.

As the second chapter shows, in the course of the eighteenth and nineteenth centuries, the aristocratic order came under assault from the rise of other castes—merchant, sage-technocrat, and worker—reinforced by Enlightenment ideas of equality. But even as the merchant's influence grew in the nineteenth century, he was normally the junior partner of an aristocratic elite that embraced a warrior ethic. An exception was the United States, where the old warrior aristocracy had always been much weaker and where the merchant emerged as a dominant caste. But by the middle of the century, formerly agrarian powers like Germany and Japan were adapting to a more commercial world—often more successfully than Britain—by building more sophisticated heavy-industrial economies with the help of the sage-technocrat and the merchant.

Even so, the warrior aristocracies maintained an important social position in many states, and they found themselves policing new hierarchies, as new workers challenged merchant-industrialists and European states tried to maintain their colonial empires. Ultimately, the warrior's pursuit of national status, honor, and heroism in the First World War wrecked the peace the merchant needed to prosper. But the mass slaughter then discredited the old aristocracy, weakened empires, and opened the way for the merchant to claim sole dominion.

The third chapter traces the efforts of the merchant to rule alone in the 1920s as the United States became the dominant global power. But his rule was to be a brief one, for his market fundamentalism and his unwillingness to work with other castes—both workers and sage-technocrats—prevented him from creating a stable order. While he brought an attractive cultural equality and short-term riches, asset bubbles, debt, and economic inequality all contributed to the collapse of 1929 and discredited the merchant just as fully as 1918 had undermined the old aristocracies.

Indeed, the economic crisis exacerbated conflicts between worker and merchant and brought vicious civil wars between left and right, imperialists and nationalists, and with them unprecedented bloodshed. For fifteen years, three rival systems—radical right-wing nationalism, Communism, and Social Democracy—struggled for dominance amid the wreckage of market liberalism. The cosmopolitan merchant's love of toleration and compromise gave way to a new, harsh world of winners and losers, of zero-sum games. In this era of warfare, all castes looked to the warrior for protection, and he returned in new, less aristocratic guises. The Nazis tried to defend social hierarchy against the left by forging all citizens into imperialistic warriors (as did the Japanese); the Communists replaced the merchant with an unstable alliance of paternalistic and martial officials and state bureaucrats. However, in Scandinavia and to some extent in the United States, a more sustainable, economically egalitarian, inclusive, and balanced model did emerge: Social Democracy. This was a nonmilitant and less authoritarian form of the Communist model, with a reduced role for the warrior and a greater role for the merchant and worker, coordinated by sage-technocrats.

It was this sagely model that gradually conquered the world after the Second World War, as the fourth chapter shows. The experience of bloody social and imperial conflicts, the memory of 1929, and the power of labor unions and Communism forced merchants and sages to compromise with workers, while European warriors gradually abandoned their old empires. The result was a more sagely era, established internationally at the Bretton Woods conference of 1944, spreading to the Communist East after Stalin's death in 1953, and also to the newly independent countries of the "Third World" in the 1950s and '60s. It was especially well entrenched in those powers, such as Germany and Japan, where caste conflict and hierarchy had been most marked. It appeared that some of the sharper divisions of caste were finally being dissolved.

However, as the fifth chapter explains, just as it seemed that Social Democracy was emerging victorious, the merchant struck back. For the sagely system had its faults. First, the Cold War order entrenched new imperial relationships—in both the American and the Soviet spheres—and triggered nationalist rebellions, most seriously in Vietnam; second, while inclusive and more equal than previous systems, it was not inclusive or equal enough, giving power to technocrats and excluding women, youth, and ethnic minorities; and third, it failed to deal with the economic crises of the 1970s and the transition to a postindustrial world. The merchant, in alliance with the 1960s creatives, took advantage and began to engineer a return to the 1920s. This time, though, he was even more powerful, especially in the traditionally more commercial societies of the United States and Britain. For, like the 1920s, this was a "postwar" age, and the tolerant soft merchant was very appealing. Not only had the Cold Warriors been weakened, so had sage-technocrats and workers. Now the merchant had few rivals to constrain him.

This merchant-dominated era saw the narrowing of some international inequalities, particularly between the West and the rising Asian powers. But others widened, and within countries economies became less equal; the financial crisis of 2008 was the consequence, at least in part. I shall argue in the epilogue that, although we have avoided the disaster of 1929, we are again entering a period that echoes the 1930s—an era of economic contraction, national rivalries, increasing inequality, and social conflict. Neglectful of economic equality and long-term development, the merchant cannot possibly resolve these tensions alone, but in much of the West the major alternatives remain unpopular. And unless we forge a new caste order, we can only await the future with trepidation.

ONE

Caste Struggles

M any a British vacationer, fleeing the dismal weather at home for the balmy climes of the Mediterranean, will perhaps be fleetingly familiar with the countryside around the northern French city of Cambrai. Its flat, prairie-like fields, sown with corn and wheat, actually hold little to snag the interest of those speeding along the autoroute toward the more dramatic landscapes of the South. However, around the year 1000 C.E., this scenery was worthy of close attention, a frightening and dangerous place. For, in common with many of the lands of the weak Holy Roman Empire, Cambrai was at the mercy of bands of mounted warriors—the knights. In the absence of central authority, these horse-mounted bandits fought their neighbors and pillaged the countryside, protected by their fortress-citadels. Particularly violent was Walter of Lens, warden of Cambrai Castle, a belligerent and brutal knight intent on imposing his will and that of his lord, the Count of Flanders.[1]

Who could restore order to this region of chaos? Two centuries before, Charlemagne and his successors had been able to establish control over a remarkably large swath of Europe by constructing a rudimentary bureaucracy and branding themselves (with the Church's help) as both representatives of God and the heirs of Rome. But since that time the empire had fragmented, and the rule of the kings of France stretched no farther than a narrow tract of land around Paris. In much of the rest of northern France, the knights battled for preeminence. Rather like modern Mafia bosses, these "big men" fought pitched battles with their rivals for territory, assisted by their "families," both real kin and a broader network of fighters. Defiantly illiterate, these bands of knights lived according to martial, heroic values.[2]

Yet while the knights could cheerfully pursue their warrior vocation, life for everybody else was made unbearably grim. Agriculture and trade suffered, and even higher nobles and kings found that the constant disorder seriously harmed their interests. But in the absence of a powerful king, who was to stop this destructive rampaging?

It might seem odd to us, but at that time the only real hope lay in the Church. The local bishop, Gerard, like many of his fellow prelates, was the scion of an aristocratic family, and the Church was as much an exploiter of peasants as the knights were. But unlike the knights, the Church had a particular interest in promoting peace, for it had no armed forces of its own. Church power was moral, not military, and its chief weapon was the threat of an eternity of hellfire for breaching the sixth commandment, "Thou shalt not kill."

By 1024 Gerard had convinced many—including the Count of Flanders—that the untrammeled rule of the warrior knights was destroying society. At a grand meeting held in the town of Douai, where each side blamed the other for the pervasive violence and chaos, Gerard, Walter, and the count came to an agreement: the "peace of God" would operate from Wednesday night until Monday morning, during which time attack and plunder would be suspended and only the king's men would be permitted to wield weapons. Those who defied this curfew would be excommunicated from the Church or confined to a monastery to do penance for their crimes.

Gerard justified this treaty by appealing to a new vision of society, and in so doing he enunciated for the first time an idea that was to become foundational in subsequent European thought.[3] "From the beginning," he declared, "mankind has been divided into three parts . . . men of prayer, farmers and men of war," and each of them had his own particular duty—to pray, to labor, and to fight.[4] Gerard was therefore accepting that war could be legitimate: warriors were needed to defend the men of prayer and labor. But, he insisted, society could become rich and righteous only if the knights accepted an implicit social contract. They had to protect the peasants, not plunder them; they had to obey the king, not defy him. The king, in turn, had to listen to the counsel of the sage-priests. This was a perfect military-moral machine: the men of violence, their hands drenched in blood, could be purified only by the prayers of the holy, and only when they were pure could their victory be assured.

Gerard's solution was but a temporary one: it was to be many years before power was effectively centralized. But the story of Gerard and Walter shows us, in microcosm, a fundamental transition in world history: the taming of the warrior and the rise of the settled agrarian caste society, ruled by an alliance of the warrior, the paternalistic aristocrat, and the sage. It was this social system that came to dominate much of the world.

From Clan to Caste

The first human societies knew little of caste, or indeed of states. Nomadic foragers lived in relatively loose-knit societies that did not require long-term and closely coordinated cooperation, because for them the living was (relatively) easy—only three to five hours of hunting and gathering per day. But this "original affluent society," as the anthropologist Marshall Sahlins famously called it, could not support substantial populations;[5] settled agriculture (emerging after about 10,000 B.C.E.), by contrast, was able to feed many more, though only with an inferior diet and at the cost of much backbreaking work.[6] People had become less free:

they were now "caged," tied to one territory and obliged to cooperate with their neighbors more closely. Investment in land, dams, and tools all demanded coordination and leadership in a way that simple hunting and gathering had not.

Even so, these early agricultural societies were still relatively equal and unspecialized. The village and the extended kin group—the clan or "tribe"—was the main organizing principle, and politics was based largely on its consent.[7] To ensure the group's survival, chiefs, or "big men," were granted the authority to resolve conflicts and redistribute food, but their power was very limited and could easily be retracted. Other specialists also emerged: shamans and spiritual experts, people thought to have special skills in performing holy and magic rituals and communicating with the gods. But just as chiefs had not yet become a separate caste of landed aristocrats, neither had these early sages become elaborate priesthoods. The castes were there in embryo, but they had not yet freed themselves from the power of kinship.

However, by about 3200 B.C.E. a new form of urban civilization had arisen, and the world was increasingly divided between the old clan-based societies and a new, more complex order: the agrarian state, founded on caste. Along the banks of the world's great flooding rivers, first in Sumer and its neighboring cities between the Tigris and Euphrates rivers (Mesopotamia, or modern Iraq) and then along the Nile (Egypt), the Indus (Pakistan), and the Yellow River (China), a more intensive agriculture supported larger populations and cities. In these more specialized societies, people were increasingly grouped by occupation rather than kin.[8] In Mesopotamia, a "Standard Professions List" included a wide range of groups, from priests and officials to merchants, artisans, and slaves.[9]

These cities were run by some of the first "states"—that is, non-kinship organizations that relied on coercion more than consent. As populations grew—Uruk, in Mesopotamia, had about fifty thousand inhabitants by 3000 B.C.E.—authority was needed not only to resolve conflicts but to organize the irrigation of land and build food warehouses.[10]

However, by the third millennium B.C.E., as rivers began to dry up, competition between cities intensified and war became more common. Simultaneously, these cities were increasingly challenged by the warrior cultures of peoples in the unsettled, non-agricultural lands: their skills as hunters and herders made them more militarily effective than their agriculturist neighbors.[11]

In about 2300 B.C.E., however, we find these warrior-nomad and agrarian-urban cultures being combined for the first time to form a new kind of state—the "agrarian empire," founded on "tribute taking."[12] The first known state of this kind was built by Sargon of Akkad, a "marcher" lord from the borderlands between settled agricultural and herder regions, who conquered the Mesopotamian cities.[13] The agrarian empire, governed by warrior-landowner elites, was to dominate much of the world for some four thousand years, until the spectacular implosion of four of its last and greatest examples in the early twentieth century—Qing China in 1912, Romanov Russia in 1917, Hapsburg Austria-Hungary in 1918, and the Ottoman Middle East in 1923 (though the residues of the European overseas empires staggered on until the 1950s and '60s).

Agrarian empires were normally run by aristocrats, who embodied both warrior and landowner values, in close alliance with priests who justified their rule, and they used officials to administer it. Together these elites lived off the labor of the mass of the population, the peasantry, who gave them "tribute" in the form of taxation. They also took tribute from weaker neighboring peoples. This kind of state was far more hierarchical than the earlier clan-based societies had been: peasants, mostly self-sufficient, were coerced into giving their produce as tax, for which they received little in return. However, the relationship was not entirely parasitic. Peasants had to be secure on their land and guaranteed at least a minimal level of peace if they were to produce a taxable surplus. Rulers protected them and, together with priests, organized grain distribution in time of famine; meanwhile, priests, through their prayers and rituals, appeased the gods to avert the ever present threats of divine displeasure in the form of natural disasters and disease. And while these so-cieties might have been culturally very hierarchical, economically they were more equal than modern capitalist societies, in which the majority of people lack the land or other productive resources necessary to secure some autonomy.

The sages justified this hierarchy by developing various versions and elaborations of the idea of caste—the notion that society was divided into fixed, inherited occupations. One of the oldest surviving schemes can be found in the Indian religious text the Rig-Veda, composed between 1700 and 1500 B.C.E.:

> When gods prepared the sacrifice with Purusha [the first man] as their
>   offering . . .
> When they divided Purusha how many portions did they make?
> What do they call his mouth, his arms? What do they call his thighs
>   and feet?
> The priest [Brahmin] was his mouth, of both his arms was the warrior
>   [Rajanya or Kshatriya] made.
> His thighs became the common people [Vaishya], from his feet the
>   servant [Shudra] was produced.[14]

Similar three- or fourfold schemes can be found in most agrarian so-cieties. Sages or priests were nearly always found at the top, largely be-cause it was they who wrote the texts; warriors and their chiefs, the kings, tended to wield the real power.[15] So Gerard of Cambrai's counterparts in the medieval Islamic world placed "men of the pen" over "men of the sword" (followed by "men of commerce" and farmers), and Confucian scholars gave preeminence to themselves, too.[16] Warriors were only rarely accepted as superior, in more militaristic societies such as Japan.

However, the apparent stability presented by these caste schemes ob-scured the tensions between the wielders of these different kinds of power. Especially fraught were the conflicts between the castes that made up

Purusha's "arms"—the warriors and landowners. The elites of agrarian empires were expected to combine both roles, for land gave wealth, but force was also a crucial element of government—for collecting tribute both from peasants and from foreign lands. However, there was also a tension between the cultures of landed aristocracy and warriors: landowners needed to "look after" their peasant subjects if they were to extract taxes from them, while warriors, though essential for defense and extracting tribute from other peoples, often developed a culture of feuding, violence, and parasitism that could destroy a productive agricultural economy.

Taming the Warrior

The first agrarian empires marked the beginning of a gradual process of taming warrior power. But warriors remained dominant and unconstrained beyond imperial borders, in the neighboring lands still occupied by animal-herding pastoralists. Particularly threatening were the nomads of the Central Asian steppe for the two millennia between 700 B.C.E. and 1350 C.E., who perfected a powerful military technology—a highly mobile cavalry—that gave them the advantage over the settled agrarian peoples to the south and east.[17] One such group was the Scythians, who overran Anatolia (modern Turkey). Their successors included the Huns, Vandals, and Goths, who destroyed the Roman Empire; the Ottoman Turks, who conquered the Middle East; and the Mongols, who at one time held sway over Russia, China, and India.

These steppe nomadic peoples lived according to a pure warrior code—the way of the comitatus, or war band.[18] Life involved a great deal of war and violence, and values of bravery and fraternity were uppermost. A core group of fighters would coalesce around a leader and swear to fight and die for one another. The second-century C.E. Roman writer Lucian gives an account of them through the Scythian character Toxaris, who declared: "We wait till we see a brave man, capable of valiant deeds, and to him we all turn our attention. . . . The engagement is concluded with the most solemn oath: 'to live together and if need be to die for one another.'" The warriors would then "draw blood from their fingers into a cup, dip the points of their sword therein, and drink of that draught together, and from that moment nothing can part them."[19]

These groups were not strictly clans, but such warrior blood bonds could be stronger than those of real family. The chief was expected to be generous to his followers—both an inner circle and a broader number of ordinary soldiers. And they, in turn, would often live with the chief, in his hall or tent, eating, drinking alcohol or other intoxicants, and listening to bards celebrate the heroes of old in epic poems, from the English *Beowulf* to the Mongol *Gesar,* while looking forward to booty and glory. In the Mongol armies of Genghis Khan, status depended entirely on military skills and bravery.[20] Genghis Khan shared simple food and quarters with ordinary soldiers, and his egalitarian and meritocratic style encouraged enormous loyalty among his troops.

This warrior social structure—with groups of fighters clustering around particularly charismatic and successful heroes—can still be seen in many societies. Even in much more bureaucratic modern armies and the police forces of today, it is a small minority of "warriors" who are the most aggressive. For example, postwar studies of the U.S. Army have shown how soldiers still tend to cluster around particularly aggressive fighters in their ranks, both in battle and in more routine contexts, and all militaries rely on—and are suspicious of—the "adrenaline junkies" who form the core of any successful fighting unit. It is these men who are the most committed to their profession and who are admired by their colleagues as members of an elite.[21]

Not all of these clannish warriors, however, came from outside the borders of agrarian empires. Even within, there were often "bandits" and renegades who rejected central authority, from Walter's knights to the groups of soldiers that fight Central Africa's civil wars today. They could be "Robin Hoods," protecting the poor peasantry against the exploitative state, but more often they were themselves predators, like the "Celalis" of seventeenth-century Ottoman Turkey or the post-1911 Chinese bandit army of Bai Lang, the "White Wolf," made up of landless peasants and demobilized soldiers.[22]

Agrarian empires sometimes used force to suppress these warrior groups, but they also sought to negotiate with them and incorporate them into their power structures. Seventeenth-century Ottoman sultans frequently appointed bandit leaders as local governors.[23] And beginning in the eighteenth century, Russian czars brought the Cossacks—a warrior people of hunters and herders on their southern borderlands—into the fold by incorporating their leaders into the Russian gentry.[24] In Russia, as elsewhere, incorporation was normally accompanied by cultural transformation: warrior chiefs were expected to abandon their exclusive concern for their "brothers" and become "fathers" of the peasants and "sons" to the emperor.

Gerard of Cambrai was calling for precisely this change in eleventh-century Flanders, and kings, with the help of priestly propagandists, promoted the transformation of warriors from violent and impulsive heroes roaming the countryside into "courteous" nobles and "chivalrous" knights adorning the emperor's court. In Europe, for instance, starting in the eleventh century, an elaborate chivalric literature inculcated knights with a paternalistic concern for the weak, a romantic love of women, and a sagely interest in literary refinement. Violence was to be used only when absolutely necessary and was increasingly to be confined to staged tournaments. Giraut de Bornelh, a southern French troubadour poet, warned his knightly audience against abandoning a courtly culture of genteel tournaments for pillage and plunder:

> Shame [on] the knight
> who dares court a lady
> after touching bleating sheep with his hands
> or robbing churches and travellers.[25]

The taming of the warrior can be seen most vividly in Japan, although it remained incomplete. The military caste—the samurai—was originally composed of herders and hunters from beyond the settled agrarian lands, and in the ninth and tenth centuries they formed bandit groups that often terrorized and looted the settled population.[26] As in many warrior castes, their lives were founded on military prowess, honor, and shame—hence the gruesome custom of self-disemboweling (*seppuku*), which samurai practiced to avoid the shame of capture and decapitation by the enemy. The aristocratic Heian court, with its culture of hereditary authority and paternalism, tried to integrate the samurai into agrarian society, granting them lands and official posts, but these inducements failed, and they stubbornly retained both their independence and their disruptive warrior culture, contributing to a long period of civil war in the fifteenth and sixteenth centuries. After 1603, the Tokugawa dynasty finally restored order; the samurai were brought to heel and transformed into hereditary landowners and, increasingly, state officials. Even so, their identity as a warrior caste was never wholly abandoned, and Bushido, or the "way of the warrior," with its ideas of honor, heroic competition, and pride, remained central to the ethos of the samurai elite.[27]

The Japanese landed class might have been particularly warrior-like, but in many agrarian states, rulers at the central and local levels continued to see themselves both as fathers of the people and as warriors. So landowners continued to dominate most armies until 1914, and indeed long after. Military sports were also common, from wrestling in the Mughal and Ottoman courts to dueling and horse racing among the European aristocracies. Hunting—both a symbol of and training for war—was almost universal, from the industrial slaughter of animals in late-nineteenth-century Europe and imperial India to the huge ceremonial autumn hunts of the Qing Manchus, involving tens of thousands of people.[28] The English writer Rebecca West was struck by the importance of hunting to the aristocrats she met in interwar Yugoslavia. As she remembered:

The old Hungarian count . . . was heard to mutter as he lay dying, "And then the Lord will say 'Count, what have you done with your life?,' and I shall have to say, 'Lord, I have shot a great many animals.' Oh, dear! Oh, dear! It doesn't seem enough!"[29]

If hunting and shooting were insufficient for entry into heaven, they certainly were not enough on their own to maintain the prestige of landed aristocrats in settled agricultural societies that increasingly set a premium on peace. In these circumstances, rulers emphasized their role as fathers and sought status not primarily in military values but in familial ones. First, they stressed the importance of their lineage and bloodline: just as the Rajputs of northern India traced their warrior prowess to their descent from the sun, moon, and fire, so European aristocrats were obsessed with ancestors, coats of arms, and "pride in race." And, second, they poured their resources into maintaining ostentatiously lavish lifestyles—a symbol of their ability to look after their "inferiors": their purses were as open as their hearts, as the Rajput warrior castes put it. Indian kings were expected to spend a certain proportion of their income, sometimes as much as a third, on festivals and ritual feasting; expensive Kashmir (cashmere) shawls, a symbol of aristocratic status, were a common currency of gift giving—as they are in Indian politics to this day—and the Mughal emperors set up special offices for collecting and grading them so they could oil the wheels of statecraft.[30]

Aristocratic generosity cultivated the loyalties of followers and retainers, of course, but it was also designed to keep the lower orders happy. In *The Leopard*, Giuseppe di Lampedusa's evocative novel about his nineteenth-century Sicilian ancestors, Prince Fabrizio earns the gratitude of his tenants by frequently "forgetting" to collect their paltry rents. And when Father Pirrone, the family priest, is asked what it is like living with the nobility, he accepts that they can be cruel, touchy, and proud but insists that this is simply the reverse side of their willingness to help the unfortunate: both are the products of a code of honor that gives them the right to rule on condition that they serve those inferior to them. So when they "treat someone badly, as they do sometimes, it is not so much their personality sinning as their class affirming itself"; but once their power is recognized, they are willing to help their inferiors—irrespective of business interests, to which they show a "contemptuous indifference."[31]

As Father Pirrone clearly implies, these aristocrats knowingly traded some of their potential wealth for the even more valuable commodities of honor and prestige.[32] The perils of ignoring this balance are apparent in the novel when the indebted Prince Fabrizio accepts the advice of the local merchant Don Calogero and tries to run his estates more efficiently. His family acquires "a reputation as extortioners of their own dependents," and their prestige is destroyed.[33] The great French commentator on the declining aristocracy, Alexis de Tocqueville, made the point more directly: "in aristocracies the hire of a farm is paid to the landlord, not only in rent, but in respect, regard and duty"; it therefore made little sense for landlords to squeeze their tenants, for "what [aristocrats] gain in money will before long be lost in power."[34]

Clerics and Clerks

If landed aristocrats valued bloodlines, generosity, and military valor, sages could not have been more different. For them, command of ideas, symbols, and culture—not weapons, land, and wealth—conferred status. In many early societies, sages had essentially two tasks: a moral one, ensuring obedience to the laws of the gods; and a technical one, the conduct of elaborate sacrifices and rituals in precise accordance with recondite rules. These tasks gradually evolved into two clearly defined roles: the sage as ideologist—the figure who interpreted the holy books and pronounced on how men and women should behave—and the sage as specialist, who used thinking and writing to solve practical problems, such as reading the stars and oracles or keeping accounts and advising on state policy. In many so-

cieties, the sage did both. The fusion of these roles can be seen in the
Confucian official who was both state administrator and public moralist,
and in the priests of Western Europe, whom rulers often employed as
functionaries.

But despite these differences in precise specialization, sages often
shared a common culture, one that was very different from the warrior's
or the landed aristocrat's. As wielders of the pen rather than the sword,
they generally did not engage in violence. In the case of India's Brahmins, this pacifism was symbolized by vegetarianism and abstinence—in
contrast to the meat-eating, hooch-loving Kshatriyas. Sages also often
abhorred aristocrats' obsession with heredity and bloodline, as well as the
warriors' risk-taking behavior and love of display. Of course, they often
had little choice: they did not generate wealth themselves and relied on
grants from landowners and merchants, or fees for their services. But
their status also depended on their moral or intellectual standing, and
that meant that they had to be—or at least appear to be—independent of
the world of wealth, comfort, and material success. And so even professionals who were connected with politics and commerce, like lawyers,
were bound by strict codes of ethics that supposedly made them incor-
ruptible.

Naturally, there were exceptions: in societies where warrior values were
strong, sage-priests were close to warriors and sometimes even became
fighters themselves. Between the eleventh and the thirteenth centuries,
the pope launched a number of "crusades," encouraging Western European knights to colonize the lands of the "infidel" in the Middle East and
in Eastern and Southern Europe.[35] The Church even established its own
"military orders" of monks, like the Teutonic Knights. Similarly, medieval Japan saw the rise of the *sōhei,* Buddhist soldier-monks who took part
in factional struggles between temples, while eighteenth-century Bengal
monastic armies confronted the British East India Company.

More common in agrarian empires, however, were sage-priests like
Gerard of Cambrai and Father Pirrone, who justified a peaceable social

hierarchy presided over by father-kings, for they naturally had little to gain from the rule of egalitarian warriors who held the priestly skills of knowledge and literacy in low esteem. Rather, they used their moral authority and their expertise in communicating with the heavens to defend the unequal social order. Among the warriors themselves, the chiefs also realized that there were benefits to be gained by an alliance with the sages. As warrior chiefs, they had to share power with other warriors; but as patriarchal kings, anointed by priests, they could wield more individual authority. We can see the mutual advantage of such an alliance of sage and warrior in medieval Indian kingship. In the Pallava kingdom of southern India, for instance, Brahmin priests would organize elaborate rituals to symbolize the king's role as upholder of the social order (*dharma*) and his place as head of a hierarchy of "little kings." In doing so, they were justifying his use of violence to subordinate potential rivals and rebels below him.[36]

If Indian Brahmin priests tried to channel the king's violence into the defense of social order, Chinese Confucian sages tried to minimize any reliance on warrior values. Confucius (551–479 B.C.E.)—the son of a knight who became a private tutor to aristocrats—was in much the same position as Gerard of Cambrai. He lived at a time of widespread clan warfare, and much of his philosophy was designed to restrain a warrior caste run riot. But his solution was even more radical than Gerard's. Everybody, he argued, including emperors and princes, should abide by a set of moral precepts established by sages: inferiors were to obey superiors, and in return superiors were to be benevolent to inferiors. So long as everybody abided by these rules, order could be maintained without the use of force:

> Lead them by political maneuvers, restrain them with punishments:
> the people will become cunning and shameless.
> Lead them by virtue, restrain them with ritual:
> they will develop a sense of shame and participation.[37]

For Confucius, it was the upholding of morality and virtue that gave rulers the right to govern, not aristocratic values of violence and bloodline inheritance.

Confucius died an obscure scholar, but his ideas lived on as a sagely ideology, passed down from sage to sage. Some three centuries later, the Han emperor Wudi (156–87 B.C.E.) saw in his teachings an ideal means to curb the powers of the regional aristocracy, and he endorsed Confucianism as a state philosophy. By the eleventh century, under the Song dynasty, Confucius's ideas were not simply justifying the power of "clerics," or priestly moralists; they had come to underpin an entire system of government by "clerks," or expert administrators, and China had by far the most sophisticated bureaucratic government of the premodern era.[38]

The landed gentry in China, unlike the gentry elsewhere, were not simply entitled to inherit power, and neither could they buy power, as was the case in more commercial societies. Rather, the gentry's sons were obliged to embark on a long, difficult education requiring the memorization of about 400,000 Chinese characters—or two hundred a day for six years.[39] After this punishing intellectual apprenticeship, their fate and status would finally be settled by a three-day exam. Following an intrusive body search to root out cheating, the candidates would sit in rows of bare, mosquito-infested cells, writing, among other things, the infamous "eight-legged essay," on themes in classical Confucian texts; in later years there was greater emphasis on essays about practical questions of public policy.[40] Hundreds of thousands took the exam, and only a few passed; in 1006, a mere 3 percent succeeded. And of those, a tiny group took the highest exam in Beijing itself, where the emperor presided over the final stage as examiner in chief.[41]

China's ruling ideology was therefore very different from that of other premodern empires. In the earliest Confucian fourfold social schemes, warriors were omitted entirely: at the top were the sage-officials (*shi*), followed by farmers, artisans, and merchants at the bottom. By the eleventh century soldiers were given a place, but they were second from the bottom of a list of eight, just above vagrants.[42] In reality, the examination system did not destroy the influence of local gentry families—it was, of course, usually only the wealthy and privileged who could afford the preparatory education (though there are examples of poor families banding together to educate a particularly able child, who, if appointed to office, could earn rewards for his sponsors). Moreover, in the localities it was the landed gentry—sometimes with and sometimes without a degree—who staffed the regional bureaucracies. However, the examinations did "sagify" the Chinese elite at all levels: it ensured that Confucian thought and a Confucian ethos saturated the culture of administration, government, and power holding. One consequence seems to have been that the state became much more interested in public works, famine relief, and welfare than in war—which possibly explains why states with Confucian cultures have been so successful in promoting economic development to this day. Chinese officials endlessly discussed how to balance the ways of the sage and the warrior—*wen* (culture) and *wu* (violence), as they put it; the emperor, who had the ultimate power of life and death, was expected to embody warrior values. Confucian officials also had to use both *wu* and *wen*, and could also exercise a great deal of violent repression, most notably during the Taiping rebellions of the mid-nineteenth century. But the selection of Chinese elites by exam, rather than by military success or aristocratic bloodline, inevitably gave them a more sagely and less militaristic attitude to the world than that of their counterparts elsewhere.[43]

Still, sagely rule did not always serve the needs of the Chinese state. Between 1125 and 1368, and again after 1644, Central Asian nomadic peoples to the north conquered the Han Chinese, in part because the Chinese had neglected defense. Warrior peoples therefore ruled China, and their values of *wu* prevailed for a time. The Mongols (1234–1368) were most extreme in their suspicion of the sage; they abolished the exams and ruled as a warrior caste. But the Manchus (ruling as the Qing dynasty, 1644–1911) eventually came to a compromise with Confucian officials. They kept their own identity as a martial elite—hunting and conducting elaborate military exercises—but they also increasingly ruled through the Confucian bureaucracy.[44] Yet this dual sagely-warrior power was not enough to defend China against the challenge from much more effective maritime warriors—the gunboat-borne soldiers of mid-nineteenth-century Western Europe.

By that time, several European countries were developing bureaucracies to match China's, though it had taken them a very long time. Since the twelfth century, the medieval universities had begun training experts in law and theology who could administer royal and noble courts and extract taxes more efficiently. However, much administration was still carried out by aristocrats—by officials who owned their positions and passed them on to their children. They were not proper "bureaucrats" in the modern sense—that is, officials selected according to their expertise and performance in examinations, organized hierarchically and following administrative rules.[45]

As the costs of war escalated in Europe from the sixteenth century onward, kings did try to "sagify" their nobilities, forging them into "service aristocracies," the better to govern their lands and extract taxes.[46] In Castiglione's influential sixteenth-century Renaissance text *The Book of the Courtier,* aristocrats were expected to be not only literate but positively erudite, capable of discoursing on the classics. They were also to be graceful, witty, and urbane, and, most important, were to show their superiority not through crude displays of power but through a more subtle *"sprezzatura,"* or nonchalant self-assurance.[47] The universities of Oxford and Cambridge became finishing schools for the aristocracy, building lavish and grandiose accommodations to make them feel at home and sweeten the bitter pill of education. Meanwhile in Russia, Peter the Great made a basic education compulsory for all noble adolescents, and aristocratic houses throughout Europe were filled with dancing masters and fencing teachers to help their sons combine the military arts with elegance.[48]

But it was only very gradually, from the late seventeenth and eighteenth centuries on, that sagely professional expertise rather than aristocratic inheritance and patronage began to penetrate state administration—again under pressure of war. And even then it happened only in some countries—in Britain, where a powerful parliament fought against aristocratic control over official posts, and in Prussia, where kings saw it as the only way of paying for their frequent wars.[49] The Prussian king Frederick II, in particular, separated the "state," run by expert officials, from the royal dynasty, and elevated the former to the supreme position; the king was merely the state's servant, and only the state was immortal. "I am thinking only of the state," he wrote in 1776, "for I know only too well that everything—even if the sky should crash in upon the earth—will be a matter of absolute indifference to me from the moment of my death."[50] By 1794 officials were no longer called "royal servants" but professional officials of the state.

This was the beginning of the warrior's disengagement from the landed aristocrat; it was also the beginning of his alliance with the sage-technocrat—one that became ever stronger in the course of the next century, as will be seen. This was particularly true in Prussia, where, as the army became professionalized, so the bureaucracy became militarized, with civil servants put in uniform and subject to harsh discipline.

In many agrarian societies, though, sages prided themselves on remaining independent of the martial values and the vested interests of the landowners. The warrior's love of competition and worldly success for its own sake was generally frowned on as likely to undermine thoughtfulness and independent judgment. As the fourteenth-century Confucian sage Sung Lien wrote, "Gentleman-sages are nourished in the hills and the woods, but may be ruined in the courts of rulers."[51] Similarly, the aristocrat's desire to promote the interests of his lineage tended to provoke sagely disapproval. Confucian sages vigorously resisted the efforts of the local gentry to dilute the rigors of the exam system, the better to promote their own children.

Even so, an obsession with rituals, examinations, or moral probity could create its own self-serving conservatism—whether a slavish subservience to bureaucratic ranks and degrees or a dogmatic love of rules. Even medieval Confucian sages understood the problem, denouncing examinees who merely "peddle their empty verbiage and trivial practices to the authorities."[52] These charges are still, of course, leveled at professionals and public sector administrators by more lordly or mercantile castes.

However, the rise of the sage-technocrat was a very gradual process: bureaucracies were small until the second half of the nineteenth century, and aristocrats dominated European armies until 1914, when the First World War began under the confident leadership of men on horses, festooned in the elaborate uniforms, swords, medals, and mustaches of their caste.

Holy Rebels

Most sages—both priests and experts—were therefore closely allied with warrior and landowner rulers, and as such were able to become elites themselves. But there was another type of sage—the "holy man"—who was less likely to be a member of the political establishment, often lived an unworldly, ascetic life, and championed transcendent spiritual values that could provide an alternative to the dominant social order. We can see these figures in a number of religions, and their independence from political and priestly power could sometimes confer on them the most remarkable influence. Indian *sadhus* have frequently led peasant movements, and in many ways Gandhi was their heir. Holy men also played an important role in the eastern part of the Roman Empire in the fifth and sixth centuries, the most famous being Simeon the Stylite, who lived on top of a pillar in the Syrian wilderness, attracted followers, and used his sacred power to intercede on behalf of disadvantaged peasants.[53]

Some holy men, however, could be more radical in their rejection of priestly power and hierarchy. Anybody, they argued, of whatever social background or religious status, could be godly if he had faith and behaved morally. Both Jesus and the Buddha were sages of this type. Jesus condemned the Jewish Pharisees for their refusal to have meals with "ritually impure" sinners and tax collectors, insisting that spiritual condition was more important than obedience to religious laws imposed by priestly figures.[54] The Buddha challenged the role of Brahmin priests more fundamentally when he declared that virtuous thought and actions brought salvation, not participation in pointless and costly rituals; he also condemned the Brahminic view that the higher castes were more religiously pure than the lower.[55]

These sagely critiques of established priesthoods and status hierarchies can be found in a number of societies. Christian "heretics" in medieval Europe often condemned the special status of priests and ridiculed their rituals, and Luther similarly criticized the Roman Church for creating a special, privileged caste of priestly intermediaries between heaven and earth who claimed the power to secure salvation for ordinary believers.[56] More radical Protestants took the Buddha's view: that every layman who could read the sacred texts had access to the holy and had no need of priests at all.

The targets of these religious reformers were normally priests, but their radical ideas had more destabilizing effects. For by seeing every virtuous person as holy, they challenged the status of priests—a group that was powerful in its own right—and, more generally, the social hierarchies that priests defended. As will be seen, merchants were one group to take advantage of these spiritual rebellions and their egalitarian implications. But so too did the peasantry, and Luther's ideas were taken up by rural rebels in Germany in the 1520s. Meanwhile, in imperial China, Buddhist-influenced religious sects that challenged the Confucian order and promised the coming of an egalitarian society played an important role in most peasant uprisings. The late-nineteenth-century anti-foreigner Boxer Rebellion in northwestern Shandong, for instance, was inspired by sects that believed everybody, including poor peasants, could be possessed by spirits and thus speak with divine authority.[57]

However, while holy rebels were a perennial challenge to the agrarian order, they found it difficult to change society in any fundamental way. Chinese secret societies and Christian heresies were put down by a mixture of priestly inquisitions and aristocratic force. And even where radical religious movements were victorious, they were often soon transformed back into the conventional agrarian-caste religions they had tried to overthrow. Thus, by the thirteenth century, Buddhism, having died out in India, survived in Sri Lanka as a religion in which monks supported an order dominated by kings and warrior-landowners.[58] Similarly, German and Scandinavian Lutheranism was as priestly as the old Roman Church; now, though, its hierarchies were presided over by kings, not popes.

Holy men, therefore, could possess an enormous amount of ideological power and deploy it to challenge the social order, but they found it difficult to achieve lasting change. The same was true of peasants, though their attitude to the social order was often more ambivalent.

Swynkers, Sweters, and Sowers

In the late fourteenth century, William Langland, a member of the gentry from the English Midlands, produced an extraordinary poem—part religious allegory, part satirical commentary on his society: *The Vision of William Concerning Piers the Plowman*. The narrator, Will, is guided toward Truth by Piers, a humble peasant with half an acre in the countryside near the Malvern Hills. Much of the poem is critical of lordly arrogance and Church corruption, but Piers still accepts the basis of the social order. His world is populated by a fourfold hierarchy of royalty, knights, clergy, and "commons." At one point Piers meets a knight who offers to help him plow his field, but Piers refuses, declaring: "I shall toil [swynke] and sweat [swete] and sow [sowe] for us both . . . on condition that you keep Holy Church and myself / from wastrels and from wicked men that destroy this world." The knight readily agrees, but Piers has one more condition: "Look you, trouble no tenant unless you have just cause / And even when you are justified in fining them, / let mercy assess the amount."[59]

Langland was describing an informal social "contract" that bound peasants to their lords—from the point of view of the masters. But in 1381, the figure of Piers the Plowman was being used for much more radical purposes. Long-established tensions between peasants and lords came to a boil when the king tried to levy a poll tax to finance his wars, and the result was a huge rebellion against gentry and Church landowners in the counties around London. Not only peasants took part— artisans did, too, and masons, tailors, and dyers were all involved.[60] A priest, John Ball, gave a fiery sermon on Blackheath, on the outskirts of the capital, and presented Piers the Plowman as an oppressed figure. Condemning all social distinctions, he asked a catchily subversive question: "When Adam delved [dug] and Eve span [spun], who was then a gentleman?"[61]

We can find both Langland's and Ball's attitudes among peasants in agrarian societies, and their relations with lords differed enormously. Occasionally peasants rose in rebellion, but much of the time, peasants and the authorities seemed to accept a set of traditional social arrangements.

Peasants were members of households that exerted a good deal of control over the land they farmed and were often self-sufficient. Even so, they faced various threats to their way of life: from warrior bandits; from landlords and officials with demands for taxes and sons for the army; from famine and predatory beasts; and from merchants driving prices up.[62]

This alarming array of existential threats that beset peasants at different times throughout the long life of the agrarian state explains the appeal of Langland's views. Gentry and governments could take part of their surplus, but in exchange peasants could expect the protection and paternalism that Piers the Plowman asked of the knight. Lords might be expected to save peasants from famines or to endow sagely institutions, such as south Indian temples or European monasteries, to do so. Meanwhile, in China the imperial bureaucracy built one of the first and most sophisticated welfare systems, establishing a complex network of granaries to distribute grain to the poor in lean times.[63]

However, if peasants believed that states and landlords had become too demanding or had reneged on traditional obligations during hard times, they could protest violently—from the 1381 English Peasants' Revolt to the massive German rebellions of 1524–25 to the peasant insurgencies of late-nineteenth and early-twentieth-century China. And at times, peasants could make a real difference—some have argued that rebellions precipitated the end of serfdom in Western Europe.[64] Peasants organized themselves in very different ways. In Europe, village communities were traditionally stronger, and kinship weaker; in India, kin was much more important; and in China, peasants organized themselves in a number of ways—through villages, clans, and religious sects.[65] Even so, the military power mustered by a dispersed peasantry was normally far weaker than the more concentrated and well-organized might of its opponents.

This difference in power also affected skilled workers in the towns. The artisans' importance to the urban economies of many societies gave them political leverage, as did their guilds.[66] But they rarely challenged the authority of the landed or the wealthy. In the sixteenth- and seventeenth-century southern Indian Vijayanagara Empire, artisan guilds took advantage of economic growth to improve their status, but they were more interested in competing with one another than in challenging royal rule.[67] And even in Europe, where guilds could exert real political influence, they often came to be dominated by the rich.[68] Like peasants, artisans did rebel, and between 1300 and 1700 European towns were rocked by protests against taxes and in favor of political representation. These revolts were sometimes successful; in the French town of Montpellier in 1645, for instance, locksmiths and millers sacked the houses of tax officials and forced the lieutenant general to abandon a tax on fruit.[69] But, like those of the peasants, their protests were essentially intended to enforce an existing set of traditional obligations; they rarely challenged the fundamental balance of power or the paternalistic philosophy that underpinned it.

We can therefore identify an "agrarian" worldview, shared by aristocrats, priests, and (sometimes) peasants, that valued hierarchy, stability, and mutual obligations. But one caste did not always share this outlook and was to be a much greater threat to the peasantry than the clannish warrior was: the merchant. And as the merchant became more powerful, an increasing number of peasants—especially in Europe beginning in about 1600, and then in the European empires—rebelled against the spread of volatile markets as well as state taxation.[70] For even though he had no weapons, the merchant's practices and values undermined the agrarian moral and social order more thoroughly than the clannish warrior ever would. And some of the most acute insights into the outlook of the trader, and the reasons for his unpopularity, can be found in the first-ever Indian autobiography, the fascinating and poignant memoir of a seventeenth-century north Indian merchant, Banarasi.

Children of Hermes

Banarasi should have been a highly successful merchant. He was born in 1586 into a prosperous family in Jaunpur, a branch of a formerly warrior caste that had long since turned to trade and Jainism—an Indian religion particularly attractive to merchants, both then and now. His father was a successful dealer in gold, silver, and the dust of precious stones, and he had given his son the education typical of a merchant. Banarasi was bright and soon learned how to read and write, keep accounts, and distinguish real coins from counterfeit ones. He also displayed many other traits of a good merchant. In a touching personal balance sheet of his virtues and vices, he described himself as a "sweet-spoken" man, friendly toward all; a man who displayed "tolerance and forbearance," "equilibrium and balance"; a devout believer in Jainism who did "not consort with other men's wives"; and a man "with little anger, pride or artifice in him." However, he admitted he had faults: "his greed for wealth is great"; "a small gain brings him great joy; and a small loss makes him worry excessively"; "he cannot refrain from telling lies"; and "he does not practise any rites or rituals, nor does he practise self-restraint."[71]

Undoubtedly, many of these virtues, and some of the vices, were useful for the merchant. Merchants were, in essence, middlemen. They provided a service to all castes by bringing goods from places where they were in surplus to areas of shortage, sometimes journeying long distances in a world where travel was difficult, expensive, and unsafe. They also provided another good in short supply to aristocrats and peasants alike: credit. In essence, they made their money by buying cheap and selling dear. And small merchants like Banarasi tended to operate in a specific form of market that is now rare in the developed world (except perhaps in the realms of property and used cars). This was the "bazaar," where the quality of goods is variable, information on their value is difficult to discover, and every deal is the result of intensive bargaining.[72]

These roles all demanded a particular set of qualities, which Banarasi and the Jains shared with many merchant communities around the world. They prized tolerance, friendliness, and politeness, which gave them the easygoing affability needed to trade with anybody, whatever his culture or religion.[73] Similarly, they disapproved of aristocratic qualities of pride, showiness, and anger. And while, as will be seen, merchants as rulers could be warlike in seizing markets, as subordinates in agrarian empires they tended to value peace—understandably, for war disrupted trade, and commerce was a peaceful form of moneymaking that depended on each side freely agreeing that the exchange was to its advantage. In this, commerce was different from aristocratic forms of moneymaking—taxation or tribute—that ultimately depended on coercion. Among most members of Indian merchant castes, this disapproval of violence was symbolized by strict vegetarianism, though Jains took this much more seriously than most, even filtering their water through muslin to make sure they did not inadvertently eat small insects. Aristocrats naturally disdained this behavior as cowardly and dishonorable; as one Gujarati saying went, "The merchant's mustache droops down"—an unfavorable contrast with the warrior Rajput, with his waxed, skyward-pointing mustache.[74]

Banarasi's love of money and his anxiety over minor gains and losses were common among merchants. The popular merchant handbook written by the fourteenth-century Italian banker Pegolotti praised similar virtues: successful merchants had to be "slow to buy, quick to sell."[75] Merchants had to be flexible to take advantage of sudden changes in the market. In 1591, for instance, famine in Southern Europe allowed the Ximenes—rich Portuguese merchants based in Antwerp—to make huge profits, some said of 300 percent, by chartering ships full of wheat and rye and sending them to Italy.[76] Merchants were therefore rarely directly involved in production—whether in agriculture or in industry—because it involved tying capital down in longer-term enterprises.[77] Also, production was often governed by rules that gave priority to the interests of peasants, lords, or artisans over that of the market.[78]

Yet there was sometimes another, deeper reason for merchants' avoidance of production: their cultural isolation from the majority of the agrarian population. As the anthropologist Clifford Geertz found in his study of 1950s Indonesia, both aristocrats (members of the Hindu majority) and merchants (a Muslim minority) set up industrial enterprises in the newly independent country. But the merchants' firms, while profitable, remained small and employed only members of the extended family. They did not want to manage large numbers of local Hindu peasants who did not share their profit-oriented value system. The Balinese nobles, on the other hand, were used to behaving as paternalistic managers and organizers, and were much more likely to set up large factories and create jobs. Their firms tended to become relief organizations for the employment of the local community, rather than profitable businesses. As the former king of Tabanan region admitted, if you went into an aristocrat's firm you would find "half-a-dozen directors, a bookkeeper or two, several clerks, and a hoard of semi-idle workers"; a Chinese merchant's firm of the same size, by contrast, would employ only the proprietor, his wife, and their ten-year-old son, but they would be getting more work done.[79]

Pegolotti similarly saw "industriousness" as an essential characteristic of the merchant.[80] Trade was competitive, and small merchants especially had to be frugal and hardworking, because success was difficult and depended on making tiny profits on many deals. All of this contrasted with aristocratic leisure, insouciance, and lavish display. The sixteenth-century Spanish traveler Luis Ortiz noted that in cities run by merchants, elites were much less interested in costly furs, silks, and perfumes than the aristocrats of the poorer Spanish imperial capital of Valladolid: "such luxury is not to be found in Florence, or Genoa, or in the Netherlands."[81] Similarly, in late-sixteenth-century merchant-ruled Venice, nobles would wear silk clothes in fashionable colors, but they would hide them under black gowns "for the modesty of that Republic."[82] When merchants did display their wealth, it was often by giving to charity or to their churches, promoting their own self-helping, literate culture. They have always been interested in financing education, and Banarasi's fellow Jains often donated enormous sums to temples and schools; indeed, there was a saying in Gujarat: "Gifts by the *lakh* [hundred thousand], accounts by the penny."[83]

A certain kind of intelligence and education was especially valuable for a merchant, for gathering information and making quick calculations were essential. In information-poor markets, trading was, in essence, a contest between buyer and seller in which the main weapon was information: the one who knew most about market conditions, who could judge the quality of the product, and who was the shrewdest judge of his competitor would be the winner.[84] More generally, intelligence and information could give merchants advantages over their competitors, and merchants were much more likely than other castes to use innovations from elsewhere in order to improve efficiency and productivity.[85]

Merchants, of course, valued intelligence as much as sages, but their attitude to learning was very different. Merchants preferred quickness and cleverness over abstract thought, complex rule-bound systems, or philosophical speculation, and they saw education as something that was practical and open to all, rather than scholarly and confined to sagely elites.[86] (These attitudes persist today, when businesspeople complain that students spend too much time parsing Latin poetry or deconstructing episodes of *The Wire* rather than learning how to spell and add.) Banarasi, however, rebelled against the narrowness of his merchant education and became absorbed in religious scholarship and love poetry. The local caste elders despaired. "Learning is meant for Brahmins and bards," they explained. "The sons of merchants sit in the marketplace. Those who spend all their time in learning go hungry. Listen, son, to what your elders tell you."[87] Eventually, Banarasi knuckled down and went along with his family's wishes. But he was never a very successful merchant: his sagely leanings (the ones that impelled him to write an autobiography in the first place) do indeed seem to have damaged his commercial acumen.

Some merchants also developed views of religion different from those of sage-priests. Banarasi's attitudes—devout and moralistic, yet hostile to priestly ritual—were typical of Jainism and of other religions popular among merchants, like Puritan Protestantism. The German father of sociology, Max Weber, famously argued that modern capitalism triumphed in the West and not elsewhere because a peculiar Puritan theology inspired people to concentrate on "rational" worldly success—the Calvinist doctrine that people were predestined to be saved or damned allegedly created anxiety and led believers to "prove" their virtue in this world. But Weber misidentified the most important ingredient of Puritanism; crucial was its critique of the priestly castes and its claim that pious laypeople could interpret the Bible without any priestly assistance. And contrary to our often rather parochial, Western-centric view of history, Puritanism was not the only "merchant-friendly" religion. Buddhism, Jainism, and some forms of Islam also appealed to merchants for similar reasons: they all rejected wasteful ceremony and priestly hierarchy and often, with them, martial glory and aristocratic display.[88] They also valued literacy and encouraged laypeople, not just priests, to read sacred texts. And they prized morality, which they saw as universal and enforced by individual conscience, not by hypocritical priests. These religions were initially holy-man alternatives to priestly religions and were often initially very hostile to trade; but they were often taken up by merchants and, as in the case of Puritanism, were adapted by them to become, in effect, merchant religions.[89]

Merchant morality also emphasized another set of values: creditworthiness, trust, frugality, and self-discipline. Merchants needed to have a reputation for caution and sobriety if they were to be seen as reliable and creditworthy by their fellows—essential when, as the eighteenth-century French minister Turgot put it, "there is no commercial centre on earth where business does not run on borrowed money."[90]

Indeed, these qualities lay at the center of the merchant's moral code: for the Gujarati merchant, the same word was used for "credit" and "honor," and the popular seventeenth-century French handbook *The Perfect Merchant* (*Le Parfait Négociant*) decreed that merchants should avoid bankruptcy at all costs because there was "nothing of which merchants should be more jealous than their honour."[91] This view of honor, of course, was opposite that of the aristocrats, which demanded generosity and display. But merchants had only contempt for these attitudes: the warriors and peasants who borrowed from them were feckless wastrels who spent money on weddings, feasting, and gambling.[92] As one twentieth-century Muslim Javanese merchant explained, "If you work hard and pray that's all you need to do." Therefore, "those who are poor are poor mainly because they are lazy, stupid or sinful. For example they gamble." Meanwhile, "those who are rich are rich because they work hard and are clever."[93]

Merchants, then, were as interested in morality, religion, and honor as other castes, but their ideas of what those were differed.[94] And this tension might help to explain why merchants were often religious or ethnic outsiders, with different customs and dress and cut off from the host community.[95] The ancient Greek god of merchants, Hermes, embodied their marginality. The messenger of the gods, he was commonly represented with winged sandals, a traveler's hat, and a herald's staff—the deity who crossed boundaries and traveled from place to place. He was clever and good at speaking, in contrast to wiser or more moralistic gods, and he was also seen as a potential trickster, the god of thieves.

Frequently, the agrarian castes welcomed a clear separation between merchant minorities and the other castes, for people often wanted to be able to negotiate free of the complicated relations of interdependence, paternalism, and deference that normally bound them. As one former Jewish shopkeeper in interwar Poland remembered:

> In the Christian store the customer had to remove his hat. . . . He had to take what he was given and pay whatever the asking price was without bargaining. The Christian customer could not endure the tension and the Christian merchant did not understand the psychology of the customers, whom one had to let bargain and bring down the price.
>
> In the Jewish store the Christian felt free to select the merchandise, test it, haggle and bargain down the price, get credit, and in general have a talk with the Jewish merchant, who was not pompous like the Christian storeowner.[96]

However, it is no surprise that merchants were often condemned by the agrarian castes. Warriors and aristocrats were major critics, as one would expect, given their prizing of honor and shame over money. We can see this hostility in its most extreme form in Tokugawa Japan, in the seventeenth and eighteenth centuries. Even though the samurai relied on merchant loans, strict demarcations between markets and politics were enforced: samurai were not allowed to engage in commerce, while merchants had to show due deference before them and were barred from politics. This was very different from the situation in France at that time, where merchants could buy noble titles and status.[97]

This hostility could be reinforced by sages, though the intensity of anti-merchant sentiment in the major religions varied. In some cultures—especially where trade was a small part of the economy—religious texts were uncompromising, insisting that any profits from trade were unnatural and the result of greed. In early medieval Europe, priests quoted Aristotle and the Old Testament to condemn trade as a whole, and particularly popular was a quotation falsely attributed to Saint John Chrysostom (literally, "Golden Mouth"): "No Christian ought to be a merchant, or if he should wish to be one, he ought to be ejected from the Church of God."[98] The Confucian tradition was also very hostile to merchants; in one text of 81 B.C.E., a Confucian sage declared that "merchants are good at deception and artisans cover up their trickery," while peasants were more virtuous because "the ancients esteemed physical effort."[99] And even the rulers of Qing China, who encouraged merchants and trade, remained fundamentally committed to an agrarian economy.[100]

However, when trade became a more significant part of the economy and sages themselves could benefit from it, they were often prepared to modify their opposition. From the thirteenth century, the Christian Church began to accept that "honest" commerce was possible and permissible. Usury—lending money at interest—remained less acceptable, though ways were found to circumvent the strict biblical prohibitions. Usury was also formally condemned in Islam, though Islam had always granted a respectable status to merchants—the Prophet Muhammad had been a merchant himself, and the bazaar was an important institution in the Islamic world.[101] The Hindu *Laws of Manu,* one of the most influen-

tial texts on social order and caste, drawn up in about 100 B.C.E., when
India was at the center of world trade, was among the most pro-merchant
and allowed members of the commoner (Vaishya) caste, though not
Brahmins or Kshatriyas, to lend money at interest.[102]

It was among peasants and artisans, though, that merchants could be
most unpopular. For merchants often had to sacrifice the social "family"
in a particular community to the market: at times of shortage, they
would export food to distant places and sell it at the market price, however high that was; they would insist that borrowers pay their interest,
whatever their circumstances; they would drive hard bargains with producers, even if they drove the peasant to hunger or threw the artisan out
of work; and they would trade with foreigners as easily as with natives.
A merchant might build a school for the poor, but he could afford his
benevolence, because he had made profits from the poor and the rich
alike. His view of bargaining—as a contest in which the cleverest and
best informed deserved to win—could also be seen by poorly educated
peasants as unscrupulous cheating. German folktales were full of simple,
honest peasants using violence to get their own back against clever, de-
ceitful Jewish traders.[103] The early-twentieth-century Thai king Rama VI
used similar arguments to condemn the Chinese mercantile minority:
"According to Chinese thought, money is the beginning and end of all
good. . . . In matters of money the Chinese are entirely devoid of morals
and mercy. They will cheat you with a smile of satisfaction at their own
perspicacity."[104]

Without military protection, merchants were often vulnerable to popular attacks. The Chinese peasant rebellions of the nineteenth century—
from the White Lotus (1796–1804) to the Taiping (1850–64)—could
involve confiscations of wealth and executions of the rich, and the civil
wars of the Taiping era destroyed the powerful Anhui merchant network.[105] In Banarasi's India, too, merchants were dependent on warrior
protection. Banarasi remembered the fear that gripped him and his fellow merchants when they heard of the death of their patron, the Mughal

emperor Akbar. Would law and order break down and leave their property vulnerable? Banarasi fainted and fell, cracking his head open and bleeding profusely; things were so bad "the word 'God' slipped from his mouth." Riots broke out, and the merchants hid their gold and buried their account books, while "men began to wear plain clothes, and casting off fine shawls, wrapped themselves in rough blankets."[106] Only when Akbar's son, Jahangir, announced he was to take the throne did the unrest subside, and the merchants were able to reopen their shops.

However, while merchants were, in most places, not ruling castes, their power waxed and waned. Indeed, throughout the premodern period, the balance between the merchants and the agrarian elites fluctuated, and with it the relative importance of power founded on "coercion," or tribute, and that based on "capital," or market relations.[107]

Afro-Eurasian trade networks expanded during the millennium after 1000 B.C.E., and after a long period of stasis or decline in the "post-classical" world, they revived between 1000 and 1350, only to be hit by the Black Death; the expansion of cities and trade was always limited by their vulnerability to deadly infections. They then saw an enormous expansion in the century after 1500.[108] Trade was also more important in some places than in others. In the medieval era, China and India were the centers of world commerce, while Europe, especially Eastern Europe, was peripheral. Moreover, at some times—when commerce was doing well and the agrarian castes were politically weak—states could become reliant on merchants, and the balance between "capital" and "coercion" could change.

For instance, when the Chinese Song dynasty (960–1276) lost control of northern China and was forced to depend on the more commercial South, it became much more reliant on trade—at times taxes on commerce amounted to more than half of revenues. It is no surprise, then, that it allowed merchants to buy official posts and encouraged foreign trade by increasing its international trading ports from one to eight.[109] At the same time, commercialization brought technical innovations, higher

agricultural productivity, and industrial development, including gun-
powder technology and the mechanization of textile manufacturing.[110]
The commercial era was brought to an end by the Mongol invasion of
1279, when once again China became primarily an agrarian empire extracting tribute from the peasantry.

Merchant power was, however, particularly strong in independent cities. In the classical period, trading city-states were to be found not only
on the Greek and Phoenician Mediterranean coasts but also in Africa,
India, and Southeast Asia. In the medieval era, cities were most autono-
mous after 1000 in the German and Italian lands of the Holy Roman
Empire, because they could take advantage of the divisions between the
sages, in the form of the Roman Church, and the warrior rulers.[111] In
Italy, these became fully independent city-states and even established
empires—most impressively those of Genoa and Venice. As one would
expect, they were run very differently from agrarian states: their merchant rulers were initially uninterested in territorial conquest at home
and had underdeveloped bureaucracies; rather, the city-states used military power—often bought from mercenaries—to establish commercial
dominance abroad.[112]

Merchants transformed economies throughout the world in the sixteenth and seventeenth centuries; western India and the Yangtze Valley
in China were particularly commercial, market-oriented places.[113] In
many regions, peasants in the areas near cities found themselves drawn
into producing for food markets and adopting commercial ways; and
merchants could become involved in production by supplying artisans
with raw materials and part of their wages.[114] Yet there were limits. Most
merchants were involved in trade and finance, but few controlled production before the eighteenth century, in either agriculture or industry. Few
parts of the world economy were therefore "capitalist"—by which is
meant an economic system in which a group of private individuals owns
the means of production absolutely; every aspect of production, includ-

ing labor, is treated as a means of producing commercial profit; and workers, now (unlike peasants) without access to productive property, survive as wage earners.[115]

When it came to political power, early-seventeenth-century merchants were probably strongest in the old city-states of Europe, though they were also becoming much more influential in India as the Mughal emperors increasingly depended on their cash.[116] However, in one region we can see a more fundamental change over the course of the century. In northwestern Europe, the merchant was to become a real partner with the warrior and the landowner. And for the first time, this would happen not just in city-states like Venice and Genoa or in a loose alliance of cities and territories like the Netherlands, but in a large agrarian state: England.

An Orange Revolution

In 1532, Georg Gisze, a thirty-three-year-old German merchant from Danzig (now Gdansk) now living in London, sat for a portrait by an ambitious painter of the same age and nationality, Hans Holbein. The result is one of the most striking and intriguing images of the early modern merchant that we have. Serious but sympathetic, he is shown standing at his desk, opening a letter and surrounded by the paraphernalia of his calling: quill pens, seals, letters, contracts, ledgers, a small timepiece, and, of course, cash in a pewter box. His expensive (if relatively sober) clothes display his wealth, as does the oriental carpet that covers the table.

And yet, look closely and there is an incongruity here. The lavish clothes sit oddly against the rough, shed-like wall of his office; and while Holbein deliberately shows Gisze as an imposing, substantial figure, he seems strangely confined, uncomfortably cramped between the desk, wall, and shelves. There are other signs that all is not as harmonious as might initially appear. A Latin motto meaning "No joy without sorrow" can be made out behind the weighing scales on the wall, and a vase on the table holds a peculiar bouquet of carnations—symbols of Gisze's forthcoming engagement—and medicinal herbs.

In trying to capture Gisze's character and circumstances, Holbein revealed the contradictory nature of the life of the early modern merchant. Danzig was a member of the Hanseatic League, a group of North Sea and Baltic trading cities, and its merchants dominated the Northern European sea trade. The league had been granted privileges by the king, and its merchants lived in the "Steelyard," a compound on the site of what is now Cannon Street Station. But their lifestyle was not in accord with their riches. As Holbein showed, they were corralled into a small area, living without their families in far from luxurious surroundings. The merchants' settlement was locked at night (Holbein shows Gisze's set of keys hanging on the wall), and fraternizing with the local population was discouraged. In part these precautions reflected the unpopularity of foreign merchants among the locals; in 1517, in the "Evil May Day" riots, a thousand artisan apprentices looted their houses. But merchants were also more widely distrusted. Foreign links brought disease, and plague stalked the Steelyard at the time of Holbein's visit (hence the medicinal plants). And merchants also brought ideas that might disrupt the status quo—on more than one occasion, royal soldiers went into the Steelyard to search for dangerous Protestant texts imported from Germany. As a foreigner, of course, Gisze held an unusual position; commerce was well established in English society, and London's merchants were a thriving group. But in the volatile economic conditions of the era, even local merchants were highly reliant on the king to provide stability and protection.[117]

Some 150 years later, the example of Nicholas Barbon, who lived only a mile away on Fleet Street, shows how much more confident and powerful the merchant had become in the intervening period. Barbon, born in 1637, was the son of the Puritan leather merchant and firebrand preacher Praise-God Barebone. He does not seem to have inherited his father's religious preoccupations, and after a training in medicine he gave up this profession to take advantage of the building boom following the Great Fire of 1666. He soon became a highly successful but notoriously unscrupulous speculative developer. As one acquaintance wrote of him, he was interested "more in economising [on] ground [floor space] for advantage . . . than the more noble aims of architecture, and all his aim was at profit."[118] He threw up shoddy tenements and ignored legal prohibitions on new building, most controversially in his development of Red Lion Square, where the neighboring lawyers of Gray's Inn attacked Barbon's builders. They won the (unarmed) fight but failed to stop Barbon, who continued to successfully bully and deceive his way to riches.[119] Even so, his enemies had to admit that he was extraordinarily inventive, and indeed he was an important pioneer of modern finance. He established the world's first fire insurance company and co-founded Britain's first land bank, which issued some of the earliest mortgages; meanwhile, he made major contributions to London's landscape (particularly along the Strand).

Barbon had clearly broken out of Gisze's confinement. He had spread merchant values and market rules beyond the Steelyards of England to other areas—from the lives of his builders to those of his tenants. He was fully conscious of the importance of his innovations, and in 1690, in his *Discourse of Trade,* he wrote an early defense of free trade and market economics.

Barbon's confidence and steely determination to ride roughshod over opposition show how politically powerful the English merchant had become by this time.[120] So what had changed in northwestern Europe between the era of Gisze and that of Barbon, and why? Long-term economic and religious changes had an impact, but politics and caste power were also crucial. England may or may not have been more commercial and capitalist than India and China, but the merchant had certainly become unusually powerful. A new caste alliance had emerged, and the merchant was an influential partner within it.[121]

At the root of the transformation were growing markets, trade, and urbanization, especially after 1500, when journeys to the New World established Europe as a new commercial hub after a long period on the Asian periphery.[122] New techniques and technologies of warfare after 1400 and the rise of mercenary armies also gave merchants more influence.[123] But it was the northwestern part of the European continent that was particularly affected: the cities on the North Sea and the Baltic had a great deal of autonomy, and the wealth of late-medieval London had conferred on its merchants an unusual degree of political influence for the time.

The Reformation was one sign of that new urban and mercantile confidence, as well as an ideological blow to the old caste order. Initially a religious revolt against the Roman Church for its neglect of spiritual values, it had a more generally corrosive effect on the agrarian castes, justifying the social and political influence of ordinary, literate, and largely urban believers. It also, paradoxically and unintentionally, had a long-term secularizing effect by placing religious power in the hands of laypeople and validating worldly labor.[124] But perhaps the most important direct effect was in England, where it licensed the king to seize monastic property and weakened the power of old Church, aristocratic, and peasant rights to the land, giving it to gentry who were more determined to exploit it in a more profitable, capitalist way.[125] In the course of the following century, land was "enclosed," to give it a single owner, and a large landless labor force was created.

A further, indirect consequence of the Reformation was the vicious religious conflict of the era and its escalating and barely manageable costs. As rulers demanded higher taxes, they met with resistance and struggled to contain the unrest as the old agrarian order came under strain. And by the middle of the seventeenth century it was becoming clear that one European power was more stable and successful than the others: the Dutch Republic. The Dutch state was an alliance of coastal cities dominated by merchants. But rather than seek to build military forces themselves, as their Italian predecessors in Genoa and Venice had, they forged an alliance with aristocrats in the agrarian hinterland. The resulting division of labor played to the strengths of each: the cities exploited their mastery of finance, raising money for the war against their Spanish Hapsburg overlords,[126] while their neighbors to the south, the princes of Orange, built on their military expertise and used merchant cash to develop new military techniques—drilling troops and mounting sieges.[127] This new "Orange" alliance of merchant and aristocratic rule was to prove extraordinarily successful, and by 1650 the Dutch had thrown off Hapsburg imperial domination, built a vast trading empire in Asia, and become the leading power in Europe, eclipsing the great agrarian powers, France and Spain.

The Dutch achievement was keenly observed elsewhere.[128] It was especially influential in neighboring England. In the 1640s, merchants and Puritan sages were joined by Protestant gentry in a parliamentary rebellion, toppling King Charles I and the bishops in 1649, but even when the old order was restored in 1660, merchants were in a strong position and continued to agitate for the promotion of their interests and status. For Nicholas Barbon, the Dutch had shown that trade earned wealth; and if England was to compete internationally, it was imperative that the previously despised merchant elite, with very different values from the old warrior landowning aristocracy, had to be given access to power. As he wrote, "Until trade became necessary to provide weapons of war, it was always thought prejudicial to the growth of empire," as commerce led to "too much softening the people by ease and luxury, which made their bodies unfit to endure the labour and hardships of war. . . ." But "now we see all corners of Europe crowded with . . . disciplined and standing armies in pay, . . . which as it cannot be done without huge funds of money, and the ancient demesnes [lands] of the king not sufficing, taxes are everywhere increased on the subject."[129] For Barbon, it was no longer the paternalistic landowner who was the warrior's best friend, but the merchant.

Not all agreed with Barbon, and the old castes—the Catholics and

High Anglicans and conservative landowners—fought back. The clash
between the two visions of society dominated English, Scottish, and Irish
politics for much of the seventeenth century. But the conflict was finally
resolved in 1688 with another "Orange revolution," the so-called Glorious Revolution. Challenging James II—a Catholic, Francophile king
who saw the future of England in its agrarian economy—rebels invited
William of Orange to take power and import the Dutch model of
merchant-aristocratic rule.[130]

The entrance of the merchant into the principal corridors of power
was finally announced with the foundation of the Bank of England, in
1694. As the pro-merchant Londoner John Toland enthused, "What
greater demonstration can the world require concerning the excellence of
our national government, or the particular power and freedom of this
city, than the Bank of England?"[131] Merchants and wealthy landowners
lent money to William and the military aristocracy to fight wars and
achieve glory, and they were paid interest in return, collected by an increasingly efficient tax-extracting bureaucracy.[132] But merchants also
achieved a decisive influence over the state. Now they were financing the
king. And the wars they paid for built a vast empire of trade and plantations, from which foreign merchants were excluded.[133] They also began
to build a merchant-friendly state at home, and men like Barbon could
flourish without routinely needing to break the law.[134] For the first time
in history, the merchant had a major influence in a powerful agrarian
state capable of building a world empire. And through that empire, the
British were to empower merchants throughout the world.

TWO

Iron Fist, Velvet Glove

Robinson Crusoe, the hero of Daniel Defoe's famous 1719 novel, is a merchant from York who finds himself shipwrecked on a desert island. Heedless of his misfortune, he applies his merchant habits to these unpromising circumstances, and through a combination of good sense, ingenious technology, and hard toil, he transforms the arid atoll into a productive paradise. His land is neatly fenced, his animals are domesticated, and he even tries to convert the "savages," who, sadly, do not share his economic or religious attitudes. Emphasizing firm kindness rather than bullying violence, he successfully teaches his native servant, Friday, to be a good Christian, and when cannibals visit the island, Crusoe forswears a resort to militaristic cruelty and vengefulness and leaves them in peace.[1] To do otherwise, he observes, would be to ape the warriorish ways of the brutal Spaniards in America, a "race of men who were without principles of tenderness."[2] What better allegory could there be for peaceful merchant colonialism? However, when the cannibals seem likely to consume a God-fearing Christian, he flies into a bellicose fury and slaughters them with unthinking violence.

Through Crusoe's example, Defoe was insisting on the essentially pacific, commercial nature of the English—in contrast to the militaristic

Spanish, ruled as they were by old agrarian castes. However, he regarded violent force as justified in the quest to spread peaceful commerce globally. For as he rose to world domination, the merchant encountered resistance to his morality and way of life, which elicited from him two very different responses. When seriously threatened by competitors and other castes, especially workers, peasants, and artisans, the merchant would adopt a hard and militant stance, determined to spread his culture by the sword if necessary—and despite his disapproval of the old warrior ethic, he could often be found forging alliances with the military aristocracy above him. But in the absence of such resistance, it was the soft merchant who won out, preferring to tempt resisters into the fold with the promise of comfort and consumption.

For much of the eighteenth and early nineteenth centuries, the British merchant alternated between these two strategies. But for a period in the mid-nineteenth century, it looked as if the soft merchant was in the ascendant, with social peace at home and a Pax Britannica abroad. That stability, however, proved illusory. By the end of the nineteenth century, the aristocratic warrior was to return to preeminence—in alliance with the hard merchant—in both commercial Britain and formerly agrarian states. But now they had the support of the sage-technocrat. And now, as rulers of much more powerful nation-states with vast armies, they were able to wreak far greater destruction than ever before.

AT THE BEGINNING of the era of British dominance, the hard merchant/warrior alliance was in the ascendant, and Defoe was among its most articulate spokesmen—unsurprisingly, perhaps, given the harsh and uncertain environment of his youth. The son of a candle dealer, he was born in 1660 into a Puritan merchant family. This was a bad year for his community, for the Puritan revolution had been defeated and Charles II had reclaimed his throne, intent on removing the religious freedoms granted to Puritans during Cromwell's republic. Defoe was now a member of a persecuted minority: he recalled that his fellow dissenters were so fearful of a return to Catholicism and the confiscation of their Bibles that they had made copies in shorthand.[3] He strongly identified with his family's and his community's ethos throughout his life. He saw the "true-bred merchant" as "the most intelligent man in the world" and denounced the landed gentry for devoting themselves to "hunt, race, game, drink etc."[4] He welcomed the Glorious Revolution of 1688 as a divinely ordained deliverance from the forces of popish sages and aristocratic tyranny.

Defoe initially traded in stockings and wine, some five minutes' walk from Georg Gisze's Steelyard, in Freeman's Yard, Cornhill. But he was hardly a model merchant in the Puritan mold. He could never resist speculative get-rich-quick schemes, cheated his mother-in-law of the huge sum (for the time) of four hundred pounds, was named in eight separate lawsuits for fraud, and finally went bankrupt. And yet he spent much of his life proselytizing for the commercial way of life, and the values he espoused were strikingly similar to those of Banarasi's Jains or Pegolotti's fourteenth-century Italian commercial travelers.

Defoe's advice manual, *The Complete English Tradesman* of 1725–27, describes his merchant ethic most clearly. Most important for the trader, Defoe insisted, was hard work; indeed, in his typically extreme language, he went so far as to accuse the slothful merchant of "murder," for he was effectively starving himself, his family, and his reputation.[5] The trader was also to be sober and sensible, not a luxury-loving "Sir Fopling Flutter."[6] And he was to be pacific, not proud and quarrelsome like the "martial warlike Princes" who ruled the Turks.[7] Most strikingly, he was to be cosmopolitan. (Defoe had approvingly described the English as a "mongrel, half-bred race.") He was to be honest—though only up to a point: he had to maintain his creditworthiness, but he could not avoid "unavoidable trading lies," and it was legitimate to persuade the customer to pay the highest price possible even when the merchant was prepared to take less.[8] Finally, he was to be shrewd and plain-speaking, equipped with practical literacy and numeracy, and not encumbered with elitist erudition and pedantry "fitter for Dancing Masters"; Defoe's educational ideal was his alma mater, Charles Morton's dissenting Academy at Newington Green (near present-day Hackney), which specialized in mathematics, science, and modern languages, not Latin and Greek.[9] Merchants had to abandon the old fusty scholarship and learn from a new breed of secular sage—the scientists and inventors who had become so prominent with the foundation of the Royal Society of London (for Improving Natural Knowledge) in 1660. As Defoe declared, "The knowledge of things, not words, makes a scholar."[10]

However, this commitment to cultural equality was not intended to justify economic equality, for that merely rewarded the lazy and the foolish—a view Defoe shared with many merchants. Indeed, he was a firm admirer of the "pump-house at Amsterdam," where beggars were given the choice to pump and remain dry or to "grow lazy" and sink beneath the water: "they may chuse which they like best." His ideal, then, was a society of competitive men who had a certain sympathy and fellow feeling with others as traders and consumers but not as part of some paternalistic extended social family. That merely led to destructive charity from above and slavish dependence below.[11]

How, though, was the merchant to propagate this new vision of society? As Defoe realized, if the merchant was to escape his confinement and create a merchant-friendly economy, he needed to convert other, potentially hostile castes to his way of thinking. But this was easier said than done. The laboring poor, thrown off the land by enclosures and deprived of their rural autonomy, resented menial, repetitive work for disciplinarian merchant-manufacturers. Meanwhile, landowners and the established church were certainly not going to give up their dominance without a fight.

When it came to the castes beneath him, Defoe was generally a firm advocate of toughness: the poor had to be compelled to work, and most forms of welfare would simply indulge their laziness and had to be banned—even begging.[12] He was equally uncompromising toward his upper-caste opponents. But in their case he preferred to forge alliances with more sympathetic members of the military caste. Defoe was always on the lookout for a powerful noble supporter of his cause. In 1685, for example, he rushed to join the charismatic Duke of Monmouth in his failed rebellion against the Catholic James II; he became an unstinting supporter of (and powerful propagandist for) William of Orange's bloody Protestant wars against the French, and he also thought force was needed to suppress the assorted pro-James "Jacobites" and reactionaries who challenged the commercial, Protestant order. In an ideal world, of course, he preferred peaceful trade to war. But at a time of vicious commercial competition between nation-states, when rulers battled to control trade routes, he became an advocate of military support for commerce.

Defoe was therefore no believer in pure merchant rule. Indeed, at times he espoused the benefits of the old agrarian caste order and argued that the merchant should be placed below the two old ruling castes of church and aristocrat. Trade, he argued, had to go "hand in hand with religion and constitution, not by way of equality, but as it is the great auxiliary, which enables us to protect, defend and preserve the other from all its opposers."[13]

Crusoe-like merchant-warriors, fired by moralistic self-righteousness, played a crucial role in spreading the merchant's influence throughout the world. The early European empires were built by such merchants in "chartered companies"—commercial organizations that had their own militias and were supported by national navies with their own troops. The most successful was the British East India Company, which took control of Bengal after the Battle of Plassey, in 1757, and brought Britain its most lucrative imperial possession. Defoe himself was a propagandist for the settlement of American colonies with slave plantations. He, like many early imperialists, was convinced of his moral right to expropriate the land of so-called "lazy natives" and "oriental despots," those most egregious examples of the martial aristocrat.[14]

However, by the middle of the eighteenth century, some were turning against the hard merchant, at least in sagely circles. Commercial society had become more secure in England following the defeat of the Jacobite rebellions of 1715 and 1745–46, and the escalating expense of wars over trade strengthened the supporters of "*doux commerce*" (soft commerce). The most powerful defender of the soft-merchant worldview was the great theorist of market society Adam Smith.

Smith, first a professor of moral philosophy at the University of Glasgow, then tutor to an aristocrat, and finally a high Edinburgh customs official, was an eighteenth-century version of the secular sage—the "enlightened philosopher" employed by reforming aristocrats and new state-sponsored universities, prepared to challenge the old agrarian order. He was born into a world both sagely and aristocratic: his father was a trained lawyer and member of the Scottish "service aristocracy," that part of the minor gentry involved in public administration. And he did not have the practical and competitive personality of the merchant; in fact, he was more like a typical absentminded professor in character, wrapped up in his thoughts and muttering to himself as he wandered the streets of Edinburgh.[15] This sagely attitude gave him a much less narrowly mercantile view of the world than Defoe; he was closer to the liberal "creative" castes of our own day, with their criticisms of the commercial bourgeoisie's supposed "narrowness," their interest in humanistic education, and their sympathy for the less fortunate. And so it is odd that during the turn to Thatcherite and Reaganite economics in the 1980s, Smith was often held up as the theorist of harsh market discipline. For Smith, while agreeing with the hard-merchant Defoe on the need to spread the merchant ethos, took a very different view of how this should be done.

But Smith, like Defoe, had close connections with commerce. His father was controller of customs in Kirkcaldy, a prosperous port town near Edinburgh, and this was the career for which his son was intended. Smith, therefore, had firsthand knowledge of how successfully a new commercial order was increasing prosperity, and *The Wealth of Nations* of 1776, his most famous work, is indeed the most powerful justification of commercial society ever written. Here, Smith went so far as to suggest that the love of trade was *the* definitive human quality—what set mankind apart from animals. For Smith, all of us, whether street porters or philosophers, are merchants by nature, for we all have two universal desires: to "truck, barter and exchange" and to "better our condition."[16] Some might see this as a rather pinched view of humanity, but Smith would have disagreed; he insisted that bartering was an elevated thing, a form of oratory or persuasion that demanded a sympathy with strangers and allowed people to achieve their goals without violence.[17] Bartering also fostered the "division of labor," the specialization of work that allowed some companies and countries to become more productive than others. The desire to better one's condition, meanwhile, was a powerful spur to hard work, and it was the competitive desire for status conferred by luxury goods that led to the virtues of commercial society.[18]

Today we would call this vision of society a "consumerist" one, and Smith insisted that everybody would benefit from it. According to him, wealth would inevitably trickle down from the rich to the poor as the rich consumed and created employment. Smith accepted that commercial societies were economically unequal, and more so than their agrarian predecessors, but he insisted that they also produced more wealth for more people. Although the wage-earning poor had to spend their time keeping the rich in "idleness and luxury," they were much wealthier than "naked savages" in precommercial societies, who enjoyed only the basics of existence.[19] And Smith, living in a Jacobite-riddled Scotland where old-style paternalistic lords were still powerful, was particularly hostile to the culture of dependency promoted by kings and aristocrats. He accepted that aristocrats might be more benevolent to their inferiors than the merchant, but in return they expected servility, sycophancy, and blind loyalty. A society in which people were bound together through competitiveness and commerce might well be less equal economically than a paternalistic one, but it would be freer, wealthier, and more peaceful. This vision lay at the root of the soft-merchant ethos, and it is no surprise that in 2007 the British "New Labour" prime minister Gordon Brown even ordered that the British twenty-pound note carry a portrait of Smith and the famous pin factory he used to illustrate the division of labor.

Defoe, of course, would have agreed entirely with many of Smith's ideas. And yet much of Smith's writing was nothing less than a sustained attack on Defoe's hard-merchant worldview. For Smith, Defoe's preferred route of spreading the merchant ethos—through an alliance between big merchants and the warrior aristocracy—was anathema. This caste configuration, Smith insisted, merely encouraged rapacious merchants to use the "violence and injustice of the rulers of mankind" to promote their own businesses at the expense of their competitors; the inevitable result would be animosity, war, and cruel, slave-owning empires.[20] Smith also strongly disapproved of merchants' harshness to the laboring castes below them—their desire to drive them as hard as possible for the lowest wages they could get away with. He believed not only that commerce flourished in conditions of peace and international concord but also that workers would be far more productive if they were treated well, with good working conditions and high wages. The rule of the merchant caste, allied with warriors—as envisioned by Defoe—was no way to promote the ideal soft-merchant ethos: as Smith made clear, "merchants and manufacturers . . . neither are, nor ought to be the rulers of mankind."[21]

For rather different reasons, then, both Smith and Defoe agreed that merchants could not rule alone. But while Defoe advocated a merchant-warrior government, Smith's ideal rulers were enlightened sagely magistrates—humanities-educated people much like himself—who could be trusted to promote the positive side of commercial values and regulate their cruelty with a sense of fairness to the whole of society, including the poor.

Smith, then, while a defender of the merchant ethos, was far from enthusiastic about real-life merchants. And this central paradox lends his work a profound ambivalence.[22] Smith admitted that the commercial spirit, in giving status to the hardworking and competitive, led people to "admire and almost worship the rich and powerful" while despising and neglecting the poor.[23] He also despaired at commercial attitudes to learning. Among the merchant classes, he noted, "education is despised"—at least the broader, humanistic education that he so valued. He also worried about the life of mindless, repetitive tasks to which factory workers were condemned by employers.[24] This is why he believed the state had to establish schools that would not only impart practical skills but also teach people to be citizens.

But despite these doubts, Smith was an optimist, like so many Enlightenment "philosophers" in Scotland and *"philosophes"* in France. He did not have any very clear solutions to the problems and injustices of commercial society he had so vividly identified; but even so, he believed that a commercial society dominated by the merchant ethos was generally superior to the alternatives, and that history was moving in a progressive direction. And crucially, unlike Defoe, he thought market economies and consumer societies would evolve without much need for violence or state intervention.

Smith's enthusiasm for commerce was shared by many of his contemporaries among the French *philosophes,* who saw it as the best way of securing Enlightenment values of social and legal equality. And many of the French revolutionaries of 1789 agreed with him that a market society would help to destroy the strict caste divisions of the aristocratic order. There was, however, another, more radical, pro-worker Enlightenment tradition that condemned not only the social inequalities of the ancien régime but also those created by the merchant. It was this form of politics that became powerful, very briefly, under the influence of Robespierre's radical Jacobins and the *sans culottes* ("without breeches") artisans in 1793–94.

This radicalism was easily defeated, and commercialization, under British hegemony, soon resumed. However, it was Defoe, not the more peaceable Smith, who was vindicated. Defoe rightly predicted that commercial society would not be built without a great deal of coercion. In the eighteenth century, the European powers were almost constantly fighting; beginning in 1757, Britain and France sought commercial dominance from the Caribbean to India—a struggle that culminated in the bloody Napoleonic Wars.

By the mid-nineteenth century, it did look as if Britain and its allies' victory over Napoleon in 1815 might at last bring Smith's dream of peaceful commerce to pass. Now Britain was in control of the world's maritime trade routes, as well as being the preeminent manufacturing exporter and importer of raw materials from abroad. It was in its interests to defend Smithian values of free trade, reinforced by the London-backed gold standard—the new international global currency.

But the British system was not as peaceful as its defenders claimed. London used force to bully governments into accepting free trade, from sending gunboats to Latin America in the 1830s to fighting the Chinese Opium Wars of 1839–42. In most years, Britain was at war somewhere in the world, with the most dramatic challenge coming in 1857 from the Indian Rebellion (or "Mutiny"). Meanwhile, coercion was enormously important to the empire's economy: even after the abolition of slavery, in 1834, much labor on colonial plantations was effectively still unfree and subject to the system of indenture.

At home, too, governments used harsh laws to impose markets: landlords' "enclosure" of lands previously controlled by rural communities was effectively a form of privatization at the barrel of a gun. It should be no surprise, therefore, that Britain was periodically racked by riots, and as late as 1869 police in parts of rural Norfolk were issued cutlasses.[25] Meanwhile, repression of peasant rebellions in Ireland continued well into the twentieth century.

However, compared with many other nations, between 1688 and 1914 Britain did make a relatively peaceful transition from a society ruled by the agrarian castes to one increasingly dominated by the merchant.[26] In part this was because as the country became richer—often at the expense of other countries—and offered more economic opportunities, many ordinary people were "converted" to commercial ways.[27]

But it was also because Britain followed the course advised by both Defoe and Smith: it was not ruled by the merchant alone. In this most dynamic period of its history, Britain suffered from a series of crises precipitated by the merchant as he tried to introduce markets to a resistant population, and each was resolved by a new caste compromise that tamed the market. This caste consensus sustained a remarkably successful economic system and provided a model for the rest of the world—for a time.

One Wedding and a Funeral

It is a truth, universally acknowledged, that the British have a flair for costume dramas. Serializations of eighteenth- and nineteenth-century novels, with their frettings over advantageous marriages, property inheritance, and petty status anxieties, are British TV's major export. And with good reason: novelists living in the first largely agrarian nation to have experienced the rise of the merchant have been endlessly fascinated by the tensions between the commercial and agrarian castes. And they were especially interested in the way those conflicts were expressed through the long-running post-Reformation "culture wars" between the aristocratic "Cavalier"—arrogant, morally lax, and cosmopolitan—and the Puritan "Roundhead," who was diligent, moralistic, and provincial.[28] Most writers were eager to show how this division could be healed, generally by a wedding. And the history of Britain can be usefully read through the prism of these marriage plots.

The alliance of aristocratic and merchant cultures in the decades after 1688 was most clearly, if rather creepily, explored by the Protestant printer and novelist Samuel Richardson in a series of somewhat odd novels. His bestseller *Pamela, or Virtue Rewarded* (1740) recounts the story of the efforts of the libertine squire Mr. B to seduce his servant, the Puri-

tan maid Pamela. Mr. B exhibits all the sins of the Cavalier aristocrat—
a classical education in dead languages, a cosmopolitan love of all things
French, and a bullying and profligate character. Pamela, by contrast, ex-
udes Roundhead virtue—pure, pious, and Scripture-schooled. And instead of responding to Mr. B's outrageous behavior with violent rebellion,
she calmly (if rather masochistically) endures his advances and converts
him to godliness and good household management.

The compromise between Mr. B and Pamela echoed the alliance between the merchant insurgents of 1688 and the commercially minded
aristocracy.[29] By the 1720s, the merchant radicalism of the early Orange
era had been diluted,[30] and Britain was ruled by a close-knit oligarchy of
wealthy urban merchants and aristocratic landowners, often quite literally joined by marriage. Landowners were major financiers of the national debt and became involved in colonial trade. Henry Lascelles, for
instance, born in 1690 to a Yorkshire landowning family, made a fortune
through importing sugar from Barbados and by investing in the national
debt.[31] The ideal English "gentleman" was emerging—part merchant,
part Cavalier aristocrat.

These compromises became central to the character of Britain's economy. Commercial firms were small and controlled by groups of owner-
partners rather than professional managers.[32] This was the world of the
inspired amateur, not the stuffy professional, and a powerful Victorian
ideal was the "merchant prince"—a swashbuckling, adventurous figure,
reliant on entrepreneurial instinct and eager to take rapid and risky decisions without interference from officials or technical experts.[33] Samuel
Smith, a successful mid-nineteenth-century merchant engaged in the Indian cotton trade, elaborated this aristocratic, generalist, and anti-sagely
ideal when he declared that a "first-class merchant does not burden his
mind with a multitude of details, and is always seemingly at leisure while
intent on great issues."[34] Meanwhile, the British state did not develop
into a powerful sagely force. Although one of the most efficient tax gath-
erers in the world and highly effective in fighting wars, it was much less

developed in other areas; government relied on local elites until the 1870s, and a central bureaucracy did not become really powerful until the 1890s.[35]

However, as Britain became the "workshop of the world" in the years after the Napoleonic Wars, a new type of merchant emerged who was to challenge this gentlemanly compromise, and who was much more difficult to integrate into the social order: the industrial manufacturer.

Many early British industrialists had either commercial or artisanal roots, and often combined the two in a set of attitudes that valued production over consumption, Puritan plain-speaking over ingratiating sociability, and inventiveness and long-term investment over smart short-term business deals. They also had a "hard" merchant attitude toward their rivals—the gentleman-merchant, whom they thought lazy and corrupt, and the factory artisan or unskilled worker, who was deemed feckless and ill disciplined. Their relations with their workers were particularly fraught, for they made their profits by mechanizing production and cutting wage costs. In some ways, they can be seen as the heirs of the old Roundheads, and indeed they often came from the nonconformist communities of the North of England.[36] Typical was the formidable Bradford worsted entrepreneur Titus Salt, who spent the first thousand pounds he had carefully saved on a gold watch—a luxury, certainly, but one that could be justified as a necessary instrument of self-discipline.[37]

The most influential spokesman for this outlook was Samuel Smiles, author of the bestselling *Self-Help* (1859) and originator of the self-help-book genre, which fills airport bookshops to this day. Smiles was born into a Calvinist Scottish family of shopkeepers in 1812 and apprenticed to an Edinburgh surgeon. But he found it difficult to earn a living in medicine, so he worked on the early railways before eventually making his fortune by writing. As a youth, he was rather a radical figure—a campaigner for social reform in a society he saw as unfair and unequal. But later in life he returned to the Calvinism of his upbringing and the evangelical conviction that anyone could transform himself through hard work and "self-help." He was always a harsh critic of the gentlemanly merchant values that prevailed among the London elites, and he turned down a knighthood in 1902. His books are best understood as "saints' lives" for the manufacturing age—inspiring stories of humble folk who raised themselves from the ranks of laborers through sheer "industry, perseverance, and self-culture."[38] His favorite subjects were inventors and poor engineers like Josiah Wedgwood, the inventor of Wedgwood porcelain, who was taken out of school at a young age to work in a pottery, and Richard Arkwright, the laborers' son who went on to revolutionize the technology of the textile industry. Smiles's lesson was that greatness came from merchant qualities of diligence and sobriety rather than high birth and a fancy education. But it also came from the artisan's pride in invention and production, rather than Adam Smith's pure merchant values, which exalted trading and bartering over consumer goods.[39]

Naturally, this ruggedly independent, self-improving figure posed a challenge to an older caste compromise, upsetting the gentlemanly elite, but particularly workers and artisans. Serious striking and unrest in the 1830s and '40s—much of it organized by artisans threatened by mechanization and the vagaries of the market—shook Britain's rulers and convinced many, including Marx and Engels, that revolution was coming. A series of new caste compromises was the result. Manufacturers became less "hard" and more paternalistic in their attitudes to their workers, and government sought to regulate working and living conditions in factories and towns.[40] An economic upturn in the 1850s helped, and many skilled workers were attracted by the culture of middle-class respectability— a merchant ideal of morality, temperance, and charity.[41]

The extension of the franchise to many in the middle classes in 1832 and landowners' willingness to accept pro-merchant free trade (1846) also defused tensions between landed elites and manufacturers. Moreover, they shared a common suspicion of the bookish sage-technocrat, whether in his incarnation as state official, professional manager, or scientist. Smiles's heroes might have helped scientific progress along, but they were practical people with little formal education, not researchers and theorists. Smiles spoke for many of the early industrial entrepreneurs when he wrote, "The highest culture is not obtained from teachers when at school or college, so much as by our own diligent self-education when we have become men."[42] And Britain's manufacturers relied a great deal on skilled workers, who managed much of the industrial process themselves and also trained new workers on the shop floor. This system enabled them to do without professional managers and elaborate technical training.[43]

So, while Britain in the 1850s and '60s was widely derided by its critics as a "nation of shopkeepers" (in Napoleon's derisive old phrase), in fact it was founded on caste compromise.[44] The landed aristocracy retained much of its political and cultural influence, benefiting from the riches of the City of London. The gentleman-merchant focused on international trade and banking, lent money for Russian railways and American steel mills, and held sway over the gold standard—a fixed global currency system that encouraged trade and became increasingly dominant toward the end of the century. The manufacturer was never as influential as the gentlemanly merchant or mercantile aristocrat—few were members of the influential London gentlemen's clubs—but they supplied products to the world.[45] Skilled workers, too, reaped the benefits of the booming economy. All of this was presided over by a relatively small central state. With few international rivals, Britain's fleet was more than capable of flushing out pirates and forcing foreigners to open their markets.

This mid-Victorian compromise was founded on an ethos of "gentlemanly" independence, which penetrated many levels of society.[46] The castes, despite tensions between them, had learned to coexist reasonably harmoniously, essentially by minimizing interference in one another's affairs. And this relatively low level of cooperation was enough because Britain was very much the *workshop* of the world, not the *factory* of the world—until the later part of the century, muscle was still more important than machinery.[47] Manufacturers ran pretty small-scale outfits and did not need much investment from gentleman-merchant bankers, who could therefore channel their funds into more lucrative opportunities in trade and foreign industry. And just as these small-scale manufacturers made few demands of their caste "superiors," they tolerated a great deal of independence below them, allowing skilled workers a measure of autonomy over the organization of the workplace.[48]

The compromise among merchant, warrior, and landed aristocrat also underlay Britain's empire. In some areas, the British ruled over what was in effect a traditional agrarian empire—most notably in India after 1857, where the British delegated much of their power to local landowners and princes, discouraged too much commercial development, and extracted tribute from the peasantry. In much of the world, though, theirs was a more "informal," commercial empire, mixing hard and soft merchant values: the warrior—in the form of the Royal Navy—defended the merchant by keeping trade largely free and making sure that countries paid their debts, while the merchant, in the form of the Bank of England, ran the gold standard in collaboration with other states and encouraged foreign investment from the City of London.

Britain was making the world safe for merchants around the world, and certainly many traders of all nationalities took advantage of this new Pax Britannica. A small group of internationally networked merchants— including the Parsis of Bombay, the Greeks of Alexandria, and the British of Rio de Janeiro—made large fortunes.[49] The British international order also allowed landowners to produce for the international market and helped them transform their economies into more capitalist ones. Beginning in the 1860s, for instance, Argentine estate owners took advantage of finance from London banks to invest in ranches and railways, exporting their meat and grain to Europe and North America. Together with trading and banking elites, they controlled governments and ensured that they supported pro-British, pro-merchant policies.[50] These were the groups condemned by nationalists as "compradors"—unpatriotic Trojan horses for foreign capital and political influence.

Argentina was one agricultural country that did well in this British informal empire; it might even have had one of the highest per capita incomes by 1900. Most others, however, did poorly, unless they had industry—and the British free-trade regime succeeded in stifling industrialization in many parts of the world as it prevented other powers from nurturing their own manufacturing industries. India was a major victim, as British policies weakened domestic industry and encouraged Indian merchants to concentrate on trade and finance.[51] Foreign pressure also damaged efforts to industrialize in China and the Ottoman Empire, though resistance from ruling castes also played a major role; in China, in particular, the sagely rulers were determined to exclude foreign influence and avoid social disruption.[52]

It was therefore in the period of British merchant influence that the gap between the industrialized "West" and much of the South became so extreme.[53] But again, not all countries fared poorly in the British system. For strong states determined to industrialize, in control of their own trade policies, and able to set high tariffs—such as the United States, Germany, and Japan after 1894—the gold standard and open trade gave them an advantage.[54]

For many elites in the 1850s and '60s, therefore, it seemed that Britain was the country of the future, and its fervent advocacy of free trade promised a world of peace, production, and plenty. "Smithianismus"— the thought of Adam Smith—was all the rage in Germany; London's Crystal Palace of 1851, a temple to the icons of Britain's technological ingenuity, was admired throughout the world, and even Lenin's favorite writer, the Russian socialist Nikolai Chernyshevsky, took the giant Hyde Park greenhouse as his model for utopia in his novel *What Is to Be Done?* Smiles's *Self-Help* became an international bestseller: millions of copies were sold in the United States, though in Japan, where it was published

in 1871 as *Stories of Successful Lives in Western Countries,* the translation
rendered it oddly sagely and Confucian in tone.[55] Meanwhile, cities from
Buenos Aires to Shanghai boasted leather-chaired and oak-paneled clubs
for Anglophile gentleman-merchants to lounge in after a hard day's gentlemanly trading.

For liberals, the British commercial order promised the dissolution of
old ancien régime caste divisions. But the racially exclusive clubs in the
British colonies represented the real nature of the British commercial empire more accurately: places designed for urbane business and political
networking, they were also imbued with the spirit of hierarchy, aristocracy, and social segregation. In Rangoon, for instance, the Pegu Club
catered to officials and senior businessmen, the Boat Club accommo-
dated engineers and shop assistants, and the Railway Institute was for the
army ranks and the mixed-race "Eurasians."[56]

However, just as the Japanese were learning how to help themselves—
British style—others were predicting the demise of the British international order. The early 1870s brought three significant challenges. The
proclamation of a new unified German state, the Second Reich, in 1871,
signaled the rise of new competitors, powerful both militarily and
economically—not only Germany and, to an extent, Japan but also the
United States; second, the creation that same year of a socialist workers'
government in Paris, the "Commune," demonstrated the power of the rising working class; and finally, 1873 brought an international banking crisis followed by a twenty-year decline in prices—the first so-called Great
Depression—and with it a backlash against British-sponsored free trade as
governments resorted to state protection for nascent industries. The depression also coincided with, and might in part have caused, fundamental
technological change—the so-called second industrial revolution. This
brought a new, larger-scale, and more technologically sophisticated industrial economy. The great beneficiary of all these changes was the sage-
technocrat—professional engineers, scientists, and teachers and, especially

in Continental Europe and Japan, state bureaucrats.[57] To compete economically and militarily, states had to expand: they needed to become more involved in managing this dramatic economic and social change—coordinating heavy-industrial investment, providing mass education, and, in Europe, building welfare systems to mitigate the worst effects of the radical upheaval. It is no surprise that the greatest social thinker of the era, Max Weber, saw "bureaucracy" as the dominant social force of the age—an inevitable but not always welcome force that imprisoned humanity in its "iron cage." State bureaucracies swelled, and the sage-technocrat's values began to penetrate all spheres—armies, commercial companies, and even labor unions.

This was a world in which the British caste alliance of the nineteenth century was at a distinct disadvantage. For while the British state did become more professionalized and intrusive after the 1870s, in the economy the sage was much less of a presence.[58] And the success of Britain's competitors at the end of the century is, at least in part, explained by their ability to incorporate him and his values into their economies.

However, the rising powers integrated the sage in very different ways, for the old division between the more commercial and agrarian states survived. Where the old warrior-aristocrat elites were still particularly strong, in Germany and Japan, sage-technocrats became their partners, along with some businessmen. And together they launched assertive, state-led projects to build industrial strength, bolstered by powerful nationalist ideologies. Warriors, aware that industry, not land, now produced wealth, gradually disengaged themselves from landowning aristocrats and allied with sage-technocrats and businessmen to build nation-states, economies, and military machines. In the United States, in contrast, the aristocrat was largely absent and the merchant was more dominant—even more so than in Britain. And there the central state remained small, the warrior was weak, and the sage-technocrat was often the junior partner of private business.

Enter the Sage: "Private Officials," "Men of Affairs," and "Company Men"

Had Samuel Smiles written *Self-Help* a little later, he might have included a biography of Werner Siemens. Born to a mildly impoverished (though originally aristocratic) family near Hanover in 1816, he joined the Prussian army and devoted himself to technological tinkering in his spare time. He achieved one of his early breakthroughs (gold-plating a silver spoon) during a short spell in prison for dueling. On the way to jail, he stopped off at a local pharmacy and managed to buy enough supplies to set up a small laboratory in his "barred but roomy cell." When he received a royal pardon, he petitioned to stay in prison with his lab for a few more months to complete his experiments, but he was refused.[59]

The Prussian army, however, realized that it could exploit his scientific pursuits, and it was while serving as an army officer that he laid the foundations for the great multinational electrical engineering firm Siemens, which survives to this day. His inventions were particularly important in making possible the "globalization" of the late nineteenth century: he built an improved "pointer telegraph," using a needle to point to letters instead of Morse code—a godsend for armies and railway companies reliant on Morse-illiterate operators; and it was his method of insulating electrical wires with a natural latex called gutta-percha gum that allowed the company to network the world. But most important for the firm was his 1867 invention, the electrical generator, a breakthrough that ushered in much of "modern" life—from electrical lighting to trams.

This was just the kind of pluck and self-helpism Smiles would have revered. But on closer inspection, the Siemens story does not fit the Smilesian template very well. First, Siemens valued his achievements as a pure research scientist as much as, if not more than, his work as an inventor and risk-taking entrepreneur: "My love always belonged to science as such, while my work and accomplishments lay mostly in the field of technology," he declared.[60] And though he had not been to university, he had received a very thorough scientific training in the army, becoming an active member of the Berlin Academy of Sciences and publishing several scientific papers.

Moreover, Siemens's career was closely bound up with the state and with an army that was becoming more bureaucratic and less aristocratic in spirit. Technological changes—the railways and new weaponry, from mass-produced guns to warships—gave states an interest in promoting industrialization, and militaries were major customers for the new technologies.[61] Siemens's first contracts came from the army and state telegraph authorities. Indeed, at one stage he even considered transferring into the civil service to help run the telegraph system, before eventually setting up his own private company in 1849.[62] Certainly, like Smiles's heroes, he was a political liberal, hostile to aristocratic rule. But he was also much more nationalistic than they were: "From earliest youth on," he wrote, "the disunion and powerlessness of the German nation pained me," and he saw "the large technical business firm" as a central weapon in Germany's efforts to compete with "England, France and America, those countries which are our most dangerous enemies in the struggle for survival."[63] He also put his money where his mouth was: in 1884 he funded a new state physics institute, which sought to benefit both German industry and the military—especially its growing navy.[64] Siemens, though certainly an entrepreneur, quick to exploit new market opportunities, was at heart a sage-technocrat and believed in the transformative role of the state.

Although Siemens was an unusually dynamic and effective figure, his commitment to serious academic education and to furthering the interests of the state was common among German businessmen. Even in his own time, entrepreneurs were more likely to have a thorough technical education than their British counterparts, and in the late nineteenth century many owner-entrepreneurs, and especially the managers they employed, had a university education in science. So, while in 1913 Britain had only nine thousand full-time university students, Germany had sixty thousand.[65] And while Germany had a capitalist economy, its government, committed as it was to competing with and overtaking its rivals, was far more willing to intervene to promote industrial development, by nationalizing railways, establishing protective tariffs, and encouraging price fixing between groups of firms (cartels).[66]

More important for business and industry than actual government intervention, however, was the influence of the state's sage-technocratic ethos. Many businessmen, for example, aspired to be honorary civil servants and described themselves as "private officials" (*Privatbeamte*), close associates of the state officials (*Beamte*). And even businessmen who did not have Werner Siemens's close relations with the civil service admired the way it was run—its ability to coordinate large enterprises; its division of management functions among specialized officials; its prioritizing of education and expertise in promotion decisions; and its ability to think in the long term rather than according to short-term market advantage. It is no surprise that while British entrepreneurs pined for knighthoods and peerages, Germans coveted the titles of "commercial councillor" and "privy commercial councillor"—titles awarded by the civil service that granted the favored businessman a status equal to that of civil servants and the military during official ceremonies.[67]

Germany was not the only country to give greater roles to the state and to academic education than Britain. All late-industrializing countries found that self-helping entrepreneurship, artisanal tinkering, and the presence of gentleman-merchants were not sufficient; it was the sagely virtues of careful planning, thinking long term, rewarding expertise, and investing in analysis and research that were crucial. Large, expensive, technologically complex corporations could not rely on Adam Smith's "invisible hand" of the market; they needed the visible hand of bureaucratic organization.[68] And that guiding hand might be found in government, in business, in the investment banks that committed long-term finance to industry (unlike Britain's more trade-oriented "merchant banks"), and in developing long-term synergies within and between businesses—a system the business historian Alfred Chandler called "cooperative capitalism."

Among the Great Powers of the European continent, it had been common for some time for rulers to harness the knowledge of sages and to train engineers and technologists for the army and civil servants for government. The French monarchy was among the most energetic in creating schools to educate civil servants, and the *grandes écoles,* founded after the Revolution, trained a highly prestigious group of technocrats, the *"énarques,"* who dominate the civil service and business to this day.[69] However, of all European states, the sage probably had the most prestige in Prussia and Germany, both as civil servant and as academic. During the eighteenth and nineteenth centuries, university examinations became increasingly important for selecting a nonaristocratic, expert civil service, and as a consequence, by the middle of the nineteenth century Germany had the most prestigious university system in Europe.[70] King and sage maintained close links after the Reformation, and beginning at the end of the eighteenth century, rulers of several German states established universities, staffed by civil servant–academics, to create highly educated and prestigious bureaucracies. These sagely values and those of the "educated middle classes" (the *Bildungsbürgertum*) held sway over business classes. German businessmen, as much as civil servants, were (and are) expected to have a good general "education," or "cultivation" (*Bildung*), in music and literature and were thus very much part of a broader middle-class culture.[71] Germany did, of course, have a powerful old-style military aristocracy—especially among the Junkers of the Prussian East—and Chancellor Bismarck entrenched its influence in Germany's new constitution. But the German middle classes had developed a powerful sagely culture to counter it. Indeed, they forged their own equivalent of Confucianism, with the polymath Johann Wolfgang von Goethe taking the place of the great Chinese sage as a spokesman for the importance of cultivation and education—in a more modern and technologically friendly form, of course.

It is perhaps no surprise that the German model of nationalistic, state-influenced development was so appealing in Japan, where both warrior (samurai) and sagely (neo-Confucian) cultures were also prevalent among elites. Stung by Japan's humiliation at the hands of the United States in 1853–54, when American naval forces compelled it to open up to foreigners and endure a regime of unequal trade treaties, a group of reforming samurai rebelled against the Tokugawa dynasty and the failing landed aristocratic order it presided over. As has been seen, under the Tokugawa, the samurai retained warrior values, but many of them were now state officials, and they imbibed Confucian notions of scholarship, intellectual meritocracy, and good governance. Once they took power in the so-called Meiji Restoration of 1868, this concern with military power, combined with a technocratic ethos, led to a strategy of "strengthening the armies" by "enriching the nation," and that meant learning from the West.

The most influential spokesman for this westernization was Yukichi Fukuzawa (1835–1901), an intellectual from a lowly samurai background. His earlier writings were influenced by the dominant commercial liberalism of the midcentury, and he even set up his own publishing enterprise, advising his nephew that one could be both sagely and mercantile: "Earn and learn, learn and earn, then you can earn both the status of a scholar and a rich man."[72] However, after 1875 his views, like those of many in the Japanese elite, became more nationalistic and statist as he responded to an increasingly competitive and imperialistic world order.[73] State bureaucrats and businessmen, therefore, often shared a patriotic sensibility, and while the Meiji built a capitalist economy, the state was always heavily involved in building infrastructure and fostering technical education.[74] Similarly, its "men of affairs," or entrepreneurs (*jitsugyoka*), adopted a sage-warrior ethic of state service (both Confucian and samurai), rather than one of individualistic "self-help." Indeed, they distanced themselves from the merchant, who had enjoyed very low status (below both samurai and peasants) in the old, pre-1868 caste system.[75] Japan's approach to industrialization was therefore closer to Germany's than to Britain's, and its large integrated financial-industrial groups (*zaibatsu*) had much in common with Germany's "coordinated capitalism."[76]

By the 1880s Germany (with the United States) had replaced Britain as the great power of the future—at least in the eyes of many politicians, journalists, and intellectuals. Popular books like Ernest Williams's *Made in Germany* (1896) warned the British of the threat from German manufacturing prowess, and vocal lobbies called for German-style protection for industry, scientific education, and greater military spending to counter the naval threat. Thus, Sergei Witte (from a Dutch Lutheran background), the architect of Russia's industrialization program, was strongly influenced by the German economic experience—though he encountered a great deal of resistance from traditional warrior-landowner elites, who still controlled the state. Meanwhile, a German-influenced Japan won the admiration of nationalists throughout Asia after its triumph over a European power in the Russo–Japanese War of 1904–5. The influence of German sagely culture was also felt in its major economic competitor, the United States. The German university, with its emphasis on scholarship and research rather than Oxbridge-style gentlemanly tutoring, had a powerful impact on American education, and indeed the highly professionalized research universities of the United States, which populate the higher reaches of the world rankings today, were founded on the German model.

The sage established his influence in many other areas of life, but his position was very different from that of his German counterparts. For the American central state was small, and while it did intervene to develop the economy, it did so indirectly and "out of sight," by collaborating with local government and business or operating through the courts;[77] as in Britain, it was the independent professional, not the state bureaucrat, who became the most influential type of sage.[78] In these circumstances, business was able to achieve a dominant position—especially in the so-called Gilded Age following the Civil War.

The career of the great steel magnate Andrew Carnegie illustrates how this peculiarly American relationship between merchant and sage was forged. Carnegie's life, unlike Siemens's, was close to Smiles's *Self-Help* ideal. Indeed, he was born only forty miles from Smiles's own birthplace, to the family of a Dunfermline weaver. Driven by poverty to Pittsburgh in the 1840s, he worked his way up from telegraph messenger boy to railway company man before setting up his own steel plants. But Carnegie was always more of a buccaneering merchant than a Smilesian artisan. Charming and irrepressibly optimistic, the diminutive, bearded "Star-Spangled Scotchman" was no craftsman, tinkerer, or artisan-inventor. He had a flair for accountancy and managing money; he also enjoyed the exhibitionism of salesmanship and the thrill of making bets in risky markets. For a time, indeed, he worked as a trader in company bonds (i.e., debt) in the rather murky world of 1850s American railway finance, and he was accused, probably justly, of mis-selling bonds, effectively cheating investors of $400,000.[79]

Carnegie had precisely the merchant qualities that would equip him for success in late-nineteenth-century America. The first American colonies had been founded by Calvinist Puritans who had rejected the sagely hierarchies of the established church in England and Scotland. And subsequently, in 1776, these revolutionaries had rejected the idea of rule by a landed aristocracy or by a centralized state. Without powerful aristocratic or sagely forces to constrain them, only two major castes were left to compete for power: farmers and merchants. The first developed a culture of cooperation, egalitarianism, and mistrust of outsiders—whether merchant elites or state officials. And some even redistributed land according to the size of families. Their love of locality and community was expressed through a "republican" ideology that stressed the virtues of the independent farmer.[80]

Starting in the early nineteenth century, however, population pressure and flourishing international trade in commodities brought more and more Americans into the market economy. And by the time Carnegie arrived in the United States, in 1848, the merchant had achieved a powerful position, bolstered by the ideologies of self-help and Protestant moral reform. And though the central state bureaucracy and the military thrived during the Civil War, in the 1860s (as they would again during the First World War), they were swiftly cut back during peacetime. The United States enjoyed the luxury of having no threatening external enemies—the Native Americans could be fought with a skeleton force— and even career officers were skeptical of the need for a large peacetime standing army. The American army was therefore much smaller than those of other great powers: in 1910 it was roughly the size of the Ethiopian army at the time, while, relative to the size of the American economy, the U.S. state bureaucracy was smaller than that of the Netherlands.[81]

So, with the influence of businessmen enhanced following the end of the Civil War and the state and the courts happy to bolster the power of private firms, the great tycoons were in a good position to use the government—both federal and local—to further their own business interests.[82] And, far from seeking to become German-style "private officials," the American tycoons saw the businessman as the ideal to which all other groups should aspire. For Carnegie, successful businessmen were themselves a rare and precious elite, with formidable "ability and energy," who deserved their staggering wealth and should be free to use it for the benefit of mankind.[83] Many agreed with them, encouraged by influential writers and preachers who lauded businessmen as the latter-day saints of a market-friendly Protestantism. So, for example, the Baptist minister Russell Conwell declared in his bestselling pamphlet of 1890, *Acres of Diamonds,* "The men who get rich may be the most honest men you find in the community," while "there is not a poor person in the United States who was not made poor by his own shortcomings."[84]

Carnegie initially flourished in this highly commercial society, and he was also fortunate to be in steel at a time when the United States was building its modern infrastructure. America's railways, unlike most of Europe's, were built by competing private banks and companies in an atmosphere of frenzied speculation and corrupt politics. And they were built in an extraordinarily chaotic and wasteful way; by 1890 six companies had laid seven railway lines in Kansas, giving that state more miles of track than New York, though it had less than a third of New York's population.[85]

However, the growing size and success of American business encouraged its tycoons to embrace a more sagely worldview. The destructive wastefulness of unbridled competition, together with hugely expensive technology and the sheer size of the American market opened up by the railways, convinced many businessmen that they needed more coordination, investment, and expertise. This, of course, was precisely what German industrialists had already discovered. But American big business developed a different set of solutions. Rather than relying so much on collaboration between firms, some of them built huge corporations that could mobilize the resources needed to sustain professional management structures and invest in research. They also relied on the new universities—established by the state but increasingly funded and controlled by business itself.[86] The merchant had been forced to give the sage a seat at the table, but the latter's place was still a subordinate one. The ideal American pen pusher was not the Prussian-style state bureaucrat but the college-educated middle manager, who had learned to combine competitiveness with teamwork on the football fields of Harvard and Yale.[87] Moreover, American scientists took pride in their "pragmatism" and closeness to corporations, in contrast to German and French scientists' concentration on pure theoretical research.[88]

Various aspects of Carnegie's personality suited him for this more sagely phase in American capitalism. His ambition had always been to be a writer and thinker, and at one time he even thought of moving to Oxford, where he expected to find intellectual luminaries to mingle with. New York, however, was a more practical place to live, and there he frequented the literary and artistic salon of the well-connected Madame Botta. Carnegie regaled his fellow salonistas with his politics and recitations from Robert Burns; he also wrote several works of social theory justifying the wealth and power of the tycoons—most famously *The Gospel of Wealth*.[89] But these broad intellectual interests were also keenly applied to his business, and he employed the latest technology while establishing an innovative accounting and managerial structure to coordinate his huge concerns.[90]

By the early twentieth century the sage-technocrat was penetrating more aspects of American life, including politics. A serious economic crisis in 1893 brought a sharp reaction against laissez-faire, and the success of Progressivism—a broad sagely ideology that called for state-led social reform, a greater role for educated professionals, and more regulation of "robber barons" like Carnegie and J. P. Morgan—suggested that the political culture of the United States was converging, to a limited extent, with Western Europe's. By 1904 the oilman John D. Rockefeller was declaring, "The day of combination is here to stay. Individualism has gone, never to return," and future generations of American tycoons were to create even more sagely structures.[91] The Massachusetts Institute of Technology–educated Pierre du Pont perhaps went furthest, employing teams of managers and scientists in his chemical engineering corporation and establishing his own research division.[92] By 1914, then, the American corporation had become a mighty bureaucratic organization. The American economy was still overwhelmingly made up of small businesses, but in the corporations, values had shifted.[93] Even Carnegie, the great rags-to-riches huckster himself, argued that businessmen's value to society lay in their "talent for organization and management."[94]

So, however different the American corporate man, the Japanese "man of affairs," and the German "private official" might have been, and however varied their relations with the sage, they were adapting successfully to the technological changes of the second industrial revolution, and together they had effectively destroyed Britain's economic primacy. By 1913

Germany had overtaken Britain in industrial output, and America's output was more than double Britain's.[95] Yet while these late-industrializing countries achieved economically effective caste alliances among sagely, warrior, and merchant elites, they had far more difficulty integrating other castes, particularly industrial workers. New conflicts were emerging, between an elite alliance of warrior, merchant, and sage—often committed to nationalist ideas and international competition—and the newly empowered worker.

The Worker Rebels, the Sage Defects: Socialism

Nikolaus Osterroth, a Catholic skilled worker in the Bavarian clay mines in the early 1890s, remembered how employers had increased their efforts to extract work from them. "Up to this time," he recalled, "the mine workers had enjoyed rather free" working conditions; "but now they were to come under strict rules with a sophisticated penalty system." These new work rules "created bad blood among the miners and stirred them to resistance, which at first found an outlet only in tavern debates." When the devout Osterroth's local priest told him he should obey his employer, because masters and servants were ordained by God, he broke with his previous ideas and converted to socialism and rebellion.[96]

Osterroth's experience was shared by many workers throughout the industrialized world after the 1880s, for businessmen were trying to exert greater control over their employees. As they invested in new machinery, they expected their employees to work at its pace and tried to replace expensive skilled workers with cheaper unskilled alternatives. And in the ideas of the American theorist of "scientific management" F. W. Taylor, with his stopwatch-wielding managers and "intensify labor" campaigns, they were given the means to do so. The merchant, with the help of the technocrat, was finally destroying the artisan and transforming the worker into pure labor power.

But Osterroth and his fellow workers had other complaints, too. Their jobs and living standards were precarious, subordinated as they were to the interests of international finance. The gold standard, adopted by the British and by most other industrial countries by the end of the nineteenth century, was great for bankers, as it kept the currency stable and guaranteed the value of their investments. But for workers and farmers it was a curse, ensuring that the ups and downs of the business cycle directly affected their lives. When trade declined, so would jobs and wages. By the rules of the gold standard, governments were not allowed to spend money to alleviate their suffering.

Given these economic and technological conditions, tension between workers and employers was inevitable, and could be found in many industries and regions. But it was much more common among the late-industrializing countries, where large factories and the latest mechanization were more widespread, and the result was often violent conflict. Skilled worker-artisans were at the forefront of strikes and protests—European metalworking industries were especially affected. But they were sometimes joined by unskilled workers, fresh from the countryside, who were angry at low wages and job insecurity. Meanwhile, in many countries peasants and farmers felt, reasonably, that their interests were being sacrificed to those of industrialists and international financiers.

It is therefore no surprise that the period saw the rise of mass working-class movements—both labor unions and political parties (though, of course, many workers were not involved). They found their ideological inspiration in the politics of the French Revolution of 1789 and the brief period of radical Jacobin rule in 1793–94, when the egalitarian artisans of Paris made common cause with anti-aristocratic professionals. But most successful in developing these ideas, and in forging a political movement founded on them, was Karl Marx (1818–83). The grandson of a German rabbi and the son of a nonreligious Enlightenment lawyer, Marx was committed to the more workerist side of the French revolutionary tradition. But he was also determined to be modern, endorsing many of the values of the sage-technocrat, and he tried to combine the two worldviews to craft a powerful critique of the merchant. Markets, he argued, were the enemies of artisan autonomy and worker democracy; but they were also irrational and volatile and had to be controlled by the rational sage-technocrat and planner. In his youth, his vision was a more ultra-egalitarian, workerist one: work would be organized democratically, without any form of subordination. Later in life, however, he became more of a technocrat, accepting that engineers and planners had to be in charge. And it was this strain, combined with a commitment to economic equality, that came to dominate the prewar European Marxist movement and attracted intellectuals and educated professionals, as well as workers, to the cause.

Marxist socialism was most successful in Germany, in part because guild traditions had survived and gave workers a tradition of collective organization;[97] there, the Social Democratic Party adopted a Marxist program in 1875, and Marxists also played a role in Russia's worker revolutions in 1905 and 1917. Elsewhere, other ideologies flourished. In the United States, worker and farmer movements protested against the great business tycoons, and Carnegie himself was one of the main targets; in 1892, his Homestead steel plant, in Pennsylvania, was the site of a bloody battle between armed workers and his hired paramilitary "Pinkertons."

Businessmen and state officials responded to this threat in different ways in different countries, their response depending on the particular caste structure. In Germany, Bismarck, an aristocrat steeped in the traditions of Prussian state paternalism, established the first rudimentary "welfare state" in the 1880s, to cushion workers from the blows of a volatile market, thus hoping (in vain) to limit socialist support. This was also the example followed in Britain and other Western European countries, and in 1911 the Japanese state introduced its own version. Russia's more hard-line warrior-aristocratic autocracy was less willing to compromise and was ultimately destroyed by revolution. American administrations were also less willing to step in to protect workers from downturns in the market, though for rather different reasons: they saw the welfare state as paternalistic and un-American. Carnegie himself argued that it was morally wrong to give money to the poor, irrespective of whether they were deserving or undeserving; rather, wealthy people like him had to give their fortunes to libraries and universities—institutions for the self-disciplined and self-helping.

In most industrialized countries, however, an alliance of the state and business confronted workers, and violence was often the result. It was most serious in repressive Russia, but America took second place in the number of workers killed during strikes, probably because of more widespread gun ownership. (Five hundred to eight hundred workers died between 1872 and 1914, compared with sixteen in Germany, about thirty-five in France, and somewhere between two thousand and five thousand in Russia.)[98]

Even so, there were differences between the more merchant-dominated America and former agrarian powers. The forces ranged against workers in Germany and Russia were much more united, and more determined to exclude them from the national community, than was the case in the more decentralized and liberal United States, where workers had full democratic rights. Also, American workers, divided by ethnicity, were much weaker than elsewhere. This helps to explain why the United States was not home to a large-scale socialist movement.[99]

The merchant-industrialist was, therefore, coming under intense pressure from below and was looking to the warrior for protection. But there were other reasons for the increasing importance of the warrior: the politics of empire and the internecine struggles between European states. In the later part of the century, the warrior and, in many cases, the traditional aristocrat, whose influence had seemed to be declining in the middle of the century, were on the march again.[100]

Valhalla

In the summer of 1909, Sir Charles Addis, head of the London office of the Hongkong and Shanghai Bank (HSBC), was invited to spend a weekend with Carl Meyer, a German Jewish diamond magnate, at his country seat, Shortgrove, in Essex. He wrote enthusiastically to his wife of his time there:

> A motor was waiting at Audley End station and drove me through the beautiful wrought iron gates of Shortgrove . . . an old Queen Anne mansion four storeys high and 13 windows wide. Two centre halls with galleries on which the bedrooms open. In the dining room a superb portrait of Mrs Meyer by Sargent . . .
>
> We went over the stables next, old and extensive like the house, saw the model cottages and the home farm and the pedigree herd of Jersey cows, and so to dress for dinner. Excellent dinner, lobster, grouse etc. . . . Coffee and cigars on verandah in open air.

Charles Addis was a Scot, a son of a church minister, and from an impeccably middle-class background. He was also a conventional, if unusually thoughtful and well-read, upholder of the liberal orthodoxies of the London financial elite of his day. He believed in the progressive nature of the British and their mission to modernize the world through free trade; he had a sympathy for non-Western cultures (he learned Mandarin), sponsored Chinese educational charities, and understood why nationalists were so resentful of the Europeans; and he favored small government and freedom at home and disliked the use of force abroad. In many ways, then, he was the epitome of the peace-loving Smithian merchant.

However, his account of his country-house weekend should give us pause. For here we find him reveling in the culture of the old European warrior aristocracy, albeit hosted by a wealthy businessman. This warrior culture redux was becoming increasingly dominant toward the end of the century and marked a striking departure from the distinctly bourgeois tastes of the mid-1800s. Addis's appreciation of John Singer Sargent's painting, with its flattering portrayal of Mrs. Meyer and her daughters as latter-day Marie Antoinettes reclining on Versailles-style chaise longues, only reinforces this impression. And this was not only a matter of aesthetics. For Addis, however much he might laud the principles of laissez-faire and the small state, was keen to involve his own state, Britain, in the business of empire. In close collaboration with the British Foreign Office, Addis sought to further British interests in Qing China as the imperialist powers—Germany, Japan, and France—scrambled for influence over the crumbling regime. In the face of nationalist opposition and foreign competition, he made sure that the British and the Hong-kong and Shanghai Bank were in the vanguard of lenders to China. And when nationalists finally overthrew the Qing in 1911, he was instrumental in making sure that a pro-British government emerged. This was not empire as military conquest, as it was in so many parts of the world, but it was loss of autonomy all the same—empire in a rather more informal guise.[101]

Addis found many of these political machinations distasteful, but he had little alternative. The British might have seen their empire as a force for globalization in the interests of all, but their competitors had disagreed, and new powers were determined to redress the balance.

It is, therefore, no surprise that Addis found himself sharing the imperial stage with rather more conventional warrior-aristocrats. Lord Curzon, viceroy of India between 1899 and 1905 and himself from an aristocratic background, pressed for Indian aristocrats to become involved in the Indian army and the imperial project. But much more bloodthirsty was the Prussian general Lothar von Trotha, who waged a ruthless war of annihilation against the Nama and Herero peoples of German South-West Africa between 1904 and 1907.

It was not only competition with neighbors and resistance from colonial subjects outside Europe that justified warrior power. Within Europe, too, new nationalist movements were challenging the multi-ethnic agrarian empires and were often supported by their rivals—most explosively in the Balkans, when the Russians backed the Serbs against the Austro-Hungarian empire. And as ethnic tensions increased, empires began to favor "majority" groups—whether the Russians in Russia or the Muslims in the Ottoman Empire. Life, as a consequence, became more difficult for minorities like the Jews in Europe and the Armenian and Assyrian Christians of the Ottoman Empire, who had become important "intermediaries" in both the professions and trade—used by imperial aristocracies to run their domains and deal with the outside world.[102]

Warrior values, therefore, began to penetrate domestic politics. This did not necessarily lead to a desire for war itself, nor did militarism extend to all middle-class groups; many businessmen tried to maintain a soft-merchant internationalism. But in Germany and elsewhere, Mars was winning over Mammon among the middle classes, whether official, professional, or commercial.[103]

The question that faced these nationalist middle classes, though, was who was to be in control: the professional or commercial bourgeoisie or the old aristocratic warrior? The power of the old aristocracy had been seriously weakened, now that industrialists were so much wealthier, and the masses had the vote. Therefore, embattled businessmen had two courses open to them. The first was to seek protection from and emulate the old aristocratic warrior caste; the second was to detach themselves from the old nobility and forge the masses, or at least some of them, into a new type of nonaristocratic warrior.

The first road was taken by Diederich Hessling, the antihero of Heinrich Mann's satirical novel of 1912–14, *Der Untertan* (*The Loyal Subject*, also known as *Man of Straw*), and one of the most unattractive businessmen in world literature. As the title makes clear, Hessling is the son of a paper-mill owner but is a slavish subordinate to the German emperor and to the landed aristocracy that still dominates the government and the military. He is a feeble, fearful child who develops a repellent personality—snivelingly sycophantic to authority and aggressively bullying toward social inferiors. He transfers his loyalty from his father to the kaiser, Wilhelm II, whom he treats as a godlike figure, while also enthusiastically embracing the politics and values of the German nationalistic right. He particularly exalts the military, and when he goes to university he joins a nationalistic dueling fraternity, the "Neo-Teutons," a group that plans to bring back the "happy middle ages," when each social order—knights, clergy, and artisans—was represented but also knew its place. After university, he returns to his father's paper mill, where he bullies and patronizes his workers. The novel ends with the unscrupulous Diederich's victory over his business rivals and his mastery over his small town. He is chosen to deliver a speech to mark the unveiling of a statue to Kaiser Wilhelm I, celebrating "the unparalleled development of commerce and of nationalism" while calling for military valor and preparedness: "A master-nation . . . does not achieve such an incomparable flowering in the slackness of peaceful ease. No . . . in the end we have been able to plant our victorious colours everywhere, and to forge the imperial crown of Germany upon the field of battle."[104]

How representative was Diederich? Mann, a writer of the left, was using his novel to make a particular political point: that business had become enmeshed in a reactionary past of emperors, barons, and wars. Diederich's path was followed by some, but many German businessmen—and the middle class more generally—had more independence and confidence in bourgeois culture than Mann suggested. Those who wanted to fight threats from abroad and from below most aggressively were therefore more likely to adopt the second strategy, that of detaching themselves from the old aristocracy. This was the approach of the new radical right, which burst onto the political scene at the end of the century. These rightists sought to use a militant nationalism to bind together the old warrior ethic with a new ethos of hard-merchant discipline and sagely achievement, distinguishing themselves from the landed aristocrats and ruling groups of the time, whom they often saw as selfish and ineffective. In Germany, where right-wing patriotic groups like the Army League and the Navy League gained mass (though far from majority) followings among the middle and upper middle classes, and especially among professionals, the modernized warrior ideal was linked with a veneration of sagely *Bildung* (cultivation).[105] But other groups were also regarded as members of the patriotic German *Volk,* though of lower status—solid peasants, hardworking artisans, and productive small-business men. Firmly excluded, however, were those deemed disloyal to the nation: socialist sages and "cosmopolitan" merchants—both identified as "Jews."

In many ways, then, the radical right was calling for the old agrarian caste order to be restored, but only once it had been made more inclusive for the age of the masses. Social hierarchies, especially between middle classes and workers, would be maintained, but the old aristocracy had to be reformed and based on middle-class "merit" rather than heredity. And that merit was defined as a tough, efficient authoritarianism. Also, hereditary right had to survive alongside achievement, though in a new, social Darwinist form.[106] If the old aristocratic warrior had inherited his high status from his ancestors, the new warrior's standing derived from his new, larger family—his "race." For the radical right, therefore, an old aristocratic hierarchy of families became an international pecking order of races, fighting for honor and glory.

These ideas had a great deal of influence in German intellectual circles, where several cultural figures were urging the overthrow of an old, corrupt, hereditary aristocracy and its replacement with a new, "meritocratic," and vigorously martial one. This was, in essence, the plot of Richard Wagner's *Ring of the Nibelung* cycle of operas (1848–74): Wotan, the old king of the gods, in his lust for power and prestige, has been corrupted by love of money and by those who possess it, the mercenary Nibelungs; he finally accepts that the gods have to give way to Siegfried— a human, not a god—and the less exalted (but more heroic) mortals. The final scene of the final opera, *Twilight of the Gods* (*Götterdämmerung*), shows the gods' abode, Valhalla (hall of the slain heroes), engulfed by flames, clearing the way for a brave new world. The message of the philosopher Friedrich Nietzsche was similar: the world needed a new order, run by the "superman," a mixture of the warrior and the sage-artist. Merchants were not highly valued in the thinking of these warrior lovers. But that did not stop businessmen from adapting these ideas, and they cast themselves as new "social aristocrats," fighting for German interests in a brutal economic war while ruling over their less able workers, or "serfs."[107]

Completely excluded from this radical-right vision, though, was the globalizing soft merchant. Indeed, the outbreak of war left him with few defenders, as shown in the success of two bestselling books by the sociologist (and future Nazi sympathizer) Werner Sombart—*The Jews and Modern Capitalism* (1911) and *Heroes and Merchants* (1915), which cast the war as a struggle between Teutonic warriors and British shopkeepers.

These ideas might have been particularly popular in Germany, but they could also be seen throughout Europe, and beyond. The cult of competitive sports, the foundation of youth groups like Robert Baden-Powell's Boy Scouts (1908), and the popularity of militarized Christian churches such as the Church Army (1882) all attest to the power of the soldierly ideal. Outside Europe, too, anticolonial nationalists—generally sages by origin—sought to turn themselves into "modern" warriors to resist the West: the young Mao Zedong, an avid reader of social Darwinist theorists, condemned the traditional Confucian culture of the Qing for neglecting warrior values. "The military spirit has not been encouraged," he complained, and he called for the mass adoption of physical education to strengthen the nation.[108] Even Mohandas Gandhi—later the great theorist of nonviolent resistance—urged his fellow Indian nationalists to study the heroic feats of General Gordon and acted as a recruiting officer for the British Army. Only by joining the military, Gandhi believed, would Indians be accepted as equal citizens.[109]

The United States was not immune to this military culture, either, though it was not nearly as powerful as in Germany and Japan. The nation's war with Spain in 1898 had bequeathed it an empire in the Philippines, Cuba, and Puerto Rico, and some, including the nationalist Progressivist Theodore Roosevelt, urged that the United States build up its state to compete with the other great powers. However, both the war and the empire were highly controversial, and even Roosevelt made sure his warrior worldview was diluted with that of the merchant. In his speech of 1899 entitled "The Strenuous Life," he was careful to praise the "captain of industry" as well as the military leader, to stress the importance of "work" as well as "strife," and to demand "competence" as well as "duty":

> All honor must be paid to the architects of our material prosperity, to the great captains of industry who have built our factories and our railroads . . . for great is the debt of the nation to these and their kind. But our debt is yet greater to the men whose highest type is to be found in a statesman like Lincoln, a soldier like Grant. They showed by their lives that they recognized the law of work, the law of strife; they toiled to win a competence for themselves and those dependent upon them; but they recognized that there were yet other and even loftier duties— duties to the nation and duties to the race.[110]

Many businessmen wholly rejected the martial ideal; Carnegie himself was a campaigner for world peace. Others, though, did see themselves as warriors in a campaign for American economic supremacy. At the World's Columbian Exposition in Chicago in 1893, a group of California fruit farmers made its commitment to the global economic struggle clear by building a striking exhibit: a statue of a medieval knight made entirely of prunes. As the farmers explained, it "metaphorically impressed the fact that the prunes of that state [California] are being introduced victoriously into all lands, to the discomfiture of the products of other countries."[111]

Left-wing critics like Heinrich Mann argued that this mixture of popular neomilitarism and cutthroat capitalism would inevitably lead to war, and when war did break out, in July 1914, they felt vindicated. In fact, there is little evidence that either factor precipitated war.[112] More responsible were reckless aristocratic militaries and state officials—especially the German civil and military authorities.[113] Of all middle-class groups, businessmen as a whole were least keen on war, having so much to lose from the disruption of trade and foreign capital flows.

But Mann's *Loyal Subject* had a kernel of truth. The values of the warrior had become influential among elites and the urban middle classes, in Germany and elsewhere, in the years before 1914. And during the war itself, whole populations, far beyond the glittering courts and chanceries of Europe, were expected to feel a deep sense of national honor. Kaiser Wilhelm, Emperor Franz Josef, and Prime Minister Asquith all justified war as a defense of national "honor," and the young, middle-class war poet Rupert Brooke welcomed war for the same reasons:

> Honour has come back, as a king, to earth,
> And paid his subjects with a royal wage;
> And Nobleness walks in our ways again;
> And we have come into our heritage.[114]

As Brooke was to discover, however, the reality of the war had little in common with these chivalric fantasies. New military technologies—trenches, machine guns, and rapid-firing artillery—gave huge advantages to those in defensive positions, and bloody, unheroic stalemate was the result. These battles could not have been more different from the knightly tournament. Most of the casualties—possibly as many as 70 percent of them—were caused by artillery, and soldiers rarely even saw their enemy, nor victims their conquerors. Even the most battle-hardened soldier-aristocrats were shocked by the industrial slaughter: Lord Kitchener, the British secretary of state for war, famously declared, "I don't know what's to be done. This isn't war." [115]

Götterdämmerung

The end of the war brought deep disillusionment with the old landowner aristocratic caste and its warrior ideology. Not only was the war not the promised opportunity for knightly heroism, but glory seemed a far from sufficient justification for such extraordinary suffering. The British novelist Ford Madox Ford explored this disenchantment in his tetralogy *Parade's End* (1924–28): its hero, the chivalric and gentlemanly Christopher Tietjens, begins the war full of patriotic fervor, but by the end he is convinced that England should never again impose its will on others— "Damn the Empire," he concludes.[116] And the defeat of the great land-based agrarian empires—Russia, Austria-Hungary, and the Ottoman Empire—and the victory of the more liberal and commercial United States, Britain, and France, further discredited aristocratic values, and with them the principle of empire. The refusal of the victors to dismantle the British, French, and Japanese empires at Versailles in 1919 brought nationalist riots and revolts in China, Korea, Libya, Egypt, Syria, Iraq, and Morocco; meanwhile in India, Gandhi's Congress Party adopted a confrontational but nonviolent stance toward the British.[117]

So as Europe's militaristic courts were consumed like so many Valhallas, its aristocracies became forever associated with self-indulgence, callousness, and failure. Many turned against violence itself, and an international peace movement vowed that the Great War would be the war to end all wars.

But the war also opened new wounds. The end of the multi-ethnic empires and the creation of new nation-states brought a host of ethnic and territorial conflicts, while the brutality of warrior elites convinced many that they had to fight for social justice. The discrediting of the old elites particularly empowered the workerist left. On the whole, the European working classes had not been as committed to the idea of national honor as the middle classes, and they resented the harsh discipline and sacrifice imposed in its name. Many also agreed with Heinrich Mann that capitalists were as responsible for the bloodshed as the aristocrats. The result was the success of a new, more anti-merchant and ultra-workerist socialist movement—Communism—that split from Social Democracy with the formation of the Communist International (Comintern) in 1919. As the artist Heinrich Vogeler explained, "The war has made a Communist of me. After my war experiences, I could no longer countenance belonging to a class that had driven millions of people to their deaths."[118] Following the example of the Russian Revolution of 1917, when the Bolsheviks took power in the name of workers' and soldiers' councils ("soviets"), Soviet republics were declared in Hungary, Bavaria, and Slovakia, and workers' councils sprang up throughout Germany. Meanwhile, Communists everywhere demanded not just higher wages but fundamental changes in power relations, including nationalization and democratic worker control over factories. This was especially the case in Soviet Russia, where workers gained significant new powers over factory management. For a brief period, the ultra-workerist side of Marxism was triumphing over the more technocratic version.

Worker rebellions only fueled the determination of a warrior right within the defeated powers to continue the war—to destroy the left, to end national humiliation, and to resolve the ethnic and territorial questions that continued to divide Europe. Ernst Rüdiger Starhemberg, an aristocrat and future member of the Austrian paramilitary Heimwehr (Home Guard), remembered the day when he was demobilized from the imperial army in November 1918:

> Women were screaming "beat them to death, the damned officers!" [A group of soldiers] took my stars and my medals for bravery as well, and the *Grosse Silberne* [a high military decoration] with the Emperor's face was thrust into the dirty street. . . . I spat out the blood and collected the pieces of my sabre. . . . "Damned rabble," I thought, "there will be a day of reckoning for you."[119]

These were precisely the feelings of a rather more junior officer in the German army, Adolf Hitler: the warrior had to prop up a disintegrating social hierarchy and defend national honor. However, as will be seen, his warrior was of a more demotic variety than the old, discredited warrior aristocracy.

Ultimately, though, the militaristic right was unable to convince defeated populations to continue the war; four years of fighting at the front and shortages in the rear were enough. The numbers of right-wing paramilitaries in Germany and Austria-Hungary were small, and after 1924 American aid to the new democratic Weimar Republic helped to marginalize them.

Communists were more numerous, but states were effective in repressing worker rebellions. Also, most significantly, Western European elites were forced to make serious concessions to working classes, for war had given workers more power—both as soldiers and as producers behind the lines. Employers took greater account of labor unions, and welfare states were expanded—especially in the new Weimar Republic.[120]

Communists also failed in their efforts to convince a majority of the working class that the radical form of worker democracy they advocated was feasible. As the Italian Communists discovered in 1919–20, when they tried to set up factory councils in the industries of northern Italy, it was very difficult for such decentralized elected bodies to run a modern industrial economy. The councils often pursued their own narrow interests and refused to deliver the supplies needed to keep the whole economy functioning.[121] The Communists, like Marx himself, had not developed an effective way of combining democracy with economic efficiency.

In the Soviet Union, war with Germany in 1917–18 and the subsequent invasion by the liberal powers and Japan ensured that worker democracy was even more difficult to achieve. The civil war of 1918–21 helped to militarize Communism, and the worker was firmly united with the warrior. But even this alliance could not bring about international revolution.

By 1921 it was clear that the revolutionary tide had ebbed. The Bolshevik Red Army had retreated from Warsaw in 1920, and the Italian factory-council movement had collapsed. The German Communist "March Action" of 1921 was a miserable failure. And, most dramatically of all, that very same month Lenin welcomed the merchant back to the USSR. He argued, to the consternation of many Bolsheviks, that the military officers, government officials, and workers' councils that had run the economy during the Great War and subsequent civil war had to give way, in particular areas of the economy, to the market; the merchant could be expelled again only when conditions had improved.

The merchant was making similar inroads elsewhere as governments, to varying degrees, dismantled the controlled economies of wartime. But warrior politics had not been completely defeated: in Western Europe, states were reluctant to go too far in restoring the free markets of the pre-1914 system, because they had to appease their rebellious working classes. And in the defeated states, warriors of the radical right also remained behind the scenes, resentful and biding their time.

However, the Americans did not have to worry about these challenges, and after 1920 they went a long way toward restoring the prewar position of the merchant in the United States. But they did not stop at that. Because America had emerged from the war as the wealthiest nation, replacing Britain as the main exporter of capital, it could be even more ambitious. For the first time in history, a serious attempt was made to spread pure merchant rule to Europe and to the international economic system as a whole.

THREE

Hubris and Catastrophe: The First Merchant Age

Bruce Barton's *The Man Nobody Knows* (1925) was the nonfiction *Da Vinci Code* of its day. Panned in the *New Republic* as "vulgar" and condemned in the *New York Times* for belittling its subject, it nevertheless soared to the top of the American bestseller lists and remained there throughout much of 1926. Rather like Dan Brown, Barton, one of the founders of the advertiser BBDO, insisted that the life of Christ had been seriously misunderstood. Far from being "meek and lowly," a "sissified," "pale young man with flabby forearms and a sad expression," he was manly, energetic, and, most important, hungry for success. For in the hypercompetitive world of ancient religions, he had no choice. At a time when there was too much religious "supply," he had to create "demand" for his new ideas, and he did so with his "advertisements"—his miracles and parables. Christ was, then, the greatest adman the world has ever known, but he was far more than that. He was none other than "the founder of modern business": he "picked up twelve men from the bottom ranks of business and forged them into an organization that conquered the world."[1]

Posterity has agreed with Barton's critics, not with his admirers: his work is normally cited as a particularly crass example of Jazz Age materialism. But this judgment is a little too dismissive, for he had captured the zeitgeist rather more astutely than his critics admitted. His book was nothing less than the gospel of a revised soft-merchant ideal suited to a new economic model: a popular, consumerist, gadget-crazy, networking-obsessed, finance-led capitalism. This was the system that had been developing in the United States since the 1880s, in parallel with a more sagely industrial capitalism; became more dominant with the reaction against the sage after the First World War; was exported to the developed world; and was in many ways the prototype of the capitalism that has reigned since the 1980s. And in doing so, Barton revealed both its allure and its dangers, the flaws that brought the world to the edge of catastrophe.

Bruce Barton was born in Tennessee in 1886 to a clergyman's family. Neurotic and driven, he graduated from college during the brief 1907 depression, and both economic environment and psychological tensions triggered a crisis. He drifted aimlessly for a while but then found his home in the expanding world of popular magazines.[2] He wrote some political articles, and, like many educated people of his generation, he advocated a diluted version of the fashionable Progressivism of the time—a sagely ideology that called for state-led social reform, a greater role for educated professionals, and strict regulation of "robber barons" like Carnegie and J. P. Morgan.[3] It was this movement that delivered victory to the moralistic Princeton sage Woodrow Wilson in the presidential election of 1912—the only president in American history to hold a PhD. After America's reluctant entry into the war in 1917, Wilson presided over the greatest expansion of state influence in the economy yet seen.

However, the war changed Barton's views. As has been seen, the warrior and the state bureaucrat were always weaker, and the merchant stronger, in the United States than across the Atlantic, and for many Americans war had brought unwelcome levels of state intervention and unacceptable working-class demands. A "Red Summer" of labor activism and ethnic conflict had brought a backlash against state and collective action. As

Barton wrote at the time, "The individual is destroyed in the mass; personal responsibility is swallowed up in organized effort."[4] As had been the case after the Civil War, it was not long before the wartime military and the central bureaucracy were cut back.

This reaction against Progressivist sagely crusades—whether intervening abroad or trying to remake society at home—was reflected in the election results of 1920. The Democrats lost, and Wilson himself was portrayed as a repressive, statist figure from a warlike past. As the antiwar socialist Eugene Debs commented, "No man in public life in American History ever retired so thoroughly discredited, so scathingly rebuked, so overwhelmingly impeached and repudiated as Woodrow Wilson."[5] The decade was to be dominated by pro-business, small-government Republicans—Harding, Coolidge, and Hoover. Economic regulations were dismantled, labor unions were neutered, and the merchant, now free from constraints, was able to broadcast the glories of capitalism to the rest of the developed world.

Behind this version of American capitalism lay an updated version of Adam Smith's soft-merchant values, and this was precisely the culture embodied by Barton's Messiah. His Christ did not approve of the bureaucratic Pharisees or arrogant Herod-style aristocrats: his God was "no Bureau, no rule maker," nor was he a "vain king who must be flattered and bribed into concessions of mercy." But Barton also made it clear that he had little time for the puritanical hard-merchant God, reminiscent of Carnegie, who had prevailed before the war, the "rigid accountant, checking up the sins against the penances and striking a cold hard balance"; Judas, not Christ, was the penny-pinching hard businessman. Rather, God was "a kindly, indulgent, joy-loving father." Christ, meanwhile, was easygoing and affable, "the most popular dinner guest in Jerusalem." He was the ideal prophet for an aspirational, unstuffy capitalism of success, sociability, and spending—a consumerism that had been developing since the late nineteenth century, with the invention of new affordable luxury goods, mass retailing, and modern advertising.[6] This was a Christ for the rapidly proliferating Rotary Clubs, those arenas for softhearted charity and hardheaded business deals. Nothing could be further from Teddy Roosevelt's "strenuous life."

However, Barton's Christ represented only half of the duo that dominated American capitalism. If Barton was the new capitalism's copywriter, behind the scenes was a more sagely figure: the inventor and entrepreneur Henry Ford. Ford was more Smilesian tinkerer and pseudo-intellectual than educated scientist. (He wrote several notorious rants about the dangers of international Jewry.) Nevertheless, he largely invented the economic model behind Barton's consumer capitalism, with the help of engineers and stopwatch-wielding time-and-motion men.[7] And so, while he doubled his workers' wages to five dollars a day, he used the efficiencies brought by his famous work-intensive production line to cut the price of his Model T to $440, half its original price.[8] Ford's motivation was one part sympathy for the workingman and two parts unsentimental realism. By paying his workers so much more, he effectively turned them into consumers of their own products. And in his efforts to hold on to his valuable skilled workers, he simultaneously created a new capitalism that was both profitable and popular. Underpinning it was an unstated contract: in return for swallowing the harsh discipline of the production line and ditching socialism and costly artisanship, the worker would be paid enough to buy himself the status lost at work. And if his wages weren't quite enough, the newly important banks and consumer credit industry would cover the deficit.

Bruce Barton, Henry Ford, and their imitators were resolving the conundrum first raised by Adam Smith: Why would workers tolerate a system that wrenched them from a poor but relatively independent life in the country and subjected them to closely supervised and repetitive work on a production line? Smith believed that wealth would "trickle down" from employers to the masses, but he was wrong; this had happened only to a very limited degree, because employers were so much more powerful in any conflict over wages. One solution, of course, was a form of socialist redistribution of wealth led by the state, but that was unacceptable to business. Employer paternalism was another option, and was still attempted—not least by Ford, who tried to police his employees' lives— but that caused resentment. Meanwhile, Carnegie-style lockouts and armed Pinkertons could not be used forever, especially when employers wanted to hang on to their skilled labor (which was relatively scarce in the United States).

The solution to the great riddle was Ford's mass consumerism. Employees would, employers hoped, lose interest in questions of class and differences between managers and labor, because they could at least aspire to have a lifestyle similar to that of their bosses—even if they would never achieve it. A 1924 advertisement for Chevrolet, "The Psychology of the Automobile," exposed the political goals of consumer society very clearly. The wordy advertising copy explained that, now that the laborer drives to work in his own car, "he is now a capitalist—the owner of a taxable asset. . . . He has become somebody, has a broader and more tolerant view of the . . . fat-cigared capitalist." "How," the ad asked, "can Bolshevism flourish in a motorized country having a standard of living and thinking too high to permit the existence of an ignorant, narrow, peasant majority?"[9]

By the 1920s many Americans were participants in the consumer society we know so well today.[10] Mass-produced goods were given attractive brand identities and marketed throughout the country; self-service supermarkets and catalogs began to edge out small shops; and new media devices—radios and telephones—proliferated. Consumers soon longed for the latest labor-saving devices and gadgets.[11] The new products ranged from little "luxuries," like Gillette razors and Frank Mars's Snickers Bars (first introduced in 1930), and larger labor-saving devices, such as washing machines and vacuum cleaners, to substantial investments like houses and cars, which were now affordable for skilled workers.[12]

The merchant-industrialist, with the help of a battery of white-collar "sage" employees—the engineer, the advertising executive, and the manager—had therefore finally overcome some of the social tensions brought about by industrialization and found a way of spreading his influence among the mass of the population in a soft, Smithian way. He had not yet penetrated the whole of the population: advertisers saw only 50 to 70 percent of Americans as potential consumers, and many unskilled workers were excluded. (Indeed, the gap between pay rates for skilled and unskilled workers was greater than in many parts of Europe.) But that still compared with potential consumer populations of between 5 and 30 percent in a much less consumerist and affluent Western Europe.[13]

Consumer capitalism transformed not only the way many Americans lived but also the way they thought. In some ways, it merely fulfilled the dreams of Adam Smith: the majority were becoming soft merchants, trading and bartering, competing for consumer goods while at the same time feeling tolerance and "sympathy" for one another because they all shared the same values. However, consumerism is a complex thing and had a much broader appeal, reaching beyond soft merchants to a more sagely constituency. Consumption was not simply a way of competing for status, as Adam Smith argued. It was—and still is—also a form of self-expression, one that went hand in hand with imagination and an almost romantic sensibility. By buying consumer goods or watching Hollywood films, ordinary people could escape older, restrictive cultures—family, village, or small town—and satisfy their desire for new identities and experiences. While some saw this in a negative light, as passive manipulation by advertisers, to many more it presented a genuine opportunity for individual creativity and aesthetic self-expression. The soft merchant had successfully retailored capitalism to suit a democratization of the romantic spirit that particularly appealed to a confident, university-educated middle class.[14] This reached its peak in the 1950s and '60s, but it was in the 1920s that we can see a flowering of "bohemian" culture as the values of the Byrons and Shelleys of a century before spread more widely among the educated middle classes.

Consumer society also bolstered a cultural democracy already present in the United States. Anybody (apart from stimatized minorities) could gain social acceptance and climb the status ladder by buying the right kinds of consumer goods. People were not held back by aristocratic heredity or sagely cultural achievements, which took at least a couple of generations to acquire. As the sociologists Robert and Helen Lynd wrote in *Middletown,* their 1929 study of Muncie, Indiana:

> In 1890 Middletown appears to have lived on a series of plateaus. . . . It was a common thing to hear a remark that so and so "is pretty good for people in our circumstances." Today the edges of the plateaus have been shaved off, and every one lives on a slope from any point of which desirable things belonging to people all the way to the top are in view.[15]

In Europe, by contrast, the plateaus were still very much intact and unshaven in the 1920s. Middle and working classes retained separate cultures and would very rarely aspire to become soft merchants. Workers instead developed powerful proletarian cultures of solidarity, and whether one was commercial or sagely on the European continent, being "bourgeois" involved *Bildung*—having "educated tastes" and speaking, dressing, and behaving in a particular way. As the academic Edmond Goblot wrote in his 1925 study of the French bourgeoisie, *The Barrier and the Level,* clothing, conversation, and deportment were all central to bourgeois identity: "One can tell a bourgeois from a man of the people simply by a look as they pass in the street. One cannot confuse a '*Monsieur*' with a 'man,' still less a '*Dame*' with a 'woman.'"[16]

Not only was the soft merchant dissolving social distinctions; he was also softening political conflict between right and left as merchant values began to penetrate all classes. Voting in national elections in the United States declined from 80 percent in the 1890s to 50 percent in the 1920s, a sure indicator that the stakes appeared to be getting much lower.[17] And more generally, the soft merchant was cultivating a more gentle, middle-class personality. In place of the self-denying, dogmatic, and charmless puritan was a figure more suited to consumer society. As Bruce Barton explained, his readers should reject "the old-fashioned notion that the chief end in life is a steadily growing savings account," for "life is to live and enjoy as you go along." As was normal with the soft merchant of this era, however, self-expression and freedom were to be confined strictly to leisure time. The soft merchant of the 1920s was pretty "hard" in the workplace, for workers had to be disciplined and obedient. If his readers wanted to succeed, Barton advised, they had to discover, and then adapt to, their bosses' likes and dislikes—even changing their dress and choice of tie to please them.[18]

Cultural democracy, though, was no guarantee of economic equality. Indeed, America became extraordinarily unequal in the 1920s. Taxes were steadily reduced—with the top marginal rate falling from a high of 77 percent in 1919 (to finance the war) to 25 percent in 1928—as successive administrations insisted that the greatest benefits of rising productivity should go the wealthy to encourage enterprise. At the same time, the wages of ordinary workers failed to keep pace, reflecting the weakness of labor unions. So while the income of the top 1 percent of the population rose by 63 percent between 1923 and 1929, that of the lowest 93 percent actually fell by 4 percent.[19] After the relative equality of wartime, the gap between the rich and the poor rose to a record peak and was to reach a similar level only in the 2000s.[20] As a consequence, ordinary Americans found themselves increasingly resorting to credit to finance their new consumer goods. Before the First World War, the debt of the average American family (excluding mortgages) was increasing by four dollars a year; by the 1920s that had more than tripled, to fourteen dollars a year.[21]

Not everybody, of course, approved of this soft-merchant world. Sagely Progressives condemned its triviality, as did more romantic champions of individual authenticity. The American writer and Nobel Prize winner Sinclair Lewis launched one of the most effective broadsides against it in his novel of 1922, *Babbitt*. George F. Babbitt, Lewis's likable antihero, is a successful real estate agent and a typical member of the rather smug commercial middle classes of Zenith City, the self-styled peak of world civilization. He is the acme of the affable salesman—"*Boobus americanus,*" as the writer H. L. Mencken called him—overconfident, philistine, and obsessed with consumer goods, especially his car. Babbitt is also a member of a hypocritical coterie of Rotary Club (or "Booster Club") cronies, who ostensibly meet to manage their charitable activities but in reality spend their time enriching themselves with corrupt business deals—all the while denouncing the "Bolshevism" of workers who ask for higher wages.[22] Babbitt was precisely the sort of person who voted for the pro-market, small-government Republican administrations of the era, demanding government by a "business administration," not a "college president" like Woodrow Wilson. Eventually, Babbitt rebels and has an affair with Tanis Judique—one of "the Bunch," a group of local bohemians. But he soon decides that they are as conformist as his Booster Club chums and realizes he has no alternative to his old, compromised life.

Though Lewis won the Nobel Prize for literature in 1930, a sign of the merchant's loss of prestige among European elites after the Crash of 1929, only five years earlier the world looked very different. The new American consumer capitalism, with its promise of modernity, liberation, cultural democracy, and self-realization, had spread its appeal across the world. And it was particularly attractive in Europe, where the warrior had been dominant for so long.

Merchants of the World, Unite!

Among the exports of Jazz Age American capitalism, one of the most influential was Babbitt's beloved Rotary Club. And this business organization was to find its unlikely champion in another Nobel Prize winner, the German writer Thomas Mann (brother of the more left-wing Heinrich). With his formal manners, stiff collars, and admiration for old-style Protestant merchant attitudes and German high culture, he embodied the idea of prewar European "cultivation." It was no surprise that he wrote in defense of German nationalism during the war. But defeat in 1918 came as a major blow to both his politics and his identity—so much so that he simply switched ideological sides and endorsed the liberal democratic Weimar Republic, and in 1928, in a matching cultural about-face, he joined the Munich Rotary Club.[23]

The style of the European Rotaries was, predictably, much more formal and elitist than in their American equivalents. The clubs were more likely to be frequented by government ministers than by real estate agents, and members addressed one another formally rather than chummily. Even so, the conversion of somebody like Thomas Mann shows how far American soft-merchant ideals had penetrated European elites. In 1920, there were 758 Rotary Clubs across the world, but by 1929 that number had grown to 3,178, of which 725 were outside North America.[24] The merchant caste was beginning to spread globally, mimicking the old internationalized aristocracy and challenging the other great network of the period, international Communism.

Rotary (so-called after the practice of rotating meetings between members' offices) was founded by a Chicago lawyer, Paul Harris, in 1905, as a place for businessmen and professionals to mix commerce and socializing—"networking," as we would call it today. Only one representative from each profession and trade could join, to avoid business competition, and they would attend weekly meetings over lunch, at which first-name informality reigned (at least in the United States); this was worlds away from the gentlemanly British club of the nineteenth century. Initially, the emphasis was on mutually beneficial business deals, but soon charity and public "service" was the focus, and after the war Rotary sought an international role. In 1921 its statutes declared that it would "promote international peace through a world fellowship of business and professional men," and in 1922 the organization was renamed Rotary

International.[25] The various conventions and policy pronouncements of the 1920s suggest genuine idealism.[26] For many Rotarians, the war and the rise of Communism had shown that soft businessmen had to take the reins of power from discredited warriors and politicians. As one delegate told the 1928 convention:

> Let me confess, the time has passed when the world trusted the politician, the statesman. One is accused of duplicity and treachery. The other with evasion and desertion. To someone somewhere civilization must turn with confidence and with hope. To whom shall it turn if it not be to such as you?[27]

The unpopularity of the sage-official and the warrior in the United States was widespread and created an alliance between an anti-statist right and an anti-imperialist left, who protested against President Wilson's efforts to use American state power to stabilize postwar Europe. So when the Democrats were defeated in the 1920 election, the Republicans— with a great deal of popular support—refused to allow the government to lend abroad; Congress had already voted to keep the United States out of the League of Nations.

American policy was seriously constrained by an isolationist Congress, but Republican leaders were anxious to project American power— although via the merchant, and especially the banker, rather than through armies or state officials. Republicans argued that grand sagely organizations, like the League of Nations, and governmental negotiations would only politicize the conflicts that continued to fester after the war.[28] Prosperity through trade and investment, not grand political schemes, would bring peace, while of course helping American business at the same time. Realizing that they needed a prosperous Europe if they were to sell their goods abroad, the Republicans knew that this meant pumping in a great deal of cash, which only the United States possessed. War had dealt a fatal blow to British financial power, had severely disrupted world trade, had destroyed Europe's infrastructure, and had created a highly unbalanced, militarized economy.[29] Massive investments were therefore needed to revive Europe's economies, but Europeans staggered under mountains of debt. The Allies had already borrowed from the United States during the war, and Washington's refusal to write off these loans (a massive $26.5 billion) led the Allies to insist on the enforcement of Germany's deeply unpopular war reparations (even larger, at $33 billion).[30]

A European revival seemed impossible, but Washington had an answer: to rely on American private bankers to funnel capital into the rest of the world. And that depended on creating a new, merchant-friendly order. At its center was a classic merchant solution: to restore a fixed currency based on gold. The theory was that the gold standard, with currencies pegged to gold at prewar rates, would stop governments from spending too much and printing money to pay for it. This, it was claimed, would encourage private bankers to invest, confident that they would be paid back in a rock-solid currency, which in turn would stimulate trade and encourage business to provide jobs for workers.

The new American-led order was hailed as a return to a version of the pre-1914, British-led global market economy, but it was actually significantly different.[31] With the exception of American tariffs to protect local industries from competition, the Washington-led system was much more merchant-oriented than the British one had been. The gold standard in the late nineteenth century had never depended on pure market mechanisms: it required a great deal of informal management and international cooperation to sustain the system.[32] But Washington, with its suspicion of "power politics" and sagely coordination, was much less willing than Britain to engage in gentlemanly negotiations and deals behind closed doors, even though international relations were so much more tense than before.[33] Herbert Hoover, commerce secretary between 1921 and 1929, president from 1929 to 1932, and a central figure in the American economic strategy of the era, expressed the new philosophy explicitly in his 1922 book *American Individualism:* "[Reactionaries and radicals] would assume that all reform and human advance must come through government. They have forgotten that . . . the measure of national idealism and progress is the quality of idealism in the individual."[34]

But Europe's politics were so fraught, and its economies so weak, that it was not always easy for the American government to remain completely aloof. The virtual collapse of the German economy during the hyperinflation of 1922–23, and the French and Belgian invasion of the Ruhr to enforce reparation payments, forced Washington to intervene more vigorously.[35] Even so, it insisted on operating through private banks. In 1924, Hoover established a commission headed by the banker and future vice president Charles Dawes to draw up a plan to rescue Germany. Arms were twisted, and eventually the banker J. P. Morgan was persuaded to lend to Germany and get the German mark back onto the gold standard. The loan proved successful, and American credit flooded into Germany. Between 1924 and 1929, the United States contributed 80 percent of the capital borrowed by German banks and other credit institutions, and 50 percent of the capital lent to large corporations.[36]

The Dawes loan was ultimately driven by the American government, but elsewhere bankers had more influence. And they found support among a new influential cadre of pro-merchant sages—the early international economic advisers, or "money doctors," as they were dubbed. Many of these advisers had served the country before the war in the American colonies in the Philippines and elsewhere. But when empire became unfashionable, they looked for new, more mercantile masters.

Edwin Kemmerer was one of the most prolific. He was a colonial administrator before becoming a well-paid financial adviser in the 1920s and the first professor of international economics at Princeton. Well connected with American banks and an excellent public relations man, he was hired by a number of poor countries to attract American investors. He would visit for a few days and then issue his prescription for economic health, which was always the same medicine: a strong dose of balanced budgets and a follow-up regime on the gold standard. After the obligatory press conference for American journalists, the money would start to flow in. He was often criticized for being an instrument of both avaricious banks and desperate governments, and with some justification. In 1926, for instance, he led a delegation to Poland, encouraged by the New York bank Dillon Read (Dillon had Polish origins) and the Polish government—with the approval of the American Federal Reserve—to recommend a package of economic policies that would attract foreign investors. His subsequent boosterish speech, which carefully obscured the shaky condition of the Polish economy, received such headlines as PRINCETON MAN, MONEY DOCTOR TO NATIONS, OPTIMISTIC OVER POLAND. It had the desired effect: American bankers bought heavily into Polish bonds.[37]

By 1926, as more countries joined the gold standard and American money flooded into Europe, it seemed as if the new soft-merchant order, centered in Washington, was indeed dragging the world out of recession. Between 1919 and 1929, more than $1 billion a year left New York, with Europe receiving just under 50 percent. And alongside this, American multinational companies like Ford, Eastman Kodak, and Gillette made direct investments in foreign plants.[38]

With loans came the first glimmerings of a new American-style consumer civilization of not just Rotary Clubs but also branded goods—from Carnation milk to Kellogg's Corn Flakes—and, of course, Hollywood films. With these came a new architecture: art deco, the ornate modernism born in Paris but forever identified with Jazz Age America was prevalent in Europe and elsewhere—including the two great trading cities of Asia, Shanghai and Bombay. These symbols of light-hearted luxury stood in stark contrast to the sober and more puritanical modernist architecture of sagely socialists like Le Corbusier and Mies van der Rohe.

American loans and merchant culture also softened the political conflicts of the immediate postwar period, at least to some degree. Two failed antiliberal German insurrections in 1923—an aborted Communist revolution and Adolf Hitler's Beer Hall Putsch—marked the end of the era of paramilitary struggles. Weimar's democracy finally seemed to have been stabilized under the pro-American leadership of Gustav Stresemann. Many nationalist Germans were still deeply resentful of the Versailles Treaty and yearned to regain lost territory. But by the mid-1920s it looked as if Versailles would survive its revisionist critics. In Japan, too, the pro-American foreign minister Kijuro Shidehara helped to persuade leaders to accept Washington's merchant view of the world and abandon their imperialistic ambitions in China and elsewhere. His arguments were strengthened by the increasing importance of American trade and investment to Japan.

A merchant-friendly Germany also helped the USSR take further steps into the capitalist fold. After 1922, Germany and Austria redirected some of their American loans to Moscow (despite Washington's disapproval), and in 1924 the ruble went onto the gold standard to encourage more foreign investment. Even politburo member Joseph Stalin—not a natural friend of merchants—strongly supported the gold standard and warned of the evils of inflation, in his usual tones of dogmatic certainty;[39] the staunchly anti-Communist Herbert Hoover would have heartily approved.

This was an era of merchant confidence in other parts of the developing world, too. After Europe, Latin America received the largest amount of American capital in the decade after 1919 ($300 million a year), while Asia took $100 million.[40] Following the war and Wilson's "betrayal" of Third World nationalists at Versailles, things had not looked so rosy for the merchant. Anticolonial nationalist movements were radicalized, especially among urban educated groups, and many condemned businessmen and landowners as "compradors"—traitors to their homelands and foreign capital's fifth columnists. It is therefore no surprise that the new warrior, anti-merchant Communist movement saw many opportunities outside Europe, and radical socialists like the Vietnamese Ho Chi Minh played key roles in nationalist parties. However, political repression and an eventual economic revival ensured that Communism remained a relatively weak force in mid-1920s Asia, as in Europe. In China, the Communists forged an alliance with nationalists, and even Ho Chi Minh would dilute his revolutionary social message.[41]

Mohandas Gandhi's Indian National Congress showed how much more effective a nonviolent form of nationalism could be in this merchant-dominated era. Gandhi himself was from a merchant *bania* subcaste, and his conception of nonviolence, *ahimsa,* was influenced by Jain thought. Convinced that "India's millions have no tradition of violence" and that only the minority warrior caste could use force effectively, he argued that civil disobedience was the only weapon that would work in India, and thus it was a much better way of expelling the British.[42] He seemed to have made the right calculation. After 1919, he built a broad alliance of the poor, wealthy peasants, and businessmen, as well as those more conventional nationalist groups—the sagely professionals. He then used his holy-man-style charisma to lead them on spectacularly impressive nonviolent campaigns, like the "Dandi March" of 1930, in protest of the government's salt monopoly, which caused acute embarrassment to the British and led them to make major political concessions. It also secured a great deal of popular sympathy abroad—particularly in the United States.[43]

However, Europe's empires were still founded on a carefully calibrated balance of force and collaboration with landed and commercial elites; this was still a world of the warrior and aristocrat. The Rotary vision of peace and commerce therefore appeared to be of little relevance to many Third World nationalists. Neither could the shaky international economy, disrupted by war and shackled by the gold standard, make it compelling. Toward the end of the 1920s, commodity prices began to fall, and with them the foundations of liberal optimism.[44]

There were serious limits to the merchant's penetration of Europe, too. In most European countries, the return to the gold standard had a depressive effect on economies, and growth was weak, while investment was not enough to revive it.[45] Living standards and consumption were much lower than across the Atlantic, while unemployment was much higher: by 1929 only 1 percent of British households had washing machines, compared with more than 30 percent in the United States. And tensions between employers and labor remained high. In Germany, in particular, the old enmities of the immediate postwar period—between the radical nationalist right and the socialist and Communist left—were never far beneath the surface.

For a while, however, greenback credit papered over the cracks in the system, and many believed America had set the world economy on the path to prosperity and peace. In 1927, the French writer and academic André Siegfried's *America Comes of Age,* a popular bestseller, declared that the United States had created a "new civilization" of mass production and consumerism, while Europe had been "relegated to a niche in the history of mankind."[46] Siegfried was not entirely happy about these changes. He was a sage of romantic inclinations and an admirer of the artisan, who he felt was expiring, crushed between the consumerist merchant and the Fordist engineer. American conformism and materialism, he argued, were destroying individual freedom, creativity, and spirituality. But he was fatalistic: "American civilization" was the way of the future.[47]

Siegfried, it turns out, was right—but only in the long run. For within two years, the American-sponsored merchant order was stumbling badly, and within five it had virtually collapsed.

Implosion

Who or what was to blame for the economic crisis of the 1930s? In recent decades, the debate over the question has been furious, for the stakes are very high: this was the greatest crisis modern capitalism has ever suffered. In recent decades, with free-market economists in the ascendant, it has been particularly fashionable to blame almost anybody but the merchant, which partly explains why we have forgotten the lessons learned so painfully by our predecessors and why we have repeated so many of the errors of the 1920s. The Chicago "monetarist" economist Milton Friedman was the first to popularize this exculpatory view, in his influential *Monetary History of the United States* of 1963.[48] According to him, the structure of the merchant-dominated economy of the 1920s was basically sound; it was the sage-official who was to blame for the crisis. The villain was the Federal Reserve, which raised interest rates and thus choked off the supply of money at the wrong time, allowing a small downturn to be unnecessarily transformed into a deep recession. Had the sage-officials at the Federal Reserve loosened the money supply, the argument goes, 1920s-style capitalism could have continued to flourish. This view is not popular among academic historians, and other, more fashionable explanations blame either warriors or workers: the war had created serious structural problems in the economies of Europe; or powerful labor unions were keeping wages and prices too high, thus preventing the free-market gold standard from working as it should have. America's selfish, anti-free-market tariff policy is also commonly condemned.[49]

Some of these arguments are more convincing than others; war was perhaps most damaging to the world economy, for it disrupted trade and left massive overproduction of industrial goods in its wake. But there is a danger that we let the real culprit off the hook: the failures of the merchant—the soft-merchant order created after 1923, followed by the hard merchant's austerity in response to the crisis. Internationally, the American-led system failed to tackle the underlying trade and financial imbalances of the era, but events in the United States also show the drawbacks of unconstrained soft-merchant rule particularly clearly. A deeply unequal postwar economy distributed grossly disproportionate rewards to an ever tinier elite. The wealthy were unable, even in this era of gross excess, to spend more than they saved, and their savings either fueled financial speculation or were lent to the mass of the population to buy consumer goods. Such a poor distribution of wealth soon brought the economy to the limits of consumption-based growth.[50] And without a significant welfare safety net, ordinary Americans cut back on spending drastically as soon as confidence fell. Housing, one of the main growth areas of the period, had already begun to stagnate in 1928, but the trigger for the final collapse came with the bursting of the stock market bubble in October 1929. As share values plummeted, Americans simply stopped buying. Factories closed, banks collapsed, and unemployment rates rose fivefold—from 3 percent to 16 percent—within two years.[51]

In Europe, indebtedness to American banks was clearly the major problem, and some of that had been built up unwisely. Germans, in particular, had borrowed to invest in consumption and unprofitable industries;[52] lavish municipal sports stadiums and swimming pools were notorious examples.[53] But international banks, eager to lend for high rates and fat commissions, had encouraged such irresponsibility. And this shortsightedness was also responsible for the disaster of 1929: as soon as higher profits could be found elsewhere—especially in the United States, where Wall Street was blowing a speculative bubble and the Federal Reserve was raising interest rates—investors pulled their cash out with little warning, leaving bankruptcy and economic devastation in their wake.

But the merchant had not yet done his worst. Once the crisis had hit, he turned a financial collapse into a grinding depression. Predictably, when merchant-oriented governments and businessmen encountered threats to their financial position, they were transformed from soft consumerists into hard advocates of austerity: fearful that governments would print money to inflate away the debt, they insisted that spending and welfare benefits be cut. This, of course, was almost the ideal policy to make the crisis much worse, as critics such as the British economist John Maynard Keynes argued at the time. Hair-shirt austerity simply fed a spiral of decline, squeezing spending power out of the economy and fueling unemployment. The state had to intervene to ensure that demand was high enough, a policy that might involve directly creating jobs.

In the United States, however, such solutions were still seen as heresy. Hoover did try active measures to tackle the crisis, encouraging businesses to join together in cartels in the hope that they could prevent prices from falling.[54] But orthodox solutions—cutting deficits and balancing the budget—took priority, and there was more than a whiff of hard-merchant puritanism in the response of Hoover's administration. His treasury secretary, Andrew Mellon, argued that the catastrophe had nothing to do with the flaws of laissez-faire capitalism but instead had been caused by individual greed and speculation. The solution, therefore, was to keep interest rates high, thus punishing the profligate and forcing "unprofitable" industries to go bust. Looking back, Hoover blamed his rigidity on the moralistic outlook of his colleagues and advisers:

> The "leave-it-alone" liquidationists headed by the Secretary of the Treasury Andrew Mellon . . . felt that government must keep its hands off and let the slump liquidate itself. . . . He held that even panic was not altogether a bad thing. He said: "It will purge the rottenness out of the system. High costs of living and high living will come down. People will work harder, live a more moral life. Values will be adjusted, and enterprising people will pick up the wrecks from less competent people."[55]

In indebted Europe, the gold standard, so beloved by merchants, initially gave governments little choice but to pursue austerity.[56] But when the international financial system began to break down in 1931 with a series of bank collapses, there was less need to obey the gold standard's rules, and from then on it was the hard-merchant ideology of orthodox liberal economics that played a greater part. So when, in mid-1931, the German finance minister, Hermann Dietrich, expressed doubts about the draconian austerity measures pursued by the "Hunger Chancellor," Heinrich Brüning, he was overruled by a cabinet convinced by economists that budgets had to balance and inflation was the real danger.[57]

The result of Brüning's austerity was the end of democracy in Germany and—indirectly—the rise of Adolf Hitler. Social tensions became acute between supporters of the hard merchant and a working class determined to preserve its benefits and jobs; soon both were turning to the warrior to protect their interests. In the 1928 elections, the two warriorish anti-Weimar parties, the Nazis and the Communists, had received relatively small percentages of the vote (2.6 percent and 10.6 percent, respectively); in the elections of November 1932, those figures had risen to 33.1 percent and 16.9 percent, respectively. Even so, parliamentary politics became increasingly irrelevant, and paramilitaries—Communist and Nazi—took to the streets. Brüning had already concluded that he could not win the parliament's agreement for his austerity program, so after 1930 chancellors ruled by decree. And it was the difficulty of securing popular consent for this hard-merchant program that explains President Paul von Hindenburg's decision to appoint Hitler chancellor three years later. Intended as a puppet, Hitler soon cut the strings and mounted a fundamental challenge to the old merchant order.

The economic crisis empowered a similar radical-right warrior reaction in Japan—though one more closely connected to traditional elites and the army than in Germany. Between 1929 and 1931, exports fell by 50 percent,[58] and at the same time Washington and London pressured Japan into limiting its naval strength. This provoked a powerful attack on parliamentarians and big business by radical right-wing groups, which accused them of capitulating before an international system that now offered no economic advantages. In November 1930, Tomeo Sagoya, a young member of a radical nationalist secret society, shot Prime Minister Osachi Hamaguchi, and by 1932 the parliament had lost power to traditional military, bureaucratic, and business elites; the army became especially dominant, launching an invasion of Manchuria in 1931 without parliamentary approval.[59] For much of the 1930s, Japan's prime ministers were generals or admirals, and by the time Japan launched a war on China in 1937, the military was seeking to create a new "national defense state," imbued with its warrior worldview.

Elsewhere, the economic collapse and sudden withdrawal of American loans helped the rise of an economic system even more hostile to the merchant: the Communist "command economy," introduced for the first time by Joseph Stalin in 1928. Lenin's 1920s market reforms had always had their weaknesses: many rank-and-file Bolsheviks felt that it was a betrayal of their ideals—the "New Exploitation of the Proletariat" rather than the "New Economic Policy"—and the politburo's plans to develop the economy with the help of grain exports were hit by plummeting commodity prices and poor harvests. Nevertheless, up until early 1928, most Soviet leaders hoped to continue the market strategy. But the rollback of American loans to Germany, and thus of German loans to the USSR, together with further falls in grain prices, contributed to a radical change of direction. Stalin and his allies concluded that the merchant strategy had failed.[60] To repay debts, fund imports, and rearm, the state had to be firmly back in charge. Planning officials, not markets, were now to determine the development of industry; meanwhile, peasants were corralled into collective farms, making grain seizures easier, so that the proceeds could be channeled into new state-owned factories. It was this economic system—where the merchant and his values were severely limited or entirely absent—that was to be the model for all future Communist states and was eventually to govern the lives of almost a third of the world's population.

By the early 1930s, the American-style merchant regime had collapsed after having wrought havoc across much of the world. The foundations of the liberal order constructed by the United States after the war—the gold standard and international trade and investment—had been shattered, and nothing had been put in their place. A global economic contraction and nationalistic, economically isolationist policies were the consequence, and these only exacerbated the problems. André Siegfried's new "American civilization" had crumbled after only a few turbulent years. As Bertolt Brecht, the German Marxist poet, commented with bitter irony in 1930: "What men they were . . . Their inventors the most adept! Their trains the swiftest!"[61] It all looked like lasting a thousand years . . . but endured a bare eight.

Three Roads to Salvation

The crisis was so sudden and catastrophic that the Jazz Age soft merchant was widely discredited. He was seen as a member of a selfish international elite, concerned more with lining his pockets than with producing for the nation and creating jobs for ordinary people. The prophets and evangelists of the 1920s were suddenly reviled. Propagandists and cartoonists saw the crisis in a remarkably similar way, whether among Soviet Communists, German Nazis, or American New Dealers: top-hatted wheeler-dealers in their pompous stock exchanges were being brought low by their own greed.

The Soviets, of course, saw the crisis as a sign that all merchants—and indeed capitalism itself—were doomed, just as Marx had predicted. In 1930, Stalin forecast, not unreasonably, an imminent civil war between a "fascicizing bourgeoisie" and a revolutionary proletariat, and a 1932 poster by the famous propaganda artist Viktor Deni showed the pillars of capitalism buckling under the force of the "October Hurricane" of 1929.[62] Hitler did not go so far: the culprit, he argued, was not capitalism itself but the Jewish financier. Nazi anti-Semitism, like its nineteenth-century predecessors, was not directed just at international commerce: the "Jew" represented a whole range of modern forces that, the Nazis claimed, were corroding national unity—whether greedy financiers, Marxist intellectuals, or subversive workers.[63] But the economic crisis allowed the Nazis to exploit older prejudices against the Jew as trader, cheating good, solid Germans.[64]

Franklin Delano Roosevelt, the new American president, also reserved his venom for the financier and trader, sparing "productive" business. Even so, he still sounds remarkably radical to modern ears. In his inauguration speech, in March 1933, he condemned the trader for the failures of the past and argued that a new group had to take over: "rulers of the exchange of mankind's goods have failed through their own stubbornness and their own incompetence, have admitted their failure, and have abdicated." His language was Christian rather than socialist or racist, comparing the bad capitalists to the "money changers" Jesus Christ had expelled from the temple: "The money changers have fled from their high seats in the temple of our civilization. We may now restore that temple to the ancient truths. The measure of the restoration lies in the extent to which we apply social values more noble than mere monetary profit."[65]

Yet if the "money changer" was to be toppled from his high seat in the temple, who was to take his place? As Roosevelt spoke, the contours of the new caste politics were becoming clear. Three rival systems competed to displace the Jazz Age merchant: the radical right, most powerfully represented by German National Socialism; Stalinist Communism; and Social Democracy, of which Roosevelt's New Deal was a milder version and Sweden's Folkhemmet ("People's Home") a stronger one. A fourth, a version of the old merchant-influenced liberalism (with strong sagely adaptations), continued in Britain and France, though it had little international appeal.[66]

Those who have characterized twentieth-century history as a struggle between two principles, "liberalism" and "totalitarianism," therefore present a one-sided view, and neglect the fact that many at the time saw the struggles as a conflict between a workerist left and a right that favored social hierarchies at home and imperial hierarchies abroad. It is true that Nazism and Stalinism shared some important features—notably the power of the warrior and of military-style hierarchies, and the importance of the sage-priest as ideological mobilizer. But they differed profoundly over a range of other major questions, such as the place of the merchant and the worker. To classify them both as simply "totalitarian" therefore highlights their mutual hatred of liberalism and bundles other crucial features, often thought far more important at the time, into the background.

The balance of caste values was therefore as important as the conflict over liberalism versus state control, and each system offered a different mix: Nazism embraced warrior, hard-merchant, and some sagely values; Stalinism, those of the sage-technocrat, the warrior, and, to a decreasing extent, the worker; Social Democracy, the sage, worker, and soft merchant; and liberalism, the merchant and the sage. But as the economic crisis destroyed consensus among nation-states and social groups, there was an increasing tendency to look to the warrior. The Rotarian dream of a peaceful world, ruled by the merchant, had been shattered. The soldier had returned, but now the old aristocrat was giving way to a more populist warrior.

Lords and Slaves

The warrior as fighter was at his most powerful within Germany, although this has been obscured in some writings. After 1945 it was common to condemn Nazism as a big-business conspiracy, its storm troopers the dupes of Ruhr bosses; today, when arrogant technocrats are under attack from the academic left and "ideology" is condemned by the right, it is fashionable to see the Nazi as a fanatical sage, obsessed with implementing a utopian program of "scientific" racism.[67]

Racial ideology certainly played a central role in Nazi rule, but the caste most respected by the Nazis was not the sage but the warrior. The German writer Wolfgang Koeppen tried to capture the worldview of a regular Nazi in his character Gottlieb Judejahn, the monstrous antihero of his novel *Death in Rome* (1954). Judejahn has fled a defeated Germany to become an arms dealer in the Middle East. But, as his vivid reminiscences of his time in the SS show, he is still a warrior at heart, with utter contempt for the "weakling," whether soft merchant or sage:

Judejahn addressed [his soldiers] in a fatherly fashion as "my lads" and Judejahn said crudely, latrine-style, "Kill the cunt," he always had the popular touch, always a hell of a guy, great sense of humor . . . in bloody charge of the Black Reichswehr [German army] camps on the estates of Mecklenburg, death's head on his steel helmet, but even they, the old gods, had turned their coats, Ehrhardt the captain dining with writers and other such shitheads . . . but he, Judejahn, had taken the right road, unwavering and straight ahead, to Führer and Reich and full military honors. . . .

Recovery, life going on fatly and prosperously after total war, total battle, and total defeat, it was betrayal, betrayal of the Führer's plans and his vision for the future, it was disgraceful collaboration with the archenemy in the West. . . . The net of the German bourgeoisie had not yet been thrown over the old warrior.[68]

Hitler himself was certainly more the "bohemian" autodidact than the hearty Wagnerian warrior. (He had, of course, harbored ambitions to be an artist, and remained fascinated by architecture.) But he wished it were otherwise. As the paramilitary leader Gerhard Rossbach described him in the early 1920s, he was "weak but wanting to be hard, half-educated wishing to be an all-rounder, a Bohemian who had to be a soldier if he wanted to impress true soldiers."[69] But Hitler's worldview was very close to Judejahn's, even if his character was not. As he explained in *Mein Kampf* (My Struggle), "a person . . . who is physically sound and robust, of a steadfast and honest character, ready and able to make decisions and endowed with strength of will, is a more useful member of the national community than a weakling who is scholarly and refined."[70] For Hitler, the ideal state would be run like the old Prussian army, though recast in an updated, less aristocratic mold. Sport would be a central element of its new education system—Hitler favored populist and virile boxing to elitist fencing and dueling. If, Hitler declared, the rulers of the old German empire had "learned boxing, it would never have been possible for bullies and deserters and other such *canaille* [rabble] to carry through a German revolution [in 1918–19]."

Hitler's warrior ethic, then, took a very particular form; it was (in theory) hostile to old elites, but it also reconciled itself with elements of the hard-merchant, anti-workerist value system. Indeed, Nazism was an updating of the ideas of the old pre-1914 radical right. It was a program intended systematically to forge all German citizens into nonaristocratic warriors, a blend of militarism and racism together with hierarchy. And unlike its prewar predecessors, the Pan-German and Navy leagues, Nazism shunned traditional bourgeois ideas of *Bildung* and refinement.[71] What Hitler and his movement envisaged was nothing less than a race of global "lords" or "masters" (*Herrenvolk*), competing with their Western rivals and ruling over the slave races of the East.

The Nazis' anti-elitism secured them considerable working-class support. But while Nazis often expressed contempt for the values of the merchant and the sage, it is no surprise that by the late 1920s Hitler was attracting supporters from the commercial and especially from the professional middle classes, as well as from small farmers.[72] For it was these groups that saw their social and national status under threat, from workers below and rivals abroad, and looked to the warrior to maintain social and economic hierarchies. As power became a real possibility, Hitler made every effort to mobilize these groups by stressing the similarities between Nazi and hard-merchant values.

Hitler tried to forge a connection between the two in a speech to an influential industrialists' club in Düsseldorf in 1932. He began by denying the "widespread" view that Nazis were "hostile to our business life." In fact, he argued, the worldviews of the Nazis and of business were very similar, for their enemies were the same: democracy, equality, and pacifism. His goal, he argued, was to create a powerful German "civilization" to compete with other Western civilizations; and that could be achieved only by a system that placed the "capable intelligences of a nation, which are always in a minority," in positions of power. "Democracy," in contrast, brought the "rule of stupidity, of mediocrity, of half-heartedness, of cowardice," because it gave power to the less talented. And this particularly applied to the economy. It was illogical, Hitler argued, for businessmen to defend a hierarchy based on "the principle of achievement" in their own companies, while accepting the rule of the masses in politics, because "whatever man in the past has achieved—all human civilizations—is conceivable only if the supremacy of this principle is admitted."[73]

There was a great deal of sympathy for Hitler's arguments among hard-merchant businessmen who believed that the left was challenging an order based on merit. Hitler's love of violence and war, though, was more of a problem. War was expensive, disrupted trade, and involved state interference in business; and property-loving businessmen hated Nazi thugs smashing up even Jewish shops. But Hitler swept such objections aside. The English view that the world had been conquered by "purely economic means" was sheer hypocrisy, he argued; the white races had become rich not through trade alone but because they had exercised an "extraordinarily brutal right to dominate others."[74] And now that the world economy had collapsed, it was clear that trade could not save the fatherland. Germany could survive only by conquering a massive empire and thus gaining "living room" (*Lebensraum*) for the German race.[75] In the meantime, violence in Germany itself was essential for creating the Germans who could win the coming international competition. The "bourgeois" woken up by rowdy Nazis outside his window might ask, "Why must the Nazis always be so provocative and run about the place at night?" But this was dangerous complacency: "Gentlemen, if everyone thought like that, then no one's sleep at night would be disturbed, it is true, but then the bourgeois today could not venture on the street."[76] The merchant might not like it, but he needed the warrior's protection.

Therefore, though many German businesspeople were dismayed when Hitler, after gaining the chancellorship in January 1933, proceeded to destroy democracy, imprison opponents, and, worst of all, impose state controls over the economy as part of rearmament, they welcomed his hard-merchant measures—the destruction of labor unions, the arrests of Communists, and the freezing of wages. Moreover, they soon discovered that they could make good profits from the protectionist Nazi economy.[77] As Hitler had promised, the new regime seemed set on restoring the power of the middle classes by removing the workerist challenge from the left.

However, while the Nazis were happy with economic inequalities, old cultural hierarchies were, in theory, anathema to their vision of a revitalized Germany; hierarchies were to be based on "merit"—at least merit as defined by the Nazis. Ideally, society was to be remodeled as one giant army unit, in which people were subordinate to the Führer and his deputies but also part of a single whole. Like the radical right of the past, the Nazis hoped to forge everybody into members of a warrior "master race," dissolving aristocratic hierarchies of blood and status within the race so they could assert them more powerfully outside it.

This Nazi ideal was played out in the thousands of military-style "camps" (*Lagern*) set up to transform Germans into warrior Nazis. Members of the Nazi Party, Hitler Youth, and League of German Maidens were most commonly trained in them, but nonparty professionals and businesspeople were also expected to attend for short educational refresher courses.[78] The Jewish diarist Victor Klemperer recorded the experiences of a friend, a professor of literature, at one of these distinctly militaristic retreats. The camp inmates were "teachers between forty and fifty. They slept six to a room, wore uniforms, did digging and sport, were given educative lectures. A headmaster talked about the character of the French; they were similar to the Jews, they did not love animals."[79] The camps also made very deliberate attempts to break down social divisions; youths of different classes were made to mix, and Nazi pedagogues urged working-class students to bring arrogant high school graduates down a peg or two by "ribbing" and "name calling" and even, in extreme cases, using violence.[80]

How did Germans respond to these efforts? In many different ways, of course. Workers, deprived of their old unions and political parties, were less likely to be enthusiastic than the middle classes. But there is evidence that the Nazis had real success in transforming the outlook of many ordinary Germans of all classes.[81] In part, they were responding to economic improvements: the Nazis put people to work on public works projects, and rearmament slashed unemployment. Simultaneously, the regime established welfare systems popular with ordinary people and sagely professionals alike. But the appeal was not only to pocketbooks and bellies. They were also responding to the powerful Nazi political message: they, as Germans, were threatened by overbearing Jews—of both the Marxist and the merchant variety—and by rapacious foreign enemies.[82] Germans could regain their self-respect only if they became more warrior-like.

This anxious and self-pitying politics seems bizarre to us today, given that it was Nazi Germany itself that behaved like the classic bully, unleashing terror and wars against weaker peoples. But to many Germans at the time, hit by economic crisis and national humiliation, the Germans were weak, and their rivals strong. A grim insight into these attitudes came from one woman who noted that it was no coincidence that one never came across any Jewish maids or servants—the Jews, she insisted, would only rule, never serve.[83]

The Nazi system of military mobilization appealed to right-wing nationalists everywhere, convinced that it made sense in the zero-sum world of the 1930s economy. But elites in Japan—both soldiers and state bureaucrats who sought to revive the economy—were in a better position than most to emulate the German example. In 1937, Hiromi Arisawa, a young economist influenced by Nazi writings, argued that military priorities had to be paramount, and that "in a semi-war situation, an economy led by the state has to be coercive."[84] However, in the absence of a

unifying Nazi-style party, the Japanese political system was far more fragmented than Germany's, and these ambitions were barely realized. Big
business did accept a "five-year plan" for key industries, but coordination
was weak and internal conflicts were rampant. Moreover, the success of
the military's "spiritual mobilization" of the population for war beginning in 1937 was limited. Women, in particular, resented (and ignored)
the "frugality" campaigns, which sought to persuade them to give up
their kimonos for simple peasant garb. It was only after Pearl Harbor,
in 1941, that war, and warrior culture, began to seriously affect ordinary lives.[85]

Warriors, Workers, and Planners

The militarization of Germany and Japan may have been precipitated by
economic crisis, but it was freely chosen. The Soviet Union, caught as it
was between these two aggressive powers, was more constrained in its
choices. As Hitler had made clear, Germany ultimately had plans to turn
the USSR into a colony. "Russia is our Africa," he later declared. Also, the
USSR was still an overwhelmingly agrarian country, richer than India
and China, for sure, but poorer than the European economic "periphery,"
whether the Slavic East or the Mediterranean South, and far poorer than
Western Europe, the United States, and Japan.[86] It was therefore no surprise that the breakdown of international trade and cooperation with the
West after 1928 should have brought about a sharp turn to warrior values, last seen during the Russian Civil War.

But the Soviet warrior ideal was a very different type from the Nazi
variety: he was to be a warrior-worker. And so for a time in the late 1920s,
Communist youth and party members found themselves mobilized into
military-style "shock-worker brigades" and "Light Cavalry" units. At this
stage, however, they were being drilled for battle only on the so-called
economic front. And unlike Nazi labor units, they were not to be founded

on the hard-merchant values of strict subordination to managers and engineers but on a more workerist, egalitarian approach. Stalinist leaders saw this as pure hardheaded pragmatism. Economic success, it was thought, would come only through harnessing a working-class heroism, which depended on proletarian collective pride, not financial incentives or top-down management discipline. As Stalin argued in 1930, the Soviet style of production transformed "labour from the shameful and heavy burden which it was thought to be previously, into a matter of *honour*, a matter of *glory*, a matter of *valour* and *heroism*. Nothing like this exists or could exist in capitalist countries."[87]

It followed from this attitude that Soviet workers could be expected to work extremely hard for very low wages, just as if they were soldiers fighting for a heartfelt cause. This attitude had some parallels with Nazi Germany, but, unlike their German counterparts, Soviet workers were also granted higher social status—though since the revolutionary period they had been deprived of real power. So, for example, workers could subject their immediate bosses to "criticism from below" (within strict limits).[88] The 1928 show trial of engineers from the Shakhty mines, in the Ukraine, signaled that workers were free to condemn managers and engineers (though not the Communist Party) for mismanagement and poor treatment—especially if they were of "bourgeois" class origin.

Soviet society in the late 1920s, then, was seen by the regime as an army, though one closer in spirit to the partisan brigade—or even the ancient warrior clan—than the modern professional officer-led army. Some workers' brigades shared wages equally between their members, while others elected their foremen.[89]

Actual workers were, understandably, often hostile to these attempts to speed up production, and some used egalitarian, workerist ideas to criticize the regime. But in places, workers responded more positively. John Scott, a twenty-year-old who escaped unemployment in the United States to work in the huge Magnitogorsk metallurgical complex in 1931, remembered the warlike appeals and the self-sacrifice they encouraged:

In 1940, Winston Churchill told the British people that they could expect nothing but blood, sweat, and tears. The country was at war. The British people did not like it, but most of them accepted it.

Ever since 1931 or thereabouts the Soviet Union has been at war. . . . In Magnitogorsk I was precipitated into a battle. . . . Tens of thousands of people were enduring the most intense hardships in order to build blast furnaces, and many of them did it willingly, with boundless enthusiasm, which infected me from the day of my arrival.[90]

However, the worker-warrior was not the only figure in the Soviet caste mix; the sage-technocrat was also a powerful presence, in the approved command-economy form of the technician, planner, and state official. Marxism-Leninism was always a much more sagely movement than Fascism or Nazism and relied on an elaborate secular "priesthood" of ideological officials—the Communist Party. Communists believed in Enlightenment ideas of science and progress. And though they might at times have accepted the necessity for revolutionary violence against class oppression, they never, unlike the radical right, thought violence a good thing in itself. Sages, of course, became particularly prominent with the institution of the command economy, in 1929. The end of Lenin's New Economic Policy and the expulsion of the merchant now left the planner in control of the economy, and every manager, engineer, and worker became an official in a huge state machine.

Unsurprisingly, given their sagely bent, most planners and managers did not approve of the worker-warrior approach. Predictability and rationality were their watchwords, while heroic "storming" to fulfill targets and "criticism from below" were seen as disruptive and destructive. And when the economy ran into crisis in the early 1930s, precisely because of overambitious target setting, planners argued that the command economy required greater discipline. The leadership now changed course, and industry became much more hierarchical.[91] Planners and engineers became more powerful under the new slogan of 1931, "Technology decides everything!" But so did rather less sagely local party bosses, who behaved more like the paternalistic aristocrats of old. Citizens were expected to bow and scrape to each local "little Stalin," who was now in a position to bestow welfare on them in displays of Sovietized *noblesse oblige*.[92] The Soviet Union was effectively ruled by a new version of the czarist "service aristocracy," a ruling stratum that mixed the sagely virtue of expert public service with the stifling paternalism of a new aristocracy.

Stalin himself was not averse to presenting a czar-like face as father of the people, receiving ritualized "thanks" and obeisance. But he and many others in the Communist Party were never comfortable with this orderly social pyramid, whether dominated by sagely planners or quasi-aristocratic bosses. Realizing it lacked real energy and dynamism, granting power to conservative officials, they often harked back to the warrior-dominated model of worker mobilization of the late 1920s—though they preferred an increasingly hierarchical approach.

If Hitler was a (third-rate) intellectual trying to be a soldier, Stalin was the reverse. He read widely and made serious efforts to master Marxist theory—as any self-respecting Bolshevik leader had to do. But among his fellow party bosses, he was either the tough leader of the gang or the convivial, toast-drinking bon vivant. Though never a soldier (unlike Hitler), Stalin had been a political commissar in the Red Army during the civil war, an experience that had shaped him. It was at this time that he jettisoned his Western-style suit and adopted his trademark military tunic and boots. But his love of the military was not just a matter of personal character and style. At the end of the 1920s, he and many other party members were convinced that the main advantage of the Soviet system over the capitalist one lay in its warrior-worker ethos. These values, they believed, were absolutely essential if the USSR was to make the economic leaps forward needed to narrow the gap with an aggressive West—leaps that would defy the staid officials and planners.[93] In capitalist societies, they argued, workers could not be truly productive, because people were more interested in moneygrubbing than in achieving heroic feats of development.[94]

Oddly for a Marxist, Stalin often saw the world less in class terms than in caste terms: it was the contrast between the "merchant" and the warrior "hero" that haunted him, and he frequently expressed contempt for the "merchant" societies of the liberal West.[95] In August 1939, he told German foreign minister Joachim von Ribbentrop that the British would not fight, because the Axis powers had "frightened principally the City of London and the small British merchants"; and in 1951, he cast doubt on the Americans' determination in the Korean War, telling the Chinese leader Zhou Enlai: "Americans are merchants. Every American soldier is a speculator, occupied with buying and selling."[96] For Stalin, merchant values were corrosive and sapped willpower. As he explained to the French Communist leader Maurice Thorez in 1947, "When a person gets dollars his head will get empty. A full pocket makes for an empty head."[97]

But at home it was the sage-technocrat and official, not the merchant, who was the real threat to Stalin's plans for warrior-worker mobilization, and Soviet politics endured many bloody battles between the two worldviews—as did many other Communist regimes.[98] Once we have this fundamental conflict in focus, it becomes easier to explain one of the most mysterious episodes in Soviet history: the "Great Terror" of 1936–38.

It is still common to see the Terror simply as the product of Stalin's vengefulness or obsessive paranoia. Certainly he was unusually fearful and vindictive, but other factors were also important, and warrior-worker ideas also help to explain some of his thinking at the time.[99] As Hitler remilitarized the Rhineland and intervened in the Spanish Civil War, and as it became evident that the liberal powers would do little to stop him, Stalin began to panic. In 1936, the USSR was still far behind Germany militarily, and already it was clear that Germany planned to invade. The answer, for Stalin, was another dose of the warrior-worker spirit to shake up the slothful sagely bureaucracy. He first targeted the officials running industry in the autumn of 1936, launching a purge of their ranks combined with worker "criticism from below"; when he found that the officials were being protected by paternalistic "big-wigs" and "princes" among the local party bosses, he arrested them, too. It was only by replacing these "conservatives" with more heroic, dynamic officials that, he believed, the Soviet people could be mobilized and the Soviet state protected.

But "purging" (expulsion from the party) was not enough for Stalin. War was imminent, and he could not take the chance that the purged— and now disaffected—might conspire with Hitler. Driven by a mixture of callousness and brutal military logic, he decided they were to be shot; and eventually he became convinced that anybody with a question mark over his commitment to the "socialist cause," from party leader to peasant, had to die, in case he should make common cause with the invading Germans.[100]

As mass repressions and denunciations escalated, state violence convulsed Soviet society. More than 700,000 people were killed, and many more sent to prison camps. Predictably, given the purge of managers and scientists, the economy descended into chaos, with officials too frightened to make decisions or impose authority. In late 1938, Stalin ended the Terror, and he never again risked a major purge of his officials.

The regime returned to its old hierarchical structure, but Stalin's fears that it would ossify proved to be misplaced. Workerist heroism might have been abandoned, but the German invasion in 1941 unleashed a Soviet-Russian nationalist heroism, which was much more powerful. "*Za Rodinu! Za Stalina!*" ("For the Motherland! For Stalin!") was the new Red Army battle cry, and Stalin halted the state persecution of Russian Orthodox Christianity. That patriotic self-sacrifice, combined with the ruthless efficiency of the sage-planners in running the war economy, had an effect; in one of the most extraordinary administrative feats of the war, the Soviets dismantled their major industrial plants and transported them thousands of miles east, to keep them from falling into the hands of the Germans. The USSR survived, very much against the odds.

The USSR of the 1930s might have been weak and deeply isolated, but the militaristic aggression of the right and the failures of the merchant gave its version of Communism some international appeal, among both sagely intellectuals and the left wing of the anticolonial movements. Western intellectuals flocked to Moscow to investigate the new experiment—most famously Beatrice and Sidney Webb. But more significant for the future were events in China, where civil war and the Japanese invasion strengthened the position of one of the most warriorish of Chinese Communists, Mao Zedong. Driven out of the cities, the Communists took to the countryside and began to mobilize the peasantry against the invader. Mao was one of the most successful guerrilla leaders, and his base at Yan'an (1936–48) was designed to be a model of equality—owing something to Marxist ideology and something to the egalitarianism of the traditional warrior band;[101] indeed, one of Mao's favorite books as a child had been *Water Margin,* a classical Chinese tale of 108 bandit "brothers" who defended the poor against unjust officials.[102] It was this guerrilla model of organization that was to make Communism so popular among anticolonial nationalists during and after the war.

In the West, however, the other, Social Democratic branch of the socialist movement responded to the crisis of the 1930s most successfully. By making peace with the merchant while ensuring that the sage and the worker controlled him, Social Democracy harnessed the power of capitalism to enrich all classes of society. It emerged in its purest form in Sweden, but in these warlike times, a rather more militaristic version was stronger, this one hatched in that most unlikely of places: the United States, the merchant's homeland.

People's Home, New Deal

In 1930, the Swiss architect Le Corbusier visited the Stockholm Exhibition of Design and Handicrafts. His radical ideas—flat roofs, horizontal lines, light interiors, and simple design—were a hit. Not only were several Swedish architects excited by the "international modernist" style of architecture, but so were the social reformers among the Scandinavian sagely classes. Possibly the most influential was the economist and sociologist Gunnar Myrdal, who was to become one of the most important sage-technocrats of the postwar West. Born the son of a laborer, Myrdal shone in the mathematical, laissez-faire economics fashionable in the 1920s, but he soon became disillusioned with its rigid certainties and adopted the Keynesian heresy.[103] Deeply committed to social reform, he saw in Le Corbusier's cheap, functional, but elegant plans a new ideal for housing the Swedish working class. An influential adviser to Social Democratic governments, after 1934 he helped launch a program of public housing in the modernist style, nicknamed "Myrdal's tenements."[104] From then on, modernism became entrenched in Swedish culture, and it is no accident that Sweden, through IKEA, is today the most successful purveyor of flat-pack modernism to the world's middle classes.

It was precisely at this moment in Sweden's history that it became the pioneer of Social Democratic politics, and it is in the modernist architecture of this era that we can see the spirit of Social Democracy most clearly, for the architecture, like the political movement, united the sage-technocrat and the worker. The style was seen as scientific and functional: it was based on pure geometrical forms, adapted for mass factory production. Its aesthetic was studiedly democratic, disdaining the grandeur of aristocratic neoclassical buildings and rejecting the fuss and ornament so beloved by the traditionalist bourgeoisie. With its clean horizontal lines and open glass-fronted facades, modernism was, quite literally, democracy in concrete. It was in the radical left-wing architectural movements in Germany and the Netherlands that this aesthetic had been born, but it was soon crushed by the Nazis, who generally favored a more monumental architecture, suitable for an imperial *Herrenvolk*. As the architect Berthold Lubetkin complained in 1937, "To design horizontal windows is to attract the attention of the secret police."[105]

The Social Democratic union of sage and worker had deep roots in Swedish society: its aristocratic state, closely connected with the Lutheran Church, had long had a paternalistic sense of duty toward the poor;[106] Sweden also had a well-organized working class by the 1920s. However, the real secret of the Social Democrats' success lay in their willingness to compromise and widen their appeal beyond the industrial working class. Unusually for Social Democratic parties, the Swedish party's workerism included the other part of the worker caste—the smallholder peasantry—and it took an interest in raising rural living standards. This was the meaning of the concept of Folkhemmet elaborated by the party leader Per Albin Hansson in 1928—Sweden was to be a cross-class *people's* home rather than simply the *workers'* home. "The good home," he explained, "does not recognize any privileged or neglected members, nor any favourite or stepchildren."[107] Much of the business and liberal establishment was therefore hostile to Social Democratic policies, but, unlike its German counterpart, it lacked the strength in numbers to resist them. But at the same time, the Swedish Social Democrats sweetened the pill and offered compromises with the merchant—notably accepting that the market had to be improved rather than destroyed. The German Social Democrats, like many Marxist movements, never made serious efforts to win over the peasantry, who became some of the Nazis' most loyal supporters; they were also much more suspicious of the market and failed to propose constructive solutions to the crisis of capitalism.

When the economic crisis struck, the Swedish socialists were therefore in a much stronger position than the German Social Democrats. Influenced by the writings of Keynes and other British left-wing liberals of the

1920s, Swedish Social Democrats tried to use the state to rescue capitalism.[108] The ideas of Keynes were founded on a deep mistrust of the merchant, with his speculative excesses in good times and destructive moralism in bad. And the Social Democrats followed Keynes in arguing that orthodox austerity measures, as adopted in the United States and Germany, would simply deepen the Depression. Rather, the state itself had to step in when the market failed and establish work programs paying market-level wage rates. In this way, a virtuous circle rather than a vicious one would be established, giving consumers spending power and, in turn, increasing production and employment. In 1932, the Social Democrats succeeded in forging an alliance with the peasant party, thus outvoting the conservative and liberal opposition; but it also won business over to its pro-growth policies.[109] By the 1936 election it was clear that the policy had worked (or at least had helped an improvement already under way).[110] The Social Democrats were able to form a majority government, and success bred success. The party ruled Sweden almost continuously until 1976.

The last place we might have expected a similar politics to emerge was the United States. If Swedish Social Democracy grew amid labor-union power and deep-rooted paternalistic state traditions, the United States possessed neither. And yet Franklin D. Roosevelt succeeded in introducing a version of Social Democracy into the United States—albeit one with a strong merchant element.

It is tempting to ascribe at least some of Roosevelt's political innovations to his social background. By American criteria he was a blue blood, both in origins and in culture. Born into a wealthy, landed family in New York State, he grew up in English-style aristocratic comfort on the ancestral Hyde Park estate. His instincts were (unsurprisingly) socially conservative, but at the same time paternalistic;[111] when, after an attack of polio, he went to recuperate in rural Georgia in the mid-1920s, he expressed shock at the poverty he saw and accepted that something had to be done about it.[112] He certainly betrayed more than a touch of aristocratic paternalism in his 1933 inauguration speech: he urged Americans to recognize the "falsity of material wealth as the standard of success," for confidence thrived on "honor, on the sacredness of obligations, on faithful protection, on unselfish performance."

As important as Roosevelt's upbringing was his experience of war. He had been the second in command in the Department of the Navy during the First World War, so he appreciated how Americans, often so skeptical of the big Progressivist state, were willing to tolerate it in wartime. He therefore made sure that his inaugural address was full of comparisons between the economic crisis and a military emergency: Americans needed to forge "a unity of duty hitherto evoked only in time of armed strife," and the government had to treat the economic crisis "as we would the emergency of a war."[113]

However, if Roosevelt's background predisposed him to more state-led, Progressivist solutions, he was no radical, nor were the economic ideas of his advisers. At first his administration pursued Hoover's ideas of business cartels, combined with a commitment to balanced budgets and sound finance. But to achieve confidence in the financial system and head off future bank collapses, he was prepared to clip the merchant's wings with revolutionary brio. In the first few weeks of his administration, he closed all the banks for a brief period, gave the government sweeping powers to restructure them, and ultimately shut down a thousand of them; he split Wall Street banks from local banks that dealt with depositors, stopping them from gambling on the financial markets with ordinary savers' money; and he took the dollar off the gold standard. He had his opponents, of course, but his supporters were far more numerous: a majority of Americans, like him, blamed the economic collapse on dishonest and feckless bankers.

Yet while these actions might have been dramatic, they did not lead to recovery, and from 1935 on, the Roosevelt administration moved rather more decisively away from the Hooverite past. It now took a more Keynesian line, concluding that the problem lay in too little spending by ordinary people and deciding that it had to take a much more interventionist and pro-labor approach.[114] An alphabet soup of government agencies set the unemployed to work on state projects. Most ambitious was the Works Progress Administration (WPA), which hired millions of Americans to build schools, hospitals, and airports; even artists and actors drew salaries from the government.[115] Roosevelt also established the rudiments of a welfare state and social security system, though they were still less generous than their European equivalents.

The New Dealers, though, still saw their project as cutting the merchant down to size rather than destroying him, or, as the economist John Galbraith put it, creating "countervailing powers" to the overweening power of business and using the federal government to raise workers, farmers, and underprivileged regions, like the South, to positions of equality in the marketplace. Hence, they intervened in the economic development of Tennessee, neglected by private business, and gave labor unions important new rights.

But Roosevelt could go only so far. He met resistance from powerful, entrenched merchants in Congress and business. His social security system was a largely contributory one, and he never had the mandate for a European-style welfare state that gave the poor benefits by rights.[116] Nor did he pump-prime the economy as much as Keynesians wanted, and his renewed commitment to a balanced budget led to a new recession in 1937.[117] The Swedish notion of a sagely state negotiating among different castes in the interests of full employment and growth was not widely accepted. It was ultimately only the massive stimulus of war and rearmament that propelled the American economy to prosperity.

THE RUSSIAN NATIONALIST POLITICIAN A. I. Savenko wrote in 1915 that "war is an exam, a great exam."[118] And if the Second World War was an exam, its main candidates—Nazi Germany, Communist Russia, Social Democratic America, and liberal Britain and France—had prepared for the test in very different ways. It may be that the Germans and their allies were doomed to lose the conflict for purely economic reasons. As British historian Adam Tooze has recently argued, the GDPs of Britain, France, and their huge empires exceeded those of Germany and Italy by 60 percent, and when America entered the war, the Axis powers could not hope to win.[119] But the different caste orders in each of the combatant powers also contributed to the outcome.

The Nazis' racism and warrior ethic not only unleashed mass violence across the continent; it also damaged their own interests. They may have helped mobilize support for war, but it was counterproductive once the Germans had conquered their empire in the East. Unlike more paternalistic imperialists, such as the British, the Nazis ruled as a "master race," enslaving rather than seeking collaborators—especially among the "inferior" Slavic peoples.[120] Inevitably, they provoked resistance. One Czech remembered why he had become a Communist at the age of sixteen: "During the German occupation . . . I lived in a state of unconscious fear. As a Czech, I knew that the Nazis considered the Czech people an inferior race, and if Hitler emerged victorious, my fate might be the same as that of my Jewish classmates."[121]

The exaltation of the warrior and the denigration of the sage had another damaging consequence: the German army had powers to insist that even scientists serve at the front, and the Germans had a much smaller and less effective civilian support structure than did the Americans, Soviets, and British. They therefore lacked the degree of expert support their competitors enjoyed, whether in the form of Soviet planners, Bletchley code breakers, or U.S. Air Force technocrats.[122]

When the conflict ended, it was these sages, as much as the soldiers, who believed they had won the war. And after 1945, they had the confidence to remake the world in their own image, while making sure that the merchant was never able to cause such chaos again.

FOUR

The Age of Whiz

On September 21, 1959, a coach full of skeptical journalists traveled to Dearborn, Michigan, to witness the unveiling of the Ford Motor Company's latest model: the Falcon. Since its glory days in the 1920s, Ford had fallen behind Chrysler and General Motors, the victim of Henry Ford II's increasingly conservative management style. But the Falcon was supposed to change all that. The brainchild of Ford's future president, Robert Strange McNamara, it marked a very deliberate departure from the chrome-laden, baroque extravaganzas of the previous few years, epitomized by the garish Edsel, launched in the teeth of McNamara's opposition in 1957. McNamara felt that the Edsel was ill suited to compete with the newly popular European cars, especially the modest and austere Volkswagen Beetle. As the business-dominated Eisenhower era came to a close, a younger generation was attracted by the streamlined and understated "European" style, seeing the status-seeking showiness of the mid-1950s as rather vulgar and crass. McNamara clearly understood the spirit of the times, and the Falcon was a runaway success, putting Ford back at the forefront of American car manufacturing; the Edsel, meanwhile, was one of the American car industry's most spectacular failures. McNamara's success in rescuing

Ford attracted the attention of the new president, John F. Kennedy, and the auto executive soon defected from the private sector and joined the Kennedy administration as secretary of defense. McNamara, the no-nonsense, no-frills technocrat, fit in well with the image of youthful dynamism and meritocracy Kennedy was anxious to project.

Yet within a few years, this representative of the early-1960s zeitgeist had become one of the most reviled leaders in the Western world. The venomous obituaries from both left and right that marked his death in 2009 suggest that he remains one of the least popular historical figures in the United States—even beating such close rivals as Henry Kissinger and Richard Nixon. McNamara's misfortune, of course, was to find himself in charge of one of the most humiliating failures of American foreign policy: the doomed effort to prevent the Communist Viet Cong of North Vietnam from taking over the non-Communist South. But his abiding unpopularity is more complex than that, for McNamara was a prime example of a specifically American version of the sage-technocrat who ruled the world in alliance with the warrior for the two decades after the Second World War. And in his biography we can find the reasons for the powerful appeal of this caste—and for its spectacular fall from grace in the 1970s.

For his 1960s student critics, McNamara, with his slicked-back hair, accountant's glasses, and close-fitting dark suits, was the epitome of complacent corporate America.[1] Yet this was always a case of mistaken identity, for McNamara was, in fact, always something of an outsider in the business world. His middle name, Strange, was an adaptation of his French American mother's family name, Étranger ("foreigner"), and he was generally regarded by businesspeople as very intellectually able, if rather arrogant and "European." He had voted for Roosevelt in 1940—a fact that he had felt compelled to conceal from his fellow faculty at Harvard Business School[2]—and he hated what he saw as the Republican conformity of the Detroit suburbs of Dearborn and Bloomfield Hills (where Ford managers were expected to live); indeed, he insisted on moving forty miles away from his colleagues, to the university town of Ann Arbor.

McNamara was therefore very much on the sagely, rather than the merchant, side of the division in the American elite. And it was the sagely caste that became increasingly powerful as the generation that had come of age in the Great Depression inherited political power. From a modest, middle-class, but pro-union family, he arrived to study economics at Berkeley in 1933, convinced that the state had to help the poor and that the chummy, know-nothing businessmen of the 1920s should cede power to educated technocrats. A few years later, he was plucked from Harvard Business School to become one of the civilian experts who did so much to boost the American war effort, and he was drafted into the U.S. Air Force to introduce statistical methods into bombing strategy.[3] It was his stats team—known as the "Whiz Kids"—that was recruited *en masse* by Henry Ford II to apply wartime expertise to car production.[4] At Ford, McNamara stood out for his lack of interest in the individualistic extravagance of 1950s American car culture, a sagely outlook entirely in keeping with his New Deal attitudes. And his technocratic ethos influenced his approach to business. He pursued efficiencies by increasing managerial control; and while he might have been committed to some degree of economic equality, he was certainly not interested in equality of power. Ford workers were paid well, but they were also expected to obey a strict line of command, at the head of which stood company president McNamara.

McNamara, then, had many features of the typical Progressivist American sage-technocrat: he hoped to make society fairer by using his knowledge in the service of the soft merchant, improving both profits and workers' living standards; and, while not a warrior himself, he was willing to resort to war in defense of the merchant against foreign threats. Indeed, it was during war that his sagely values were most likely to be accepted by a majority of Americans—as Roosevelt had appreciated when he employed martial rhetoric to justify the New Deal. McNamara was therefore at an advantage after 1945 compared with his post-1918 predecessors, for peace had not been fully declared: the United States was now fighting a new kind of long-term war, against the Soviet Union, and was building a global informal empire to counter the threat of anti-Western nationalism and Communism. So if George Babbitt, *Boobus americanus,* typified American influence after the First World War, Robert McNamara—"the leading specimen of *Homo mathematicus,*" as one acquaintance described him—represented the second American coming.[5]

Today historians look back on this era of economic growth and relative social harmony as a golden age, or "Les Trente Glorieuses" (the glorious thirty years), and that success owed a great deal to people like McNamara. By granting the sage-technocrat so much more power over the merchant and permitting him to bring the worker into the corridors of power, the new Western caste order was much more resilient than the failed experiment of the 1920s; and the Communist East and the newly decolonized South, where the sage was even more dominant, also did well. But the flaws in the new international caste order were evident from the time of its birth, in the final years of the war. For the American warrior, determined to preserve the West's power over the postcolonial South, disrupted the compromises required to maintain the system; the merchant's fetters were not strong enough; and overconfident sage-technocrats like McNamara alienated castes that felt excluded. By the late 1960s caste tensions had returned, and it was only a matter of time before the Western warrior decided to abandon the sage and restore the power of the merchant.

Prophet in the Wilderness

On July 1, 1944, 730 academics, politicians, and officials from forty-four countries, accompanied by armies of clerical staff, arrived at a huge Spanish Renaissance–style hotel in the ski resort of Bretton Woods, New

Hampshire. Built by a railway tycoon, with stunning views over the surrounding countryside, the Mount Washington Hotel was the most luxurious of its day, though somewhat worse for wear when the delegates to the United Nations Monetary and Financial Conference arrived. It had been closed during the war and was being refurbished, or "built around us, while we sit on our appointed perches," as Keynes put it.[6] But the complaints were few, for these were not Gilded Age industrialists or pampered princes but sages, who claimed to be driven only by an ethic of public service. Even the rather grand Dean Acheson, the chief delegate from the State Department, was only mildly annoyed that he had to use a former hotel bar as his office and a sink as a filing cabinet.[7] And it was war that had propelled the sage-technocrat—and especially the economist—to this Olympian summit of world power. Keynes, in particular, owed his influence to war. After publishing his famous *General Theory of Employment, Interest and Money,* in 1936, he was viewed as a heretic by the free-market British establishment, but with the outbreak of war, the kind of state intervention Keynes had been advocating suddenly became the norm, and his ideas became the new orthodoxy. By 1944 he had been appointed London's chief economic policy maker and delegate at Bretton Woods.

However, this sagely ascendancy obscured sharp differences. Bretton Woods followed months of difficult negotiations between Keynes and the American economist Harry Dexter White, and the key bone of contention was the role of the merchant—how much power would he have in the new sagely order?

White and Keynes could not have been more different, and it is no surprise that they disliked each other. White, an energetic and clever man, though often seen as pushy and aggressive, was the son of Lithuanian Jewish immigrants to Boston. He had worked in one of his family's hardware shops and went to university later in life, before becoming an official in the Treasury Department. He had supported the Socialist candidate in the 1924 presidential election, had little love for the British

Empire, and had learned Russian so he could study Soviet planning.[8] During the war, he had even passed information to American Communists—his exposure at the House Un-American Activities Committee hearings would lead to his death from a heart attack in 1948. But when he joined the government, he moderated his economic radicalism. As a typical New Dealer working for the Roosevelt administration, he was reluctant to limit markets too fundamentally.[9]

Keynes's origins, by contrast, were more solidly sagely: his father was an academic, and his mother came from a long line of nonconformist preachers. But there were other, distinctly unsagely aspects to his character. He won, lost, and recovered a great deal of money gambling in the City of London; he was a member of the Bloomsbury circle, a bohemian group that prized aestheticism and friendship over material success; and he was a committed Oxbridge don, a member of that most gentlemanly and paternalistic branch of the sagely caste.[10] (He even missed the opening sessions at Bretton Woods because he was hosting a dinner to celebrate the fifth centenary of the Amicabilis Concordia, between his college, King's Cambridge, and its "sister," New College, Oxford.)[11] This rich experience of diverse worlds had shaped an unusually complex view of life. His City adventures gave him a strong skepticism of markets—capitalism, he noted in 1930, rewarded "some of the most distasteful human qualities."[12] But he also had little of the puritanical disapproval of wealth common among sages: for him, both Christianity and Marxism were "pseudo social service religions."[13] His preference was for a tough sagely control of capitalism, enabling the soft merchant to spread his bounty as widely as possible while creating as little chaos as possible. And as the representative of Britain, a heavily indebted country, he had particular reason to be suspicious of markets, for left unfettered, they would benefit only the wealthy, which—in the context of the global economy— meant the United States.

White, as much as Keynes, had learned the lessons of the 1920s. They both saw the need to restore global trade and investment after the col-

lapse of the 1930s, but they were also convinced that there should be no
return to the laissez-faire world of a pure gold standard or a poorly regulated international market in capital. The devastation of Europe reinforced their view: in 1939, the American economy had been only half the
size of those of the main belligerents in Europe, Japan, and the USSR,
whereas by 1946 it was larger than all of them combined.[14] Washington
rightly feared that the restrictive and deflationary gold standard demanded by Wall Street would prevent the Europeans from achieving the
growth that American exporters needed so much. They also realized that
rigid and deflationary free-market policies in war-blighted Western
Europe could lead to social unrest and drive its peoples into the arms of
Communists.

However, Keynes and White differed over how far capitalism should
be controlled. One of the most striking things from today's perspective is
how radical Keynes's program was and how far he was prepared to depart
from free-market orthodoxies. He developed a scheme that transferred
power over the global economy to a new international bank, run by sages
and charged with managing currencies and preventing large imbalances
between rich and poor countries. Successful trading countries like the
United States would be required to invest their surpluses, and countries
with trade deficits would be entitled to take out limited "overdrafts," to
see them through difficulties.[15] Keynes's proposals, of course, baffled and
infuriated his merchant critics, who believed that successful countries
should be free to do what they liked with their wealth. But for Keynes,
deficit countries were the virtuous ones, as they were importing goods
and allowing the exporters to create jobs; surplus countries, meanwhile,
had a duty to recycle their wealth into productive investments. Keynes
also wanted to bring developing countries into the new economic order:
by buying up commodities such as oil, wheat, and rubber, the global economic government would stabilize prices and avoid the unpredictable
price swings that had inflicted such poverty and instability on less developed countries between the wars.

White hated Keynes's plan—partly, of course, because it conflicted with the economic interests of the United States, as well as with Washington's plans to forestall a new Nazism by creating an American-led postwar order. But Keynes's ideas also clashed with his fundamentally merchant worldview. For White, virtue lay in hard work and competitiveness, and it had to be rewarded—at the global as well as the national level. He accepted the need for a safety net for the poorer nations—the International Monetary Fund (IMF)—but it had to be a limited and parsimonious, New Deal–style contributory insurance scheme, not a generous and universal Swedish-style welfare state. Moreover, he had little interest in cooperative global economic government: the United States would be in charge of the new system, and it would run a new, more flexible version of the gold standard, based on the dollar.

The negotiations between the American and British teams were often bitterly acrimonious. Keynes deployed his Oxbridge style of intellectual acuity combined with aristocratic condescension, and White, perhaps understandably, responded with aggressive stonewalling. After one session, White commented, "Your Baron Keynes sure pees perfume," and he found Keynes's rudeness so upsetting that it began to affect his health; he soon avoided meetings and sent a deputy in his place.[16]

But while Keynes might have won the psychological battle, White won the economic war—inevitably, as the Americans had all the cash. Under the compromise announced at Bretton Woods, international business achieved the currency stability it wanted, while poorer governments were given the currency flexibility to expand their economies and build welfare states. (The dollar was linked to gold, and other currencies to the dollar, but weaker countries were allowed to devalue and stimulate their economies by agreement.) At the same time, trade was to be freed, but gradually (through the General Agreement on Tariffs and Trade) and in a way that did not destroy domestic industries.

So even though Bretton Woods was too beholden to both the American merchant and the American warrior for Keynes's liking, it might be seen as the high point of sagely influence in the modern world: cut off from ordinary mortals below, gazing out onto Mount Washington, these intellectual Olympians were forging fetters for merchants. Governments, not markets, would set currency rates, and the old freedom of investors to switch their capital from country to country at will—which had caused so much of the instability of the 1920s—was no more. The Bretton Woods framers were not prepared to give private bankers the upper hand over governments by allowing them the right to "strike"—that is, withdraw their capital if they disapproved of government spending. Ultimately, they wagered, business would tolerate these restrictions, because it could make higher profits through long-term stable investment than through short-term risky speculation.

When he left Bretton Woods for London, Keynes could therefore congratulate himself on a series of remarkable achievements.[17] Yet he felt like a prophet spurned, and rightly so. For White's victory left the system with a series of fatal flaws. First, the system was entirely reliant on the United States and the dollar, and designed to help the growth of American global power, so as soon as Washington ceased to believe Bretton Woods was to its advantage, it would collapse; second, Keynes's strict rules about controlling private international finance were never implemented in full and became weaker as time went on;[18] and third, the system largely excluded the newly developing countries of the postcolonial world. As we shall see, all three weaknesses were fully exploited by the merchant, and ultimately were to destroy the system.

In one area, though, the problems with White's system became evident rather more rapidly, and Washington was forced to accept that Keynes had been right. By the end of 1946, war-devastated Europe was in such deep economic trouble that even skeptical American officials began to admit that more had to be done to avoid disaster. But, as is so often the case in American politics, the sage was not powerful enough alone to convince Washington of the need for more help—only the warrior could do that. As relations with its former ally the USSR deteriorated after the war, Washington feared that Communist parties would exploit Europe's economic difficulties and become Moscow's fifth column in the West.[19] The American government therefore became increasingly open to the idea of spending money to build up the Western European economies as a first line of defense against Soviet influence.[20]

Under Marshall Aid, America gave about $14 billion, or 5 percent of its GDP, to Western European countries—the same share in 2011 would have amounted to about three-quarters of a trillion dollars (roughly the amount Congress originally authorized for bailing out U.S. banks in the 2008 crisis).[21] But less important than the money were the strings attached. For the sagely officials implementing the Marshall Plan became directly involved in the details of European economic policy, and they were determined that there should be no repetition of the vicious social conflicts of the past. In effect, they were exporting the New Deal, making Europe more Social Democratic in nature. Both employers and unions were expected to make compromises: workers had to accept the market and give up their demands for wholesale nationalization and democracy in the workplace. Meanwhile, business had to allow a degree of state economic planning, strategic nationalization, some labor involvement in economic policy, and the creation of welfare states.[22]

In fact, American Marshall Aid planners were strengthening forces that were already present in Europe itself. The war had fundamentally shifted the balance between sage and merchant: international trade had been suspended, and states had become skilled at running huge swaths of the economy. The Second World War, with its carpet bombing and ethnic cleansings, affected civilians much more than any previous war, and in these dire conditions state officials had become confident, accustomed to both taking and implementing far-reaching and complex decisions to protect their home populations. At the same time, many big businesses—from Renault to Bayer—had been discredited by collaboration with the Nazis. On both the left and the right of the political spectrum, state planning, direction by technocrats, and class collaboration were seen as good things. There were, of course, critics. The London School of Economics professor Friedrich von Hayek published his *Road to Serfdom* in 1944 as a free marketeer's counterblast to the confident sages of Bretton Woods. But while the book sold well, it had little impact.[23]

Yet while the whole of the developed world moved toward the sagely and worker values of state planning and welfarism and greater equality, the precise balance of forces differed depending on national conditions. The merchant was weakest and the worker strongest in Scandinavian countries where Social Democrats were in power. In these societies, workers enjoyed some of the most generous welfare states in the world: benefits were high and given to all, regardless of how much they had contributed through work. More common on the European continent was the species of capitalism favored by the center-right Christian Democratic parties that dominated European politics after 1945. Here the worker and sage were weaker than in Scandinavia, and old paternalistic ideas with their roots in Bismarck's social insurance or Catholic visions of the caring society prevailed. And so in countries like Germany, Austria, the Netherlands, and Belgium, welfare states were less egalitarian, founded on social insurance schemes that maintained distinctions between classes, and far more generous to the middle than to the working classes and the poor.[24] These countries also encouraged a more conservative attitude to women and the family.

The socialist left remained highly critical of a European economic order it saw as too market-oriented. But there was no denying that both Social Democratic and Christian Democratic systems had seriously fettered the merchant and established a successful caste compromise. The defeat of the Nazis and the threat of Communism had finally forced elites to incorporate the working classes into a new caste order; Germany and other states that had found it so difficult to achieve integration had finally achieved some degree of social peace.

Even more radical workers were prepared to support the new system. Valtéro Peppoloni, an Italian industrial worker from Terni, a Commu-

nist, and a self-confessed "rebel," enthusiastically joined strikes and organized factory occupations in the late 1940s and '50s. But he still saw the
Christian Democratic order as worth preserving; certainly it was infi-
nitely preferable to Fascism. When he first started as a steelworker under
Mussolini, the factory was full of "company guards": "The guards were
the real bosses at the plant. They would stand behind your shoulder and
watch, even if you were doing your work all right. . . . They saw you wash
your hands a minute ahead of quitting time—you were [fined]." But despite his anger at this "oppression," he refused to support the overthrow
of capitalism once the Fascists had been defeated—unlike the former
partisan fighters who had returned to factory work. "They said: 'We
must get rid of the bosses, kill them all—isn't this what we fought the
war for?' Myself, though, I never could stand the bosses, yet I have always
tried to do my duty."[25]

The new caste compromise, balancing worker and soft merchant—
all organized by the rational sage-technocrat—also brought economic
growth. Centralized wage negotiations brokered by governments, employers, and unions fostered increases in both employment and wage
equality while keeping a firm lid on inflationary labor demands. Moreover, the sagely tradition in business, combined with the old artisanal
culture among workers, developed the kind of education and apprenticeship systems that are indispensable in technologically sophisticated industries. Meanwhile, businesses felt sufficiently confident in their long-term
future to invest in expensive innovation, relying on stable relationships
with banks and freed from the vagaries of the international money markets.[26] The "Fordist" system of mass production and mass consumption
that had been so successful in the United States was finally being exported to Europe, though now under the control of the sage-technocrat.

Fordism, of course, was a hierarchical form of organization, one that
empowered managers rather than ordinary workers.[27] But in Germany,
managers took greater account of worker views and interests, certainly
compared with prewar industrialists. Meanwhile, Japanese industrialists

went even further, making real efforts to involve blue-collar workers in decision making (at least in the larger firms), and by the 1970s the use of their experience had given Japan a real competitive advantage over the United States in high-tech industries.[28] It was this system of "coordinated capitalism"—a more socially inclusive and less elitist form of the "cooperative" capitalism of the late nineteenth century—that helped make northern Continental Europe and Japan into industrial powerhouses.

The sage-technocrat and worker, however, enjoyed only a muted and short-lived ascendancy in the more merchant-dominated societies of Britain and the United States. While William Beveridge and other progressive intellectuals pushed for an ambitious universal welfare state in Britain, they could not create the collaborative economy to go with it. Britain had not established the new, deeper social compromises seen on the Continent; relations between employers and workers remained poor, the cultural divisions sharp.[29] For all the talk of modernity, breakthroughs, and the "white heat of technology," Britain's economic performance was not spectacular.[30] And when the Bretton Woods system started to crumble, Britain's middle classes were among the first to rebel.

In the United States, the turn against the worker came earlier, with the end of the Second World War—as had happened after the First. With the Taft-Hartley Act of 1947, Congress diluted many of the labor unions' gains under the New Deal, and a new Red Scare—McCarthyism— pushed popular politics to the right. Even so, there was no return to the pure-market, bank-dominated system of the 1920s—memories of 1929 were too fresh. In the mid-1950s, the New York Stock Exchange commissioned an opinion poll and discovered, to its dismay, that the public view of investment bankers had changed little since the Crash—they were "paunchy, silk-hatted tycoons" and "selfish, conniving schemers." Its response was not to defend the bankers of the 1920s but to mount a PR campaign to convince the public that they were actually sagely, "professional" investment specialists.[31] And that was not too far from the truth; as Steve Fraser, a cultural historian of Wall Street, has described them,

"The fund manager emerged as a new Wall Street type; soberly turned out, reassuringly unflashy carrier of the Street's featureless 'institutionalization.'"[32] Bankers were trying to imitate the McNamaras of corporate America—unsurprisingly, for the latter had the real power. Until the 1970s, corporations funded themselves out of profits and did not rely on stock markets or banks to finance them.[33] When shareholders, seeking high profits in the short term, clashed with managers, who preferred stability and steady growth, it was normally the managers who won.[34] And managers were only helped by their claim to embody the sage-technocratic zeitgeist of the era. As the editors of *Fortune* declared in 1951, "The manager is becoming a professional in the sense that like all professional men he has a responsibility to society as a whole."[35]

The epic struggle with the Soviet Union, and the resulting decisive influence of the warrior on America, also ensured there would be no straightforward return to the pure merchant era of Hooverism. The huge spending of the "military-industrial complex"—more than 10 percent of GDP during the 1950s—bolstered the role of the state, and especially of the enormous sagely establishments of the research universities that contributed to major breakthroughs in computer technology and played a major role in the growth of corporations like IBM.[36] As the historian Richard Hofstadter argued at the time, "We are living under a curious military Keynesianism, in which Mars has rushed in to fill the gap left by the decline of the market economy."[37]

Certainly, American military spending boosted the economy—its own and that of its allies—most notably during the Korean War (1950–53). Yet Mars was not the only god to benefit from the new order; Hermes, the consumerist soft merchant, also came into his own, and as America became the main guarantor of European security, Europe itself could give precedence to Hermes over the somewhat discredited Mars. European institutions such as the European Coal and Steel Community and the European Economic Community—the precursors of the European Union—were expressly designed to overcome the warlike ethos of the past and channel energies into creating a huge integrated market, similar to the one that had brought the United States such prosperity. As the (unusually) pro-American French intellectual Raymond Aron declared, "The affluent society banks the fires of indignation."[38]

Aron had a point. Unlike their parents in the aftermath of the First World War, Europe's citizens were much less likely to look to the warrior for salvation, for they had been offered a capitalist system that healed society rather than dividing it. As weakened European powers loosened their grip on glory and empire, Europeans and Americans traded the parade ground for the physics lab. And their competitive instincts found an outlet in a more mundane but no less thrilling arena: the kitchen.

Kitchen Wars

At the Berlin Industrial Trade Fair of 1950, American Marshall Plan officials took time off from rebuilding Europe to order a new house, delivered from the United States: a six-room prefabricated affair, complete with snazzy kitchen appliances and modern fitted furniture. In this alluring edifice they installed attractive female American-studies students recruited from Berlin's Free University, who delivered mini-lectures on washing machines and refrigerators. The exhibition—and especially the appliance-packed kitchen—was a sensation: forty-three thousand Germans visited, fifteen thousand of them from the Communist East, attracted by specially discounted tickets. (The trip was a relatively easy one before the Berlin Wall was built, in 1961.)[39]

The model house was only the first in a series of PR stunts designed to promote the "American democratic way of life" in Europe, as the Marshall Aiders were convinced that kitchen displays were the ideal way of challenging Communism. These objects of desire would both prove the superiority of the goods produced by the capitalist system and whet people's appetites for more consumer goods—creating an economic virtuous circle. And this was indeed the era when American brands finally conquered Europe. The postwar generation became addicted to Coca-Cola, Hershey bars, and rock and roll, while multinational companies like McNamara's Ford set up more and more plants in Europe to make use of cheap labor and exploit virgin markets.

But the West Berlin kitchen was about far more than cooking; it was about ethics and aesthetics. For the Marshall administrators deliberately chose the modernist style once so closely associated with the European left. Indeed, these Marshall kitchens were clones of the famous "Frankfurt kitchen" of 1926, created by the Viennese feminist Margarete Schütte-Lihotzky, who was to be imprisoned under the Nazis for Communist activity.[40] The kitchen's aesthetics were functional, scientific, and egalitarian, in contrast to a showier American design. The Americans were determined that this should be a soft-merchant, "democratic" consumerism, destroying the cultural divisions between bourgeoisie and working class. Anybody, whatever his class, education, or cultural capital, could participate—as long as he had the money, of course.

This consumerist modernism also informed the thinking behind another Marshall-sponsored project: the building of the Hilton Hotels brand across Europe. Conrad Hilton, a devout Catholic, explicitly described his hotels as "a challenge . . . to the way of life preached in the Communist world," and Marshall Aid was now employed to build them in Cold War hot spots—Rome, Athens, Istanbul, Cairo, and Tehran. Adopting the international modernist style, now increasingly associated with corporate America, they were luxurious but accessible. The State Department's Foreign Buildings Operations program was to finance such modernist buildings as "architectural calling cards" for the postwar United States government and its sagely and soft-merchant values.[41]

Despite this American enthusiasm for exporting its bounty, it took some time before ordinary Europeans could afford American-style consumption. Even so, European societies were beginning to converge with the United States. Peasants were becoming urban workers, and small-scale capitalists and independent professionals were being absorbed into corporations and state bureaucracies. And all groups had more leisure time, much of it spent in front of the TV, an American cultural import that was less connected with class status than were older entertainments. Meanwhile, Hollywood stars like Ava Gardner and rock-and-roll idols like Elvis Presley formed a new elite of celebrity, with little connection to the old social divisions of prewar Europe.[42]

Predictably, perhaps, there was opposition to this consumer culture from the traditional right and left—typical was the Communist writer Louis Aragon's denigration of the new "civilization of bathtubs and frigidaires." The left had particular reason to fear the allure of a consumerism so corrosive of old egalitarian blue-collar cultures, a value system that turned the worker into a merchant obsessed with competing for status by accumulating consumer goods.[43] The sociologists Michael Young and Peter Willmott warned of the same thing in their postwar study of the inner-London Bethnal Green working-class community, rehoused in the low-density Essex town of Debden. They found that the sociability and sharing—as well as the quarrelsomeness and lack of privacy—that had been a feature of Bethnal Green had given way to a greater sense of individualism and competitiveness. One of their interviewees complained, "I don't like it, the atmosphere. People are not the same; I don't know if they get big-headed because they've got a house."[44]

The nascent mass consumer culture was certainly effective at marginalizing the Communists and Soviet influence. After the war, Stalin, recognizing the USSR's fundamental vulnerability, had hoped for peace with the West, going so far as to accept broad "popular front" left-wing coalitions in the states of Eastern Europe that the Soviets occupied. But trust broke down between the former allies throughout 1946 and 1947, and he increasingly suspected the West of trying to undermine Soviet influence; the Americans' offer of Marshall Aid to Soviet-occupied Czechoslovakia convinced him that they were using the mighty dollar to tempt his satellites away. The response of this old warrior to the threat was predictable: the Third Wayism of the popular fronts was dropped, and back came the martial system of the 1930s and the wartime imposition of top-down military-style command economies—plans, collective farms, and labor mobilization—from the Baltic to the Black Sea. Convincing Czechs and Poles to become self-sacrificing warriors was a much more effective way of defending socialism, Stalin believed, than lily-livered consumerism. As he told his loyal lieutenant Andrei Zhdanov in 1947, "There is only one thing which these gentlemen who long for the 'Western way of life' cannot explain: why we beat Hitler."[45]

For a short period after the war, Communists were indeed widely admired for their bravery in resisting the Nazis. But it is no surprise that their popularity receded as Europeans, both Eastern and Western, hoped for a new age of peace and plenty. Stalinist Communism seemed to many to be an overcentralized, crudely martial system that had outlived its purpose. It survived in several Western countries, but only in Italy, where it was reformulated by the more intellectual and tolerant Palmiro Togliatti, did it retain extensive support. Stalinism appeared old-fashioned in other ways, too. There had always been an element of consumerism in the USSR of the 1930s and '40s, but it took a bizarrely aristocratic form.[46] Ideally, the Stalinist state wanted its citizens to live like characters in a Tolstoy novel: when they weren't performing feats of military or labor heroism, they were to sup on caviar and quaff champagne, watch ballet and opera, and mingle in palatial metro stations decked out with neoclassical statues and sparkling chandeliers. The more mundane ambition of providing families with their own simple housing in place of decaying communal apartments was not a priority. Given these tastes, it is unsurprising that the East German Stalinist leader Walter Ulbricht had little time for the American model kitchen, for, as he noted, "furniture manufactured in the Bauhaus style does not correspond to the sensitivity to beauty of the new Germany's progressive beings."[47]

This aristocratic Soviet style was not entirely bizarre, however, as it reflected an increasingly hierarchical society. Elites—whether party bosses or educated technicians—held all the power and status, while the labor of poorly paid workers and peasants was mere fodder for the Soviet imperial machine. But imposing this new order on Eastern Europeans was to prove a far more difficult task than in the Soviet heartland, and it required a great deal of repression; it has been estimated that by 1955, between 6 percent and 8 percent of all adult males in Soviet Eastern Europe—most of them workers and peasants—were in prison.

Beginning in the early 1950s, as an end to the Stalin era became conceivable, a younger generation of Soviet leaders became convinced that the Communist system could not survive as a vast, armed camp; it had to promise better living standards. Stalin's ultimate successor, Nikita Khrushchev, therefore sought to increase consumption without succumbing to the merchant's competitive consumerism. This was to be "socialist," not capitalist, consumption. Kitchens, for instance, were to be modern but small (a mere fifty square feet), and housewives were to use collective services like public laundries; they were not to have their own private washing machines or succumb to individualistic competition and selfish desire. The paradoxical objective, then, was to fulfill consumer wants and needs while also forging collectivist communities.

Khrushchev's pro-consumer policies began to bring the Soviet bloc into line with the West: the warrior's prestige was falling, and the sage-technocrat was presiding over a more equal society. Unlike in the West, however, there was no place for the merchant, and Khrushchev was determined, to an even greater extent than Stalin, to squeeze merchant influence out of Soviet society. Yet by embracing consumption as a valid goal, even promising that the USSR would "catch up and overtake America," Khrushchev was sowing a wind that would soon become a whirlwind. For while Communism might aspire to provide a perfectly comfortable and reasonably egalitarian standard of living, it disapproved of the forces that drive the growth in consumption: merchant competition for status and an individualistic desire for self-fulfillment. In this battlefield, therefore, the USSR would find it impossible to triumph.

But in 1959, Khrushchev's promises did not seem so ridiculous. In the twenty-five years after 1948, the centrally planned economies did well: some argue that the Soviet Union and Eastern Europe grew faster than Western Europe, and China grew faster than India.[48] Yet there were also weaknesses that made it difficult to compete with the West over living standards: the sage-technocrat and the warrior were simply too powerful, and the merchant was too weak. Some Communist regimes tried to remedy this with minor market reforms, such as Hungary's "New Economic Mechanism" of 1968. But in general, political opposition from party officials was too great. And by the late 1960s such liberalizers had become disillusioned. It was clear that the merchant was not going to be widely integrated into the Communist system, and the persistent martial aspects of the Soviet system became impossible to ignore after the Red Army's invasions of Hungary and Czechoslovakia in 1956 and 1968, respectively.

Though this warrior element of the Soviet system lost it friends in Europe, it proved to be attractive in the developing world. In Asia, anticolonial military struggles continued throughout the 1940s and '50s, first against the European powers that sought to restore their empires, and finally against the Americans, who were defending old imperial "collaborator" elites. Communist warriordom in the form of guerrilla leaders like Mao, Ho Chi Minh, and the Korean Kim Il-Sung flourished in these circumstances. So did other elements of the Communist caste package: worker collectivism appealed to many peasants, while the promise of planned economic development attracted intellectuals; both were intended to exclude merchants, whose wartime collaboration with the Japanese had made many of them deeply unpopular. And by 1949, international Communism had received a huge boost with the creation of three new states, in China, North Vietnam, and North Korea.

War in East Asia continued into the early 1950s—in Korea and Vietnam, against Western powers, and within China, where Mao pursued violent "class struggle" against "bourgeois" groups. However, by the mid-1950s the sage-technocrat was beginning to reassert himself in this new

Communist world, as he had in the capitalist one. The end of the Korean War, in 1953, and the interruption of hostilities in Vietnam, in 1954, brought a military hiatus when thoughts turned to economic development. In China, for example, as in the USSR in the 1930s, the archetypal Communist tension between warrior-worker and sage-technocrat asserted itself again: the prestige of Mao—a warrior leader—declined, and in his place the more sagely Zhou Enlai and Liu Shaoqi emerged, while the old worker-warrior equality of Mao's Yan'an guerrilla camp gave way to a mixture of technocratic and older Confucian-style hierarchies. These were only reinforced after the catastrophic "Great Leap Forward" of 1958–61, when Mao's attempts to apply the Yan'an model to the rural economy led to one of the most devastating famines of modern history. The sagely politics of the mid-1950s and early 1960s therefore promoted orderly development after periods of chaos. But the bureaucratic obsession with rank and expertise had its own drawbacks. Particularly unpopular was a rigid eight-grade wage system applied to all areas of political and economic life. In one Shanghai department store, assistants selling tobacco were given a "taste test," designed to find out how well they could discern different grades of cigarettes so they could be paid accordingly.[49]

Bandung Brothers

If Communist China in the mid-1950s was governed by a sagely marriage of old Confucianism and new technocracy, pursuing broadly egalitarian goals, its archrival in this period, India, was ruled by its own version of the same alliance. The first prime minister after independence from the British, Jawaharlal Nehru, came from a family that straddled the old and new sagely, or Brahminic, worlds. Descended from one of the most prestigious Brahmin castes, Nehru's uncle had followed the traditional Brahmin profession of *dewan* (chief minister) to a semi-autonomous Indian prince, while his father had a British-style education and became a well-known lawyer. Nehru himself was popularly dubbed *pandit* (teacher), had a rather pedagogical attitude toward politics, and admitted that he could be "a bit of a prig."[50] He was sent to a British private school, Harrow, and then to Cambridge, where he studied natural sciences, and science was always his main love. An unstinting commitment to "rationality" can be found in his strong advocacy of state planning. As he explained, Indian politicians had to "proceed scientifically and methodically without leaving things to chance or fate. . . . The room for what we called ideological debate on matters like planning and development becomes less and less. The whole thing becomes a mathematical formula."[51]

Nehru's vision, then, was a highly technocratic and elitist one. India was to be run by a cadre of modernizing technocrats. The old British "steel frame" of empire, the Indian Civil Service and its ethos, was to survive in all but name as the "Indian Administrative Service." And presiding over this technocracy was the Indian Planning Commission, headed by P. C. Mahalanobis—another science-loving Brahmin and former physics professor. It was he who directed efforts intended to transform the country from agricultural backwater to industrial powerhouse.

Nehru's ambitions for a modern, industrial India were therefore poles apart from those of his patron during the anticolonial phase of the Congress Party's ascendancy, Gandhi. And unlike Gandhi, Nehru had fraught relations with India's merchants and industrialists. However, in one respect he was in complete agreement with Gandhi: he was determined that the warrior should be excluded from Indian politics. Nehru admired Soviet economic planning, but not its political system or its martial style. He accepted that India was a pluralistic society and that the modernizing technocracy had to rely on persuasion and liberal democracy, not compulsion, to get its way.

Naturally, Nehru found it extremely difficult to reconcile modernization with respect for democracy in a country of such extraordinary diversity. For neither the British Raj, nor its predecessor, the Mughal Empire, had really tried to create an integrated Indian society, and in 1947 India entered the community of independent nation-states as a loose group of communities—social, religious, cultural, and linguistic. Nehru's sagely state-led development was therefore very difficult to achieve: planning and land redistribution were subverted by powerful pro-market industrialists and rich peasants, and popular educational programs ran into the sands of regional political rivalries. Nehru's efforts to overcome India's deep social and economic inequalities were consequently much less effective than those of his fellow sage-technocrats in the West and in China. The sharp contrast between ambition and reality was shown in his efforts to build a huge memorial to the new India: the city of Chandigarh. Punjab had lost its capital, Lahore, to Pakistan in the 1947 partition of the subcontinent, and Nehru commissioned Le Corbusier to design a new city, "unfettered by the traditions of the past, a symbol of the nation's faith in the future." Le Corbusier had always been one of the more grandiose of modernist architects, and, now that low-rise, democratic international modernism had been co-opted by the U.S. State Department and Hilton Hotels, he had moved on to a more monumental, primitivist style, dubbed, rather unfortunately, "brutalism" (named after *béton brut,* or raw concrete).[52] Even so, Le Corbusier saw Chandigarh as a rational, modern city, and sought to eliminate the winding alleyways and chaotic but colorful streetscapes of the typical Indian town—"What is the significance of Indian style in the world today if you accept machines, trousers and democracy?" he arrogantly demanded.[53] The new city also celebrated the power of politicians and technocrats—it had a special sagely district of government, legal, and administrative buildings, the "Capitol," separate from and raised above the rest of the city. The district still exists, though Le Corbusier's pristine lines do not, erased by the rapid expansion of the population and the determination of the inhabitants to remain "fettered" by traditional ways of life. The intimidating grandeur of the vast public spaces is now spoiled—or humanized—by shacks, small shops, and pavement clutter.

Yet despite the failures of Nehru's more ambitious projects, the Indian

economy grew at the fastest pace in its history up until then, with industry performing particularly well (though agriculture less so).[54] It would
therefore be wrong to see Nehru's policies simply as sagely utopianism, or
a crazy and unrealistic commitment to the dream of modernity. There
were good reasons why the Indian governing elite—and many others in
the global South—believed it was so vital to industrialize. The 1920s and
'30s, when commodity prices were at rock bottom, suggested that pre-
dominantly agrarian countries were condemned to poverty. And Nehru
was merely one of many leaders who followed the reasoning of the Argentine economist Raúl Prebisch: because prices in a semi-monopolistic industrial sector would always be higher and more stable than those in a
more competitive agricultural sector, any country wanting to maintain
its economic independence and avoid colonialism had to pursue a strategy
of "import substitution industrialization"—establishing tariffs against
foreign imports to build up its own infant industries.[55] This, of course,
was precisely what the United States and Germany had done in the
nineteenth century, though, unlike those major Western exporters, these
developing countries had little interest in competing in foreign markets.
Merchant values were therefore much less compelling, and domestic industries with captive, tariff-protected markets had few incentives to become globally efficient. Despite efforts to diversify, these economies also
remained highly dependent on exports of agricultural commodities and
other raw materials. The "Asian Tiger" economies of Taiwan and South
Korea, which followed the nineteenth-century export-led model, were
much more successful in using the state to drive economic development.

Even so, all newly independent industrializing countries were doing
well in the mid-1950s. Commodity prices fluctuated but were relatively
high—benefiting from the boom in the developed world as well as from
the Korean War.[56] And the modernizer Nehru, like the socialists Sukarno
of Indonesia, Kwame Nkrumah of Ghana, and Gamal Nasser of Egypt,
became a decisive figure in leading a new emerging "Third World"—
distinct from both the "First" Western and the "Second" Communist

worlds. Nehru's style of indigenous, non-Communist socialism reached the high point of its influence in April 1955, when twenty-nine delegates from Asian and African countries assembled in the West Javan city of Bandung and declared independence not only from the old empires but also from the new empires of American-sponsored capitalism and Soviet-style Communism.[57] Even Zhou Enlai, from China—still very much in the Soviet orbit—was willing to support this Third World socialist idealism.[58]

In 1955, therefore, prospects for the sage-technocrat/worker alliance looked rosy in all three worlds. The merchant was firmly under control; the warrior was still powerful but was confined to guarding borders frozen by the Cold War—at least in Europe. And prosperity was rising in the East, the West, and, to a lesser extent, the South. Influential Western writers declared "the end of ideology"—a theory similar in structure, if not in content, to the American academic Francis Fukuyama's pro-merchant "end of history" thesis. As the Canadian sociologist Seymour Martin Lipset put it, "The ideological issues dividing left and right have been reduced to a little more or a little less government ownership and economic planning."[59] Technocratic tinkering provided a solution for everything.

The post-1945 sage-dominated system therefore appeared remarkably resilient, and few foresaw its demise. Even though the first signs of tension were evident in the late 1950s, it took until 1968 for it to come under strain, and it was fully replaced by an alternative only in 1979–80 in the West and in 1989 in much of the rest of the world; it even survives today, albeit severely weakened, in its old homeland, Northern Europe.

And yet the system had deep structural flaws, as Keynes had recognized at Bretton Woods. Rather than being a genuinely collaborative effort, in which governments combined sagely planning with merchant competition to achieve sustainable economic growth, it was founded on a paternalistic deal, brokered by warrior interests in the victorious American government. The United States was prepared to make economic sacrifices to help its Cold War allies in Europe and Japan recover and fight Communism; it therefore encouraged its multinationals to build plants abroad, thus exporting jobs, and tolerated an overvalued dollar, which harmed exports. But on the other side, Europe and Japan used their more sagely models to compete ruthlessly for world markets. The result, from the mid-1960s on, was a glut of industrial goods and an American industry that found it difficult to compete against its new, more efficient, and cheaper rivals.[60] At the same time, Washington's warriorish determination to fight for control of the Third World brought budget deficits, which inevitably imperiled the stability of the Bretton Woods currency system. But the West's elites, bound together by the Cold War alliance, were determined to shore up its crumbling foundations.

It was therefore outsiders, not insiders, who precipitated the crisis of the postwar order—three groups that seemingly had very little in common but forged an alliance in the great revolution of 1968 against the sage-technocrat and the Western warrior. The first group was made up of those in the Third World who saw America's global dominance as a continuation of the European empires and protested at their exclusion from postwar prosperity; the second was those workers in the West who felt they were not benefiting enough from the social compact of the era; and the third was Western youth, who had done well out of the affluent and relatively egalitarian order but wanted to go further and bring other types of equality, too—social, political, and sexual. This was to be a brief alliance, but while it lasted it was heady—an intoxicating blend of Marxism and romanticism.

Marx and Coca-Cola

In April 1959, Fidel Castro, the thirty-one-year-old guerrilla leader of the Cuban revolution, visited New York as the guest of the American Society of Newspaper Editors. He had just seized power from the Washington-backed right-wing dictator Fulgencio Batista, and he was eager to convince the Americans, who wielded so much economic power on the island, that he was no Communist and was not planning to join the Soviet bloc. He hired a good PR firm and staged a number of media appearances that highlighted his revolutionary charisma, but also his ideological flexibility. Castro and his associates all wore beards and olive-green fatigues; but he also made a trip to the zoo rather than visiting Picasso's anti-Fascist painting *Guernica,* then on display in New York, and took the advice of his PR firm: "smiles, lots of smiles." Yet, while the PR company thought the trip had gone well, with acres of press coverage and affectionate commentary on his eccentric "fidelenglish," Castro was not happy with the result. He was praised by center-left journalists and academics, while the students of Harvard and Princeton received him rapturously, but President Eisenhower refused to meet him, and his discussions with the strongly anti-Communist vice president, Nixon, were frosty.[61] They were clearly still convinced that he was, or would soon become, a Communist. Washington's verdict was no surprise: Castro had to go. In June, Eisenhower decided not to ask Congress to renew the law that granted 70 percent of American sugar imports to Cuba, thus crippling the island's economic prospects, and by November he had secretly decided that Castro was to be overthrown.

But Nixon and Eisenhower were wrong—Castro was not a Communist, although his brother, Raúl, and his friend Che Guevara were. He was from a prosperous farming family and had grown up in the region of Cuba most dominated by the vast American multinational the United Fruit Company, which used local sheriffs to impose its will on the peasantry, often violently. Castro always had something of the warrior about him: he won an award for the best sports all-rounder in Cuba for 1943–44 and liked the "military spirit" imposed by his Jesuit teachers, valuing the "kind of healthy, austere life I lived in those schools."[62] And when he went to university in Havana, he threw himself into a violent student politics that was always in danger of degenerating into gang warfare. He was therefore well suited to life as a nationalistic guerrilla leader, defending his people against the foreigner. However, in 1959 he had little interest in Marxism-Leninism; he saw it as a rigid, cheerless doctrine, famously declaring that "capitalism can kill a man with hunger, while Communism kills a man by destroying his freedom."[63] His early policies were left-wing nationalist, not Communist. He called for industrialization and land redistribution but not mass expropriation. Yet popular pressure, combined with American antagonism, soon led him to a more radical politics, and he was eventually forced into the Soviet embrace.

Castro's 1959 visit to New York reveals much about international caste struggles as they were to unfold during the 1960s. Washington was suspicious of left-wing nationalists who sought to limit the power of the merchant in the Third World, seeing them as Communists who would take the Soviets' side in the Cold War. At the same time, a new, more radical generation in the Third World became disillusioned with the failure to achieve the economic breakthroughs promised by the older generation of nationalist leaders at Bandung. By 1959 it was clear that the social conflicts between embattled middle classes and the laboring poor that had caused so much violence in interwar Europe were affecting the postcolonial world. Like their European predecessors, both sides began to look to the warrior for support—whether Communists or right-wing paramilitaries at home or Soviet and American military aid abroad. But these battles were not to be confined to the Third World. As Castro had discovered in New York, he had an ally in the West: students. For students had their own reasons to protest against the prevailing castes—a protest that would become angrier in the late 1960s, when large numbers of them were being conscripted to fight wars to maintain Western control over South Vietnam and other parts of the Third World.

Cuba's radicalization, like that of several other Third World countries, owed much to a nationalist resentment of big-power interference. But economics, and the flaws that Keynes identified in Bretton Woods, also had a role. Harry White and the Americans had agreed to Keynes's idea of an "International Trade Organization" to stabilize the prices of commodities—both agricultural and mineral resources—but the idea fell victim to an obstructively conservative Congress. Sagely regulation of markets therefore extended only to the developed West; the merchant had more power over the Third World, in the form of volatile commodity prices. And as the commodity boom ran out of steam over the course of the 1950s, peasants, workers, and educated nationalists increasingly embraced more egalitarian solutions, which in turn provoked a hard-merchant backlash in the United States. In retrospect, Congress was extraordinarily shortsighted: it knew very well that social catastrophe in Europe could be averted only by limiting the merchant, but it refused to do the same in the developing world.

Castro and Che Guevara were thus only the first of this new generation of post-Bandung leaders who resented the second-class status to which the international order had consigned them. They came to power promising to free Cuba from dependence on ever less valuable sugar exports to the United States.[64] And by 1966 they had so many sympathizers across the postcolonial world that they could organize their own radical rival to Bandung—the "Tricontinental Conference" in Havana. For the largely Marxist-Leninist delegates, the Bandung leaders had allowed old "tribal" and business elites (the so-called compradors) to flourish and to serve the "neocolonial" interests of the West.[65] Only a radical rejection of the merchant order—through nationalization and "class struggle" against compradors and landowners—could secure real independence, wealth, and justice.

In response, regimes backed by businessmen and landowners looked for support in the United States, and they found a particularly sympathetic audience in Lyndon Johnson's White House. For some time, Washington had used military aid and CIA-assisted coups d'état to defend the merchant against the tide of left-wing nationalism and Communism, but as Khrushchev's USSR became involved, the tension escalated. President Johnson was particularly keen on military solutions, and he revealed his somewhat paranoid and lurid machismo in a lecture to his aides on the lessons of interwar appeasement: "If you let a bully come into your front yard one day, the next day he will be up on your porch and the day after that he will rape your wife in your own bed."[66] Beginning in 1963, Johnson supported a wave of anti-nationalist and anti-Communist coups and invasions: in Brazil (coup, 1964), the Dominican Republic (invasion, 1965), Congo-Léopoldville (aiding seizure of power, 1965), Algeria (welcoming coup, 1965), Indonesia (support for the massacre of Communists, 1965), and Ghana (coup, 1966). And in 1965 he made the fateful decision to increase military support for the American-backed regime in South Vietnam.

By the early 1970s, much of the Third World was becoming a war zone. Virtually every region of the South saw the rise of the worker-warrior guerrilla band—whether the "Maoist" peasant group or the more centralized "vanguard party" often supported by the USSR.[67] In India, the Maoist "Naxalites" were most prominent—an alliance of poor peasants and students founded in 1967 and demanding further land reforms from the post-Nehruvian state. (They are still conducting a major guerrilla insurgency to this day.) And this leftward shift also affected the ruling Congress Party. Nehru's daughter and successor, Indira Gandhi, was always a much more militantly romantic socialist than her father, and in 1971 she waged her campaign to "abolish poverty" (*garibi hatao*), having proved her warrior credentials earlier that year in India's war with Pakistan.

China experienced a rather different form of radicalism when, in 1966, Mao staged his own "revolution" against the sage-technocrats, in the name of revitalized worker-warrior values and the egalitarian ethos of the guerrilla past. Mao, that old scourge of Confucianism, had been unhappy with the influence of his technocratic colleagues Liu Shaoqi, Zhou Enlai, and Deng Xiaoping for some time, and he believed that tolerance for sagely hierarchies would soon lead to a taste for merchant inequality. As he explained in December 1965, "The class of bureaucrats is a class sharply opposed to the working class and poor . . . peasants," and these leaders were becoming "capitalists who suck the workers' blood."[68] In his "Cultural Revolution," beginning in 1966, Mao urged students and workers to purge educated intellectuals—the so-called ninth stinking category of class enemies—and replace them with ideologically committed "Reds." His main objective was to save socialism from the sage-technocrat and, ultimately, the merchant. But Mao was also responding to the American escalation of the Vietnam War. For Mao, the Cultural Revolution was a way of mobilizing the country to defend against "capitalists" abroad and "capitalist roaders" within.

However, it was in the Middle East that the revolutionary warrior found the warmest welcome. This was arguably the region most subject to the colonial-style influence of America, along with the continuing presence of the old imperial powers—Britain and France. Its misfortune was its strategic importance and, in some cases, the possession of oil. The Americans and the British supported Arab monarchies, and Western oil companies had a major presence in the region; in the absence of Keynes's commodity-price stabilization scheme, oil prices remained low. American support for Israel in the 1960s was also seen by its Arab neighbors as a further sign that they were under the thumb of a new Western imperialist power.

Warrior politics was the main beneficiary. Gamal Nasser, an Egyptian army officer, had built himself up as the main champion of the Middle East against the West and the traditional monarchies. But the humiliating defeat of the Arab armies in the 1967 war against Israel led many to argue that Nasserism had had its day and that more militant solutions were needed.

The rise of Yasser Arafat—a strong advocate of Vietnam-style guerrilla struggle—to prominence in the Palestinian nationalist movement was one sign of this shift; another was the 1969 Libyan coup against the monarchy of King Idris, which brought a young, charismatic army officer to power—Muammar Gaddafi. Gaddafi was precisely the type of warrior who flourished at such a time of nationalist turmoil. Born to a poor Bedouin known as Abu Meniar ("father of the knife"), he was brought up on stories of war, heroism, and resistance to foreigners.[69] He grew up at a time when the Idris regime had become extremely unpopular for hosting American military bases, privileging Western oil companies, and favoring a small, often foreign or Jewish merchant elite. And while at school, he became absorbed in Nasserite nationalist politics—his friends even carried around a stool so that he could stand on it and make impromptu speeches to his fellow students. He then joined the army, where he treated his British trainers with proud resentment. He came to power as a follower of Nasser, but with Egypt's move toward the West in the 1970s, he developed his own state model—the "Jamahiriya" or "mass state"—in 1977. He also became one of the most militantly anti-Western of leaders, becoming a key figure in efforts to turn the terms of the oil trade in favor of its Arab producers and against its Western consumers.

Gaddafi was not a Marxist-Leninist: he developed his own philosophy—a combination of indigenous socialism and Islam—and his ideas had relatively little resonance in the West. But Third World Marxists had more appeal, not because of their warrior culture—about which many young Western sympathizers were decidedly ambivalent—but because of their antagonism to the sage-technocrat, a figure the students of the 1960s saw as their enemy, too.

Castro's welcome by students and academics during his New York visit was one of the first signs of how strong the alliance between First World antiauthoritarian students and the new generation of Third World guerrillas was to become. But it was arguably forged the following year by a Columbia University sociologist, C. Wright Mills. A large, imposing Texan, Mills played up his James Dean–like image as a rebel—though one with a cause—annoying his staid colleagues by wearing his biker boots and leather jacket around the campus.[70] Mills was already an established radical critic of American society when he was invited to Cuba in

1960 to report on the revolution, and he wrote a book about his experiences, *Listen, Yankee,* that sold half a million copies.

For Mills, Cuba was a living example of a spontaneous, authentic revolution, avoiding the "impersonal bureaucracies" that now controlled Western capitalism and Soviet Communism alike. As such it served as a model for the First and Second worlds. Both the United States and the Soviet Union were highly bureaucratic systems, Mills argued, dominated by the military on the one hand and either the Communist Party or corporate commercial interests on the other. Technology had become a "cultural and social fetish," and both systems suppressed creativity: "in neither is there significant craftsmanship at work or significant leisure in the working life."[71] People might have economic security, but they paid for it with subordination. As Herbert Marcuse, a German Marxist who became the intellectual leader of the student rebels in the mid-1960s, put it, "the Welfare state and the Warfare state" were creating a "mechanics of conformity" and "one-dimensional men."[72]

Mills and Marcuse were only two of the "New Left" intellectuals who served as spokesmen for this new generation of romantic bohemians, the heirs of the Rousseaus, Byrons, and Shelleys of previous centuries and also the advocates of a more humble artisanal creativity. The radical filmmaker Jean-Luc Godard dubbed them "the children of Marx and Coca-Cola" in his 1966 film *Masculin Féminin,* and the description is a good one.[73] There might seem to be a contradiction between consumerism and left-wing politics, but actually, as in the 1920s, they were closely related. Consumer society and prosperity gave young people greater freedom to choose their own way of life, breaking from the disciplines of the military, work, and bureaucracy. And at the same time, many more people were going to university and gaining greater self-confidence. That very freedom made them more likely to value a politics of self-expression, autonomy, authenticity, and democracy—that is, a democracy of participation rather than one simply involving a vote every few years.

The 1960s and '70s activists targeted all hierarchies—whether technocratic, corporate, ethnic, sexual, military, or aristocratic—but the university became a particularly fraught battleground. The vast expansions in higher education after the war brought an explosive clash between student expectations and the reality of university life: self-confident students demanding individual attention and intellectual fulfillment were herded into overcrowded classes taught by aloof academics. One American student remembered: "We really did speak of Berkeley as a factory. Classes were immense, and you didn't feel that you could get near professors, because they were this presence way up in front of the lectern."[74]

Student activists interpreted their experience as part of a more general bureaucratization of the world, and they saw themselves as victims of the all-powerful technocrat. As Luigi Bobbio, a student at Turin University, explained, "We really believed that the university had become a machine for producing . . . managers and technicians of capital . . . in its new stage of rationalization and planning."[75] And in some countries—most notably Italy and France—they forged a bond with managers and younger unskilled workers who were rebelling against regimentation in the workplace.[76] The "Fordist" system, which put technocratic managers in charge of the factory and deprived workers of control over the way they worked, was under assault. Both students and workers could therefore unite under the old romantic Marxist platform of the 1840s—exalting both the visionary sage and the artisan.

While the sage-technocrat was the main target of the 1960s militants, they also had another *bête noire:* the warrior. Of course, some of the rebellions did involve violence, and a number of small terrorist groups—the Red Brigades, the Baader-Meinhof gang, and the Weathermen—emerged in the aftermath of 1968. But the sit-in, not the bomb blast, was the norm: 80 percent of the 1,767 protests in West Germany between 1965 and 1989 involved no violence whatsoever, while people were seriously injured in fewer than 2 percent of them.[77] At the same time, the students saw military, warrior values as a major enemy—whether in the

American army or, in Europe, lurking in the consciousness of their ex-Fascist or ex-Nazi parents. The poet Allen Ginsberg coined the term "flower power" to describe the students' attitude, and student demonstrators tried to embarrass the police by proffering blooms rather than throwing bombs.

The American filmmaker Stanley Kubrick captured this demonology most powerfully in his 1968 film *2001: A Space Odyssey*. He shows technology and violence as inextricably interlinked, from the dawn of human "civilization," when apes invent stone tools to defeat their enemies in battle, to a futuristic era in which a spaceship computer called HAL (a one-letter shift away from IBM) escapes the astronauts' control and uses various high-tech methods to murder them one by one.

Twilight of the Technocrats

All of these rebellions came to a head in the extraordinary year of 1968, when the postwar settlement—domestic and international, economic and social—began to buckle. And at the center of the storm was that representative of everything the 1960s radicals loathed: Robert McNamara. By the mid-1960s McNamara was himself behaving like a character in a Kubrick film. An early enthusiast for the Vietnam War, he approached his task as defense secretary with his typical sagely technocratic energy and blind self-confidence. He ran the campaign like the Ford production line: "kill ratios" had to be calculated, new "inputs" (such as napalm) deployed, bombs ordered at lowest possible cost. McNamara's regular press conferences, where he blandly reported "body counts" and claimed bogus victories, seemed to show the innate cruelty and mendacity of big bureaucracy and big science.

Ironically, as early as 1965, McNamara had become convinced that the war was unwinnable (though he did not make his doubts public, out of loyalty to President Johnson). Militarily, there was stalemate, public opposition to the war was increasing, and he was deeply affected by the constant demonstrations. Always a respecter of academic hierarchies, he was particularly worried when he visited Amherst College and Harvard University and discovered that opposition to Vietnam "increased with the institution's prestige and the educational attainments of its students." Even more traumatic was the self-immolation of one protester outside his office window. By the end of 1967 McNamara was collapsing under the strain; at one cabinet meeting, he rambled for five minutes "in rage and grief and almost disorientation."[78]

Relations with Johnson deteriorated, and McNamara announced his resignation at the end of 1967 to become head of the World Bank; but he was still in his post when disaster struck: the Vietnamese Tet Offensive of January 1968. Although the Viet Cong troops were repulsed, the news pictures of serious fighting in South Vietnam's cities were a PR disaster. McNamara's successor, Clark Clifford, remembered the atmosphere of crisis in the Johnson administration as "something approaching paralysis, and a sense of events spiraling out of control of the nation's leaders."[79] Johnson was forced into a partial retreat, and in March he announced that the American military escalation was over, bombing was to be limited, and peace talks would be offered. The students sensed victory and took to the streets all across the world, from Paris to Buenos Aires, from Tokyo to West Berlin. In the United States, meanwhile, where students had forged alliances with the African American civil rights movement, the assassination of Martin Luther King Jr. in April sparked riots in 126 cities. Students were active even behind the Iron Curtain, in rebellions against Soviet rule in Poland and Czechoslovakia (the "Prague Spring").

In fact, neither the Vietnamese peasant-warriors nor the students had really won in 1968—indeed, the unrest brought a sharp swing to the right in public opinion, with General de Gaulle and Richard Nixon winning elections in France and America. But the 1968 insurgencies, in both the Third and First worlds, had brutally exposed the fault lines in the postwar, Bretton Woods order, and its warrior and sagely underpinnings. Workers, strengthened by low unemployment, were demanding more; the excluded South was rebelling; and Western youth were supporting their insurgencies. And even more important, Americans seemed increasingly unwilling to pay both for the war against Communism, in Southeast Asia and elsewhere, and for Lyndon Johnson's "War on Poverty"—his campaign to create a European-style welfare system in the United States. Johnson combined his warrior values with a welfarist paternalism, but he simply could not persuade Congress to agree to the higher taxes he so desperately needed for his "warfare-welfare state."

The immediate casualty of the 1968 crisis was the economic system established at Bretton Woods. The American government was spending too much to preserve the dollar's link with gold, and it was relaxed in March 1968 and finally broken by Nixon in 1971.[80] It seemed that American profligacy had destroyed the postwar order.

Yet while the causes of Bretton Woods' demise seem simple, it was actually a rather complex affair. Bretton Woods had many assassins. Harry White bears some of the responsibility. In his determination to defend the interests of stronger countries and make it difficult for weaker countries to devalue, he ironically made it more difficult for the United States to stay in.[81]

Another culprit, though, was a new, rising caste: the merchant, in the form of the international banks. Since 1944, Keynes's stringent controls on international flows of capital had been progressively and surreptitiously relaxed. In 1957, the United States (supporting its banks and multinationals), together with Britain (eager to restore the City of London's financial power), had discreetly allowed the emergence of an unregulated money market in dollars held in European banks (so-called Eurodollars) based in London.[82] In doing so, they had released an uncontainable force, for they had allowed the merchant to regain at least some of the power he had enjoyed in the 1920s. International banks, moribund since the 1930s, began to revive, mounting speculative attacks on currencies (including the dollar) if they thought that governments were spending too much. Fears of bankers also deterred any attempts to revalue currencies within the system and began to turn Bretton Woods into a rigid gold standard.[83]

It was certainly the bankers whom IMF staff blamed for Bretton Woods' demise, mourning its death in a rather bitter obituary circulated confidentially around their Washington offices:

> R.I.P. We regretfully announce the not unexpected passing away after a long illness of Bretton Woods at 9 P.M. last Sunday. Bretton was born in New Hampshire in 1944 and died a few days after his 27th birthday. . . . The fatal stroke occurred this month when parasites called speculators inflated his most important member and caused a rupture of his vital element, dollar–gold convertibility.[84]

Another caste, though, bears greater responsibility for the system's collapse: the American warrior—together, of course, with his Soviet rival. For in his zero-sum politics, and his neo-imperial perception of any nationalist movement in the Third World as a threat to American prestige, he was determined to mobilize massive resources for war. Bretton Woods prevented him from doing that, and so he destroyed it. In its stead he pursued an alternative policy of untrammeled deficits and inflation, which triggered international economic chaos and social conflict.

The end of Bretton Woods might seem like a rather arcane issue, of interest only to economists and bankers. But it was, in fact, quite momentous, for it marked the beginning of the end of the sage-technocratic order that had brought some stability to global capitalism since 1945. In the West, economic growth had rested upon an implicit understanding: business would invest if workers restrained wage demands. But with the dollar released from the sage's control, inflation soared, and this trust broke down. Workers demanded full compensation for inflation, and capitalists cut investments—leading to even higher inflation.[85] In coordinated capitalist systems—like Germany's—the sage-technocrat still had some influence, and tensions could be managed through negotiation. But in Britain and the United States, where there was little tradition of state-led negotiation between employers and unions, industrial relations rapidly deteriorated.[86] In 1970, the United States lost more working days per person to strikes than any other developed country,[87] and in Britain prices rose on average by more than 12 percent a year in the 1970s, compared with only 5.4 percent in Germany.[88]

Relations between business and labor were not the only casualties of the crisis of 1968. Tensions between the West and the South also worsened as Soviet-backed Communists exploited American weakness, and a wounded United States fought back. Muammar Gaddafi was particularly active in supporting militant anti-American groups such as the Palestine Liberation Organization, but these were minor pinpricks. The real blow came when he helped to persuade the oil-rich Arab monarchs to punish the United States for supporting Israel during the Yom Kippur War of 1973. The Organization of Petroleum Exporting Countries (OPEC) quadrupled the price of oil, and with one stroke, 2 percent of the industrialized countries' GDP was transferred to the oil producers.[89] Inflation spiraled ever higher, while the oil-producing Soviets were now able to finance a more aggressive presence in the Third World, especially in Africa.

Despite this catalog of crises, the sage-technocrats of the West still believed they could make the old system work. They expanded welfare systems and printed money to drive up employment levels. But now that the consensus between capital and labor had collapsed, these measures simply made the crisis worse; inflation continued to rise, while investment and productivity fell.[90] Meanwhile it was becoming clear that the world was undergoing a fundamental technological revolution. A glut of industrial goods indicated a serious overcapacity in old, metal-bashing manufacturing. Ultimately, the future lay in the new world of computers and high-tech communications, but that was not yet clear to all. The world was at a turning point, perhaps one more like the major economic transformation of heavy industrialization in the 1870s and '80s than the more political and cultural transitions of 1918 or 1945.

The enormousness of these challenges made a new form of Bretton Woods/Marshall Aid–style social compromise even more vital: investment had to be directed into new technologies, and workers and employers had to agree on how to share the pain of major economic restructuring, as did the industrial powers. This was, in principle, possible, though it was more feasible at a national level: some states did succeed in preserving the Social Democracy or Christian Democracy of the past, most notably Germany and the Scandinavian countries. But only the United States could mold the international order, and the Americans were in no mood for compromise, statesmanship, and calm negotiation. They were at war: employers against workers; whites against blacks; 1960s radicals against Christian conservatives; and the military and the CIA against a resurgent Communism in the Third World. Meanwhile, the whiz-kid technocrat, who might have brokered social consensus, was deeply mistrusted by the pro-market right and the countercultural left alike.

In place of caste compromise, then, the 1970s ended in caste struggle, and the world experienced yet another revolutionary change. The merchant became harder and looked to the warrior for help, and this militant movement—"neoconservative" in foreign policy and "neoliberal" in economics—was to topple the technocrat and worker from their brief period at the summit of the global system. Only a generation after the sages of Bretton Woods had vowed to learn the lessons of the Great Depression, the world was about to endure another experiment with the economics of the 1920s.

The Merchant Militant

In 1952, a twenty-six-year-old financial consultant, Alan Greenspan, entered the Manhattan apartment of Ayn Rand—the fiercely pro-capitalist writer and intellectual—for the first time. The atmosphere was Russian in its intellectual intensity, and the scene a rather 1920s one, as might be expected from the salon of a woman who had spent her youth in early Soviet Leningrad. Her rooms were stark, with a dramatic view of the Manhattan skyline—befitting the author of *The Fountainhead* (1943), a bestselling novel heroizing a modern architect. And she herself adopted the rather masculine "modern" style popular among female students in the USSR in the 1920s; as Greenspan described her, "her face was dramatic, almost severe, with a wide mouth, broad brow, and great dark intelligent eyes—she kept her dark hair in a pageboy that emphasized them."[91] Greenspan visited her weekly for several years, and there is something slightly incongruous about this straitlaced "undertaker," as Rand called him, becoming involved with a group notorious for its cultish atmosphere and sexual intrigues.

Greenspan was the most famous of Rand's disciples, becoming the hugely influential head of the Federal Reserve in the 1990s and 2000s, but her ideas spread widely among the still small American pro-market right. In the 1960s, a young Republican activist and lawyer, David Bergland, remembered championing her views at party meetings in Orange County, California—one of the early heartlands of the conservative movement and a region that helped bring Ronald Reagan to power as governor of California in 1966.[92]

Why did this eccentric Russian émigré have such appeal among these right-wing free-marketeers? (Her books are still bestsellers, especially in the United States and India.)[93] The answer lies, paradoxically, in the fit between the Russian society in which she grew up, rent by social and cultural conflict, and her new American home. For post-1960s America was also experiencing sharp political and ideological divisions—even if not quite as intense as those of revolutionary Russia. And it was her personal experience that enabled her to reclothe the old militant hard-merchant ideologies that had been influential before the Second World War in more modern garb, suitable for the second half of the twentieth century.

Ayn Rand was a very angry person, and her fury was understandable. She was born Alisa Rosenbaum to the family of a prosperous St. Petersburg pharmacist in the revolutionary year of 1905; the family's shop was taken by the Bolsheviks in 1918, and they were forced to leave St. Petersburg (Petrograd) for south Russia. On their return, Rand became a student at Leningrad University—a place riven with class and political conflict—and she was expelled for a time as punishment for her "bourgeois" origins.[94] Given this background, it is no surprise that Rand should have developed a deep hatred for socialism. But, of course, she had also imbibed the militant culture of that time. Her novels owe a particular debt to early Soviet culture: their melodramatic plots, in which ideologically polarized characters struggle for dominance, are strongly reminiscent of the socialist realist novels of the 1920s USSR.

But Rand's main achievement was political, not literary: it was to create a militant hard-merchant ideology that was free of the nationalistic and explicitly militaristic themes so prominent in the thinking of men such as Heinrich Mann's Diederich Hessling. She did so by adapting the aristocratic ideas of the German philosopher Friedrich Nietzsche, applying them to merchants, and linking them to the "rationality" of the market. (Her philosophy was boldly named Objectivism.) For her, as for Nietzsche, socialism was a passive-aggressive ideology, fashioned by the weak and envious to control the strong and talented. For Rand and Nietzsche, the Christian virtue of altruism was actually a vice: it stifled creativity and empowered interfering bureaucrats and belligerent trade unionists. This was why Rand insisted that any state intervention in the economy was unacceptable; for her, even the free-market enthusiast Hayek was a semi-Communist "middle of the roader."[95]

The positive characters in Rand's novels were utterly Nietzschean in their improbable heroism, their contempt for the untalented, and, sometimes, their cold cruelty. And by the time of her second major novel, *Atlas Shrugged* (1957), they were all businessmen, not Nietzsche's warrior-artists. But they boasted many romantic Nietzschean attributes—a free spirit, creativity, and a flair for innovation. In contrast, her villains were all bureaucrats: stodgy, obstructive, and fearful of change. As one declares, "We can manage to exist as and where we are, but we can't afford to move! So we've got to stand still. . . . We've got to make those bastards stand still!" [96] In this world, the able commercial middle classes are the real victims, crushed by the "man at the bottom who, left to himself, would starve in hopeless ineptitude." [97]

Rand's heroes courageously defy their bureaucratic and worker enemies, and *Atlas Shrugged* is, essentially, a fantasy of heroic businessmen struggling to free themselves from stifling state regulation. Yet, interestingly, their preferred weapon is not the warrior's force. Instead it is a version of the workers' strike—though one in which they withdraw not their labor but their enterprise. America's businessmen boycott their country, following the mysterious leader, John Galt, into "Galt's Gulch"—a utopian market society established deep beneath the mountains of Colorado—thus depriving the world above of their practical competence and vigorous intelligence. After great sufferings, including Galt's torture at the hands of the evil state, they bring the economy to a condition of total collapse and prepare to take back America.

Randian neoliberalism, or "libertarianism," as it is sometimes called, was not a major electoral force in 1970s or 1980s America (though in recent years its influence has probably increased). More popular was a form of Christian conservatism that valorized a rather more traditional kind of hard merchant, rooted in evangelical Protestant morality, and attacked 1960s bohemianism and its elevation of race and sexual equality. [98] Also influential among political elites was a more explicitly warrior group concerned with the threat of Communism—the neoconservatives, many of them, like the journalist and writer Irving Kristol, ex-Trotskyists. Rand, however, was offering something particularly alluring: an ideology that gave the businessperson an aura of romantic glamour while at the same time showing that his activities were founded on a scientific economics. [99] Rand also captured the strong feeling among the commercial middle

classes in America that they were engaged in a life-and-death battle with
the sage-technocrat and the worker, as inflation eroded their living standards. As one of her readers, the head of an Ohio-based steel company,
enthused:

> For twenty-five years I have been yelling my head off about the little
> realized fact that eggheads, socialists, communists, professors, and so-
> called liberals do not understand how goods are produced. Even the
> men who work at the machines do not understand it. It was with great
> pleasure, therefore, that I read "Atlas."[100]

It was this antagonism, rooted in deep social conflict, that lay at the
root of neoliberalism—a hard-merchant movement with strong warrior
elements that sought to roll back state influence and marketize all areas
of life. Margaret Thatcher, one of its most forceful proponents, famously
declared there was no alternative to her policies, and it is common now to
see this international turn to purer market capitalism as something driven
entirely by global economics. But that interpretation is difficult to square
with the actual history of neoliberalism's rise in the 1970s and '80s. It is
true that the post–Bretton Woods inflationary order was unsustainable,
but states responded to this new international environment in very different ways—some more neoliberal than others. Neoliberalism triumphed
earliest and took its most radical form where caste conflict was greatest;
it found it much more difficult to secure a foothold where the postwar
consensus had survived, as in Germany, Scandinavia, and even France
and Mexico.[101]

If neoliberalism found its electoral support in divided societies among
the angry middle classes—both commercial and professional—who saw
no prospect for a consensus between business and labor, its origins lay
elsewhere. Its ideas were not new: they were the old orthodoxies of the
1920s, and the flame had been kept alive by economists, like Hayek in
the 1930s, and intellectual coteries such as the Rand circle in the 1950s.[102]

But it really came into its own in the United States in the 1970s, when new devotees could be found among grassroots conservative anti-tax activists, as well as academics, intellectuals, and journalists; the economics profession was particularly important in providing it with an ideology.[103]

However, if neoliberalism was to have any effect on the real world, it needed political power, and American business—both big and small— was central to its growing influence. Hit by the economic crises of the late 1960s and early 1970s, resentful of government taxes and regulations, and fearful of consumer activists, businesspeople were determined to organize to curb the power of the worker and the sage. They were helped by changes in political funding law: between 1974 and 1980, corporate contributions to campaigns rose from $4.4 million to $19.2 million, and most of this was given to free marketeers; meanwhile, between 1976 and 1980, the number of corporate political action committees (lobbying groups) rose from fewer than three hundred to more than twelve hundred.[104] At the same time, funds were poured into free-market think tanks like the Heritage Foundation and the Hoover Institution. Armed with these new instruments of influence, business became extraordinarily effective at pushing anti-tax legislation through Congress; it was also influential in changing the nature of economic debate. By the end of the 1970s, pro-market sages in the worlds of academia and think tanks had a substantial following in the financial press, particularly in the United States and Britain.[105] The angry middle class now had a militant merchant ideology to justify its efforts to break the compromise of the 1940s and return to the 1920s.

Chile was the first country to experience a neoliberal revolution, and it provided an ideal environment for the movement. It had suffered from particularly deep social divisions and poor levels of growth for some years, and in 1970 the Marxist Salvador Allende was elected to introduce left-wing economic policies that were popular among the poor but resented by business and landowners. Augusto Pinochet, a conservative army officer who had risen to the rank of general, organized the violent

backlash. A coup was staged in 1973, and many leftists and trade unionists were killed, including President Allende.

Once in power, Pinochet handed economic policy over to the "Chicago
Boys"—students of the neoliberal economist Milton Friedman, from the
University of Chicago. They imposed extremely radical free-market policies as part of a "shock treatment," as Friedman called it. They freed
trade and banks from state regulation, raised interest rates to "squeeze
out" inflation, slashed state spending (in 1980 it was half the 1973 level),
privatized health care, and introduced education vouchers.[106]

It took some years before the economic problems of the 1970s broke
the postwar consensus in the West, and neoliberalism's first European
success was in Britain. In retrospect, its triumph there should not have
been surprising—slow growth, deficits, and poor industrial relations
poisoned politics, and many could look to its merchant traditions to
revive national greatness. Margaret Thatcher was also the ideal leader,
with her combination of "Britannia" warrior manner and merchant
values. She saw herself as the courageous defender of the small-business
values embodied by her shopkeeper father against effete Oxbridge
elites and disruptive workers, and she relished the battle. She pursued
a draconian anti-inflationary policy with extraordinary determination,
despite protests at the devastation it brought to Britain's industrial
base; she "rejoiced" at Britain's victory over Argentina in the Falkland
Islands; and she confronted the mining unions, or "the enemy within,"
as she called them.[107] It is no surprise that under her premiership, Britain saw some of its most serious rioting in the twentieth century, and
the police fought pitched battles with miners striking to keep their
pits open.

Her extreme style antagonized some of her supporters: John Major,
her successor as Tory leader and prime minister, condemned her "warrior
characteristics," which he saw as "profoundly un-Conservative."[108] Mrs.
Thatcher's personality might have been unusually confrontational, but
she was not alone in her approach; her great adversary, the miners' leader

Arthur Scargill, had an equally militant approach, and she was merely channeling the extraordinarily high levels of social conflict in Britain at the time. She had come to power in 1979 largely because a substantial proportion of the population blamed the labor unions for strikes and inflation and despaired of social consensus. And while there was deep disquiet at some of her economic policies in the early 1980s, she had a great deal of support for her assaults on the unions and the public sector.

In 1980, Thatcher's and Pinochet's lead was followed by Ronald Reagan, and neoliberalism took root in the largest economy on the globe. On the face of it, Reagan seemed to be a worthy successor to the warrior/hard merchant Pinochet and the hard merchant/warrior Thatcher. A former actor who specialized in playing heroic swashbucklers—from cowboys to sportsmen—he had come into politics as a committed Cold Warrior, and as governor of California in 1968 he had ordered the police to take a tough line against student protesters. As soon as he became president, this true believer in the virtues of American capitalism delighted the right by deregulating business, attacking labor unions, and trimming the public sector. And he combined this domestic war making with a new belligerence in the international arena. The first time the Soviet general secretary, Mikhail Gorbachev, met Reagan, he described him as having the diplomatic subtlety of a "caveman." Denouncing Communism as "the focus of evil in the world," Reagan ordered major military escalations in Afghanistan, Nicaragua, El Salvador, the Philippines, Angola, and Ethiopia—largely through covert military forces or aid to local insurgents. After Vietnam, American public opinion would not accept an explicit revival of the military state. Only guerrilla wars—the euphemistically termed "low-intensity conflicts"—were feasible. Even so, like Thatcher in Britain, Reagan skillfully articulated a nationalist message: the hard merchant could revive American greatness by cutting through sagely sclerosis and confronting worker selfishness.

Yet arguably more important than either Reagan or Thatcher in furthering this hard-merchant and warrior agenda, and in restoring Anglo-

American power, was the rather less charismatic figure of Paul Volcker, who from 1979 to 1987 was the head of the Federal Reserve. An economist with close connections to Wall Street, he had for a long time been a convinced economic liberal.[109] However, his hand was also forced by the merchant—in the form of the international banks. Nixon's contradictory strategy—using deficit spending to finance America's warfare-welfare state while at the same time freeing up controls on international capital—had brought the country, and the West, to a crisis. Financial markets were rebelling, refusing to buy American bonds and casting doubt on the position of the dollar as the world's leading currency. Volcker was determined to take decisive measures to maintain American preeminence, and that meant appeasing the financial markets. In October 1979, he raised interest rates to painfully high levels to attract international capital back to the dollar.[110] Employers, he argued, would be forced to cut costs and hold down wages; inflation would thus be squeezed out of the system, money would regain its value, and investors would return to the United States.

The decision was a crucial one, and it marks the true beginning of the neoliberal era. The American warrior had finally abandoned his Bretton Woods alliance with the sage-technocrat and the worker and thrown in his lot with the merchant. Volcker believed that the whole economy would benefit in the long term, and certainly inflation was driven down to below 4 percent and remained at this level or lower for the next two decades, while capital flowed into the United States. But the costs for industry were very high, as it faced expensive borrowing costs and an overvalued dollar damaged the export sector. Meanwhile, falling wages and rising unemployment weakened labor unions. (By 1993, real wages had fallen 15 percent below 1978 levels.)[111]

Ultimately, though, industrial decline did not matter to America's warriors, for they had another source of funds to finance the Cold War: the international merchant. Capital fled the indebted parts of the Third and Second worlds, including Communist Eastern Europe. Poland and

Romania were effectively bankrupted, and the 1980 Polish Solidarity uprising was only the most dramatic sign of the crisis in the Soviet bloc.
Meanwhile, funds flooded into the United States—a $46.8 billion out-
flow from the G7 countries in the 1970s became a $347.4 billion inflow
in the 1980s—and much of Reagan's "Second Cold War" was financed
by Japanese loans.[112]

Volcker's policies and the high cost of credit did much to strengthen
merchant power throughout the world. To attract capital, countries were
forced to adopt policies demanded by the financial markets, and a newly
assertive and neoliberal IMF and World Bank insisted on the same
agenda. "Structural adjustment loan" programs were offered to indebted
countries, but only on condition that they "stabilize, privatize and liberalize." After 1989, this was regularly termed the "Washington Consensus"—
a set of one-size-fits-all merchant-friendly policy prescriptions. Examples
of egregious defiance—like that of France in 1981–83—could be punished by a withdrawal of capital. Other states, like Communist Mozam-
bique in 1987, accepted these policies voluntarily, in exchange for IMF
loans.

Volcker's commitment to combating inflation and serving international financial markets set the course of global economic policy for some
thirty years. But the hard-merchant radicalism of the early years was difficult to sustain, for hair-shirt austerity hit not only labor but also the
middle classes. Of course, economists like Paul Volcker, Milton Friedman, and Alan Greenspan insisted that this belt tightening would not last
very long: once the American economy was back in balance, capitalists
would invest, jobs would be created, and everybody would prosper. But in
early 1980s Britain and America, that clearly was not happening, and
electorates were becoming restive. Volcker himself was forced to temper
his harshness in 1982, lowering interest rates in response to a serious
banking crisis in Latin America, though he remained a true believer in
neoliberal orthodoxies. But it was Ronald Reagan who was to lead the real
retreat. Indeed, Reagan turned out to be rather less committed to the hard

merchant/warrior creed than his supporters had hoped, and by the mid-1980s he was making concessions to his old enemies, the 1960s radicals.

Flower Power Triumphant

Reagan's biographer Edmund Morris described him as "truly one of the strangest men who's ever lived." "Nobody around him understood him. Every person I interviewed, almost without exception, eventually would say, 'You know, I could never really figure him out.'"[113] And historians have had the same problem. This was somebody who called the Soviet Union an "evil empire" and yet was determined to negotiate with the Communist Satan; and this was a believer in free-market economics who massively increased government debt.

Some have pointed to his character to explain the contradictions. Reagan might have cast himself as a warrior hero from a young age, but he had a compulsive need to be popular. Certainly, for all his talk of good and evil, this affable man did not feel comfortable as an embattled ideologue. Others have looked to his upbringing. His mother was a member of a pacifist Protestant sect, the Disciples of Christ, and he seems to have inherited much of her optimistic theology—so different from the puritanical self-sacrifice (and other-sacrifice) of the Thatcherite hard merchants.[114] In 1983, he astounded pollster Richard Wirthlin when he asked:

> You know, Dick, what I *really* want to be remembered for? I want to be remembered as the president of the United States who brought a sense and reality of peace and security. I want to eliminate the awful fear that each of us feels sometimes when we get up in the morning knowing that the world could be destroyed through a nuclear holocaust.

Wirthlin was shocked: this scourge of the 1960s peaceniks was now "obsessed with peace."[115] Reagan was not fighting for the merchant against his enemies as aggressively as hard-line neoconservatives and neo-liberals had hoped. This was a figure much more comfortable with a soft-merchant world of easygoing consumption and compromise than with Thatcher's unbending toughness.

In economic policy, Reagan dismayed hard-merchant neoliberals, including Friedman and Greenspan, when he cut taxes and raised military spending but conspicuously failed to reduce welfare programs.[116] "Supply-side" economists ("voodoo economists" to their enemies) told Reagan he could afford this largesse because tax cuts would unleash entrepreneurship and boost real economic growth, and he doubtless believed them. But he also wanted to believe them. He wanted to be a popular president, not to make unpleasant choices. And he could afford to do so, because America could now rely on its new powerful ally—the international banks—attracted by high interest rates and low inflation and no longer worried about deficits. By the mid-1980s America was booming, but it was also deeply in the red. So while in 1980 Reagan seemed to be the ideal champion of the new hard-merchant ideology, his presidency invented a very different, much softer merchant order—ideal for the thrusting entrepreneur, for sure, but also delivering high living standards to the middle classes.

In foreign policy, too, Reagan radically modified his confrontational warriorish approach after 1983–84. Precisely why is not entirely clear. There is some evidence that he was profoundly shocked when, in November 1983, the USSR misinterpreted an American military exercise, Operation Able Archer, as an attack, and the world came its closest to nuclear conflagration since the Cuban Missile Crisis;[117] or he might have been responding to the unpopularity of his covert support for the brutal Nicaraguan "contras." Certainly, the Reagan administration realized that the American public no longer took the Communist threat as seriously as before and, as Soviet weakness became clear in the 1980s, was no longer willing to listen to Cold War demands for sacrifice.[118] As Peggy Noonan, one of Reagan's speechwriters, remembered, when focus groups were asked to register which phrases they liked, they showed positive feelings toward words such as "reach," "free," and "America" but did not want to hear those worrying words "Afghanistan" and "Nicaragua."[119] Reagan got the message, and by 1986 he was proposing complete nuclear disarmament, whether in response to public opinion or out of deep conviction— something that appalled Washington's Cold Warriors. By the late 1980s he had established a good relationship with Mikhail Gorbachev, despite his membership in the "evil" Communist Party.

If the old Cold Warrior Reagan was now appealing to a maturing (and voting) 1960s generation, Gorbachev, born in 1931, was a bona fide 1960s person himself. He was a member of the generation that was too young to fight in the Second World War and attended university during the liberalizing "thaw" after Stalin's death, between 1953 and 1964—the age cohort that Russians call the *shestidesiatniki* ("sixties people"). And he was the only Communist leader of that age to have made it into the gerontocratic politburo by the mid-1980s.

The slogan most associated with Gorbachev is the rather technocratic term *perestroika,* or "restructuring," and that captures his early policies well: he represented a group of party reformers who believed that if the USSR was to compete with the West, the system needed to be more "rational" and freed from inefficiencies. But perhaps more representative of his worldview was one of his favorite words: *tvorchestvo,* or "creativity." Gorbachev was not a Western-style liberal, as many thought at the time. He was a Russian version of the 1960s romantic—initially a Marxist and then a sort of democratic socialist—whose main bêtes noires were militarism and the Communist "bureaucrats," the stiflers of the "creativity" he believed was so necessary for economic and political success. And he was determined to destroy them even if that meant removing the framework that kept the Soviet state together. Gorbachev's revolution, then, was 1960s philosophy in action: he brought an end to Moscow's empire in Eastern Europe, much to the dismay of the Kremlin's Cold Warriors; and when the USSR began to break up, he refused to use extensive force (though he might have sanctioned the failed hard-line coup of 1991).[120] He was also initially popular among younger, educated white-collar workers, precisely the type of people who had rebelled against milita rism and bureaucratic regimentation in the West in the 1960s.[121] Sixties values might have failed to conquer the political sphere in the West of 1968, but they succeeded in the East of 1989: Gorbachev brought an end to the power of the sage-technocrat and sage-priest party ideologist and—inadvertently—destroyed the Soviet state.

Most observers failed to discern Gorbachev's real radicalism because they were fooled by his balding pate and drab suits. He hardly looked like a 1960s person. But the picture was different on the streets of Eastern Europe. There, the 1989 revolutions were carnivals, and young activists often used the techniques of the West's 1968 radicals, preferring to ridicule the warrior-bureaucrats rather than confront them.[122] Poland's "Orange Alternative," for instance, mounted elaborately staged "happenings." Embracing their status as "little people" ranged against the mighty state, they dressed up as elves in orange hats, danced around military equipment, and provoked the police with slogans such as "Citizens, help the militia, beat yourself up!"[123] The police naturally looked ridiculous: when they arrested the ironically nicknamed "Major"—the leader of the movement, Waldemar Fydrych—they had to charge him with "public agitation by impersonating an elf."[124]

The climax came with the peaceful breaching of the Berlin Wall and Communist leaders' realization that they could not stop it by force. Flower power, or elf power, had won, and neoconservative attempts to take credit are the complete opposite of the truth. Reagan, and subsequently George H. W. Bush, took an emollient stance toward the USSR; had they not, they would undoubtedly have provoked the Soviet hardliners and possibly a coup.

However, while the bohemians might have participated in the revolutions of 1989, they did not take control. The odd radical figure might have come to power—the playwright Václav Havel, elected to the Czechoslovak presidency, was one—but it was the merchant who reaped the rewards, and especially the soft, globalizing merchant, rather than the warriorish hard-liner of the 1970s and early 1980s. Reagan's legacy was ultimately one of peace, free markets, and debt—much as in the 1920s, of course. In 1989, as in 1918 America, there was a powerful sense in both the West and the East that the old era of violent warriors and supposedly "utopian" sages was over; it was giving way to a world of globalizing and tolerant merchants. As Francis Fukuyama wrote, "history" had ended; Nietzsche's "last man"—a rather passionless figure obsessed with his own comfort—had inherited the earth.

Fukuyama, of course, came in for harsh criticism by predicting the eternal rule of the merchant, but his 1992 book lasted longer than André Siegfried's ill-starred effort of 1927. For this time the soft merchant's position was much more commanding; his enemies were weaker, and he had won over a number of former adversaries to his side, including the bohemians of 1968 and 1989.

FIVE

Davos Man

Magic Mountain

The Swiss ski resort of Davos was once best known to literary types, as the setting for *The Magic Mountain,* Thomas Mann's great 1924 novel of ideas tracing Europe's path to the carnage of the First World War. There, in a tuberculosis sanatorium, its characters engage in feverish and distinctly highbrow debate about the future of Europe and the crisis of liberalism. Seventy years later, however, the association of Davos with intellectual intensity and warring ideologies had been completely erased. For since the 1970s, the resort has been home to the World Economic Forum—the annual gathering of the world's commercial and political elites.

The contrast tells us a great deal about the differences between the last era of global merchant power—the 1920s—and the one we are still living through. In the 1920s, Thomas Mann—although himself a Rotarian and born-again liberal—realized how weak the merchant order really was, and he understood the enduring appeal of the alternatives. Mann also believed in the power of ideas and the genuine importance of the clashes and controversies between them. Today Davos, though it grandly claims to be a place of serious thinking and big-issue debates, is in fact an arena of ideological consensus. If Bretton Woods was the Mount Olympus of the sagely postwar era, then Davos is the Valhalla of the new merchant gods. This is a Rotary Club for plutocrats (the 2012 admission price was $71,000), and just as the Rotarian embodied the global merchant of the 1920s, so the forum gave its name to the 1990s and 2000s version: "Davos Man."

Of course, the merchant, the consummate negotiator, has not excluded other castes; he has realized that he cannot conquer the whole world immediately, for many countries are still ruled by sages or warriors. The forum has over time issued invitations to a diverse group, from military dictators to Communist apparatchiks. But there are limits, and most delegates accept the merchant's view that deregulated markets are the future, even if they do not always share his belief in the inevitable triumph of liberal democracy.

Many of these skeptics have been very willing to accept the Davos consensus, partly because there have been concrete benefits in trade and investment but also because the sage-technocrat, warrior, and worker castes have found themselves so apparently discredited around the world, after the crises of the 1970s and the fall of Communism, that they have little alternative. Most countries, of all ideological stripes, have therefore seen some increase in merchant influence; only fortress-like North Korea has held true to the Stalinist faith in a total anti-merchant vision.

Yet the lack of real debate has had its costs. For unlike the Rotarians, Davos Man has had three decades to extend his dominion without any serious check from other castes. In that period he has made many millions richer, mainly in China and India. But he has also created a crisis that might become even more serious than that of the 1920s. And it is no surprise that the 2008 meltdown was initially so devastating where the merchant has historically been strongest, and where his influence on society has been deepest: the United States and Britain.

In February 1999, *Time* magazine awarded its famed front cover to a besuited trio of rather smug-looking men whom it dubbed the "Three Marketeers." Most prominent was Alan Greenspan; flanking him were Robert Rubin, President Bill Clinton's treasury secretary, and Larry Summers, Rubin's deputy, protégé, and successor. *Time*'s article could not have been more fulsome in its praise: the three were gushingly credited with "saving the world" from the financial crisis that hit Asia and Russia in 1997–98 and threatened to destroy the whole global economy.

More than a decade later, of course, their glittering reputations are distinctly tarnished. They have not quite suffered the disgrace of McNamara—yet. Indeed, Larry Summers enjoyed a second coming as a key economic strategist in the Obama administration. But Greenspan is widely blamed for the 2008 meltdown, Rubin was humiliated by it, and in its wake Summers has recanted many of his ultra-free-market beliefs. And while it would be unfair to blame three individuals (however powerful) for the flaws in a whole model of capitalism, there is some justice to this censure. For it would be difficult to find a troika who had more influence on the post–Cold War, American-driven model of global markets.

The Three Marketeers, despite their shared free-market faith, were rather different in their politics. Greenspan was still, at root, a hard-merchant Republican, a recognizable survivor from the militant era of the 1980s; Rubin and Summers, on the other hand, had Democrat sympathies. As a young academic economist, the abrasive Summers had even criticized the dogma that markets always knew best. But it was the more emollient Rubin who was the best representative of the soft-merchant style and values that were dominant in the West in the 1990s and 2000s. A banker with a profound faith in free markets, he impressed people with his sociability, low-key charm, and democratic tolerance. He also expressed a sympathy for the poor and aligned himself with the new center-left ruling political ideology of the 1990s: the "Third Way," or *Neue Mitte* ("New Middle"). Unlike the welfare-skeptic Greenspan, Rubin insisted that globalized financial capitalism both should and could be reconciled with a concern for the less fortunate. While he insisted that the commanding heights of the economy would be ceded to the banks, welfarism would share at least some of the benefits brought by lightly regulated capitalism. The deserving poor would be protected from the full force of global competition and given the wherewithal to become full participants in the market.[1]

However, the soft merchant had learned lessons since he was last in control, in the 1920s. No longer was he the know-nothing Rotarian; he had accepted the need for some sagely expertise appropriate for an age of greater professionalism. (Rubin was an economics summa cum laude and Phi Beta Kappa from Harvard, with a law degree from Yale.) He had also learned the lessons of the McNamara era and had adapted to the romanticism of the 1960s. Though Rubin was no bohemian, his memoirs present a picture-perfect version of early-1960s student life: sitting in Parisian cafés, discussing Kerouac and existentialism and worrying about Vietnam.[2] Rubin was certainly more cerebral than was the norm on Wall Street, but he was blazing the trail for future generations of "smart," liberal, highly qualified Ivy Leaguers in an increasingly high-status profession. With his mixture of heavily attested ability and steely ambition, he rose to be head of Goldman Sachs, then joined the Clinton administration, before moving on to become director of Citibank, where he remained a powerful fixer in the Democratic Party and patron of President Barack Obama's economic team.

But Rubin had much the same objectives as Greenspan and the neoliberal economic elites of the era: to transform the sagely, managerial capitalism of Bretton Woods into a purer merchant version. The merchant's flexibility, competitiveness, and search for maximum profit, they were convinced, would bring prosperity to all. Capital, they insisted, had been tied down in dead-end, unprofitable enterprises by complacent managers and selfish workers. And allowing capital's owners to pursue profit, and profit alone, could liberate that capital and redirect it into new productive industries anywhere in the world—even if they were in China, India, or Southeast Asia. Barriers to high profits, whether union agreements at home or restrictions on trade and capital flows abroad, had to be removed. In practice, that meant giving more power to the owners of capital and their agents, the banks.

With this objective, Greenspan and Rubin took a hatchet to the regulations so painstakingly constructed in the aftermath of the debacle of 1929. Bank deregulation had already begun in the United States and Britain in the 1970s, but Greenspan and Rubin made the decisive contribution, eroding and finally abolishing the New Deal Glass-Steagall Act and thus, for the first time since the 1920s, permitting international banks to use the savings of ordinary depositors to make high-risk investments in international financial markets. Simultaneously, Rubin, acting in concert with the IMF, pressed other countries to open their financial markets to foreign investment banks.

The main objection, of course, was that this new merchant capitalism could not be the foundation for long-term investment and jobs. Capital needed to be tied down if it was to finance the research and skills needed for complex high-tech industries; if the merchant was allowed to extract his profits and switch his capital at will, he would merely bring back the international financial chaos of the 1920s. He might even bring an even more drastic return to the pre–Siemens/Carnegie, less sagely British Victorian model of capitalism, which had so dramatically failed to adapt to the modern industrial world.

But the castes who might have resisted the merchant assault were becoming weaker. Unemployment in the West and the massive expansion of a new labor force in China undermined union power.

Equally important, though, was a loss of faith in old solutions among sagely elites, and one group in particular: the economists. Since the 1970s, Keynesian support for economic management by technocrats had become deeply unfashionable, and a much more merchant-friendly version of the discipline was conquering the field.[3] According to this new orthodoxy, the market was much more efficient than any group of experts could possibly be, because it responded to signals from millions of "rationally acting" individuals. This assumption—the so-called Efficient Market Hypothesis—justified the marketeers' faith in banks and financial markets: only they could respond to the rational market and invest capital where it would be most productive.[4] And even though China might be the main beneficiary, humanity as a whole would benefit from the more efficient use of resources.

In 1979, Larry Summers pointed to a major flaw in the theory with one simple riposte: "THERE ARE IDIOTS. Look around."[5] One only had to observe traders to see that they were not cool, rational beings, assessing all the available information; they were victims of fads, fashions, and panics. However, this rather obvious insight did little to dent economists' faith in the elegant idea; indeed, Summers himself moved increasingly toward a market fundamentalist position. Perhaps we should not be surprised, for sage-technocrats can become sage-priests: left to their own devices, they can develop elaborate, internally coherent theologies that they enforce with the dogmatic certainty of medieval clerics, and once they are established it is difficult to shake them out of their certainties.

The pro-market sages undoubtedly made an enormous difference to merchant power. Their influence was considerable—in the op-ed pages of the newspapers, in governments, in international organizations, and in powerful private institutions like the credit-rating agencies, which assessed governments' economic policies and could trigger capital flights by "downgrading" them. They also had an elegant and internally coherent set of ideas that could be understood by ordinary people, at least at a basic level. This was much more impressive than the institutes of Marxism-Leninism that peppered the capitals of the Communist world.

Merchant Bankers and Vampire Squids

But if the economists laid the intellectual ground for the merchant advance, the assault itself was led by those purest embodiments of merchant values, the bankers. It was they who were to be the shock troops of the new capitalism.

Bankers have not always been pure merchants. Following its humiliations of the late 1920s, Anglo-Saxon finance had lost much of its brash commercialism. London's merchant banks had retreated into a sleepy gentlemanliness, and a highly regulated Wall Street had a distinctly sagely atmosphere, its banker-bureaucrats paying fixed salaries, managing safe investments, and playing second fiddle to the McNamaras of the corporate world.[6] But from the 1970s onward, the investment banks, with their allies the big pension funds, began to regain their merchant character.[7]

By the late 1980s they had become the almost pure merchant institutions they are today—that is, organizations perfectly in tune with the volatile fluctuations of the market. During booms, they would rush into flourishing sectors, increasing their staffs and scattering massive bonuses like so much confetti; during bad times, they would make a very rapid exit, drawing in their horns and laying off their employees. There is very little long-term planning or investment in this business plan, nor much concern for one's staff beyond their short-term ability to turn a fast buck. As one banker told Karen Ho, an academic anthropologist studying the culture of Wall Street in the late 1990s: "Wall Street firms could [not] care less about their employees. Easy come, easy go. When times are good, times are great. . . . You get big bonus checks. When times are bad, you are gone. They couldn't care. So it's a high risk."[8]

To some, this might seem to be a horribly unstable and inhumane working life, in which personal relationships are reduced to nothing beyond the bottom line. But most bankers, like merchants throughout the ages, accept it willingly—partly, of course, because of the money but also because they believe it is inevitable and even virtuous, for it encourages flexibility and efficiency and drives economic prosperity by rewarding the strong and punishing the weak, as they see them. Another banker told Ho:

It is a business where there is no tenure. There is no union protection. Basically, if things change you could be out. That's one reason why people are very flexible. So you need flexible people, and people who can deal with it every day. Some people would hate that. I don't mind that. . . . Most businesses have five-year plans—What are we going to be producing?—and have long product life-cycles. [We] have very short product life-cycles. How do you plan when you never know what the market is going to do?[9]

Investment bankers, then, lived their lives according to market rules because they did well out of them but also, perhaps more important, because they *believed* in them. And they were determined to spread their values—including their preference for a profitable but deeply unstable way of life—to other castes. Deregulation gave them just the leverage they needed, and since the 1980s they have successfully imposed merchant values on the rest of the economy.

The first redoubt to be conquered was the gentlemanly City of London. Margaret Thatcher's "Big Bang" deregulation of 1986 allowed foreign ownership of financial institutions, and British-owned merchant banks were soon swallowed by their bigger Wall Street and European rivals. London now became a transatlantic outpost for the global merchant vanguard.

Even more significant than the victory over the City was the merchant's conquest of American and British manufacturing industry. His initial instruments were not the older investment banks but a new phenomenon, the independent, swashbuckling "corporate raiders"—men like the flamboyant Anglo-French financier James Goldsmith. In the 1980s, warriorish hard merchants of this type launched aggressive takeovers of large firms that they thought were undervalued on the stock market, judging that such businesses would be worth more broken up, or squeezed by "efficiencies" to produce more profit. Corporate raiders' weapon of choice was borrowed money, with which they bought shares in the hapless victim companies (hence "leveraged buyouts"); they then cut wages and sold off assets, drove up the share price, and sold the company for a fat profit.

Of course, this behavior looked opportunistic and selfish, and the raiders, as well as the bankers who lent them the money (Michael Milken and other salesmen of risky "junk bonds'), were targets of sharp criticism for destroying jobs and communities. Oliver Stone's 1987 film *Wall Street* was a powerful broadside against such practices, with its amoral antihero Gordon Gekko and his famous speech to the shareholders of the Teldar Paper corporation: "The point is, ladies and gentlemen, that greed, for lack of a better word, is good. Greed is right. Greed works." But it is often forgotten that Gekko was not simply acting the pantomime villain; he was describing the management philosophy of the era: only "greed," or self-interest, would make capitalism work properly, and the self-interested had to seize control from the bureaucratic managers who cared about other things, like jobs, innovation, and quality. As Gekko insisted, "Greed will save not only Teldar Paper but that other malfunctioning corporation called the USA."[10]

James Goldsmith used a more revolutionary language of market liberation: "Let the market free, and . . . cleanse [these bloated firms] through market action." The "do-gooder" manager might claim that "he is in business for all these constituencies, of suppliers, communities, employees, and everybody else." But that was untrue, and even "if it's true, it's a mistake." For Goldsmith, profit and "shareholder value" were paramount and would ultimately help the economy as a whole by allocating capital correctly. Even the high levels of debt incurred were good for the takeover victims, the raiders insisted, because they forced them to become efficient in order to pay it off.[11]

Corporate raiders and junk-bond dealers fell out of favor after a series of scandals and the stock market crash of 1987—Milken even ended up in jail for fraud. But the merchant assault on the corporate world continued in the softer 1990s, albeit in less buccaneering form and accompanied by less brutally honest language. "Private equity" replaced "leveraged buyouts," "junk bonds" became "high-yield bonds," and now corporations themselves, rather than raiders, did the taking over, presenting these deals as technical-sounding "mergers and acquisitions."[12] But the pattern was the same, and throughout the 1990s and 2000s investment bankers were the real force behind the takeovers, insisting, against mounting evidence, that they would "add value" to the firms they bought.

In fact, in many cases, little if any value was added. Studies of the firms themselves show that they tended to perform better for three or four years, then fall back to previous levels.[13] And many mergers were catastrophic failures, most notoriously the DaimlerChrysler debacle of 1997. The principal effect of many of the buyouts was to suck resources out of the firm and funnel them upward, to shareholders, bankers, and the top managers involved in the deal. The main losers, of course, were ordinary workers, who lost their jobs or were "outsourced" and rehired for lower wages and benefits; the swaths of middle management who were also "downsized"; and the local suppliers who lost their main markets.[14]

In 2010, the journalist Matt Taibbi memorably described the investment bank Goldman Sachs as a "great vampire squid wrapped around the face of humanity, relentlessly jamming its blood funnel into anything that smells like money."[15] He was sharply criticized for reducing a complex question to moralizing polemic, and reasonably so, for while there is a good deal of corruption in the financial industry, most bankers cannot simply be dismissed as greedy people; many are true believers, convinced that what they are doing is good according to their merchant ethic. But Taibbi's metaphor captures the economic process with lurid accuracy: capital, carefully amassed over time through steady investment and sagely decision making, was being sucked out of the industrial economy and then regurgitated into the bank accounts of wealthy investors or, as often as not, those of the investment bankers themselves.

Though the takeover movement affected only a minority of companies directly, it marked a major victory for the merchant in his strug-

gle for control of the economy. For the movement's sheer aggression
intimidated all: every big firm feared that it might be targeted next,
and adopted asset-stripping and pro-shareholder strategies to avoid it.[16]
Managers, desperate for shareholder approval (and often with their
own salaries closely linked to the share price), took a relentlessly short-
term approach designed to maximize profits and so look good for the
investment banks' quarterly figures.[17] Research and development was
neglected—American investment was considerably lower than the average between 1952 and 1979, and the stock of fixed capital today is
32 percent lower than it would have been had the "golden age" continued;[18] industry hemorrhaged jobs, both white-collar and (especially) blue-
collar, many of which were exported to China; and the wages of ordinary
workers stagnated—those of the bottom 10 percent of American workers
did not rise at all between 1979 and 2003. At the same time, a higher
proportion of profits went to shareholders, and the wages of the top
10 percent of the population grew by 27.2 percent in the same period.[19]

The one exception was the extraordinary success of the new information technology (IT) industries—particularly in Silicon Valley at the
end of the 1990s. Here, as will be seen, the freewheeling culture of merchant capitalism fit well with the new creative and flexible computer
world. And venture capitalists piled into these new industries, even if
much of the money was wasted in the dot-com bubble. However, it is
often forgotten that much of the investment in these technologies was
made by the American military and the government-subsidized higher-
education system. Also, the new industries were not adequate replace-
ments for the old ones. Most of the jobs created were for small groups of
highly educated people. The actual production of computers and mobile
phones was exported to more industry-friendly countries in Asia.

As we see 1920s levels of inequality return after thirty years of merchant rule, we seem to be mystified as to how and why this extraordinary
transfer of wealth could have occurred under our very noses. Why did so
few of us notice it? But we should not be surprised: the merchant, unfet-

tered, loves flexibility and hates tying down his capital, for fear of missing out on higher profits. Handing over corporate control from sage to merchant was bound to create a super-rich elite with little interest in the other castes below.

But power over the commanding heights of the economy, through banks and boardrooms, has also given the merchant an even greater prize: the propagation of his ethos to increasing numbers in the population. The educated middle classes were expected to imitate the bankers themselves and become more "flexible," moving from project to project in response to the needs of the market. As 1990s French management literature advised, the successful person in the new economy had to be "adaptable, physically and intellectually mobile"—a serial member of "flexible" teams and "networks," "rarely made up of the same people." Naturally, this has imperiled economic security as well as the ability to build a career and to develop expertise and skills.[20]

At the same time, however, the merchant's drive for efficiency and cost cutting has subjected ever more of us to the quarterly balance sheet, the short-term target, and the petty tyranny of the line manager—an updating of the "Taylorism" of the 1920s for the digital age.[21] This has been particularly true for those in unskilled jobs, but it has also started to affect managers and professionals. As one senior British supermarket manager recently explained, the head office's "[computer] systems monitor everything. . . . Every little thing is monitored, so there is no place to hide."[22]

The merchant, however, did not confine his attention to industry. Having remodeled the economy, he began to expel his rivals—sage-technocrats, workers, and warriors—from their other redoubts. This was perhaps most noticeable, and unexpected, in European football—once the home of warrior honor ("fair play") and local community pride. By the 1990s the media coverage of sport had made certain teams and competitions commercially valuable, and the merchant saw his opportunity to make and take the profits. Manchester United, the richest football club in the world, was the battleground of one of the most acrimonious struggles for control when, in 2005, it was taken over by American businessman Malcolm Glazer in a hedge-fund-financed leveraged buyout, much to the anger of its fans.[23] They have recently tried to wrest control of the debt-laden club by pooling their resources with those of a group of wealthy "Red Knights" (after the team colors). But even with considerable financial backing, this new chivalric order has so far failed to dislodge the new owners.

The greatest victims of the merchant's renaissance, though, have been the workers' citadel—the labor union—and the sage's stronghold: the state and the public sector. Unemployment as well as labor-market deregulation have destroyed much union power. And as in the 1920s, bankers used their financial muscle to force governments to keep budget deficits and inflation low; if they refused, financiers would punish them by refusing to lend and undermining their currencies. Only Social Democratic and Christian Democratic governments, which could maintain a healthy economy though effective "social contracts" and "coordinated capitalism," could maintain their generous welfare states without being punished by the financial markets. James Carville, a political adviser to Bill Clinton, famously paid homage to the power of international finance when he complained: "I used to think that if there was reincarnation, I wanted to come back as the president or the pope or as a .400 baseball hitter. But now I would like to come back as the bond market. You can intimidate everybody."[24]

In fact, the hard merchants in the bond markets did not succeed in cutting welfare as much as they would have liked. But they were, to some extent, comforted by the efforts of soft-merchant governments on both the left and the right to extend merchant influence to the old sagely strongholds of education and health care. In Britain, that has involved introducing "internal markets" into the health service and treating students as "consumers" and academics as "service providers." In the United States, it has gone much further—for instance, with the rise of for-profit universities. Their defenders argue, with some justice, that they provide a more flexible form of education for people who have to work, thus serving a group neglected by more conventional, sage-run universities. However, the corrosive effects of markets on education have been entirely predictable. Some of the universities have been accused of "high-pressure sales techniques," "inflated claims about career placement to increase student enrollment," and toleration of low standards for fear of losing lucrative students.[25] If professionals are worried about meeting targets and maximizing profit, they are likely to be less interested in the welfare of their individual patients or students.

Merchant penetration into the public sector has therefore spoiled relations between professional sages and merchants in recent years. But that was not always the case, for merchant rule initially found a ready sympathizer in the "creative" castes—heirs of the Romantic artist, committed to artisanal autonomy—who had come to the fore in the sit-ins of 1968 and were now taking their positions in the economy. It was this new caste alliance that gave the marketeers the real advantage over the Rotarians of the 1920s. As always, Davos was in tune with the zeitgeist: its 2006 session, co-chaired by Larry Summers, was devoted to the theme "The Creative Imperative."

New Romantics

A shuffling column of tired, depressed-looking men, shaven-headed and drab in cheap gray uniforms, makes its way along a tunnel monitored by TV screens. Cut to policemen in riot helmets chasing a young female athlete wielding a large hammer. Cut to an intense, sinister face on a screen, his eyes shielded by reflective glasses, berating a hypnotized mass, seated in close ranks, Orwell style:

Today, we celebrate the first glorious anniversary of the Information
Purification Directives. We have created, for the first time in all history, a garden of pure ideology—where each worker may bloom, secure
from the pests purveying contradictory truths. Our Unification of
Thoughts is more powerful a weapon than any fleet or army on earth.
We are one people, with one will, one resolve, one cause. Our enemies
shall talk themselves to death, and we will bury them with their own
confusion. We *shall* prevail!

As Big Brother reaches his climax, the athlete reaches the hall and
hurls her hammer at the screen. It explodes; shock and anguish grip the
narcotized audience. A voice-over then intones: "On January 24, Apple
Computer will introduce Macintosh. And you'll see why 1984 won't be
like 1984."

This one-minute advertisement for Apple Computers, directed by
Ridley Scott (maker of the cult film *Blade Runner*), was screened only
once, on January 22, 1984, in a prime-time slot during the Super Bowl.[26]
But once was enough, and this inspired pastiche of Orwell's *1984* struck
a mythic chord with the public. Apple became a household name in the
United States, and by the 2000s its controversial boss, Steve Jobs, had
emerged as a figure of almost cultlike veneration, his products symbols of
today's globalized capitalism. And with his death from cancer in 2011,
Jobs attained the status of a secular saint. Many people, if asked to make
a choice between a deeply unstable globalized economy with iPhones
and a safer, more regulated one without them, would prefer to take their
chances.

But as the *1984* advertisement shows, Apple was not just about sleekly
designed gadgets. It had a clear values agenda: the reconciliation of the
bohemian sage of the 1960s with the unbound merchant of the 1980s.
The "Big Brother" of Apple's advertisement was a thinly veiled dig at its
rival IBM, the corporate computing behemoth Stanley Kubrick had
railed against in *2001*. But Steve Jobs, unlike Kubrick, had nothing

against corporations or machines. Indeed, he was convinced that creative companies like his own, and postmodern technology, were the best antidote to Big Brother's sagely "garden of pure ideology"—whether state or corporate. Markets, far from contradicting the romantic, creative values of the 1960s, embodied them.

Apple's commercial, then, revealed the fundamental difference between merchant rule in the 1920s and its longer-lasting successor, which seems still to dominate the West today, despite numerous disasters. George Babbitt had to make a choice between the Booster Club and the "Bunch," the countercultural bohemians on the other side of town. But by the 1990s they would all be drinking together in one great cybercafé. The 1960s creatives could endorse markets in good conscience, for merchants and romantic sages were brothers-in-arms against their natural enemies: the Big Brother bureaucrats.

Steve Jobs, born in 1955, was the embodiment of this merchant/creative alliance. Like many innovative people, he combined different caste values. Growing up in what became known as Silicon Valley, California—the home of America's giant Cold War defense corporations—he was surrounded by technologically savvy artisans, tinkering away with gadgets and gizmos in their garages, and he absorbed not only their interest in electronics but also their perfectionist pride in craft.[27] Equally central to his personality, though, were his romantic values, which prized self-fulfillment and creativity. Another highly successful advertising campaign of 1997 took the form of images of a series of "geniuses," including Bob Dylan and Albert Einstein, over which a voice intoned, "Here's to the crazy ones, the misfits, the rebels, the troublemakers . . ." Jobs, like many other hippies, had become absorbed in Zen Buddhism, and he used his company to spread his countercultural 1960s vision of the world. Apple did not just sell goods—it urged its customers to "think different." But Jobs had also been brought up in the market-friendly California that gave birth to the Reagan revolution, and he was interested in making money. Famously, when Steve Wozniak, Jobs's collaborator and the engineer who actually invented the first Apple personal computers, wanted to give away his computers for free, it was Jobs who dissuaded him.[28]

This unique caste alliance of the romantic sage, the artisan, and the merchant was hugely important for the legitimacy of the new free-market capitalism, for the "creatives" were becoming a much more influential caste in the developed world than had ever been the case before. The export of heavy industry to the former Third World, the expansion of welfare states, and the growth in the service industries all reduced the power of the sage-technocrat among the professional middle classes. The old hierarchies survived in many places—largely among technicians and managers in the corporate world—but elsewhere, organizations became flatter, and the values of their professionals had to change. The new "creative" professionals had to interact with people (clients, patients, or students) rather than with machines and organizations, and they could demand more freedom from managerial decrees. Their everyday work therefore reinforced the lessons they had learned in their liberal arts courses: the value of communication, self-expression, artisanal autonomy, and tolerance.[29]

This new caste was the ideal ally for the soft merchant. Both hated the whiz-kid bureaucrat, and each found much it could admire in the other. The creative enjoyed the freedoms brought by consumer society, while businesspeople recast themselves as bohemian creatives; a 2007 advertisement for the *Financial Times* even celebrated the British serial entrepreneur Richard Branson as a reincarnated Che Guevara, an example of the "business revolutionary."

Of course, the new alliance had its tensions when it came to the role of the market economy. The "creative" professionals (doctors, teachers, and social workers in the public sector) were more skeptical of markets than were soft merchants, who were more likely to be found among educated professionals in the private sector—such as lawyers or accountants—who had more respect for market disciplines. The creatives therefore became the stalwarts of the culturally liberal but market-skeptical (though not anti-market) "New Left"—the European Greens, the American Rainbow Coalition Democrats, and the British Lib-Dems.[30] Soft merchants, meanwhile, populated European "liberal" parties such as the German Free Democrats, the American "New Democrats," and British "New Labour"—as well as the center of some conservative parties.

The creatives and the soft merchants were often willing to overlook their differences. Prizing individual autonomy and cultural freedoms over economic equality, the romantic sage-creatives found they had more in common with the cosmopolitan soft merchant than with the egalitarian worker. And now that the culturally conservative 1980s hard merchant was no longer in the ascendant, it seemed to these new romantics that it was not (as they had thought in the 1960s) the worker or the Third World peasant who was the real bearer of the politics they craved, but the freewheeling, entrepreneurial merchant. The ethnic and gender hierarchies tolerated by the Whiz Kids of the 1950s and '60s and defended by the hard merchants of the 1980s could now be consigned to the bad old days of McNamara. Meanwhile, the warrior's love of social discipline, hierarchy, and occasional violence was condemned, by the world's rulers at least, as relics of an old "totalitarian" past.

These changes had their effect on the politics of the developed world.[31] For much of the twentieth century, the main political battle lines had been drawn on questions of economic equality, between a market-skeptical left and a pro-market right. With the rise of the "sixties people" and the reaction against them by conservatives who prized social discipline and traditional values, cultural issues and identity politics had become much more important.[32] Electorates now came to be divided into four broad groups: the culturally liberal and market-skeptical "New Left"; a more economically egalitarian "Old Left" that was less interested in these cultural issues; the culturally liberal, pro-market soft merchant; and the more culturally conservative hard merchant (more common among small businesspeople and white-collar employees in the corporate sector).

The old socialist alliance between sage and worker, forged in the nineteenth century and committed to economic equality, was therefore withering, just as the industrial working class was declining.

One extreme response to this cosmopolitanism came from the radical nationalist right—a warriorish, authoritarian, and hierarchical movement that attracted small businesspeople as well as a marginalized working class. But in the 1980s, even they had to make concessions to the merchant, rejecting the suspicion of markets common among the Fascists and Nazis of the 1930s. Among the most successful of these right-wing parties were those that could boast charismatic leaders, like the flamboyant Dutch ex-Marxist Pim Fortuyn and Jörg Haider, the son of a Nazi shoemaker who became head of the Austrian Freedom Party and joined the governing coalition in 2000. But the radical right began to do well everywhere—from the French National Front to the Scandinavian Progress parties. These parties now constituted one of the few political forces available to channel resentment against Davos Man and the complacent, globalized elite he represented; but they were also pragmatic and "modern" enough to understand the importance of markets.[33] Unlike their Fascist forebears, they had clearly subordinated the warrior to the hard merchant.

The merchant's enemies therefore presented few dangers. For many groups, merchant rule seemed both moral and exciting. Meanwhile, soft-merchant qualities—tolerance, networking, connectivity, and the ability to "sell" oneself, combined with bohemian creativity—became increasingly fashionable among all castes. In 2008, a survey asking British parents which role models (outside the family) their children should follow was topped by Richard Branson (beating Nelson Mandela and well ahead of Jesus Christ).[34]

The high point of merchant rule came in the late 1990s. "Third Way" governments were in power in Bill Clinton's United States and Tony Blair's Britain, and they seemed to have struck a balance between markets and welfare. Moreover, the American economy seemed in vibrant good health, posting major productivity increases in the new high-tech industries. The IMF and the World Bank spread the "Washington Consensus" with evangelical fervor on all continents, just as the "money doctors" had in the 1920s, and their recipes had some similarities: small states, privatization, budget discipline, and liberalization of financial flows. The main specter at the feast was the world's deteriorating ecology, but the merchant was convinced that it could be solved with market fixes—such as the 1997 Kyoto Protocol's use of traded carbon allowances. Otherwise, naysayers were largely ignored.

There were signs that not all was well. The Asian and Russian financial crises of 1997–98 were highly reminiscent of the 1930s. Gold-standard-style fixed, or effectively fixed, exchange rates, combined with financial liberalization, brought floods of foreign capital, speculative bubbles, and sudden collapse. Even more serious was the Japanese implosion of the early 1990s. The government, following the 1980s fashion of financial deregulation, allowed banks to fuel a massive property bubble, which then burst; investment collapsed, and the economy has still not recovered.[35] It did not take long for the resurgent merchant to destroy the successes of the post-1945 caste compromise. However, the Three Marketeers and their cheerleaders in Washington refused to accept that these disasters had anything to do with the merchant; it was the fault of false, corrupt merchants—"crony capitalists," as Larry Summers described them—doing deals with local politicians.[36] The merchant continued to control the main international financial institutions, such as the IMF and the banks, and with them the brain and nervous system of the international economy.

The merchant also seemed to be winning over the warrior. Certainly the United States was intervening in wars throughout the world—a Thor striking down its enemies with high-tech thunderbolts in Yugoslavia, Somalia, and Iraq. Also, the American military remained influential and well funded. But this was more like Britain's "light-touch" "gunboat diplomacy" of the mid-nineteenth century than the mass-conscription wars of the Johnson-Nixon era. In the absence of the Soviet threat, *doux commerce,* not militarism, prevailed.

There was, however, one rising power that started to cause Washington anxiety: China. And as it became more economically successful, it began to threaten American supremacy in Asia. Even so, the United States had good reasons to avoid confrontation. For the merchant had forged an important alliance with a once bitter enemy: the heirs of the old Confucian Mandarins in the Chinese Communist Party.

Merchant Mandarins

Amid the discussions on "the creative imperative" at the January 2006 World Economic Forum, one of the keynote speakers at Davos seemed rather out of place: a member of the politburo of the Chinese Communist Party and formerly China's chief state planner, Zeng Peiyan. This was a figure who would not have been welcome fifteen years earlier. His audience, though, had nothing to worry about. For the speech given by the mild-mannered, rather professorial Zeng was a paean to capitalist globalization and China's place in the new market order. Indeed, Zeng, one of the pro-market, so-called Shanghai clique in the Chinese Communist Party, was one of the leaders who was instrumental in forging a crucial alliance between the Chinese sage-technocrats and foreign merchants—both Western and diaspora Chinese. The bargain was a simple one. As chair of the State Planning Commission, he enticed Western firms like General Motors and Volkswagen to the Middle Kingdom with promises of a cheap labor force and high profits.[37] In return he was given Western investment and markets. Ultimately, Zeng hoped, the deal would work in Beijing's favor. After the failure of Maoism, China could finally reverse the humiliations of the colonial past and take its rightful place as a world power.

Zeng, an engineer by training, could be seen as the heir to China's

Confucian bureaucrats, the Mandarins, and was typical of the new Chinese elite. The crisis of Communism in the 1970s and '80s had led to very different outcomes in China and the USSR, for although they were both Communist, strongly anti-merchant regimes, they were not ruled by the same caste alliance, and therefore new generations learned different lessons from their predecessors' failure. While Gorbachev and his supporters were 1960s romantics, reacting against the sage-technocrats and warriors who had dominated the gerontocratic Brezhnev regime, the Chinese Communist reformers, by contrast, were trying to find alternatives to Mao's romantic, anti-bureaucratic Communism, and after his death it was to the sage-technocrat that they turned. Unlike their Soviet counterparts, the Chinese reformers were convinced that democracy would only bring back the instability of the 1960s.

Deng Xiaoping, one of those disgraced as a "bureaucrat" and a "capitalist roader" during the Cultural Revolution, had led the return to sagely order when he assumed the party leadership in 1978. He had already shown his determination to reverse Mao's favoritism toward the working class and ideologically pure "reds" over the educated "experts," by restoring the college examinations that had been abolished under Mao. Now the academically able would rise to the top. A history of Beijing's universities recalled how rapidly the relative status of "reds" and "experts" had changed: the formerly influential "worker-peasant-soldier students were in a sorry situation. They were older and their knowledge base was weak." Meanwhile, "the previously submissive 'stinking' intellectuals were suddenly wearing Western clothes, leather shoes, and gold-rimmed glasses . . . and walked to class in a self-assured and haughty manner."[38] During the Cultural Revolution, educated Chinese had frequently complained that the "body had been placed on top of the head"; now the world had been turned right side up again.[39]

Mao had been perceptive about Deng's "bureaucratic" tendencies; he was also right in suspecting him of "capitalist roader" instincts. The Chinese Communists, including Mao, had always seen Communism as a tool of nationalist ambitions, and when it became clear, in the 1970s, that the neighboring "Asian Tigers"—Taiwan, Singapore, and South Korea—were overtaking them by building state led but capitalistic export economies, they looked to the merchant for help. Deng legalized small businesses, especially in the countryside, and a certain Chinese entrepreneurialism, never entirely stifled by Mao, exploded: by the end of the 1980s, less than 40 percent of national income came from the state sector—similar to levels in France and Italy. Naturally, the old guard of local party bureaucrats and industrial managers objected, as they had in the USSR. But unlike Gorbachev, Deng did not try to fight them; instead, he tried to win them over by giving them a stake in the market reforms, allowing them to set up private firms and profit from them. He was trying to persuade the old Communist sage-technocrats to become more like merchants.

Of course, the market created losers as well as winners—especially the Chinese workers who had benefited from "iron rice bowl" welfarism. The tensions exploded in the social unrest of 1989, brutally suppressed in Tiananmen Square. But the 1980s market was still relatively limited, and Chinese capitalism was fueled by small household and village enterprises in the countryside; a previously poor peasantry therefore grew richer, and growth coexisted with relative equality.[40]

In the early 1990s, however, everything changed. The turbocharged Chinese economic model we know today emerged not in 1978 with the rise of Deng, nor in 1989 with the fall of the Berlin Wall, but in January 1992—in the aftermath of the Soviet collapse. On Christmas Day 1991, the red flag that had flown above the Kremlin for seventy-four years was lowered forever, and that forced the Chinese politburo to accept, finally, that American-led global capitalism was victorious. Deng, who had been obstructed by anti-merchant opposition in the Communist Party since the Tiananmen massacre, pressed his advantage and embarked on his famous "southern tour" to Guangdong Province.[41] There he launched a new model of capitalist development: no longer were village enterprises to be the driving force of growth; rather, China was to rely on giant corporations, based on Western and expatriate Chinese models, capable of competing in world markets. China was the latest, largest, and most formidable country to join the long line of state-led, export-oriented, and nationalistic industrializing countries—from Germany and Japan in the late nineteenth century to the Asian Tigers of the mid-twentieth.

It was Deng's successors—Jiang Zemin and protégés like Zeng Peiyan—who implemented the plan after 1993. Unlike Mao and Deng's generation of leaders, who had spent most of their careers in a militant, underground Communist Party, Jiang's "third" generation had joined in the 1940s and been trained at universities, often as engineers, during the technocratic 1950s.[42] Like the rulers of imperial Germany or Japan, these sage-technocrats decided that China could be a great power only if it copied its Western rivals and built huge, technologically sophisticated industries to compete in export markets. But they were operating in a new world where merchant values were much more dominant than ever before. The third leadership generation, many of whom had made their careers in China's historically commercial Shanghai, therefore made many more concessions to the merchant than had their predecessors, whether the Asian Tigers, Germany, or Japan.

China's hybrid of merchant and sage-technocrat is therefore unique. Power is ultimately in the hands of a sagely Communist Party: it keeps strict control of government appointments and sets regional official targets (such as for GDP growth and tax collection). And this bureaucratic system is justified with reference to the old Confucian ideology of hierarchy and expertise—a statue of Confucius even joined the portrait of Mao in Tiananmen Square in January 2011 (though it was removed four months later). However, the party also expects merchant-type behavior from officials: they receive bonuses of about 30 percent of their salary

for fulfilling their targets,[43] and party leaders and their children are inti-
mately connected with business. Entrepreneurs can become influential
only if they join the Communist Party, and party bosses have a great deal
of influence over major industries—in 2006, 90 percent of China's ultra-
wealthy were the children of high-ranking officials.[44] This merging of
sage-technocrat and merchant explains the high levels of corruption evident in China today.

Beijing's reforms were less sagely than the conventional East Asian
development model in other ways as well. It rejected a centralized,
Beijing-driven model, encouraging China's regions to compete with one
another to grow as quickly as possible, and it relied on foreign investment
and partnerships with Western and Asian multinationals. Wall Street
banks were crucial in advising the Chinese on how to make their companies internationally competitive. As the American financiers Carl Walter
and Fraser Howie put it, "It is not an exaggeration to say that Goldman
Sachs and Morgan Stanley made China's state-owned corporate sector
what it is today."[45]

The Chinese also gave much less power to the warrior than the Germans and Japanese had in the nineteenth century, reflecting the combined influence of Confucian bureaucrat and post-1989 soft merchant. Yet
the People's Liberation Army remains a powerful interest group, and, like
Europeans before the First World War, the Communist leadership argues
that it has to engage in cutthroat Darwinist competition with other
states.[46] This has encouraged a nationalism that erupts occasionally—for
instance, when the Americans bombed the Chinese embassy in Belgrade
in 1999 (accidentally, Washington claims) or when territorial disputes
with Japan come to the fore, as in 2005 and 2012.[47] But the Communist
Party—supported by some of the successful middle classes—is determined to keep a lid on angry nationalism. It is not above the use of a little
saber rattling to appease hard-liners, and it is engaged in the ruthless sup-
pression of Tibetan and Uighur nationalist groups. Its Confucian tech-

nocratic culture, though, favors peaceable *wen* over military *wu*. Also, its whole model of development depends on international trade, and the warrior cannot be allowed to disrupt it.

The new strategy has been extraordinarily successful. Industrial output grew by an astonishing annual rate of 9.3 percent between 1978 and 1993, and then rose to 11 percent between 1993 and 2004;[48] Chinese manufactured goods flooded world markets, helping to destroy much of Western manufacturing industry; and by 2010 forty-four Chinese companies were on the Fortune 500 list of the largest global companies. Much of this growth was in low-tech products, but China was also moving up the value chain and mastering more sophisticated technologies. The country was reversing the humiliations of the nineteenth century. It had learned the lessons of the Charles Addis era: no longer would it submit to Western banks; now it would become a world economic power.

China replaced the United States as the largest car producer in the world. Shanghai became the center of the car industry and operated like a mini–developmental state. Competing successfully with Beijing and other rivals, its well-educated and worldly bureaucrats were particularly effective, offering cheap loans, building infrastructure, educating engineers, and providing a pliant and cheap workforce. All this was irresistible to American, German, and Japanese firms, which were happy to close down their Western factories and deliver technology and know-how to Beijing.[49]

Within a decade China had created a car culture that had taken the United States forty years to achieve. In 1993, China still had only 37,000 private cars, but seven years later 200,000 Chinese cars a year were being sold to private citizens, with another 400,000 going to the state and to companies. As in the United States of the 1950s, cars are important status symbols, and the more elaborate they are, the better—German manufacturers even produce special extra-long cars to appeal to the Chinese market. And with the cars have come a massive road-building program, congestion, and pollution. Moreover, while Chinese car brands have not yet penetrated Western markets, that might be about to change.

The "Chery" (Qirui) might become as common in the West as Chinese toys and clothes are, with similarly catastrophic effects on the car industries of the developed world.[50]

The Chinese Communist Party's willingness to make so many concessions to the merchant may have been disastrous for Western industrialists and workers, but it paid real dividends to others in the West, most notably multinationals and investors; it also boosted the position of the Communist Party, an enriched Chinese middle class, and Chinese workers seeking an escape from rural poverty. It should come as no surprise, therefore, that the Chinese commercial middle classes generally support the Communist regime and have little interest in liberal democracy.[51] However, while apparently politically sustainable, the party's strategy has contributed to serious economic instability—in the world as a whole and potentially in China itself. First, by encouraging regions to compete rather than concentrating investment in a few select enterprises—as was normal in the Asian Tiger countries—Beijing encouraged state-owned companies to overborrow, indulge in wasteful investment, and create excess industrial capacity. Second, the economic strategy was much like the neoliberal one in the West, suppressing workers' wages and permitting grotesque social inequalities (in contrast to the relatively egalitarian Japan and Asian Tigers).[52] Moreover, by neglecting the countryside and suppressing labor unrest there, the party has encouraged mass migration to the cities and given employers a large, cheap, and politically weak urban workforce. Between the mid-1990s and the late 2000s, wages have fallen from 53 percent to 20 percent of GDP, while profits have risen from 19 percent to 31 percent.[53] China has therefore intensified all three major flaws in the post-1979 world economy: too many goods, too few people with the means to consume them, and too much profit available for speculation and bubble lending. Indeed, China has lent much of its surplus (via international banks) to underpaid Western consumers so they can buy Chinese exports, contributing to the dangerous buildup of Western debt.

The Chinese Communists, therefore, were crucial allies in Davos Man's efforts to sustain the unequal, debt-fueled capitalism of the neoliberal era. But not all Chinese leaders were entirely happy about it. In 2002, a so-called populist faction came to power, led by Hu Jintao and Wen Jiabao, who promised a new, more egalitarian course than the one pursued by the more pro-merchant Jiang Zemin and the so-called elitists. They were as technocratic in background as their predecessors, but they came from the poorer interior provinces rather than from Shanghai and the prosperous commercial seaboard. They had greater sympathy for the losers from breakneck industrialization and argued that the Chinese had to rely on higher domestic consumption and not just exports. Their solution was to strengthen the welfare state and introduce minimum wages. But China's export lobby is a powerful one and has successfully blocked any substantial changes that might damage their interests. Moreover, since the excesses of Mao, the Chinese leadership has been a consensual one and remains balanced between provincial "populists" and Shanghai-faction "elitists."

The post-1992 strategy therefore remains in place, and China remains very unequal. Chinese managers, in particular, continue to run their factories with the harshness of their Dickensian forebears. Particularly notorious is Foxconn, a major producer of iPads and iPhones for Apple, whose factories are uncannily reminiscent of the Orwellian dystopia in the *1984* advertisement. Workers often labor for twelve hours a day, six days a week, and are forced to stand at their workstations for so long that their legs swell. Meanwhile, banners on the wall warn, "Work hard on the job today or work hard to find a job tomorrow," and workers who arrive late are expected to write Maoist-style letters of confession and self-criticism. After a great deal of negative publicity, Foxconn raised its wages in February 2012. But in the hypercompetitive world of the merchant—even the most bohemian one—profit and flexibility are still of central importance. As one Apple executive explained, with brutal honesty, "You can either manufacture in comfortable, worker-friendly factories or you can reinvent the product every year, and make it better and faster and cheaper, which requires factories that seem harsh by American standards."[54]

It is no surprise, then, that China is regularly rocked by worker strikes for better conditions and by peasant protests against corrupt officials who sell off their land for development.[55] In 2010, some 180,000 riots, protests, and strikes broke out in China, some of them very violent; in Dongguan in November 2011, police clashed with some seven thousand strikers, and dozens of workers were injured.[56] Rural unrest is easily suppressed, but urban workers, even though very divided, pose more of a threat. Like its nineteenth-century European predecessors, the Chinese working class is developing a workerist culture combined with a militant warriorism, encouraged by close dormitory living. One 2007 strike leaflet at a German-owned factory appealed both to Cultural Revolution Maoism and nationalist sentiment:

> If you want to be a piece of meat on a cutting board or a shameful traitor to the Han [Chinese], then you can sell your body before we get our wage demand! We believe absolutely none of us is this kind of person. . . . Brother and sister . . . employees of the whole factory, for the sake of our own interests, let's unite together. Chairman Mao said: our revolution has not been successful, struggle should continue, insist! Insist . . . and insist.[57]

Chinese workers, many of them migrants from the countryside, are often divided, yet strike waves since 2010 have had some effect, as has a growing labor shortage, and wages have risen. But businesses are determined not to lose their profits or their competitive advantage, and local Communist officials support them. There is, then, a real danger that a global economic downturn will intensify conflict, harden the merchant middle classes, and propel them into the arms of the nationalist warrior.

Unstable Dominion

Davos Man may have considered the Chinese Communists his most useful allies, but he did not pretend they were his closest friends. Geopolitical rivalries and the fundamental differences between the outlooks of American merchants and Chinese sage-technocrats inevitably created tensions. But the leaders of another rising power felt rather more at home on the new magic mountain: the Indians. Zeng Peiyan might have been granted a keynote address at the 2006 forum, but the Indians had a higher status—the Mumbai business oligarch and billionaire Mukesh Ambani was one of four conference co-chairs, alongside Larry Summers. Western leaders felt much more comfortable with the new Indian business elite, partly because of language but also because they were purer merchant types, apparently unaccompanied by any Chinese-style sagely-political alliances.

The Ambanis were members of an old Hindu merchant subcaste (the *banias*), and their puritanical view of life would have been recognizable to the sixteenth-century Banarasi. Mukesh is a vegetarian and a teetotaler, and at one time he rejected the aristocratic display of some of his more luxury-loving competitors—preferring lentils and roti to fancy restaurants, and simple clothes over Western brands. He also had a very different upbringing from the Brahmin officials who now have to kowtow to him. His father had a typically merchant hostility to academic education, and rather than send his sons to school, he employed a private tutor charged with teaching them the practicalities of life. Mukesh did go to Stanford for an MBA, but he was summoned back by his father halfway through the course to take charge of a yarn-spinning enterprise. This might explain why he lacks the presence, confidence, and speaking skills one might expect in such a successful and influential figure.[58]

Mukesh's father, Dhirubhai, began his career as a typical merchant trader in spices and other goods, based in the British-controlled commercial entrepôt of Aden (Yemen). On returning to India in 1958, he set up the Reliance Commercial Corporation, which began in textiles and then diversified into energy and other industries. He was a canny political operator, and Reliance was one of those "insider" businesses that flourished under the state-regulated "license raj" of the 1960s and '70s. But the Ambanis were pleased when the Nehru-Gandhi family showed their remarkable ability to adapt to the zeitgeist yet again. Rajiv, Indira Gandhi's son and successor, rejected both his grandfather's technocratic socialism and his mother's romantic leftism, embracing the free-market ideas that were becoming so popular among his generation. He began to dismantle the license raj beginning in the mid-1980s, but the real change came after his assassination, during the world economic downturn of the early 1990s. Rajiv's successor as Congress leader, Narasimha Rao, responded to a serious debt and currency crisis by cutting a swath through Nehru's regulations, liberating the corporate sector and encouraging foreign investment—a policy that has continued, with some interruptions, to this day.

The Ambanis were major beneficiaries (and Mukesh has become India's richest man), but so too were other big industrialists, many (though not all) of them from the old merchant castes and subcastes, including the Mittals (Marwari subcaste), the Tatas (Parsi), and the Birlas (Marwari).[59] The Indian economy as a whole also did well, posting an average of about 4 percent per capita annual income growth in the 1990s and 2000s, and in the last five years it has ranged between 5.8 percent and 9.7 percent.[60] However, India's type of development has been very different from China's, as would be expected, given their very different societies and caste relations. China, with its powerful sagely-technocratic caste, has been able to coordinate—or bully—other groups and follows the standard export-led industrialization trail blazed by Germany and Japan, with predictable benefits. In India, by contrast, the sages are much weaker, and the coordination needed to develop large-scale, high-tech industries is absent. India, of course, has successful sagely groups that have collaborated with merchants and local politicians—as in the internationally competitive IT sector. But they have not built the infrastructure needed to spread the wealth beyond high-tech enclaves to the poorly educated peasant and working classes.

A good example is "Cyberabad"—a high-tech development built in the 1990s outside the southern city of Hyderabad. Like a traditional Hindu king, the state's chief minister, Chandrababu Naidu (from a Kshatriya "warrior" caste of village headmen), enticed various merchants and sages to his new futuristic hub—foreign and World Bank investors, Indian businessmen, and educated technicians. But he failed to include poor rural groups in his patronage. And when they found out that they would have to pay higher electricity and transportation prices to finance the project, they rioted.[61] This pattern has been repeated throughout India, and the benefits of development have been very unevenly distributed. Inequality increased in the 1990s and 2000s—even more than in China—and poverty reduction has been slow.[62]

The merchant has benefited most from the liberalization of the era, as he has in so many parts of the world; having been subordinate to the politician and civil servant under the license raj, he now has the whip hand and can buy favors from corrupt politicians. However, India's castes[63] are too balanced, its politics too pluralist, and its society too fragmented to allow the merchant to take complete control. Pro-business governments have therefore run up against insuperable opposition in their efforts to liberalize the economy—for instance, their recent failure to open up the Indian retail market to large foreign chains. Meanwhile, much of central India is controlled by Maoist Naxalites, who resist any efforts to "privatize" their land.

Mukesh Ambani's most recent project illustrates this brittle merchant supremacy. In 2010, he completed a twenty-seven-story home in the center of Mumbai, at the cost of more than $1 billion—supposedly the most expensive private house ever built. With three helipads, a six-story parking garage, and a series of hanging gardens, the strangely ugly and unstable-looking skyscraper soars over its neighbors. But even in this most commercial city, it sparked accusations of brashness and insensitivity to India's inequalities. When the time came for the Ambanis to occupy their palatial accommodation, they delayed the move. Some speculated that it violated the principles of the ancient Hindu architectural doctrines, the Vastu Shastra, and that the Ambanis feared it would bring bad luck, but others suggested that they were upset by the accusations of arrogance and were worried the building might be attacked by terrorists.[64] Even in these merchant-dominated times, some things have not changed since the age of Banarasi: Indian merchants who live like kings in lofty palaces attract strong disapproval, and they have to take care not to flaunt their wealth.

India and China were by far the greatest beneficiaries of the Davos era—at least in aggregate. No other region did as well in 1980–2000 compared with the previous twenty-year period, when Bandung-style industrialization prevailed. So while China and India grew by only 1.74 percent annually between 1960 and 1980, compared with 4.86 percent in the last two decades of the twentieth century, the equivalent figures for the rest of the developing world were 2.51 percent and 0.69 percent, and for the industrialized world, 3.27 percent and 1.55 percent.[65] It is therefore no surprise that China's and India's elites have been such enthusiastic participants in the annual Davos jamborees.

Continental Europe's rulers, in contrast, have been rather more ambivalent about the merchant's rise. For they still remember the destructive effects of merchant rule in the 1920s, and many have been determined to hold on to the old Social Democratic and Christian Democratic model of sagely dominance and social compromise. But while some nations—most notably Germany and the Scandinavian countries—succeeded in preserving this model at home, at the level of Brussels and the European Union the merchant made much more headway.[66] As we shall see, Europe's sages did try to forge a Continental "Third Way," but it soon became clear that they had made too many concessions to the mer-

chant—with the disastrous consequences that we are struggling to resolve today.

A Flawed "Third Way"

Jacques Delors, the president of the European Commission between 1985
and 1995, was seen by foreigners as a rather forbidding version of the
typical French mandarin, combining analytical rigor with a certain aristocratic haughtiness. One interviewer described his "usual, impeccable,
elegant self, a burgundy pullover over his shirt and tie, every hair in place
despite a working day which had already lasted 12 hours."[67] He was certainly an austere and workaholic intellectual who believed that politics
was about rigorous analysis, formulating coherent projects, and forcefully
pressing one's case—somebody who had the "will to control everything,"
as one Eurocrat complained.[68] Naturally, his self-confident intellectual-
ism enraged his rather less sagely but equally determined bête noire, Margaret Thatcher, who saw herself as "some kind of resistance fighter in the
mountains that's simply not going to let Big Brother take over [in] Brussels," as the British opposition leader, Neil Kinnock, put it.[69]

To the French, however, Delors did not seem like the typical member
of their administrative elite. He was a good deal more popular than that.
He had not attended one of the *grandes écoles* ("great schools") that produced the *énarques,* nor had he even been to university. He had worked
his way up as a career civil servant through the Bank of France while at-
tending night school;[70] he was a Christian socialist, a rare breed in a
country where the left is largely secular; and he was rather more pro-
market than most socialists. But despite his outsider status, the Socialist
presidential candidate in 1981, François Mitterrand, recruited him as an
economic adviser for his campaign, then appointed him minister of finance when he won.

Delors's job was an unenviable one: he was in charge of rescuing an uncompetitive and indebted France by means of a left-wing socialist program of which he was deeply skeptical—a policy of Keynesian stimulus and state intervention. When, as was inevitable, the international money markets punished the franc, France had a choice: to become a socialist fortress, cutting itself off from the international market, or to capitulate to global finance. In 1983, after two years of socialism, President Mitterrand accepted defeat, and Delors led the retreat, implementing a series of pro-market reforms. For Delors—and indeed for Mitterrand— the lesson was clear: France could not buck the markets in this new finance-dominated order. It was this insight that lay behind Delors's extraordinarily ambitious *grands projets:* the European single market, the European Monetary Union, and its 1999 offspring, the euro.

The French humiliation of 1983 convinced Delors that if his beloved European Social Democratic compromise among sage, merchant, and worker was to survive the onslaught of American-led free-market capitalism, Europe would have to pool its resources; individual nation-states were simply too weak to resist. Europe would have to make serious concessions to the merchant: removing controls on the flow of capital; creating a single market; and ultimately creating a single, fixed currency, to guarantee his investments. But together, European governments would be powerful enough to preserve their welfare states and state-led industrial policies from the power of the international financial markets.[71] This, then, was a European version of the Third Way.[72]

Delors's vision had some appeal to the French: they hoped that the euro would be a more market-oriented version of Bretton Woods, combining the currency stability and trade demanded by the markets with pro-growth policies that would help weaker economies like their own. But instead it became a 1920s-style gold standard—the ultimate merchant-friendly, anti-inflationary straitjacket. And France was one of the main victims.

The euro had that potential from the very beginning: Bretton Woods allowed less successful countries to devalue their currencies and increase exports, while the euro inevitably set the different exchange rates in stone forever, removing the devaluation option. But the euro became a particularly restrictive anti-inflationary institution, because, although originally more French in design, it was hijacked by the Germans.[73]

The German economy was much stronger than all the others in Europe, partly because it had preserved its sagely "coordinated capitalism" more successfully. And as the most powerful European exporters, the Germans had an interest in stable currencies and low inflation—just like the Americans in the 1920s and '40s. But how could weaker countries grow enough to buy German goods if they were locked into this restrictive system? Unfortunately, the Germans chose the disastrous American course of the 1920s rather than the more enlightened and successful one of the 1940s. They insisted that the European Central Bank be based in Frankfurt and follow a rigorous anti-inflationary policy; and they refused to give any help to the weaker economies—whether in Marshall-style aid or regular tax transfers (as happens between richer and poorer regions within nation-states).

While times were good and the world economy was doing well in the mid-2000s, the compromise between Delors and the Germans seemed to be working. The markets loved the euro, banks invested across borders, and trade grew. At the same time, Europe kept its welfare states, and inequality remained much lower than in Britain and the United States.

However, growth was still sluggish, and weaker economies struggled, especially those on Europe's periphery in the Mediterranean South, the Atlantic West, and the post-Communist East. But rather than encouraging these regions to restructure their economies, the euro offered them an easy way out of their difficulties: debt. As in the 1920s, the euro "gold standard" brought back the destabilizing flows of capital and credit—except that this time Germany was one of the "perpetrators" of the loans, rather than the principal "victim." The euro brought excessively low interest rates to the weaker peripheral economies, and deregulated banks took full advantage, piling into Spanish housing and Greek and Italian government debt. But few of these countries had achieved the postwar social compromises that Germans now took for granted, and, like interwar Weimar, they were unable to transform the easy credit into long-term growth. Greece, with its "offshore" business elite and its patron-client politics, was particularly vulnerable. Debt-fueled bubbles were being blown, and a crisis was brewing.

Post-Communist Central Europe was also blighted by debt, even in countries outside the Euro Zone, like Hungary, where thousands are still struggling to pay back mortgages borrowed from foreign banks. But the region has been rather more of a success since the collapse of the early 1990s. In many ways the closest parallel with these countries is China: the fall of Communism in 1989 did not bring a class of merchant entrepreneurs to political or economic power—they were simply too weak. Rather, it provided an opportunity for the sage-technocrats—the old Communist managers and engineers—to free themselves from the workerist past and benefit from the new market opportunities.[74] They became either company owners themselves or managers for the foreign (mainly German) firms looking to invest in the region. These technocrats certainly used their expertise to create a low-cost market economy, but unlike pure merchant entrepreneurs, they knew how to restructure the old plants and coordinate an industrial economy.

However, the fall of Communism had very different effects in Russia and the rest of the former USSR. The Russian sage-technocrat had always been much weaker than the Chinese mandarin and the German- and Austrian-style "official" in Central Europe. And Gorbachev's revolutionary assault on the Soviet state was the final blow. The military had been discredited, and the trade unions had been corrupted by years of subservience to the Communist Party. But there was one caste that could claim to be on the side of history. Paradoxically, it was Russia, where the merchant had always been so feeble and cowed, that now launched the late twentieth century's most radical experiment with business rule.

Oligarchs and "Men of Force"

In 1987, the grand Stalinist buildings of Moscow State University seemed more like a high-security installation than an educational institution. Police guarded the entrance and checked passes with grim-faced thoroughness, and students inviting guests to their rooms had to engage in endless form filling. There were reasons for this suspiciousness: the university building, a massive Stalinist "wedding cake" edifice on the Lenin Hills, had some six thousand rooms, and at a time of acute housing shortage, students were known to sublet or allow friends to squat. Even so, this high-security attitude seemed excessive, and very much the consequence of the military and bureaucratic culture of the Soviet state.

Three years later, however, the atmosphere had changed dramatically. In 1990, the USSR still existed, and there were still police at the gate, but now they could be bribed. And after the Soviet collapse in 1991, they would disappear to supplement their declining salaries, leaving the entrance unguarded. The numbers of people living in the building grew rapidly, and it was not only the rooms that could be had for cash—so could university admission and degrees. Although the university coped without police security, elsewhere it was replaced by new security guards—usually heavily muscled, leather-jacketed, and intimidating. In the absence of the state, Moscow's businesses were clearly recruiting their own protection.

In the course of only four years, a powerful state had collapsed, and with it the warrior, technocratic, and workerist values that had sustained it; the sage-priests of the Communist Party had abandoned their efforts to control what people said and thought, and commerce had penetrated every area of life, including the state, the military, academia, and the media. The evolution of security at Moscow State University was merely one sign of the merchant's complete victory over the warrior. In the security sphere, a new business opportunity was eagerly seized by entrepre-

neurs who began assembling groups of privatized warriors, recruited from
sports clubs or from the police and the KGB.[75] These were the so-called
mafias, who warred over territory like so many medieval freebooters and
blighted Russian urban life in the mid-1990s. In many ways, they were
the modern version of the knights of Cambrai—more commercially
minded, to be sure, but still predators on the rest of society.

More ambitious businessmen soon realized, however, that far greater
riches were to be had by buying political rather than soldierly power. One
of the most able and determined of these was Mikhail Khodorkovsky.
From an early age, Khodorkovsky had understood the close connection
between economics and politics in Russia. Born in 1963 to a family of
engineers, he claims that he was a true devotee of the Communist ideal
and "totally believed that capitalism was decaying."[76] However, as a
Communist Youth League (Komsomol) organizer at his university, he
took advantage of Gorbachev's new policy of allowing semi-private enterprise, and he soon decided to pursue business rather than the academic career he had originally planned. His course was partly determined
by the discrimination he suffered on account of his Jewishness—the
USSR followed the czarist state in enforcing informal quotas on Jews
to prevent their supposedly "unfair" domination of professional life. (A
high proportion of the oligarchs were Jewish.) However, Khodorkovsky
also realized that he possessed in abundance the classic gifts of the
merchant—networking, information gathering, and the ability to spot
profitable opportunities in obscure places. He began his business career
with a brilliant ruse he designed for manipulating the complex financial
system of Soviet scientific research institutes to turn paper assets, which
were not supposed to be spent, into ready cash, thus making profits for
both himself and the institute bosses.[77] Khodorkovsky had no qualms
about the dubious legality of his actions. As he once boasted, "It is possible to find loopholes in every law, and I will use them without an in-
stant of hesitation."[78]

In the process, Khodorkovsky abandoned his old Communist commitments and became a true believer in merchant values, with all the zealousness of the convert. As he recalls, he had become a completely different person, and "if the new Mikhail had met the old one, he would have shot him."[79] Like many others of his age, he saw the new capitalism not only in economic terms but as a cultural revolution, a revolt against a failed older generation. That did not stop him, however, from using his contacts high up in the Komsomol, which enabled him to navigate the "wild capitalism" that had taken hold of President Boris Yeltsin's Russia. By the mid-1990s Khodorkovsky had not only founded his own bank; he had also joined the tiny club of super-tycoons who met regularly in a villa near Moscow State University in the Lenin Hills (now Sparrow Hills). Capitalism was so new that they had not yet managed to define themselves: some used Marxist language to brand their club Bolshoi Kapital ("Big Capital").[80] But their favorite newspaper had a rather more medieval title: *Kommersant,* or *The Merchant.* The general public, however, eschewed both and adopted a more archaic and sinister term to describe them: *oligarkhi*—"oligarchs."

By 1995 the oligarchs had accumulated fabulous wealth, while the remnants of the old Soviet state structures they hated so much were battered beyond repair. The so-called *siloviki,* or "men of force," in the military, the KGB, and the police were particularly affected, but so was the state economic system, devastated first by Gorbachev's reforms of the 1980s and then by harsh neoliberal "shock therapy" in the early 1990s. Thousands of managers and businesspeople had followed Khodorkovsky and "self-privatized" the Russian economy—stripping assets and lodging the profits in shady offshore accounts (Khodorkovsky was one of the most egregious funnelers of capital abroad)[81]—while very little restructuring of the old economy took place, partly because many old Communist managers were still in place and resisted reforms of their decaying enterprises. Meanwhile, a now hopelessly corrupt bureaucracy could no longer collect state taxes, pay wages, or fund pensions. The financial vacuum was filled by the state borrowing short-term money from foreign banks, and by selling off enormously valuable stakes in the economy to the oligarchs for knockdown prices. The state's weakness was shown most clearly in the Russian defeats during the first Chechen War, in 1994 96, and the volatile, depressive, and heavy drinking Boris Yeltsin was a rather too vivid reminder of how low the once mighty Soviet state had fallen.

Many of the new merchant entrepreneurs and their political and intellectual allies saw these extraordinary developments as necessary for achieving progress toward a market, and even a stateless utopia; Ayn Rand would certainly have found herself right at home among the new Russian elites of the 1990s. The rather chilling slogan "Everything that is economically efficient is morally acceptable" became widespread, and the new rich made abundantly clear their utter contempt for the "people worship" of the old Communists.[82] A 1991 quote from the evangelical Larry Summers—typical of the deterministic triumphalism of the era— also made the rounds: "Spread the truth—the laws of economics are like the laws of engineering. One set of laws works everywhere."[83] Russia had fallen prey to a kind of inverted Marxism-Leninism, according to which the bearers of absolute truth and progress—the merchant bourgeoisie— smashed their warrior, worker, and sagely enemies, confident that history, reason, and morality were on their side.[84]

The drawback, of course, was that the merchant's militancy and apparent callousness were alienating the vast majority of the population. The failure to create a properly regulated market economy had reduced vast swaths of Russia's population to penury,[85] and the losers from the reforms quickly found a champion: a revived and now more workerist, warriorish, and nationalist Communist Party under Gennady Zyuganov. Exploiting the widespread hatred of the "Jewish" oligarchs and their supporters in the IMF and Washington, he was riding high in the polls. And even Davos Man, sensing Zyuganov's imminent victory in the 1996 presidential elections, invited him to that year's forum, where he joined the more usual array of Russian oligarchs at the gathering. The sight of

Zyuganov being feted by the commercially minded delegates proved to be a turning point. As the pro-market politician Anatoly Chubais remembered: "I saw many of my good friends, presidents of major American companies, European companies, who were simply dancing round Zyuganov . . . because it was clear that Zyuganov was going to be the future president of Russia. . . . So, this shook me up."[86]

Zyuganov's Davos coronation alarmed the oligarchs, too. One of them, the car-sales and media entrepreneur Boris Berezovsky, immediately began phoning around from his hotel room, trying to assemble an alliance of oligarchs to save Yeltsin. In the so-called Davos Pact, the oligarchs promised to put aside their business differences and use their money—and, crucially, their control of the media—to defeat the resurgent Communists. And they were successful: Yeltsin won by 53.8 percent of the vote to 40.3 percent.

The oligarchs saved Yeltsin, but they could not save the new merchant order. The unreformed, hollowed-out, asset-stripped economy was too weak, and too reliant on debt. And when in August 1998 Wall Street began to worry about Asian indebtedness, Russia suffered in the slipstream. Foreign credit was withdrawn, the ruble collapsed, and Russia had to default. The seven-year experiment with merchant rule was over.

Communist support had soared on the back of the widespread unpopularity of the oligarchs, Yeltsin, and Davos Man. But this revival depended heavily on peasants, workers, and the older generation; Communism just seemed too collectivist and backward-looking to gain overwhelming support among managers, professionals, and younger generations.[87] The trade unions were also weak. And so ultimately it was the warrior—the "power people"—not the workerist Communists, who filled the vacuum. A year after the financial collapse, in August 1999, an Islamist Chechen group launched a major attack on neighboring Dagestan, and Yeltsin, stung by the humiliation, appointed a figure to the premiership who had made his career in the KGB and its successor, the Federal Security Service (FSB): Vladimir Putin. Observers were surprised by the sudden rise of this little-known figure, but if Yeltsin was seeking a fearless pugilist to fight the Chechens, he had certainly found his man.

Major Putin had been the KGB "resident" in Dresden, East Germany, and had absorbed the mixture of warrior and sagely values that permeated that organization. The KGB, like its predecessor the Cheka, saw itself as a type of army, but a peculiarly intellectual type: a fighting force that used its hardheaded analytical abilities to defeat the enemy. Putin's favorite film, a Russian Second World War adventure, *The Shield and the Sword* (1968), illustrated the ideal, with its story of a cool, intelligent Russian with flawless German penetrating SS headquarters in Berlin. The judo-loving, weight-pumping Putin was perhaps rather more macho than this, but he had much in common with the classic type, combining shrewd intelligence, warrior brutishness, and a hard-nosed, unsentimental view of the world. It was these qualities, he believed, that would be essential if he was to rescue the Russian state from the merchant-inflicted chaos of the 1990s. That did not mean the end of the market, but it did require the restoration of state and military power. The "men of force" had replaced the merchants.

Putin's first priority, though, was war and revenge. Only a month after coming to power, a terrorist attack in Russia, blamed on the Chechens but probably organized by Putin himself, gave him an excuse to launch the Second Chechen War. And he pursued it with the crude barrack profanities that have become his trademark: "We'll track [the terrorists] down everywhere. If we catch them in the toilet—excuse the expression—we'll whack them in the shithouse."

Putin's next war was against the oligarchs. His first field of battle was over control of the media, especially TV, which he rightly believed was an essential pillar of state power. The media barons Berezovsky and Vladimir Gusinsky fled into exile, while other oligarchs were firmly informed that they could keep their wealth just so long as they obeyed the state, kept out of politics, and paid their taxes. Mikhail Khodorkovsky thought he could defy Putin and continue to play by the old 1990s rules, donating money to parliamentary deputies in exchange for favors. The result was a standoff between the oligarch and the warrior, both equally strong-willed. Khodorkovsky's businesses were raided and he was accused of tax evasion, but he still refused to leave Russia and give up his energy company, Yukos. Ultimately he was sent to prison, where he languishes to this day, still refusing to acknowledge the supremacy of Putin and the state.

Putin had no qualms about using brutal methods against his opponents—indeed, he reveled in his image as a "man of force." He was the warrior father figure protecting ordinary people against foreign threats and disloyal merchants. The lyrics of the propagandistic dance song "Someone Like Putin" (2002) encapsulated the theme: a woman ditches her boyfriend because he drinks and beats her, and she decides to find someone strong but benign to replace him. As the chorus goes, she wants

> Someone like Putin, full of strength;
> Someone like Putin, who won't be a drunk;
> Someone like Putin, who won't hurt me;
> Someone like Putin, who won't run away.[88]

This message had less appeal to wealthier and more educated parts of the population—both merchants and the heirs of Gorbachev's "sixties people." However, among the majority, hit by the economic collapse of the 1990s, Putin's popularity soared. Most were happy to sacrifice the liberal freedoms of the 1990s for a paternalistic warrior figure who would protect them against destitution and raise their status and that of their country abroad. As one opinion poll of 2010 showed, although a majority of Russians favored "democracy," 72 percent were willing to accept "certain violations of democratic principles and restrictions of personal freedoms" if they were needed to preserve "order" and the "social protection" of the whole population's living standards.[89] It was this appeal that Davos

Man, with his Fukuyaman view of history as a gradual progress toward liberal capitalism and democracy, failed to understand. Putin certainly used intimidation and censorship to impose his rule, but in the post-1998 atmosphere of penury and humiliation, they were largely unnecessary.

Russia, then, was one of the great failures of the post-1979 market revolution; and as in 1930s Germany and the USSR, the instability brought by the implosion of merchant rule was swiftly followed by a victorious return of the warrior. But the merchant did not even achieve this level of penetration in the Middle East. There, continuing tensions over the American presence and Israel, together with deep-rooted internal ethnic, religious, and social divisions, ensured that the warrior remained a permanent and dominant presence in most states, both among the West's allies—from the Gulf monarchies to republican Egypt—and among its nationalist enemies Iran, Iraq, and Syria. Ultimately, those conflicts were to explode around the world and bring the warrior back to power in the United States. However, Middle Eastern instability left Davos Man in a quandary. For, in the interests of oil, he had to support regimes with little sympathy for the merchant values of free markets and liberal democracy. And his efforts to hide that fact led to one of the most embarrassing episodes in the history of Davos: the Gaddafi affair.

Swords of Islam

Zeng Peiyan was not the most surprising figure to be celebrated at the 2006 World Economic Forum. That prize must go to Saif al-Islam ("Sword of Islam") Gaddafi, the son of that revolutionary scourge of the West, Muammar. He was awarded the title of Young Global Leader and remained a member of this exclusive club until he was ignominiously stripped of the honor during the 2011 "Arab Spring."

Saif's appearance was the culmination of a long campaign, on the parts of Libya and Britain, to present the Gaddafi regime as Davos-friendly. Libya had been under sanctions for its alleged involvement in the bombing of the Pan Am flight over Lockerbie in 1988 and was desperate to rejoin the world economy, while Tony Blair's government was eager to take advantage of the business opportunities potentially available in Libya. And when in 2003 Gaddafi gave up his weapons of mass destruction, Blair and Gaddafi insisted that Libya should be seen as a reliable member of the global merchant order—its old warrior past was over.

Saif was central to this image makeover. He was widely presented as a wise reformer and became the darling of the New Labour establishment. Anthony Giddens, the Blairite head of the London School of Economics, even predicted that Libya would become the "Norway of North Africa." In 2002, Saif sought to burnish his reputation as a sagely ally of Davos Man by embarking on a master's degree and then a doctorate at the LSE on "The Role of Civil Society in the Democratization of Global Governance Institutions." His fellow students soon realized that he was not one of them. One remembered that he thought him dim at first but then realized that Saif simply had very different concerns: "While the rest of us were arguing about the ideal theoretical way to run a government, Saif was going to run an actual government. . . . Abstractions were clearly of minimal interest to him." He said little in seminars, but he revealed his true self when, after the first-year exams, he invited his fellow students and professors to a distinctly unacademic celebration:

> Saif threw a party at a posh club in Mayfair. . . . The cast of characters was familiar: classmates and professors whom I'd normally see in utilitarian and well-lit lecture halls. But now they looked as if they'd been placed onto the set of a rap video. Dancing models in miniskirts roamed the area pressing drinks on guests. An Austrian friend and I started ordering shots of Johnnie Walker Blue Label, mainly because it was the most expensive thing we could think of at the time. Things just went downhill from there. I recall trying to talk about my thesis with my 60-year-old advisor while sitting on a circular leather bed.[90]

These environs were, of course, much more in keeping with the princely son of a warrior-king, the tamer of pet tigers and trainer of falcons, than the cramped seminar room was. But Saif's political friends in London did not want to see the reality. During the 2011 rebellions that brought the end of the Gaddafi regime, they were deeply shocked to turn on their TVs and see this expert on global civil society standing on a tank, holding a rifle, and urging his supporters to "kill the rats."

The Libyan debacle has been seen as a typical example of academic naïveté, Tony Blair's lack of principle, and the Gaddafi regime's incorrigible eccentricity. But it tells us rather more about the broader relationship between the merchant-dominated West and a conflict-ridden Middle East, where the warrior still held sway. With the toppling of the apartheid regime in South Africa in 1994, the Middle East remained the one region of the world where the issue of Western empire and anticolonialism continued to divide states from one another, while setting the "Arab Street" against pro-American rulers. It was therefore no surprise that it continued to be a highly militarized area, dominated by strongmen and authoritarian monarchs; the region spent more than any other on the military throughout the 1990s and 2000s (as a proportion of GDP).[91] And while Gaddafi was undoubtedly a particularly flamboyant figure, the Libyan state was much like its neighbors in its combination of military, paternalistic, and bureaucratic politics. So in abandoning anti-Western nationalism and embracing Davos, Gaddafi was merely following the path of the post-Nasser Egyptians and a number of other leaders.

Davos Man, of course, did not relish doing deals with these rulers, but he was determined to keep oil supplies secure and to defend the state of Israel against the challenge of nationalist neighbors. To this end, the Americans supported a number of Arab military regimes—like Egypt— and efforts were made to entice others to defect from the nationalist camp. After the fall of the USSR, Washington had no powerful rivals in the region and could apply more pressure.

The merchant also made some headway, and the United States promoted the "Washington Consensus" of free markets and privatization in the region. After the failures of Bandung-era industrialization, some Middle Eastern elites, like their counterparts in most other parts of the world, were willing to try neoliberal experiments. However, they were not terribly successful, as was the case elsewhere outside of China and India: the Middle East's GDP grew by only 0.15 percent a year between 1980 and 2000, compared with 3.21 percent between 1960 and 1980. Moreover, privatization in countries like Egypt tended to lead to a crony capitalism of oligarchs with connections to the rulers. Marketization also (paradoxically) further entrenched the power of armies, which now became "entrepreneurs" themselves and built powerful army-controlled business enclaves within the economy.[92]

The United States therefore found itself supporting a curious patchwork of authoritarian regimes—pre-1950s monarchs, 1950s Bandung-era regimes, and more radical 1960s figures like Gaddafi—to counter the threat from anti-Western nationalists. However, it merely made the instability worse: to the majority of Middle Eastern populations, the United States and its loyal ally Britain seemed too reminiscent of the old imperialists; they had simply co-opted the nationalists of the anticolonial era to join them. This widespread view, whatever its objective merits, explains the appeal of a new "nationalist" force: political Islam, or "Islamism." And Islamism, unlike its socialist and Marxist-Leninist predecessors, proved highly attractive to many of the region's business communities. Ironically, the Americans' tortuous maneuverings had driven the Middle Eastern merchant into the arms of their nationalist enemy.

The career of Osama bin Laden shows how far the issue of imperialism still poisoned Middle Eastern politics, and how powerful the appeal of warlike resistance was, even among its normally peaceable commercial classes. Bin Laden's father, born in Yemen, had been a poor laborer but managed to build a highly successful construction business by following a classic merchant strategy in an aristocrat-dominated society. He made himself a useful intermediary between foreign investors and the Saudi monarchy, and he also curried favor by lending the royal family money. After this, lucrative contracts were granted to renovate the mosques in the holy places of Mecca and Medina, and it was these projects that made him fabulously rich. His son Osama, born in 1957, was brought up in the pious environment common among Saudi merchants, and he also worked in the family business. But Osama's political attitudes were far more radical than those of his father, as he came of age in the turbulent aftermath of the Arabs' double defeat at the hands of Israel, in 1967 and 1973. This was an era when many young people in the Middle East—particularly of his middle-class background—began to see in puritanical, militant Islam a powerful form of nationalism that could be a real alternative to its failed leftist predecessors of the 1950s and '60s. A student friend from that time recalled him saying, "Unless we, the new generation, change and become stronger and more educated and more dedicated, we will never reclaim Palestine."[93]

It was the Soviet invasion of Afghanistan in 1979 that provoked bin Laden to act on his beliefs and launch a "holy war," or *jihad,* with the support of warriors in the Saudi monarchy. But when a United Nations–authorized force intervened in Kuwait to expel the Iraqi invasion of 1990, he broke with the ruling Saudi aristocrats and vowed to wage war against them and their American protectors. For in permitting foreign boots in the land of the holy places, the Saudis had forfeited all legitimacy as warrior-defenders of Islam.

In the aftermath of the September 11, 2001, terrorist attacks, it became common to see Islamism as a coherent ideology. But it is in fact an extremely broad movement. It can be of the "left," offering a powerful challenge to existing social hierarchies, or of the "right," reinforcing them. Understandably, these contrasting versions of Islamism were taken up by two very different groups: the young urban poor, blighted by bad economic prospects, embraced a populist Islamism; and the pious middle classes, both business and professional, who felt shut out by the neoliberal crony capitalism prevailing in much of the Middle East, preferred a more right-wing, hard-merchant version. This division seriously weakened the movement—most dramatically in Algeria, where the two branches of Islamism fought a civil war between 1992 and 1998. It also helps to explain why the Islamists failed to take power from unpopular regimes in the 1980s and '90s.[94] Yet despite these political failures, conditions were ideal for the growth of the Islamist movements across the Middle East. Low oil prices, sluggish economic growth, youthful populations, government repression, attempts at neoliberal reforms, and a feeling that Arab governments had abased themselves before America and Israel created a vast group of the excluded and angry.

Bin Laden's version of Islamism was a particularly warriorish version, though with elements designed to appeal to a hard-merchant audience. His *Declaration of Jihad Against the Americans Occupying the Land of the Two Holy Places* of 1996 was aimed mainly at the devout middle classes of Saudi Arabia, and pointedly praised the "great merchants" as the leading force of the kingdom.[95] But most of his message evoked a classic warrior code of honor: the soldier of Islam had to fight *jihad* to protect the Muslim community and redress the injustice of "Zionist-crusader" colonialism. Interestingly, bin Laden was even willing to privilege aristocratic ideas of bloodline over a priestly emphasis on Islamic doctrine; as he explained in the part of the *Declaration* addressed to William Cohen, U. S. secretary of defense:

> I'm telling you, William: these young men love death as much as you love life. They have inherited honor, pride, bravery, generosity, sincerity, courage, and a spirit of sacrifice. These things are handed down from father to son, and their steadfastness in combat will show when the confrontation comes, because they inherited these qualities from

their ancestors since the pre-Islamic period, before Islam took root in them.[96]

Bin Laden's soldierly ethos came as no surprise to those who knew him. One of his childhood friends remembered that, despite his calm, pacific manner, "he was a natural leader," enjoyed Bruce Lee's kung fu movies, and loved riding horses.[97] He had gained more confidence by the 2000s, but his character had not changed. As Abu Walid al-Masri, a journalist working for a Taliban newspaper in Afghanistan, put it: "Control of bin Laden was not easy. His gentle disposition hides a wild horse that no one can control, nor can he control himself."[98] Bin Laden was a modern figure who used his knowledge of engineering to build his cave hideouts, but there was more than a touch of the reckless Homeric hero about him.

Bin Laden may have seen himself as a warrior fighting for justice, but after Al Qaeda's terrorist attacks on the United States on 9/11, George W. Bush and his speechwriters interpreted the Islamists very differently: this was a movement of sagely fanatics, rather like the "totalitarians" of the interwar era. As President Bush explained in a speech to Congress and the American people nine days after the attacks:

> We have seen their kind before. They are the heirs of all the murderous ideologies of the 20th century. By sacrificing human life to serve their radical visions—by abandoning every value except the will to power—they follow the path of fascism, and Nazism, and totalitarianism. And they will follow that path all the way, to where it ends: in history's unmarked grave of discarded lies.[99]

Invoking the concept of "totalitarianism" cast little light on the phenomenon of political Islam. But it did allow the Bush administration to reject the idea that Al Qaeda was fighting *for* anything. This had nothing to do with American bases in the Middle East or with the Palestinians; it was simply a group of power-crazed utopians intent on killing people who didn't agree with them. Sagely efforts to understand causes or resolve problems were angrily denounced as a justification of "evil." The only solution was war, and the complete destruction of the enemy.

Jihad, therefore, had brought the wars of the Middle East to the doorstep of the United States, and, predictably, the warrior returned to power in Washington. Samuel Huntington's *Clash of Civilizations* supplanted Fukuyama's *End of History,* and we were all told to hunker down for a decades-long struggle against the Islamic threat.

George W. Bush threw himself into his new warrior role with gusto. Though he had come to power as the son of the colorless East Coast "Brahmin" bureaucrat George H. W. Bush, it soon became clear that his personality was very different from his father's—attributed by some to the influence of swashbuckling aristocratic types on his mother's side, by others to his adopted state of Texas.[100] The more sagely in his administration despaired at his lack of "intellectual curiosity." Richard Clarke, his counterterrorism adviser, remembered his astonishment at the new president's style:

> To be told, frankly, early in the administration, by [national security adviser] Condi Rice and [her deputy] Steve Hadley, you know, Don't give the president a lot of long memos, he's not a big reader—well, shit. I mean, the president of the United States is not a big reader?[101]

Nor was Václav Havel impressed when Bush quipped, "Contrary to my image as a Texan with two guns on my side, I'm more comfortable with a posse."[102] Bush thought he was modeling himself on Ronald Reagan, but he actually had much more in common with a rather more bellicose and ill-starred president—the last real Texan in the White House, Lyndon Johnson.

But for most Americans, President Bush was precisely the type of leader needed at a threatening time. Once under military attack (as 9/11 was regarded), many look to the warrior for protection and willingly embrace his values. Bush's popularity soared, and the phrase "9/11 changed everything" became a cliché. The age of 1990s soft-merchant capitalism, it was widely felt, had passed: frivolous consumption had to yield to a culture of self-sacrifice; the times demanded a "hero," a "decider," not the self-indulgent softness of the pleasure-loving Bill Clinton.

It seemed that the warrior was in the driver's seat for the first time since the early 1980s. Even that endlessly flexible, ideology-light soft merchant Tony Blair sensed the change in mood and embarked on a dramatic style makeover. His adviser Jonathan Powell remembered that, on hearing the news of the attacks, "he realised that things had changed. . . . He really became very steely, very focused."[103] Never the most convincing warrior, Blair nevertheless attempted to reshape himself as Bush's main ally, hilariously aping his cowboy swagger at Camp David summits. But in reality he settled into a more suitable role as Bush's most articulate spokesman, using his diplomatic gifts to temper his master's big-stick machismo.

Predictably, the unfettered rule of the warrior spread conflict, rather than resolving it. This became clear as early as the night of September 11, when Bush, his bellicose secretary of defense, Donald Rumsfeld, his more dovish secretary of state, Colin Powell, and various other officials met to plan a response. Richard Clarke remembers:

> Rumsfeld said, You know, we've got to do Iraq, and everyone looked at him—at least I looked at him and Powell looked at him—like, What the hell are you talking about? And he said—I'll never forget this— There just aren't enough targets in Afghanistan. We need to bomb something else to prove that we're, you know, big and strong and not going to be pushed around by these kind of attacks.[104]

So bizarre was the 2003 invasion of Saddam Hussein's Iraq that bewildered pundits and analysts have been arguing about its true rationale ever since. Marxists blamed oil lust; Bush family watchers detected a son's revenge on "the guy who tried to kill my dad" in a 1993 assassination plot; others—myself included—saw the influence of Francis Fukuyama and a fanatical sagely clique of democracy-spreading neoconservatives. But Clarke's extraordinary testimony shows that we had all failed to understand the main motivations of America's leaders. Bush, Rumsfeld, and Vice President Dick Cheney were operating according to an impeccable warrior logic: in war you have to show who is boss; any weakness and the enemy will be "up on your porch" and raping your wife in your own bed, as Lyndon Johnson had so vividly put it. Most commentators and academics reacted as Clarke and Powell did—with utter astonishment—for according to sagely logic, attacking Iraq simply did not compute. But to the warrior, the invasion seemed perfectly rational—and indeed necessary.

The problem with this warrior logic was that it threatened to bring war without end. Predictably, its brutal amorality reinforced the view in the Middle East that America was an imperialist bully. Washington was now seen as not only buttressing deeply unpopular Middle Eastern regimes but allowing and even encouraging them to torture and repress with impunity; Muslims in Europe became deeply disaffected; and further terrorist attacks, such as on London in July 2005, led governments to become even more security-obsessed, alienating these groups still further. Meanwhile, Washington's cavalier disregard for sagely niceties—like how to build a post-invasion Afghanistan and Iraq—merely intensified the chaos. American military spending almost doubled in real terms between 2001 and 2010, to an annual $698 billion (only a little less than Marshall Aid and the bank bailouts), but it still could not prevail over nationalist insurgencies.[105] Indeed, the warrior trio of Bush, Cheney, and Rumsfeld became bin Laden's biggest recruiting officers.

However, Washington's new Three Musketeers did not displace the old Three Marketeers. For, despite all the hyperbole, the truth was that 9/11 did not change everything. The Al Qaeda threat was vastly exaggerated, and it did not have the organization or depth of support of international Communism in its heyday, nor did it have major state backers like the USSR, Cuba, and China. Iran, Iraq, and Syria had no relations with Al Qaeda; the Afghan Taliban were easily toppled; and only the Pakistani military continued to be a thorn in Washington's side. The defeat of American forces in Iraq did not have major implications for America's worldwide power, and it is unlikely that the imminent withdrawal from Afghanistan will either. And as the wars started going badly, former neoconservative cheerleaders began to criticize the Bush approach, with Francis Fukuyama leading the defections.

The warrior also found it difficult to avoid the fact that American military power still depended on the soft merchant and the consumerist, debt-fueled economy he had built—the deal forged in the 1980s. America was suffering through the post-dot-com-bubble downturn in 2000–2001, and even the bellicose Bush was aware that the shock of the terrorist attacks might undermine the consumption that powered the economy. His steely message of military self-sacrifice was therefore always rather incongruously combined with an exaltation of consumerist hedonism. As he told an audience of airline workers at Chicago's O'Hare Airport a couple of weeks after the attacks:

> When [the terrorists] struck, they wanted to create an atmosphere of fear. And one of the great goals of this nation's war is to restore public confidence in the airline industry. It's to tell the traveling public: Get on board. . . . Get down to Disney World in Florida. Take your families and enjoy life, the way we want it to be enjoyed.[106]

For the first time in history, a visit to Disney World counted as a patriotic act.

Despite the absurdity of Bush's rhetoric, he had little choice, for the

Three Marketeers had left the United States a hollowed-out economy reliant on spending and debt. Bush therefore had no alternative but to restart the cycle of borrowing and spending. After a year or so of anxious soul-searching, the good times began to roll again, despite increasing evidence of imminent disaster.

Nemesis

In 2005, the year before Alan Greenspan's retirement, the annual Federal Reserve conference in Jackson Hole, Wyoming, organized a meeting grandiosely entitled "The Greenspan Era: Lessons for the Future." Most of the papers were sycophantic in their praise of the great Greenspan's wisdom and foresight, but the chief IMF economist, Raghuran Rajan, spoiled the celebratory atmosphere. He warned of the dangers of a "catastrophic meltdown" in the financial markets: the bonus system and the new complexity of financial products, he argued, encouraged financiers to take enormous risks with other people's money without penalizing them if they failed.[107]

Rajan's heresies did not go down well, and Larry Summers leaped to the defense of Greenspan and the financial deregulation he had done so much to encourage. Rajan's speech was Luddite, Summers insisted,[108] and would only give succor to the enemies of progress. He was followed by a procession of colleagues who drove home his point with gladiatorial glee. Rajan, understandably, "felt like an early Christian who had wandered into a convention of half-starved lions," as he later recalled.[109]

He was not alone; others were also telling Greenspan of the dangerous buildup of debt in the American housing market.[110] But the Three Marketeers were determined not to listen—understandably, because they would have been forced to reconsider the free-market model they had been defending since the 1980s. They would have had to relearn the lessons of the 1920s: that trusting private banks to make the most rational investment choices merely brought financial crashes, low investment levels, and debt.

The marketeers, of course, had been right to argue in the 1980s that change could not be resisted: wealthy countries needed to adapt to a new globalized world as heavy industries were moving to the global South, and that involved creating jobs in new service and high-tech sectors. But the merchant's dogmatic refusal to accept a serious degree of sagely coordination—whether at the international or the national level—ultimately led to collapse. Bankers' funneling of capital from American and British industries into the pockets of shareholders and the loss of industrial jobs to Asia were so rapid, there was little time to adapt. And within Britain and the United States, a pared-down state had little interest in coordinating the massive effort needed to invest in new industries and train the workforce. Meanwhile, little effort was made at the international level to control America's borrowing from Asia.

Debt was the inevitable result, for the massive transfer of wealth from ordinary wage earners to rich investors had a major depressive effect on the economy. The 1920s were repeating themselves. The wealthy were investing their cash in high-return financial speculation; they were not spending to keep up demand, nor were they investing enough in job-creating industries.[111]

Inevitably, politicians faced a dilemma: How could they satisfy their electorates when growth was so sluggish? Reagan had solved the problem with military spending and tax cuts, and the result was a massive national debt by the end of the 1980s. But Alan Greenspan, with his hard-merchant suspicion of government spending and hatred of inflation, closed off that escape route in 1993, threatening President Clinton and his treasury secretary, Rubin, with high interest rates unless they brought the deficit down.[112] They obliged, but the problem of low consumption remained.

The solution found was, again, an eerie reprise of the 1920s: the banks stepped into the breach. States certainly played their part in increasing debt levels in many countries, but state debt was also replaced with private debt: American (and British) consumers preserved their living standards, and economic growth more generally, by loading themselves up with debt, encouraged by low interest rates, egged on by deregulated banks, and free of old government controls on borrowing. We might have expected Greenspan to use higher interest rates to prick the bubbles and restrain indebtedness, but he refused: in the new world of hands-off economic policy, he no longer saw it as his job to control private borrowing, so long as national debt and inflation were low. But he also did not want to, as he realized that it would have caused a "severe contraction of economic output with indeterminate consequences," as he put it.[113] The old hard merchant had mellowed with age.

And he was absolutely right: without debt, the 1990s and 2000s would have been decades of recession and falling living standards, not the high tide of neoliberal confidence we all experienced. The economist Graham Turner has used the Oxford Economic Forecasting model to calculate what would have happened between 1997 and 2007 had governments kept the controls on domestic debt they had used in the past (the so-called corset in Britain). His discoveries were shocking. Consumption would have been 20 percent lower;[114] American wages would have been 21.4 percent lower and British wages 12.5 percent lower;[115] inflation would have averaged 0.2 percent in Britain, rather than the actual 1.5 percent (with figures of 0.7 percent and 2.6 percent for the United States), and in both there would have been several years of outright deflation—this would have gripped the economy of the United States for six years, between 2002 and 2007. Both economies would have shrunk, and unemployment would have swelled. We have therefore not been indulging ourselves with our credit cards; we have been staving off a slump.

This extraordinary piece of economic analysis cuts through today's partisan economic debates at a stroke. Since the crash of 2007–8, we

have argued endlessly over who was to blame for the buildup of debt—
was it Greenspan and the hard-merchant Republicans, Gordon Brown
and soft-merchant New Labour, or was it the state's sagely wastefulness,
the banks' merchant greed, or the workers' feckless consumption? But if
we see the bigger picture, it is clear that all of them were powerless before
the real culprit: the post-1970s economic system and the merchant values
that sustained it. Once the system was in place, we all had little choice
but to play by its rules. Governments and central bankers simply had to
allow us to get into debt if they were to keep the economy going at rea-
sonable capacity.[116] Without credit, the neoliberal economic model could
not maintain living standards for the mass of people. But borrowing from
the international money markets is dangerous, for they are capricious and
can rapidly lose confidence—as so many have learned, including, most
tragically, the Germans in 1929.

The gaudy "breaking news" streaming across the TV channels on September 15, 2008, was a rather prosaic herald of a modern apocalypse, but
it was terrifying all the same. Where Marxist broadsides, Soviet rockets,
and suicidal *jihadists* had failed, the merchant's hubris had almost succeeded. The bankers were humbled, and so were the Three Marketeers.
Robert Rubin's Citibank, with debts of $45 billion, had to be rescued by
the government; Larry Summers survived for a time, but his tenure as
President Obama's economics guru was deeply unpopular. It was Greenspan, however, who was the butt of most criticism, and he offered an apol-
ogy of sorts: he had, he admitted, found a "flaw" in his ideology of rational
markets, and it had shocked him, "because I have been going for forty
years or more with very considerable evidence that it was working excep-
tionally well."[117]

If Greenspan had looked back eighty rather than forty years, he might
have had a glimmer of insight into the causes of the crisis. Bankers' greed,
reckless borrowing, and Chinese lending were only symptoms of the disease. In their desperation to escape the crisis of the 1970s, two genera-

tions had elevated the merchant to godlike status. And the world he created was entirely predictable: glittering and tolerant, but beset by social tension and prone to economic implosion.

However, Greenspan's confession was a temporary wobble. He was soon back on the op-ed pages, defending his record and his vision of merchant rule. And the merchant, too, survived. Fortunately, some of the lessons of 1929 were learned. In the immediate aftermath of the crisis, the puritanical, hard-merchant response was defeated—for a time. Austerity was avoided, money was pumped into the economy, and the worst aspects of the crisis were averted. The heirs of the old "Committee That Saved the World," now led by Treasury Secretary Timothy Geithner, expertly saved the system, as their predecessors had done in 1997–98.

Resilience

Many expected that the crisis of merchant rule would bring a decisive swing away from free-market solutions: the state's rescue of the banks would be a decisive blow to merchant influence and would lead seamlessly to a new New Deal. That is not, however, what has happened. The Obama administration appealed to the ghost of Keynes and pursued a program of direct government spending, which has had some success in reducing unemployment. But it was an extremely moderate package that could not hope to fully address the collapse in demand as Americans were forced to pay back debt. Meanwhile, Geithner and the Obama team refused to countenance any serious state controls over the investment banks.[118]

Compared with its European counterparts, however, the American government has been positively courageous. The European Central Bank, like the American Federal Reserve, did keep the show on the road by flooding the economy with money. But European governments have pursued a counterproductive austerity to please international financial markets—and, in the case of the European Union, the German electorate. Paradoxically, given its history as a victim of hard-merchant austerity between the wars, Angela Merkel's Germany is behaving remarkably like Hoover's America, insisting that debt be repaid and the euro "gold standard" be sustained. Predictably, the result has been serious social disorder in parts of indebted Southern Europe. The Germans are fixated on the lessons of the Weimar hyperinflation of 1922–23; the rather more worrying lessons of 1933 seem to have been wholly forgotten.

So why has the 2008 crisis not brought greater change? One reason is that the immediate crisis was overcome so much more quickly than in the 1930s; middle-class Americans do not have to walk past large groups of the homeless in the subway, as they did during the worst years of the Depression. But crucial, too, is the power the merchant has built up since the 1970s. He has vastly greater political, economic, and cultural resources than was the case in the 1920s. He can rely on global networks of merchant-friendly islands and tax havens, to which he threatens to decamp (along with his tax revenues) if he doesn't get his way.[119] He has spent decades penetrating the political arena—especially in the United States, where money is so central to the political process[120]—and his commitment to low taxes, privatization, and deficit reduction has become ideologically dominant. The spread of a flexible, market-oriented private sector since the 1970s has also given him many more allies among the mass of the population—employees in the private sector are much more likely to accept market values than others.[121] The rise of the militantly free-market Tea Party in America is only the most extreme example of this populist support for the merchant.

The crisis of 2008 has unexpectedly even helped the merchant *expand* his global influence and penetrate previously inhospitable regions of the world. While the economic downturn hurt the warriorish Vladimir Putin in Russia and laid the foundations for the 2011–12 liberal demonstrations against his rule, it is in the Middle East, paradoxically, that the merchant's prospects now seem most promising. The ocean of money created to overcome the financial crisis fueled worldwide inflation, and rising food prices united opposition to the rickety militaristic regimes of the region. Muammar Gaddafi was toppled, as were regimes in Tunisia, Yemen, and the pivotal state of Egypt. The victors in recent elections in the region—routinely seen in the West as sinister, potentially totalitarian Islamists—are actually a mixed collection of populist, pro-poor radicals and the pro-merchant Muslim Brotherhood—the largest and best-organized party. Arguably its most influential leader is Khairat al-Shater, a multimillionaire who owns a famous furniture business, and its program is a resolutely free-market one.[122] The Muslim Brotherhood's leaders and supporters are the equivalent of the pious, nonconformist businessmen of nineteenth-century England, not bin Laden–type warriors; and were it not for the United States' support for Israel, they would be Washington's natural ally.

The 2008 crisis has therefore resolved nothing. The West has restored the old pro-merchant world order, but the underlying problems that caused the crisis are still there. Meanwhile, as society frays, the warrior is waiting in the wings.

Epilogue

s Russians reconsidered the foundations of their ailing aristocratic society in the mid-nineteenth century, two books became
particularly influential: Alexander Herzen's *Who Is to Blame?*
(1846) and Nikolai Chernyshevsky's *What Is to Be Done?* (1862). And it
is these two questions that lie at the center of the debate today as we confront the need to fundamentally reassess our social and cultural order.

Unfortunately, there is little agreement on either question. A majority—
possibly even "the 99 percent"—accept that bankers are to blame. But we
do not agree about *why*. Is it because they are *pseudo*-capitalists, forging
cronyish connections so that they can pay themselves far more than their
"real" market worth? Or is it because they are *ultra*-capitalists, imposing
ever harsher market disciplines on the rest of society and raking off their
share of the resulting profits?

Banks must certainly shoulder part of the blame for the recent economic crisis. But this book has argued that more important has been the
pervasive merchant value system that has underpinned their current
power. For more than thirty years, the merchant has been on the offensive. Having first conquered commerce and industry in the Anglo-Saxon
world, he has gradually rolled back the power of other castes, spreading

his value system to virtually every sphere of life—from sports to schools, from TV to music, from welfare to warfare. And he has sought to transform other societies throughout the world, though with only varying levels of success.

In many ways, the merchant's victory was not surprising: by the late 1960s, the postwar sagely caste alliance was clearly failing to adapt to new social and economic conditions, while its cultural rigidity made it incapable of responding to newly vocal groups—women, youth, and ethnic and sexual minorities. The merchant, in contrast, promised an alternative to the militarization of the Cold War era, just as he had in the 1920s. Moreover, he liberated a new post-1960s creative class and broke down old social hierarchies.

However, in the twentieth century, all castes have had a strong tendency to overreach themselves. Violence is necessary in some circumstances—for self-defense or overthrowing unjust regimes—but the disadvantages of excessive warrior power are particularly obvious to us today, whether in the slaughter of the trenches of the First World War, the bloodshed of Nazi-occupied Eastern Europe, or the torture chambers of Abu Ghraib. And even if they do not bring actual violence, warriors can generate a xenophobic, "brothers-in-arms," us-versus-outsider-"them" culture. The sage-technocrat's addiction to established procedure can kill creativity and self-fulfillment, as was so evident in the big, top-down corporations of the postwar era, while his pride in professional expertise can lead to arrogance. And although the communitarian and economically egalitarian worker has rarely achieved power, where he has governed alone he has found it difficult to coordinate a modern economy—as the short-lived workers' councils of post-1918 Europe showed.

The disadvantages of the rule of the merchant, however, are often less apparent, and now, in the wake of the 2008 crisis, may be the moment when people begin to see them more clearly. In compelling everybody, in all spheres of human endeavor, to operate according to his ethos of short-term efficiency and drop-of-a-hat flexibility, the merchant risks destroying the other caste values that are essential to human well-being—whether it is the artisan's and worker's pride in creativity, skill, community, and equality or the sage-technocrat's commitment to long-term, coordinated development. Along with this intolerance for other ways of doing, being, and living, merchant rule brings growing economic insecurity, corrosive inequality, and potential environmental catastrophe.

Yet the merchant is rarely overthrown by revolutions—he is far too pragmatic and adaptable to allow himself to become seriously unpopular, and he has a convenient and persuasive answer to the problem of economic losers: blame the victim. History suggests that merchant rule tends to be defeated by its inner flaws—as happened in 1929.

Its main economic weakness lies in the difficulty of reconciling the merchant ethos with a modern economy. The flip side of the merchant's virtues—his flexibility and sensitivity to the changing culture and needs of society (as consumers)—is an unwillingness to be tied down or to commit capital for the long haul, as is essential for major industrial development or restructuring.[1] He tends to want to keep his options open and his capital liquid for the next deal. This did not matter much in the premodern era, when most of the population worked on the land and was not beholden to merchants. It was not even a serious problem in the British-dominated early-nineteenth-century world, when manufacturing industry did not need large infusions of finance. But since at least the 1880s, industry has required high levels of infrastructure and education for workers, technicians, and managers, and all of those demand long-term investment of various kinds. If investors are allowed to seek the highest short-term profit, they will choose trade and finance over production and jobs; they will liquidate capital invested in industry rather than redeploying it; they will drive wages down or flee rich, liberal democratic countries that pay a living wage to the many, for low-wage regimes that are more willing to deny their workforces rights; and they will resist any attempts to manage world trade and finance, despite dangerous trade imbalances and international debt.

The triple crisis of stagnation, debt, and international trade and financial imbalances that affects us today was therefore the predictable consequence of merchant rule. In the 1970s, when the world economy forged at Bretton Woods was in crisis, the answer was restructuring and investment, driven by a new caste compromise at the national and international levels. But instead, from the 1980s to the 2000s (as in the 1920s before), the merchant attacked his rivals, and his ideology of "efficient markets" and "shareholder capitalism" prevailed. This allowed the banks to funnel resources out of productive investment, to blow speculative bubbles, and also to lend to Westerners to compensate them for falling real incomes. And democratic politicians were only too happy to encourage ever more outlandish forms of debt to finance desperately needed "growth." For in modern capitalist economies, lower growth means greater inequality, more social conflict, and lost elections.

Valhalla, Bretton Woods, Davos . . . Nagarkot?

It is, then, not too difficult to discover who is to blame. But the second question—what is to be done?—is much more challenging. It is clear that austerity is not the answer and that state spending is needed in the short to medium term. But if we are to find long-term solutions to this major crisis, a little bank regulation here, state spending there, and tinkering with schools and universities will not be enough. We need a more fundamental change in both values and power relations.

Perhaps we could start to think of solutions on a new "magic mountain," an alternative resort to merchant Davos, violent Valhalla, and technocratic Bretton Woods. The stunning Nepalese Himalayan hill station of Nagarkot would serve well, as it is close to both the Indian and Chinese borders and so to the new dynamos of economic power.

So what would Nagarkot Man and Woman do? This short book cannot hope to go into any detail, but my analysis suggests a few broad principles. Nagarkot would start by asking how to fulfill both requirements of a successful caste order: delivering economic prosperity and satisfying prevailing values of equality and social justice. This would require that the merchant, hard and soft, be reined in, and the worker (egalitarian and artisanal) and sage (technocratic and creative) be given greater influence in our society.

As far as the economy is concerned, we have to accept more sage-technocratic power, though without the rigid and centralized system of the Social Democratic era. Complex, globalized economies require coordination, and as Marx and the post-1917 Communist movement realized, that is very difficult to achieve through local democratic councils. Markets have worked best when sage-technocrats have played an important role, as in the "golden age" of the 1950s and '60s. And it is those societies that have largely preserved their "coordinated capitalism"—such as Germany and the Scandinavian countries—that have weathered recent economic storms most successfully. Meanwhile, in the developing world, sagely Confucian traditions have contributed to China's phenomenal growth, just as they underpinned the success of the Asian Tigers and Meiji Japan before them. It is no surprise that "Anglo-Saxon" countries, with their historical vulnerability to merchant domination, have done much less well.

State involvement and sagely coordination remain as important for the "knowledge economy" today as they were for the old industrial order; indeed, it was Cold War collaboration among universities, governments, and businesses that originally created the computer technologies that have revolutionized our lives. But the state's role cannot be just an economic one; it has to be social as well. High-tech firms cannot offer the numbers of jobs that the old industries did: having uprooted much of the population from the countryside during the industrial revolution, the merchant is now unable to sustain them.[2] The harder members of the caste want to limit the state's responsibility for the unemployed, but that is a recipe for mass suffering and social crisis. Technological change therefore compels us to accept more state involvement in the economy—in the form of training, education, and welfare, as well as industrial policy—not less.

Finance—the citadel of merchant power—would have to be at the heart of any reform: the past three decades have shown that we cannot trust banks, unfettered, to be the allocators of society's wealth; without considerable state intervention, banks and their shareholders will not make costly long-term investments in new technologies. The state itself needs to regain the confidence lost in the crises of the 1960s and '70s, though it needs to behave in a less centralized way; for instance, local publicly owned institutions such as mutual savings banks can be much more responsive and accountable to local needs than the state or big banks.

The sage-technocrat in his various forms, from scientist to coordinator, also needs to have more power in business itself. As even free-market economists are beginning to accept, productive economies need to combine two forms of capitalism: the "entrepreneurial" kind, which encourages fleet-footed flexibility, and the "big-firm" type, which drives the effective mass production of innovations—for it is the latter type that provides jobs for most of any society's population.[3] The first needs a dose of the merchant's adaptability, for without it large organizations, whether private or state, can stifle fresh thinking; the second requires a more expert culture of coordination, costly research, and long-term investment.

However, as Keynes realized, it is not enough for the sage to assume greater power at the level of the nation-state. If we are to reap the benefits of international trade and finance, globalization has to be managed.[4] We therefore need much stricter regulation of international capital movements. Even the Bank of England—hardly a center of radical economic thinking—has recently published an alarming prediction that global account imbalances between surplus and deficit countries will continue to rise, from the current 4 percent of world GDP to 8 percent in 2030.

Given that these imbalances were a major cause of the 2008 financial crisis, the Bank of England accepts that much more international financial coordination will be needed if we are to avoid another collapse.[5] Even Nagarkot Man cannot hope for global government, but globalization certainly demands much more cooperation.

The decisive argument for more sagely intervention, though, is the state of the environment. How can the world's forests, water supply, and atmosphere—or, indeed, other species—cope with the population of China, let alone the whole of humanity, consuming resources at the rates Western middle classes currently do, which only a tiny minority of aristocrats could do in the past? A small example of the devastation caused by the economic development of China is the cashmere industry. This soft wool, a product of the finest hairs of the cashmere goat, was once so rare that it changed hands only as part of the diplomacy of Asian kings and aristocrats. But since Deng Xiaoping's market reforms in the late 1970s, cashmere has been transformed into a mass-produced consumer good. Farmers in the northern Chinese grasslands were encouraged to rear millions of goats, and cashmere was then sold in huge quantities to Western consumers: in 2005, 10.5 million sweaters were exported to the United States alone. But allowing the Western middle classes to dress like the aristocrats of old has had a frighteningly high cost. Each cashmere sweater uses the hair of two or three animals, and millions of cashmere goats have eaten the vegetation that protects the topsoil; now much of the northern grasslands is desert, and this is partly why Beijing is increasingly plagued by choking red sandstorms.[6] This is something that Adam Smith could never have predicted: we are clearly facing problems that the merchant, however flexible and pragmatic, cannot solve.

Indeed, the environment is likely to force us to challenge more fundamentally the foundations of the merchant worldview, with its assumption that economic growth, driven by the competitive desire for more and more consumer goods, is a good thing. We might have to set limits to growth in the developed world, and that in turn will require a much greater role for the state. For low growth hits the poor, and without a much more substantial redistribution of wealth, zero growth will lead to even wider inequalities.[7]

However, alongside the sage, the worker—with his values of economic equality—also needs to play a major role if the world economy is to operate successfully. For even if it were possible to transform all economies into export powerhouses like Germany and China, who would buy all this stuff? We would merely create an ever greater glut of manufactured goods, as happened in the 1970s, with the trade wars and dumping that would likely follow. As Keynes realized, it is not just indebted countries, such as the United States and Britain, running trade deficits that destabilize the world economy; exporting countries also have to be stopped from building up massive surpluses, and that might require very radical measures—like moving toward a global minimum wage—which would allow poorly paid Chinese and other workers to buy goods rather than simply making and exporting them.[8] Economic inequality, both within and between nations, is not merely socially unjust and psychologically corrosive;[9] it damages the sustainability of the world economy.

So far, this looks like nothing so much as a return to the Bretton Woods sage/worker alliance, but that is not the solution. There is no need to return to the age of the Whiz Kids, as those nostalgic for the old Social Democratic order sometimes argue. The economy has changed since then, and new technologies demand the autonomy brought by the creative caste—especially in an era of such rapid innovation. In poorer countries, the old top-down model of the Bandung era has been rightly discredited, and it is also economically counterproductive in the industrialized world. This was something Japanese industrialists realized as early as the 1960s, when they raised productivity by involving workers in decision making, which gave them an advantage over their more hierarchical American competitors. Today the success of enterprises like Mondragon

Corporation—now the fourth-largest industrial group in Spain—also shows that worker participation can be combined with high levels of productivity and large-scale organizations.[10] Similarly, in local government, the Brazilian city of Porto Alegre has shown how civic involvement in drawing up city budgets can be made to work in the interests of the whole population and not just the wealthy.[11]

However, the culturally liberal values of the creatives and the egalitarianism of workers are not crucial only for the economy—they are even more important for the legitimacy of Western caste orders. As societies have moved from the old aristocratic world and as new, rising castes have become more insistent on the need for equality, liberal democratic institutions have helped to resolve many of the destructive conflicts of the past. But this type of democracy is not enough. Cross-national surveys suggest that as societies have become richer and moved into the postindustrial world, more people have become culturally liberal, valuing the importance of autonomy and self-expression over hierarchy at work.[12] There is also growing evidence that well-being among all social groups depends to a large extent on autonomy and dignity in the workplace—a fact that the merchant tends to ignore. A 2012 national survey showed that British workers were significantly happier if they had "more responsibility and control over their work, as well as higher incomes."[13] Subordination at work causes a great deal of psychological suffering: a study of the British Civil Service has shown that those on the lower rungs of the hierarchy suffer greater stress, worse health, and significantly diminished life expectancy than those higher up the ladder who have more control over their work.[14] Other research shows that employees with little control in the workplace have a 23 percent higher risk of heart attacks.[15] This all provides a strong argument for more worker and creative-sage influence in all areas of society.[16]

It is sometimes claimed that the new capitalism has solved this problem, and we often hear of new flexible workplaces at companies such as

Google and Facebook. But while some of us have benefited from them, it is a very small elite.[17] Since the 1980s, work has become more regimented for most of us, especially the least privileged; outsourcing and the decline of labor-union power have made many workplaces more authoritarian than they were, and the new managerialism, imposed by accountants and invasive computer systems, is now affecting even the "creative" occupations.[18] Fukuyama's claim that today's model of liberal capitalism is the system best able to provide dignity to all members of society is therefore deeply unconvincing.

This suggests that we need to think much more radically about the way in which work is organized and bring the democratization of the workplace back onto the political agenda. The Communist workers' council movement did not succeed in marrying democracy with productivity, but today, with improvements in technology and experience in how to organize economic democracy, we can be more optimistic; we can begin to challenge the contract established by Henry Ford—authoritarianism in the factory in return for freedom to consume outside of it. Not only would changes in the workplace improve human well-being, but they would also create the conditions for real universalism and equality and undermine the caste differences that divide our societies.

These Nagarkot solutions might seem attractive in theory, but they seem very far away. Is this new caste order ever likely to emerge, given the current disposition of social and geopolitical forces? The situation is not hopeless, but there are serious obstacles. One is the legacy of the era of European aristocracy. International collaboration will be difficult to achieve as long as many in China, the Middle East, and elsewhere believe that they have to redress the inequities of empire—and the behavior of the West, and especially Washington's warriors, often confirms their convictions.

A more significant impediment, though, is the new caste alignment that emerged in the post-1960s West and has spread elsewhere since. The sage/worker alliance, which once fought for economic equality and fettered the merchant, has withered. Instead, a sharp division has emerged between less skilled workers, on the one side—who are primarily interested in economic equality and want some state action to regulate markets—and creatives and soft merchants on the other, who prize cultural over economic equality, share a strong individualism, and are deeply skeptical of a technocratic state. This conflict is often expressed in divisions over globalization and multiculturalism: workers, hit by stagnating incomes and job insecurity, blame liberal elites for neglecting their interests and favoring foreigners; meanwhile, creatives resent any limitations on their freedom. It is no surprise that workers often feel more sympathy for the nationalist and culturally illiberal hard merchant, even though they might disagree on economic issues. This new caste configuration is particularly evident in the West, and especially in the United States. But in poorer countries, too, a globalized, culturally liberal creative and soft-merchant middle class is drifting away from poorer groups, who use nationalism and cultural identity to assert themselves. We can see this in many places—from the continuing support for the authoritarian Putin in provincial and working-class Russia, to the appeal of radical Islamism among the Middle Eastern poor, to the rise of national assertiveness among less privileged urban Chinese.

We therefore face a major dilemma: the market, to be successful, requires more collective action; but too many of us, excessively influenced by merchant and creative values, deny its importance. The two central requirements of a successful caste order—the capacity to deliver economic prosperity and the ability to meet contemporary social ideals—are therefore in tension. The prospects for a Nagarkot-style caste consensus are far from rosy, at least in the medium term.

Even in more collectivist times, it has proved difficult to build sustainable caste orders. The Bretton Woods compromise was possible only after the implosion of merchant rule in 1929 had brought sixteen years of chaos and the deaths of some fifty million people. But even then, intellectual change was not enough on its own; it took the power of labor and the fear of a working-class rebellion to bring Marshall Aid to Europe, and with it a more equitable and effective economic system. An external threat and warrior influence also played a role. The Cold War forced the castes in Western countries to collaborate to confront Communism, just as imperial and national rivalries in the nineteenth century brought merchants and sages into the ruling alliance.

The situation today could not be more different. The entry of millions of new workers into the global labor market has severely weakened organized labor. Communism is no longer seen as a threat, and in much of the world elites are, understandably, not enthusiastic about giving the warrior more power.

Neither has there been much real intellectual or cultural change—at least among elites—despite much pious moralizing about capitalist greed. The current generation of politicians, whether of the soft-merchant left, like much of the American Democratic Party, or the hard-merchant Republican right, came to maturity when the sagely Social Democratic consensus was under siege in the 1970s, and the fall of Communism only reinforced their intense suspicion of the old technocrat/worker alliance. And paradoxically, the immediate crisis of 2008 was, in a sense, overcome too quickly and easily for our long-term good. While there has been some loss of faith in the merchant, we remain much more skeptical of state coordination and collective action than the generation of the 1930s and '40s was. This is why the current cohort of politicians appears so confused and directionless, trying to restore a system that it half accepts is ethically and intellectually bankrupt and yet still regards as inevitable.

So, given this intellectual vacuum and the likelihood of several years of economic stagnation, what can we expect in the future? Historians should be wary of predictions, but if we examine caste relations today, we can see the main forces at work. And the outlook is far from reassuring.

The 1930s Redux?

As the experience of the 1930s should have taught us, debt crises bring social polarization and disputes over who should pay for past mistakes, and in the midst of such conflict, the warrior often reemerges. Perhaps the closest parallels with Weimar Germany are to be found in crisis-ridden Greece today, but the United States is suffering from some of its problems. Indebted to foreigners, adjusting to geopolitical decline, and struggling to create jobs, it is becoming increasingly divided—especially at the level of elites—between the socially liberal sagely creatives like Obama and the more authoritarian hard merchants of the Tea Party right. These take the form of sharp differences in political culture, which are worryingly reminiscent of 1920s Germany, when each town had its nationalist and leftist suburbs, football clubs, and choirs; Americans are also increasingly living in politically homogeneous neighborhoods and watching their own partisan TV news channels.

The warrior is certainly returning in the militant politics of the right. The Tea Party is a classic hard-merchant response to the failures of the soft merchant/creative alliance over the past few decades, though it also has strong nationalistic, warriorish elements, using angry martial language and blaming immigrants for milking the welfare system.[19] Its analysis is a simple one: the mass of hardworking, honest people are the victims of an arrogant, oversophisticated, and technocratic elite, which squanders taxpayers' money on bailed-out bankers, the feckless poor, and sponging immigrants while exporting American jobs to foreigners. Barack Obama—not only a cerebral, sagely type but also a "foreigner" by virtue of his African descent—is their worst nightmare.

The Tea Party has some similarities with the European radical right, though there are also sharp differences. In particular, the European right has become more workerist; it is now much less enamored of the market than it was in the 1990s, and attracts a more blue-collar electorate than before.[20] Understandably, the radical right has benefited from the recent political and economic disarray: the Austrian Freedom Party took 17 percent of the vote in 2008, the French National Front scored some 18 percent in the 2012 presidential elections, the Netherlands Party for Freedom 15.5 percent (in 2010), and the Hungarian Jobbik 16.7 percent (also in 2010).

Warrior values have been much less powerful on the left in the developed world—as one would expect, given the defection of many workers to the right and the influence of creatives who particularly prize peace. Most left-wing protest has been peaceful and democratic—notably the Occupy movement. But more angry conflicts between left and right are possible in some countries. China's working class is likely to remain militant, and Maoist rebels seem set to flourish in India.

In rich countries, too, increasing numbers of people have little stake in the current political and economic system, especially in Southern Europe, where the debt-fueled economies of the 2000s have imploded and youth unemployment has reached stratospheric levels (an extraordinary 46.2 percent in Spain).[21] As Melina, a twenty-one-year-old Greek Communist, explained, "Everybody thought they could be like the richest countries. [But] after the 80s the factories were closing, and the youth of Greece found it had nothing."[22]

Not all of these social tensions, however, will necessarily be expressed in organized politics. Deprived of decent-paying jobs and with low status in a consumer society, the poor in some countries could drift in increasing numbers into the illegal economy, with its own illicit militias. Several countries suffer from the heirs of the warrior band—the drug gang—and the prison population of the United States increased fivefold between 1980 and 2009.[23] The looting of shops in the English urban riots of 2011 was another example of depoliticized protest by people on the margins of a merchant-dominated society, but still imbued with consumerist values.

We are likely to see somewhat more conventional unrest in many parts of the developing world as populations increase, cities swell, and neither merchants nor state sages are able to provide economic security for the mass of the population. Environmental exhaustion and financial volatility will bring more of the food riots that were so important in triggering the Arab Spring.

If social conflicts are likely to intensify as economies stagnate and unemployment soars, so too are 1930s-style trade tensions at the international level. Washington complains about unfair Chinese "dumping" of goods in American markets, while the Chinese angrily accuse the Americans of trying to artificially "maintain its superpower status" and its unjustifiably high living standards.[24]

These frictions are likely to get worse. Leaders of developed countries are under pressure to increase employment through protection, and the Chinese leadership will find it very difficult to change its export-led policies and concentrate on raising living standards at home. The Communist Party's new leadership may even exacerbate tensions. Xi Jinping, who took over as president and party general secretary in 2012, is on the merchant—possibly even the hard-merchant—wing of the Communist Party. A "princeling"—the privileged son of a party official—he is associated with the "elitist," commercial- and export-oriented group, rather than the more sagely and workerist "populist" faction of the current president, Hu Jintao.[25] Behind the bland face presented to foreigners, Xi also seems to be a more assertive figure. Dismissive of Western complaints about China's economic dominance and poor human rights record, he regaled an audience of Chinese expatriates in Mexico in 2009 with a tirade against "a few foreigners, with full stomachs, who have nothing better to do than try to be backseat drivers of our own country's affairs"; "China," he added, "does not export revolution, hunger, poverty, nor does China cause you any headaches. Just what else do you want?"[26]

This type of outburst is, of course, uncommon—at least it is rarely exposed to foreign eyes; China needs good relations with its trading partners, and there are strong reasons for it to avoid a warrior-inflected, nationalist politics. Moreover, China's political leadership continues to be carefully balanced; Xi Jinping's newly appointed prime minister is Li Keqiang, who is from the more egalitarian "populist" faction. Even so, for the first time since the late nineteenth century, the dominant liberal, pro-merchant power, whether Britain or the United States, is facing an economic challenge from a nation pursuing a more sagely, export-led capitalism. Its equivalents in the twentieth century—post-1945 Germany, Japan, and the Asian Tigers—had all been part of the American informal empire, which made tensions much easier to manage. China has greater similarities with Wilhelmine Germany, in that it too has used an export-led capitalism to challenge the dominant merchant-led power. At the moment, China's internal politics do not resemble those of its German predecessor: China's poorer groups, not its middle classes, are the most nationalistic, as we would expect, since they are benefiting less from China's integration into the global economy.[27] It is also highly unlikely that China will become as militaristic as pre-1914 Germany—for reasons of tradition and interest. But that could change if China suffers an economic downturn. And it will certainly be very difficult indeed to reach a Nagarkot-style consensus that would inevitably require China to grow more sustainably, and the United States to make sacrifices on its side, too.

Like 1929, therefore, the year 2008 has set the world on a course toward potential conflict, and the domestic and international forces that brought us the violence of the 1930s and '40s are with us today—albeit still in embryonic form. Unfortunately, most of our rulers today seem as oblivious to those forces as they were then. All we need to do, they believe, is tighten our belts and pay down our debt and we can go back to the 1990s. To which only one response is possible: Dream on.

However, the situation is not hopeless, and there are strong forces resisting a return to the 1930s. The global economy is much more integrated than it was between the wars, and our rulers are determined to avoid its collapse; welfare states exist in developed countries and cushion the economic blows; democratic institutions are more resilient in many countries; Europe, at least, is not beset by major territorial disputes; and as "creative" values have become more widespread, the warrior is much less fashionable a figure than he was in some countries in the aftermath of the First World War.

It is also possible that new caste alliances will bring change over time. As white-collar workers' living standards decline and they increasingly lose autonomy at work, they might have less sympathy with merchant values and embrace a more egalitarian politics, reconciling them to the worker. This is certainly more probable than a significant increase in worker power, and is the most likely route to a remodeled worker/sage alliance. There are indeed some signs, admittedly very mixed, that popular views are changing and our post-1970s love affair with the merchant is cooling. In 2012, support in Britain for higher taxes and a greater role for the state rose, for the first time in a decade (though support for welfare spending fell).[28] It might also be that the generation coming to political maturity in the years since 2008 will be willing to challenge the ideas of its forebears, just as it was the generation that lived through the Depression that finally jettisoned damaging economic orthodoxies after 1945. A Pew Center poll published at the end of 2011 might be a sign of things to come. It showed that a surprisingly large proportion of Americans between the ages of eighteen and twenty-nine have a positive view of the term "socialism" (49 percent), versus 46 percent who had a positive reaction to "capitalism"; this is in contrast to Americans as a whole, and especially to Americans between fifty and sixty-four, for whom the figures are very different (25 percent in favor of "socialism" and 53 percent for "capitalism").[29]

These figures suggest that it may be the 2030s—when this generation begins to reach positions of power—before we undergo the type of rethinking that might produce a more equal, stable, and prosperous order. And we can only hope that is not too late. Social unrest and international competition could well persuade enough people that they need the warrior's protection yet again.

An End to Caste?

The disciples of the German philosopher Georg Hegel famously saw the course of history as both a zigzag and an ascent. Humanity progressed through sharp conflict, followed by reconciliation: one political principle (the revolutionary liberty of 1789, for instance) would generate its "antithesis" (the Jacobin Terror), which in turn would lead to a happy "synthesis" (constitutional liberty). As my narrative of twentieth-century history shows, the Hegelians were certainly right about the zigzags, but they were rather overoptimistic about the synthesis. The real flaw in their argument came from their failure to understand that individuals have limited memories. People do learn from history, but they are most affected by what is happening around them when they are young adults; earlier history seems rather too remote, abstract, and irrelevant. Thus, policy makers in 2008 learned some limited lessons from 1929: that they should not impose austerity at a time of financial crisis. But the experiences most imprinted on their minds were those of the 1970s and '80s, and they are convinced that the power of the state must be constrained at all costs. They find it very difficult to combine these experiences with the lessons that are really relevant—those from the 1920s.

Hegel's "synthesis" is therefore very difficult to achieve, and humanity repeatedly overshoots, zigzagging from one extreme to another. We often see politics through the prism of generational conflict: daughters and sons turn against the castes fashionable when their mothers and fathers were young; future generations then find themselves rediscovering the virtues of those vilified two or three generations earlier.

This book, therefore, has argued that we need to be more aware of our history. Only if we see the broader picture can we escape the limits of our personal experience. The history of the West between the 1880s and the 1970s shows that we can overcome the conflicts of the past and achieve greater caste balance—and with it the economic security and so-cial equality that modern societies demand.

But balancing castes and their values is only a first step; if we are to take equality seriously, we need to challenge the inequalities and divi-sions of caste more fundamentally. This is what the young Marx argued: that "man should be able to do one thing today and another tomorrow, to hunt in the morning, fish in the afternoon, rear cattle in the evening, criticize after dinner . . . without ever becoming hunter, shepherd, fisher-man or critic."[30] As Marx himself recognized in later life, such a radical rejection of specialization and the division of labor is difficult to reconcile with the economic efficiency we need if we are to raise the living stan-dards of the whole of the world's population. But experiments with the democratization of the workplace and the possibility of greater leisure for the whole of society show that steps in the direction of the young Marx's vision are feasible. Given mankind's extraordinary productivity and sci-entific achievements, it may not be too utopian to imagine we can at least *begin* to extricate ourselves from the divisions of caste, and question the choices made by our hunter-gatherer ancestors some twelve thousand years ago.

ACKNOWLEDGMENTS

This is a work of historical synthesis, and many of my debts are to the work of numerous historians in a wide range of areas. I am also extremely grateful to my editor; Virginia Smith, for her detailed reading and invaluable suggestions; to Simon Winder, for his enthusiastic encouragement and incisive comments; to Gill Coleridge, for all her advice and support; to Stephen Whitefield, Rory Macleod, Emile Chabal, and Jonathan Waterlow, for comments on various parts of the text; to Bruce Charlton in New York, Will Palmer in Arizona, and Charlotte Ridings and Sarah Hunt Cooke in London, for all their help with the publication of the book; and to Duncan Abbot, for his help and hospitality. Most of all, my thanks go to Maria Misra, who read several drafts, vastly improved my prose, and made a huge contribution to the development of the ideas and the argument. It is to her that I dedicate the book, with all my love.

APPENDIX

Caste and Power:
The Academic Foundations

Who controls society, and who has the power to drive historical change? The question of power and how it is distributed in society has been at the center of debate ever since Marx propounded his extraordinarily influential theory of "class," and this book is founded on a huge and sophisticated literature by sociologists, historians, and historical sociologists. In particular, it is indebted to the classical sociological tradition of Marx and Weber, the historical sociology of Michael Mann and Charles Tilly, the French cultural sociology of Pierre Bourdieu and Luc Boltanski, and the political sociology of the German American Herbert Kitschelt and others.

There are many different definitions of "power," but I follow Michael Mann in using the term to mean the ability to pursue human goals—of any type— by controlling the environment and dominating or collaborating with other people.[1] For Marx, economics—and specifically ownership of property—was key. Whether somebody had power or not depended on whether or not he owned "the means of production," and in any society economic "classes" of owners confronted classes of those they exploited.[2] In agrarian societies, land produced wealth, so the fundamental social division lay between landowners and peasants; in capitalist societies, capital was primary, and therefore a "bourgeoisie" of capital owners confronted a "proletariat" who owned nothing but their labor.

One of Marx's main critics was the German "father of sociology," Max Weber (1864–1920). He accepted that classes, founded on economic interests, could struggle for power in some places and at some times, but he insisted that economics was not always, or even often, paramount. Men and women do not live by bread alone: they also seek meaning in life. Ideas can be as important as economics, and churches or theologies as central as classes. This Weberian approach has been developed most fully by the historical sociologist Michael Mann, in his now classic work *The Sources of Social Power* (2 vols., 1986 and 1993). For Mann, there are a number of different sources of power, which are both social networks and institutions; they struggle for dominance, and some have more success at certain times than others.[3]

So what are these power networks? Weber identified three: economic (wielded by "classes"), ideological (by "status groups"), and political (by "parties"). Most sociologists, of all stripes, accept this tripartite division. Mann, however, has divided political power into two: civilian political power and military power. And others have added "associational" power, to refer to collective forms of organization used, for instance, by labor unions and civic society organizations.[4]

As Mann argues, the specific power institutions change over time, often substantially. So, for instance, the "political" power exercised by Western nations was once exercised by officials who were members of the ruler's extended household; Weber called them "patrimonial" states. Now states are run by bureaucracies, staffed by experts selected through educational attainments and exams.

Mann's approach, then, combines aspects of both Marx's and Weber's theories. Like Marx, this approach sees human societies as riven by conflicts over power and argues that these, together with more objective developments (economic, technological), drive historical change. But like Weber, it sees economic classes as only one of several important power networks:[5] landowners or capitalists are not all-powerful, and not all conflicts are over economic interests.

This fivefold categorization maps reasonably well onto standard ancient and medieval attempts to analyze society, and it is the root of my "caste" analysis.

Merchants wield economic power; soldiers, military power; sage-priests and sage–holy men, ideological power (the former often justifying the political status quo and the latter often taking a more critical view that transcends political structures). Associational power can be exercised by many groups but is often used by non-elites—that is, peasants and workers—who are weak in hierarchical societies. Meanwhile, political power is wielded at different times by landowner aristocrats and sage-technocrats.

Indeed, as Mann argues, different power networks compete for state power, and the result has been a variety of state forms. As Charles Tilly has shown in his study of the European state between 900 and 1992, a fundamental tension developed between two types of states: those founded on "capital," where rulers gained revenues from taxing trade, and merchants were therefore powerful; and those founded on "coercion," where rulers took "tribute" from peasants, and landowning aristocrats were more dominant.[6] More generally, Mann argues that power networks do not confine themselves to their "own" sphere. So, for instance, state bureaucracies do not merely concern themselves with politics; they can "invade" economic and ideological spheres, too (as they did in the developed world after the Second World War).[7]

Also, power groups rarely rule alone; they forge alliances and are often bound together by means of ideologies or institutional rules and frameworks.

This joint Marxian-Weberian sociological approach is extraordinarily insightful, and it is the foundation for this book. However, there is one weakness: it is overly concerned with social structures and organizations and has too little to say about subjective experience, ideas, and culture. If we are to understand power, we need to appreciate how members of power networks think and behave, and why their values might have a broader appeal beyond their own group—the cultural dominance that the Marxist thinker Antonio Gramsci called "hegemony." As I argue in this book, it is not only the political and economic power of business that explains the influence of free-market economics since the 1970s; it is also its ability to convince elites and electorates that its worldview is the correct one.

It is in order to capture this cultural, subjective side that I have used the term "caste." When ancient Indian writers used the word "caste" (*varna*), they argued that occupational groups had different lifestyles and values, or forms of "proper behavior" (*dharma*); medieval Western European writers similarly believed that the "orders" of society would behave and think differently.

However, "caste" also implies social segmentation and rigid hierarchy (this is how modern sociologists tend to use the term), and modern societies are clearly not "caste societies" in the ancient sense; they are much more mobile and equal, and universalist values are dominant. Yet using the word "caste" does allow us to think about the continued presence of hierarchies, inequalities of power, and differences of value based on occupation in societies today.

The concept of caste has further advantages over other forms of categorization: it is more inclusive than class, incorporating various different types of groups (bureaucrats and priests as well as capitalists and workers); and it includes both cultural outlooks and economic interests. Castes are therefore members of different power networks and institutions, which have particular cultures, encourage particular lifestyles, and give them particular attitudes toward authority, organization, and politics. A member of a priesthood will have a very different lifestyle and values from a soldier in a military unit. But one's position in an organization also matters: an educated professional in the higher reaches of a bureaucracy will have much more autonomy than a clerical worker.

The caste concepts I use—"merchant," sage-technocrat," "soldier," and "worker"—are, of course, very generalized ones, but as "ideal types," to use Weber's term, they are helpful in showing how our occupations can relate to our values. Of course, there is no inevitable correlation between the occupational structure and values, and I am not defending a materialist approach to history; many other factors can affect values, including ideological change.

The French sociologist Pierre Bourdieu made a similar attempt to show how objective social structures are related to views of the world. For Bourdieu, people operate in social networks, or "fields," in which different forms of power operate; so, for instance, they might work in markets, where economic capital is dominant, or in university departments, where "cultural capital" is more important. And each field generates its own set of unexamined assumptions (*doxa*) and practices and dispositions (*habitus*), though a person's *habitus* also emerges from his or her upbringing and education.[8]

For Bourdieu, there were countless fields with their own *doxas,* but one of his former associates, Luc Boltanski, has sought to develop a scheme of dominant moral orders. Along with Laurent Thévenot, he identified six views of the "common good" in the contemporary world, each of which can be related to my caste scheme: "market" (merchant); "inspired" (sage–holy man); "domestic" (paternalistic aristocrat); "fame" (warrior); "civic" (worker); "industrial" (sage-technocrat).[9]

Bourdieu and Thévenot developed their ideas by studying particular communities—whether French academia or industrial management. But does empirical survey research on societies as a whole bear out the argument that people's occupations are related to their worldviews? Recent cross-national research suggests that it does. The sociologist Herbert Kitschelt has argued that occupational experience is crucial to the formation of political attitudes—although he also accepts that gender and life stage have an effect. These, he suggests, are more important in modern Western societies than Marxist "class"—that is, property ownership. (Other sociologists, such as Robert Erikson and John Goldthorpe, have also stressed the importance of occupation, though they have developed different schemes.)[10]

Kitschelt and others argue that two occupational factors are particularly important in the formation of political views. The first is one's relation to the market: people who work in the private sector and are more subject to market forces are likely to have a more pro-market worldview than public sector employees who are not. The other is one's place in job hierarchies and education: those with a high level of education who have a great deal of autonomy in their work—especially those involving "creative" communication or relations with individuals that cannot be subjected to too much managerial control (for instance, copywriters or teachers)—are more likely to have a culturally liberal set of attitudes on issues like multiculturalism, while those who are engaged in technical or administrative work or who deal with clients in a routine way (for instance, retail and public administration) are more subject to hierarchy at work and are less likely to have these attitudes.

Kitschelt therefore suggests that we can relate occupation to the four political positions that dominate modern liberal democratic societies: those in the liberal professions and educated corporate managers are likely to be on the libertarian right (soft merchant in my scheme); small shopkeepers and independent salespeople (the "petite bourgeoisie" for Marxists) are likely to be on the anticultural liberal right (hard merchant); those in administrative or manual public sector jobs are likely to be skeptical of the market; while educated professionals in the public sector tend to vote for the culturally liberal "New Left" (the "creative"). However, as Romain Lachat and Daniel Oesch have argued, these relationships are not always present, and there are strong national differences, suggesting that variations in party systems and other factors have a strong influence.[11]

NOTES

Introduction

1 See, for instance, *Financial Times,* January 10–29, 2012.

2 For an economic-historical view comparing this financial crisis with those of the past, see C. Reinhart and K. Rogoff, *This Time Is Different: Eight Centuries of Financial Folly* (Princeton, N.J.: Princeton University Press, 2009).

3 See, for instance, the work of Francis Fukuyama. Fukuyama is an unusual "Whig historian," in that he is a political philosopher, not a historian; his intellectual roots are Hegelian; and his ideas are inflected with a Nietzschean pessimism about modern liberal societies. But his "universal history," as he calls it, is, at heart, an optimistic, Whiggish one. See Francis Fukuyama, *The End of History and the Last Man* (London: Penguin, 1992), p. xiii.

4 This is the implication of the excellent history of post-1980s finance by Robert Brenner: *The Boom and the Bubble: The US in the World Economy* (London: Verso, 2002).

5 See, for instance, Fukuyama, *The End of History,* pp. 7–11. Fukuyama is strongly influenced by Hegel's emphasis on the central role of ideas in history.

6 Samuel Huntington, *The Clash of Civilizations and the Remaking of World Order* (New York: Simon and Schuster, 1996).

7 Thomas Friedman, *The Lexus and the Olive Tree* (London: HarperCollins, 1999).

8 J. Jensen, P. Sum, and D. Flynn, "Political Orientations and Behavior of Public Employees: A Cross-National Comparison," *Journal of Public Administration Research and Theory,* vol. 19 (2009), pp. 709–30.

9 Herbert Kitschelt, *The Transformation of European Social Democracy* (Cambridge: Cambridge University Press, 1994), pp. 12–18.

10 Marx himself was sometimes ambiguous about the relationship between economics and "consciousness" in defining class, and many Marxist scholars have tried to incor-

porate ideas and culture into the concept. A classic attempt was made by E. P. Thompson in *The Making of the English Working Class* (Harmondsworth: Penguin, 1980).

11 By "caste," therefore, I do not mean *jati*—the thousands of endogamous social groups that dominate Indian politics today, which are also frequently called castes, and are often seen as parts of the larger *varnas*.

12 *Banias* are a *jati* rather than a *varna*.

13 For the cultures of military groups, see Randall Collins, *Violence: A Micro-Sociological Theory* (Princeton, N.J.: Princeton University Press, 2008).

14 This distinction is similar to Michael Mann's division between "immanent" (power-supporting) and "transcendent" (ideological) power. See Michael Mann, *The Sources of Social Power*, vol. 1, *A History of Power from the Beginning to A.D. 1760* (Cambridge: Cambridge University Press, 1986).

15 For this conception of power, see Mann, *Sources of Social Power*, vol. 1, chap. 1.

16 Neil Robinson, "Russian Patrimonial Capitalism and the International Financial Crisis," *Journal of Communist Studies and Transition Politics*, vol. 27 (2011), pp. 434–55.

17 Mann, *Sources of Social Power*, vol. 1, pp. 14–15.

18 This is not to suggest that all existing caste orders succeed in justifying themselves or have "legitimacy" among their populations. As Mann argues, "It is rare to find power that is largely legitimate or largely illegitimate" Ibid., vol. 1, p. 7.

19 The relationship between these occupations and values is discussed by Kitschelt in *Transformation*, chap. 1.

20 On the role of money in American politics, see Jacob Hacker and Paul Pierson, *Winner-Take-All Politics: How Washington Made the Rich Richer—and Turned Its Back on the Middle Class* (New York: Simon and Schuster, 2010), chap. 7.

Chapter 1: Caste Struggles

1 Georges Duby, *The Three Orders: Feudal Society Imagined,* trans. A. Goldhammer (Chicago: University of Chicago Press, 1982), chap. 2.

2 Ibid., pp. 40–41.

3 Duby argues that Gerard was the first to use this terminology, at least in northern France. Ibid., p. 7.

4 Ibid., p. 13.

5 Mann, *The Sources of Social Power*, vol. 1, *A History of Power from the Beginning to A.D. 1760* (Cambridge: Cambridge University Press, 1986), p. 42; Marshall Sahlins, *Stone Age Economics* (London: Tavistock, 1974).

6 J. Coatsworth, "Welfare," *American Historical Review,* vol. 101, no. 1 (1996), p. 2.

7 This account is largely based on David Christian, *Maps of Time: An Introduction to Big History* (Berkeley: University of California Press, 2005), chaps. 8–9.

8 Ibid., p. 375.

9 Hans Nissen, *The Early History of the Ancient Near East, 9000–2000 B.C.* (Chicago: University of Chicago Press, 1988), pp. 80–81.

10 This is argued by Mann in *Sources of Social Power*, vol. 1, chap. 3.

11 Ibid., vol. 1, pp. 132–33.

12 For a definition of "agrarian empire," see Christian, *Maps of Time*, pp. 278–81, 391. See also Peter Bang and Christopher Bayly, eds., *Tributary Empires in Global History* (Basingstoke, U.K.: Macmillan, 2011).

13 Mann, *Sources of Social Power*, vol. 1, pp. 130–31.

14 Ralph Griffith, trans., *The Hymns of the Rigveda* (4 vols.) (Benares, India: E. J. Lazarus and Co., 1889–92), vol. 4, pp. 289–93.

15 Bruce Trigger, *Understanding Early Civilizations* (Cambridge: Cambridge University Press, 2003), p. 508.

16 Anthony Black, "European and Middle Eastern Views," in Jeffrey Denton, ed., *Orders and Hierarchies in Late Medieval and Renaissance Europe* (Basingstoke, U.K.: Macmillan, 1999), p. 29; Derk Bodde, *Chinese Thought, Society and Science: The Intellectual and Social Background of Science and Technology in Pre-modern China* (Honolulu: University of Hawaii Press, 1991), p. 203.

17 William McNeill, *The Pursuit of Power: Technology, Armed Force, and Society Since A.D. 1000* (Chicago: University of Chicago Press, 1982), pp. 14–18.

18 For this form of organization, see Christopher Beckwith, *Empires of the Silk Road: A History of Central Asia from the Bronze Age to the Present* (Princeton, N.J.: Princeton University Press, 2009), pp. 1–28.

19 Cited ibid., p. 13.

20 Dieter Kuhn, *The Age of Confucian Rule: The Song Transformation of China* (Cambridge, Mass.: Harvard University Press, 2009), pp. 88–89.

21 Randall Collins, *Violence: A Micro-Sociological Theory* (Princeton, N.J.: Princeton University Press, 2008), pp. 375–80. This applies to police forces, too. For similar findings in studies of the American police, see Geoffrey Alpert and Roger Dunham, *Understanding Police Use of Force: Officers, Suspects and Reciprocity* (Cambridge: Cambridge University Press, 2004).

22 For the distinction between "protective" and "predatory" bands, see Elizabeth Perry, *Rebels and Revolutionaries in North China, 1845–1945* (Stanford, Calif.: Stanford University Press, 1980), chaps. 1, 3. See also Elizabeth Perry, "Collective Violence in China, 1880–1980," *Theory and Society*, vol. 13 (1984), pp. 439–40; Karen Barkey, *Bandits and Bureaucrats: The Ottoman Route to State Centralization* (Ithaca, N.Y.: Cornell University Press, 1994), chap. 5.

23 Barkey, *Bandits and Bureaucrats*, chap. 6.

24 Bruce Menning, "The Emergence of a Military-Administrative Elite in the Don Cossack Land, 1708–1836," in Walter Pintner and Don Rowney, eds., *Russian Officialdom: The Bureaucratization of Russian Society from the Seventeenth to the Twentieth Century* (Chapel Hill: University of North Carolina Press, 1980), p. 130.

25 Giraut de Bornelh, "Per Solatz Revelhar," cited in Aldo Scaglione, *Knights at Court: Courtliness, Chivalry, and Courtesy from Ottonian Germany to the Italian Renaissance* (Berkeley: University of California Press, 1991), p. 99.

26 This is argued by Eiko Ikegami in *The Taming of the Samurai: Honorific Individualism and the Making of Modern Japan* (Cambridge, Mass.: Harvard University Press, 1995), chap. 2.

27 This is argued by Ikegami in ibid., part 4.

28 Joanna Waley-Cohen, *The Culture of War in China: Empire and the Military Under the Qing Dynasty* (London: I. B. Tauris, 2006), p. 84.

29 Rebecca West, *Black Lamb and Grey Falcon: A Journey Through Yugoslavia,* vol. 1 (New York: Viking Press, 1941), p. 73.

30 Christopher Bayly, *Rulers, Townsmen and Bazaars: North Indian Society in the Age of British Expansion, 1770–1870* (Cambridge: Cambridge University Press, 1983), pp. 59–60.

31 Giuseppe Tomasi di Lampedusa, *The Leopard* (London: David Campbell, 1998), pp. 99, 142–44.

32 See also D. Spring, "An Outsider's View: Alexis de Tocqueville on Aristocratic Society and Politics in 19th-Century England," *Albion,* vol. 12 (1980), p. 129.

33 Di Lampedusa, *The Leopard,* pp. 99–100.

34 Alexis de Tocqueville, *Democracy in America,* trans. H. Reeve (2 vols.) (New York: Knopf, 1945), vol. 1, pp. 218, 279.

35 Robert Bartlett, *The Making of Europe: Conquest, Colonization and Cultural Change, 950–1350* (London: Penguin, 1994), chap. 1.

36 On Brahminic "ritual kingship" and contrasts with "heroic" and "moral" kingship, see Burton Stein, "All the King's *Mana:* Perspectives on Kingship in Medieval South India," in John Richards, ed., *Kingship and Authority in South Asia* (Delhi: Oxford University Press, 1998), pp. 133–88.

37 Valerie Hansen, *The Open Empire: A History of China to 1600* (New York: Norton, 2000), p. 73.

38 For comparisons, see Roy Bin Wong, *China Transformed: Historical Change and the Limits of European Experience* (Ithaca, N.Y.: Cornell University Press, 1997).

39 Benjamin Elman, *A Cultural History of Civil Examinations in Late Imperial China* (Berkeley: University of California Press, 2000), p. 268. Of course, many of these characters were repeating, but whole texts had to be memorized by rote.

40 Ibid., p. 41.

41 See ibid., chaps. 4, 7.

42 Kuhn, *The Age of Confucian Rule,* p. 121.

43 For the complex relations between *wen* and *wu,* see John Fairbank and Merle Goldman, *China: A New History* (Cambridge, Mass.: Harvard University Press, 1998), pp. 108–10. For an argument in favor of greater military influence in Chinese culture, see Nicola Di Cosmo, *Military Culture in Imperial China* (Cambridge, Mass.: Harvard University Press, 2009).

44 Joanna Waley-Cohen, "Militarization of Culture in Eighteenth-Century China," in Di Cosmo, ed., *Military Culture,* chap. 12.

45 For the distinction between old regime and modern officialdom, see Michael Mann, *The Sources of Social Power,* vol. 2, *The Rise of Classes and Nation-States, 1760–1914* (Cambridge: Cambridge University Press, 1993), pp. 444–46.

46 For the debate over the "military revolution" and its periodization, see David Eltis, *The Military Revolution in Sixteenth-Century Europe* (London: I. B. Tauris, 1998), chap. 2.

47 Scaglione, *Knights at Court,* p. 233.

48 Nicholas Henshall, *The Zenith of European Monarchy and Its Elites: The Politics of Culture, 1650–1750* (Basingstoke, U.K.: Macmillan, 2010), p. 65.

49 For the reasons for the emergence of professional bureaucracies in Britain and Prussia and not elsewhere, see Thomas Ertman, *Birth of the Leviathan: Building States and Regimes in Medieval and Early Modern Europe* (Cambridge: Cambridge University Press, 1997), chaps. 4–5.

50 Cited in Christopher Clark, *Iron Kingdom: The Rise and Downfall of Prussia, 1600– 1917* (London: Allen Lane, 2007), p. 240.

51 Cited in John Dardess, *Confucianism and Autocracy: Professional Elites and the Founding of the Ming Dynasty* (Berkeley: University of California Press, 1983), p. 166.

52 Ibid., p. 58.

53 Peter Brown, "The Rise and Function of the Holy Man in Late Antiquity," *Journal of Roman Studies,* vol. 61 (1971), pp. 80–101.

54 Craig A. Evans, "Who Touched Me? Jesus and the Ritually Impure," in Bruce Chilton and Craig A. Evans, eds., *Jesus in Context: Temple, Purity, and Restoration* (Leiden, Netherlands: Brill, 1997), pp. 353–76; M. Pickup, "Matthew's and Mark's Pharisees," in Jacob Neusner and Bruce Chilton, eds., *In Quest of the Historical Pharisees* (Waco, Tex.: Baylor University Press, 2007), pp. 67–113.

55 Richard Gombrich, *Theravada Buddhism: A Social History from Ancient Benares to Modern Columbo* (London: Routledge, 1988), pp. 49–52.

56 Diarmaid MacCulloch, *Reformation: Europe's House Divided, 1490–1700* (London: Allen Lane, 2003), pp. 115–32.

57 Stevan Harrell and Elizabeth Perry, "Syncretic Sects in Chinese Society: An Introduction," *Modern China,* vol. 8 (1982), p. 298; Joseph Esherick, *The Origins of the Boxer Uprising* (Berkeley: University of California Press, 1988), chap. 5.

58 André Wink, *Al-Hind: The Making of the Indo-Islamic World,* vol. 2, *The Slave Kings and the Islamic Conquest, 11th–13th Centuries* (Leiden, Netherlands: Brill, 1997), chap. 11.

59 William Langland, *The Vision of Piers the Plowman,* ed. A. V. C. Schmidt, 2nd ed. (London: Everyman, 1995), p. 96. I have tried to retain the flavor of the original and have translated the Middle English only where it is difficult to understand.

60 J. Farr, *Artisans in Europe, 1300–1914* (Cambridge: Cambridge University Press, 2000), p. 173.

61 S. Justice, *Writing and Rebellion: England in 1381* (Berkeley: University of California Press, 1994), p. 111.

62 For threats to peasants, see Charles Tilly, "Rural Collective Action in Modern Europe" (working paper no. 96, Center for Research on Social Organization, University of Michigan, 1974), pp. 22–25.

63 Bin Wong, *China Transformed,* chap. 4.

64 For the "Brenner Thesis" and the debate surrounding it, see T. Aston, *The Brenner Debate: Agrarian Class Structure and Economic Development in Pre-Industrial Europe* (Cambridge: Cambridge University Press, 1987).

65 On Europe, see Tilly, "Rural Collective Action," pp. 5–7; on China, see Perry, "Collective Violence in China," pp. 427–54; on India, see B. Chaudhuri, *Peasant History of Late Pre-Colonial and Colonial India* (New Delhi: Pearson, 2008), chap. 4.

66 On Chinese guilds, see Christine Moll-Murata, "Chinese Guilds from the Seventeenth to the Twentieth Centuries: An Overview," *International Review of Social History,* vol. 53 (2008), pp. 213–47; on European guilds, see Farr, *Artisans,* pp. 159–64.

67 Vijaya Ramaswamy, "Artisans in Vijayanagar Society," *Indian Social and Economic Review,* vol. 22 (1985), pp. 417–44.

68 Farr, *Artisans,* p. 188.

69 Ibid., p. 174.

70 Tilly, "Rural Collective Action," pp. 20–22; Steve Stern, "New Approaches to the Study of Peasant Rebellion and Consciousness: Implications of the Andean Experience," in Steve Stern, ed., *Resistance, Rebellion and Consciousness in the Andean Peasant World* (Madison: University of Wisconsin Press, 1987), chap. 1.

71 Banarasidas, *Ardhakathanak,* trans. Rohini Chowdhury (New Delhi: Penguin, 2009), pp. 271–73.

72 For the "bazaar" market type, see Clifford Geertz, "The Bazaar Economy: Information and Search in Peasant Marketing," *American Economic Review,* vol. 68 (1978), pp. 28–32; Clifford Geertz, "Suq: The Bazaar Economy in Sefrou," in Clifford Geertz, Hildred Geertz, and Lawrence Rosen, *Meaning and Order in Moroccan Society: Three Essays in Cultural Analysis* (Cambridge: Cambridge University Press, 1979), pp. 123–313.

73 On Jain manners, see David Hardiman, *Feeding the Baniya: Peasants and Usurers in Western India* (New Delhi: Oxford University Press, 2000), p. 71. On "politeness" among English merchants, see Natasha Glaisyer, *The Culture of Commerce in England, 1660–1720* (Woodridge; U.K. Boydell Press, 2006), p. 127.

74 Hardiman, *Feeding the Baniya,* p. 74.

75 Giacomo Todeschini, "Theological Roots of the Medieval/Modern Merchants' Self-Representation," in Margaret Jacob and Christine Secretan, eds., *The Self-Perception of Early Modern Capitalists* (New York: Palgrave Macmillan, 2008), p. 28.

76 Fernand Braudel, *Civilization and Capitalism, 15th–18th Century,* vol. 2, *The Wheels of Commerce* (London: Collins, 1983), p. 405.

77 For the unprofitability of manufacturing and agriculture in Europe before the "industrial revolution," see ibid., vol. 2, chap. 3.

78 Ibid., vol. 2, pp. 316–21, 372–73.

79 Clifford Geertz, *Peddlers and Princes: Social Development and Economic Change in Two Indonesian Towns* (Chicago: University of Chicago Press, 1963), p. 123. The study was a comparison of a Balinese and a Javanese region.

80 Todeschini, "Theological Roots," p. 28.

81 Braudel, *Civilization and Capitalism,* vol. 2, p. 491.

82 Ibid., vol. 2, p. 489.

83 Hardiman, *Feeding the Baniya,* p. 78.

84 Geertz, "Suq," pp. 124–25.

85 For this point, see Christian, *Maps of Time,* pp. 358–59.

86 On Russian merchant education, for instance, see M. V. Briantsev, *Kul'tura Russkogo Kupechestva (Vospitanie i Obrazovanie)* (Moscow: Kursiv, 1999). For medieval merchants in Europe, see Jean Favier, *Gold and Spices: The Rise of Commerce in the Middle Ages* (New York: Holmes and Meier, 1998), chap. 19. However, for overlaps between merchant and more scholarly learning, see D. Harkness, "Accounting for Science: How a Merchant Kept His Books in Elizabethan London," in Jacob and Secretan, eds., *Self-Perception,* pp. 205–28.

87 Banarasidas, *Ardhakathanak,* p. 85.

88 On the attractiveness of Buddhism to merchants, see Gombrich, *Theravada Buddhism,*
    pp. 57–59; Wink, *Al-Hind,* vol. 2, chap. 10. On commerce and morality in Jainism,
    see James Laidlow, *Riches and Renunciation: Religion, Economy and Society Among the
    Jains* (Oxford: Oxford University Press, 1995), pp. 360–64. For the popularity of a
    "puritan" reformed Islam among Java's merchants in the modern era, see Geertz, *Ped-
    dlers and Princes,* pp. 49ff.

89 For the development of Puritanism in the United States from a religion that was skep-
    tical of commerce into one that fully embraced it, see Mark Valeri, *Heavenly Merchan-
    dize: How Religion Shaped Commerce in Puritan America* (Princeton, N.J.: Princeton
    University Press, 2010).

90 On the role of credit, see Braudel, *Civilization and Capitalism,* vol. 2, pp. 384–85.

91 For this concept of *"abru"* see Hardiman, *Feeding the Baniya,* pp. 74–75; on the impor-
    tance of trust in business, see Craig Muldrew, *The Economy of Obligation: The Culture
    of Credit and Social Relations in Early Modern England* (Basingstoke, U.K.: Macmillan,
    1998), p. 2. Jacques Savary, *Le Parfait Négociant,* cited in N. Z. Davis, "Religion and
    Capitalism Once Again?" in Jeremy Adelman and Stephen Aron, eds., *Trading Cul-
    tures: The Worlds of Western Merchants* (Turnhout, Belgium: Brepols, 2001), p. 75.

92 Hardiman, *Feeding the Baniya,* pp. 88ff.

93 Merchant interviewed in 1952–54 by Clifford Geertz; *Peddlers and Princes,* p. 51.

94 I am therefore not arguing that merchants were more "rational" or less interested in
    religion, morality, or honor than other castes. For a challenge to these older views, see
    Adelman and Aron, eds., *Trading Cultures,* pp. 1–6.

95 There is a large literature on the relationship between ethnicity and middleman mi-
    norities. See especially Irwin Rinder, "Strangers in the Land: Social Relations in the
    Status Gap," *Social Problems,* vol. 6 (1958–59), pp. 253–60; Jonathan Turner and
    Edna Bonacich, "Toward a Composite Theory of Middleman Minorities," *Ethnicity,*
    vol. 7 (1980), pp. 144–58; Ernest Gellner, *Nations and Nationalism* (Ithaca, N.Y.: Cor-
    nell University Press, 1983), pp. 102–103. For a more culturalist view of relations be-
    tween host and middleman minorities, see Hillel Kieval, "Middleman Minorities and
    Blood: Is There a Natural Economy of the Ritual Murder Accusation in Europe?" in
    Daniel Chirot and Anthony Reid, eds., *Essential Outsiders: Chinese and Jews in the
    Modern Transformation of Southeast Asia and Central Europe* (Seattle: University of
    Washington Press, 1997), pp. 208–33. There were, of course, also economic advan-
    tages for merchants in being a separate, close-knit community, as they could establish
    relations of trust, essential for credit.

96 Sefer Biala Podlaska, interview by Jack Kugelmass (Tel Aviv, 1961), in Jack Kugelmass,
    "Native Aliens: The Jews of Poland As a Middleman Minority" (PhD dissertation, New
    School for Social Research, 1980), p. 38, cited in Kieval, "Middleman Minorities," p. 215.

97 Ikegami, *The Taming of the Samurai,* pp. 193–94; Johannes Hirschmeier and Tsune-
    hiko Yui, *The Development of Japanese Business, 1600–1973* (Cambridge, Mass.: Har-
    vard University Press, 1975).

98 Raymond de Roover, "The Scholastic Attitude Toward Trade and Entrepreneurship,"
    in Raymond de Roover, *Business, Banking, and Economic Thought in Late Medieval and
    Early Modern Europe* (Chicago: University of Chicago Press, 1974), p. 336.

99 Bodde, *Chinese Thought,* p. 211.

100 Bin Wong, *China Transformed*, pp. 146–47.

101 For the varied attitudes of Islamic traditions, see Max Rodinson, *Islam and Capitalism* (London: Allen Lane, 1974).

102 Hardiman, *Feeding the Baniya*, p. 15.

103 Laura Martin, "The Jew in the Thornbush: German Fairy Tales and Anti-Semitism in the Late Eighteenth and Early Nineteenth Centuries: Musaus, Naubert and the Grimms," in Helen Chambers, ed., *Violence, Culture and Identity: Essays on German and Austrian Literature* (Oxford: Lang, 2005), pp. 123–41.

104 Kenneth Landon, *The Chinese in Thailand* (Oxford: Oxford University Press, 1941), pp. 38–39.

105 Ho-fung Hung, "Agricultural Revolution and Elite Reproduction in Qing China: The Transition to Capitalism Debate Revisited," *American Sociological Review*, vol. 73 (2008), p. 581.

106 Banarasidas, *Ardhakathanak*, p. 107.

107 Charles Tilly, *Capital, Coercion and European States, A.D. 900–1992* (Oxford: Blackwell, 1992), chap. 2.

108 Christian, *Maps of Time*, pp. 326–27, 367–69.

109 Ibid., p. 375.

110 Mark Elvin, *The Pattern of the Chinese Past* (Stanford, Calif.: Stanford University Press, 1973), chaps. 7, 9; Janet Abu-Lughod, *Before European Hegemony: The World System, AD 1250–1350* (Oxford: Oxford University Press, 1989), chap. 10.

111 Thomas Brady, "The Rise of Merchant Empires," in James Tracy, ed., *The Political Economy of Merchant Empires, 1400–1700* (Cambridge: Cambridge University Press, 1991), p. 155.

112 Giorgio Chittolini, "Cities, 'City-States' and Regional States in Italy," in Charles Tilly and Wim Blockmans, eds., *Cities and the Rise of States in Europe, A.D. 1000–1300* (Boulder, Colo.: Westview, 1989), pp. 33–38.

113 For comparisons between commercialization in China and Europe, see Keith Pomeranz, *The Great Divergence: China, Europe and the Making of the Modern World Economy* (Princeton, N.J.: Princeton University Press, 2001); for commercialization and the increasing cohesion of merchants in northern India in the eighteenth century, see Bayly, *Rulers, Townsmen and Bazaars*, pp. 30–34.

114 Braudel, *Civilization and Capitalism*, vol. 2, pp. 316–21.

115 For this definition of capitalism, see Mann, *Sources of Social Power*, vol. 1, pp. 374–75. For the absence of powerful, monopolistic capitalists in China, see Bin Wong, *China Transformed*, pp. 146–47.

116 Bayly, *Rulers, Townsmen and Bazaars*, pp. 171–72. Bayly accepts, though, that merchants exercised their power subtly and could never become rulers. For the stronger argument that there was no difference between India and Western Europe, see Prasannan Parthasarathi, *Why Europe Grew Rich and Asia Did Not: Global Economic Divergence, 1600–1850* (Cambridge: Cambridge University Press, 2011), pp. 66–67. For restrictions on merchant power in China, see Ho-fung Hung, "Agricultural Revolution," pp. 578, 580.

117   Robert Brenner, *Merchants and Revolution: Commercial Change, Political Conflict, and London's Ocverseas Traders, 1550–1653* (London: Verso, 2003), pp. 52–61.

118   Richard Sheldon, "Nicholas Barbon," *Oxford Dictionary of National Biography* (Oxford: Oxford University Press, 2004).

119   William Letwin, *The Origins of Scientific Economics: English Economic Thought, 1660–1776* (London: Routledge, 2003), p. 51.

120   For this point, see Christian, *Maps of Time,* pp. 412–13.

121   I am therefore addressing issue of merchant power, not the thorny question of why Europe became so much richer than the rest of the world. For some, Europe was precociously capitalist from the sixteenth century; for others, it was late-eighteenth-century industrialization and empire that created the "great divergence" between East and West. For those who claim that Europe was more capitalist, see E. L. Jones, *The European Miracle: Economies and Geopolitics in the History of Europe and Asia* (Cambridge: Cambridge University Press, 1981). For the alternative view, see Parthasarathi, *Why Europe Grew Rich;* and Pomeranz, *The Great Divergence.*

122   Christian, *Maps of Time,* 361.

123   Tilly, *Capital, Coercion and European States,* pp. 86–87.

124   Valeri, *Heavenly Merchandize,* p. 7.

125   For this process in England, see Richard Lachmann, *Capitalists in Spite of Themselves: Elite Conflict and Economic Transitions in Early Modern Europe* (New York: Oxford University Press, 2000), pp. 172–76.

126   On Dutch finance, see James Tracy, *The Founding of the Dutch Republic: War Finance and Politics in Holland 1572–1588* (Oxford: Oxford University Press, 2008), parts 3–4.

127   On Dutch military innovation, see McNeill, *The Pursuit of Power,* p. 130.

128   Much of this analysis of the influence of the Dutch model derives from Steven Pincus, *1688: The First Modern Revolution* (New Haven, Conn.: Yale University Press, 2009). See also Jonathan Israel, *Dutch Primacy in World Trade, 1585–1740* (Oxford: Oxford University Press, 1989), p. 384.

129   Nicholas Barbon, *A Discourse of Trade* (1690), cited in Pincus, *1688,* p. 382.

130   For the conflict between these two views of political economy, see Pincus, *1688,* chap. 12.

131   Cited ibid., p. 366.

132   For this process, see John Brewer, *The Sinews of Power: War, Money and the English State, 1688–1783* (London: Routledge, 1989).

133   For the ways in which foreign adventures benefited the British economy, see Patrick O'Brien, "Political Preconditions for the Industrial Revolution," in Patrick O'Brien and Roland Quinault, eds., *The Industrial Revolution and British Society* (Cambridge: Cambridge University Press, 1993), pp. 136–44.

134   For the complex ways in which English law benefited commercial interests in the eighteenth century, see J. Hoppit, "Compulsion, Compensation and Property Rights, 1688–1833," *Past and Present,* vol. 210 (2011), pp. 93–128.

Chapter 2: Iron Fist, Velvet Glove

1 Daniel Defoe, *Robinson Crusoe,* ed. Donald Crowley (Oxford: Oxford University Press, 1983), pp. 171–72.

2 Ibid., pp. 231–37.

3 Maximillian Novak, *Daniel Defoe, Master of Fictions* (Oxford: Oxford University Press, 2001), pp. 28–29.

4 Daniel Defoe, *An Essay on Projects,* ed. Joyce Kennedy, Michael Seidel, and Maximillian Novak (New York: AMS Press, 1999), p. 9; Daniel Defoe, *Defoe's Review,* ed. Arthur Secord (New York: AMS Press, 1938), vol. 5, p. 406; Daniel Defoe, *A Plan of the English Commerce* (Oxford: Oxford University Press, 1927), pp. 67–68.

5 Daniel Defoe, *Religious and Didactic Writings of Daniel Defoe,* ed. W. Owens and P. Furbank (London: Pickering and Chatto, 2007), vol. 7, p. 66.

6 Ibid., p. 111.

7 Ibid., vol. 8, p. 138.

8 Ibid., vol. 7, p. 181.

9 Novak, *Daniel Defoe,* pp. 40–41.

10 Daniel Defoe, *The Complete English Tradesman,* cited in Michael Shinagel, *Daniel Defoe and Middle-Class Gentility* (Cambridge, Mass.: Harvard University Press, 1968), p. 236.

11 Defoe, *A Plan of the English Commerce,* pp. 35–36.

12 Defoe, *Review,* vol. 4, p. 35. Though Defoe was not an advocate of low living standards for the poor and argued that workers had to be paid well if they were to buy consumer goods.

13 Ibid., vol. 4, p. 588.

14 For the ideology of the early American colonists, see David Armitage, *The Ideological Origins of the British Empire* (Cambridge: Cambridge University Press, 2000). On the East India Company, see Robert Travers, "Ideology and British Expansion in Bengal, 1757–72," *Journal of Imperial and Commonwealth History,* vol. 33, no. 1 (2005), pp. 7–27.

15 Nicholas Phillipson, *Adam Smith: An Enlightened Life* (London: Allen Lane, 2010), p. 260.

16 Adam Smith, *Wealth of Nations,* Library of Economics and Liberty (http://www.econlib.org/library/Smith/smMS.html), book 2, chap. 3, pp. 28–36.

17 Emma Rothschild and Amartya Sen, "Adam Smith's Economics," in Knud Haakonssen, *The Cambridge Companion to Adam Smith* (Cambridge: Cambridge University Press, 2006), p. 322.

18 Adam Smith, *Theory of Moral Sentiments,* book 1, section 3, chap. 2, p. 1.

19 Adam Smith, "Lectures on Jurisprudence: Report of 1762–3," in Adam Smith, *Lectures of Jurispridence,* ed. R. Meek, D. Raphael, and P. Stein (Oxford: Oxford University Press, 1978), pp. 340–41; see also Tony Aspromourgos, *The Science of Wealth: Adam Smith and the Framing of Political Economy* (London: Routledge, 2009), pp. 205–12.

20 Smith, *Wealth of Nations,* book 4, chap. 3, p. 307.

21 Ibid.

22 I therefore disagree with those who claim there is no "Adam Smith problem"—an

internal contradiction within Smith's works. This contradiction might not be as crude as was once assumed: clearly Smith saw that the market could be a moral force, and he did not straightforwardly counterpose the "market" to "morality." But he did believe that commercial culture had various drawbacks, and his proposed solution to them—the inculcation of virtue—does not constitute a particularly coherent or well-worked-out program. For this argument, see Ryan Hanley, *Adam Smith and the Character of Virtue* (Cambridge: Cambridge University Press, 2009).

23 Adam Smith, *Theory of Moral Sentiments,* book 1, section 3, chap. 2.

24 For evidence of Smith's pessimism, see Hanley, *Adam Smith,* pp. 31, 36.

25 See Richard Price, *British Society, 1680–1880* (Cambridge: Cambridge University Press, 1999), pp. 319–22.

26 The debate over the degree of change in British economic and social order in the eighteenth and nineteenth centuries is a fierce one. Here I steer a course between older "Whiggish" views that overemphasized the degree of modernity, such as Asa Briggs's *Age of Improvement* (Harlow, U.K.: Longman, 1959), and those "revisionist" works that argued for the persistence of the *"ancien régime,"* such as J. C. D. Clark's *English Society, 1688–1832: Ideology, Social Structure and Political Practice During the Ancien Régime* (Cambridge: Cambridge University Press, 1985). My view is closest to that of Richard Price, in seeing both middle-class and aristocratic forces coexisting within a fundamentally commercial and manufacturing—rather than fully "industrial"—system. See Price, *British Society,* pp. 1–16.

27 See Frank Trentmann, *Free Trade Nation* (Oxford: Oxford University Press, 2008).

28 See Patrick Parrinder, *Nation and Novel: The English Novel from Its Origins to the Present Day* (Oxford: Oxford University Press, 2006), especially chap. 1.

29 Samuel Richardson, *Pamela, or Virtue Rewarded* (London: Penguin, 2003). See Ewha Chung, *Samuel Richardson's New Nation: Paragons of the Domestic Sphere and "Native" Virtue* (New York: P. Lang, 1998), chap. 1; Parrinder, *Nation and Novel,* pp. 93–97; Terry Eagleton, *The Rape of Clarissa: Writing, Sexuality, and Class Struggle in Samuel Richardson* (Minneapolis: University of Minnesota Press, 1982).

30 Price, *British Society,* p. 241.

31 S. D. Smith, *Slavery, Family and Gentry Capitalism in the British Atlantic: The World of the Lascelles, 1648–1834* (Cambridge: Cambridge University Press, 2006), chap. 7; Peter Cain and Anthony Hopkins, *British Imperialism: Innovation and Expansion, 1688–1914* (London: Longman, 1993), p. 68.

32 For the small-scale nature of British enterprise, see Bernard Elbaum and William Lazonick, "An Institutional Perspective on British Decline," in Bernard Elbaum and William Lazonick, *The Decline of the British Economy* (Oxford: Oxford University Press, 1986); Stanley Chapman, *Merchant Enterprise in Britain: From the Industrial Revolution to World War I* (Cambridge: Cambridge University Press, 1992).

33 For this self-image in the British-Indian managing agency houses, see Anna-Maria Misra, *Business, Race and Politics in British India, c. 1860–1960* (Oxford: Oxford University Press, 1998), chap. 1.

34 Chapman, *Merchant Enterprise,* p. 10.

35 For this characterization of the British state, see Price, *British Society,* chaps. 4–5, especially pp. 130, 186.

36 For the culture of these "self-made" entrepreneurs, see Theodore Koditschek, *Class Formation and Urban-Industrial Society: Bradford, 1750–1850* (Cambridge: Cambridge University Press, 1990), chaps. 7–8.

37 Ibid., p. 206.

38 Samuel Smiles, *Self-Help: With Illustrations of Conduct and Perseverance* (London: Murray, 1958), p. xi. For entrepreneurs' attitudes to education, see Koditschek, *Class Formation*, p. 192.

39 Samuel Smiles, *The Lives of the Engineers* (London: The Folio Society, 2006), p. 334.

40 For changes in middle-class views, see Richard Price, *Labour in British Society: An Interpretataive History* (London: Croom Helm, 1986), pp. 59–65.

41 For Bradford workers, see Koditschek, *Class Formation*, pp. 551–65.

42 Samuel Smiles, *Self-Help: With Illustrations of Character and Conduct* (Boston: Ticknor and Fields, 1861), p. 369.

43 For this argument, see Elbaum and Lazonick, "An Institutional Perspective on British Decline."

44 For this relationship between finance and manufacture, see Price, *British Society*, pp. 75–87.

45 Yussuf Cassis, "Businessmen and Bourgeoisie in Western Europe," in Jurgen Kocka and Allan Mitchell, eds., *Bourgeois Society in Nineteenth Century Europe* (Oxford: Oxford University Press, 1993), pp. 114–15.

46 For ideas of "gentlemanliness," see Philip Mason, *The English Gentleman: The Rise and Fall of an Ideal* (London: Pimlico, 1982); Mark Girouard, *The Return to Camelot: Chivalry and the English Gentleman* (New Haven, Conn.: Yale University Press, 1981); Cain and Hopkins, *British Imperialism*, pp. 22–37.

47 Price, *British Society*, pp. 22–39.

48 Price, *Labour*, pp. 73–83.

49 Christopher Bayly, *The Birth of the Modern World, 1780–1914: Global Connections and Comparisons* (Oxford: Blackwell, 2004), pp. 129–30, 135.

50 For "informal empire" in Argentina, see Anthony Hopkins, "Informal Empire: An Alternative View," *Journal of Latin American Studies,* vol. 26 (1994), pp. 469–84.

51 David Washbrook, "Progress and Problems: South Asian Social and Economic History, c. 1720–1860," *Modern Asian Studies,* vol. 22 (1988), pp. 57–96.

52 For Chinese resistance to industrialization, see Wellington Chan, *Merchants, Mandarins and Modern Enterprise in Late Ch'ing China* (Cambridge Mass.: Harvard University Press, 1977); Susan Mann, *Local Merchants and the Chinese Bureaucracy, 1750–1950* (Stanford, Calif.: Stanford University Press, 1987). For Ottoman failures in industrial policy, see Roger Owen, *The Middle East in the World Economy, 1800–1914* (London: I. B. Tauris, 1993), chap. 2. For the effect of British trade policies, see Bayly, *The Birth of the Modern World,* pp. 177–83.

53 Bayly, *The Birth of the Modern World,* p. 182.

54 For the role of the gold standard in the development of the newly industrializing powers, see S. Bryan, *The Gold Standard at the Turn of the Twentieth Century: Rising Powers, Global Money and the End of Empire* (New York: Columbia University Press, 2010).

55 Earl Kinmouth, "Nakamura Keiu and Samuel Smiles: A Victorian Confucian and a Confucian Victorian," *American Historical Review,* vol. 85, no. 3 (1980), pp. 535–56.

56 Misra, *Business, Race and Politics,* p. 42.

57 For the differences between "bureaucratic" state organizations, where the state had more control over promotions and education of officials (in France, Germany, and Japan), and systems where professions had more control and autonomy from the state (in Britain and the United States), see Bernard Silberman, *Cages of Reason: The Rise of the Rational State in France, Japan, the United States and Great Britain* (Chicago: University of Chicago Press, 1993).

58 On the state, see Price, *British Society,* p. 131. The question of British relative economic decline has generated a great deal of debate, and many scholars contest the notion that the British economy had long-term structural faults; see Jim Tomlinson, "Thrice Denied: Declinism as a Long-Term Theme in British History in the Long Twentieth Century," *Twentieth Century British History,* vol. 20 (2009), pp. 227–51. Much of this literature rightly contests an older view that British elites were hostile to industry per se because they were imbued with gentlemanly prejudices; see, for instance, F. M. L. Thompson, *Gentrification and the Enterprise Culture: Britain 1780–1980* (Oxford: Oxford University Press, 2001). But this does not invalidate the argument that there were social and cultural reasons for the continued adherence to a particular, small-scale type of business, as some economic historians argue. See, for instance, the detailed study of the attitudes of British businessmen in India by Anna-Maria Misra, *Business, Race and Politics,* and an attempt to revive culturalist arguments on attitudes to business more broadly by contrasting British and American Jews' experiences in Andrew Godley, *Jewish Immigrant Entrepreneurship in New York and London* (Basingstoke, U.K.: Palgrave, 2001). For the alternative argument that British industrialists were making rational decisions, given their economic position and investments at the time, see Donald McCloskey and Lars Sandberg, "From Damnation to Redemption: Judgments on the Late Victorian Entrepreneur," *Explorations in Economic History,* vol. 9 (1971), pp. 89–108. Others have argued that Britain was not set on long-term decline in 1870, and David Edgerton has convincingly shown that the British state responded to German competition and war by improving investment in science in the twentieth century. David Edgerton, *Science, Technology and British Industrial "Decline," 1870–1970* (Cambridge: Cambridge University Press, 1996).

59 Werner von Siemens, *Personal Recollections of Werner von Siemens,* trans. W. C. Coupland (New York: D. Appleton, 1893), pp. 33–34.

60 David Cahan, *An Institute for an Empire: The Physikalisch-Technische Reichsanstalt, 1871–1918* (Cambridge: Cambridge University Press, 2004), p. 36.

61 William McNeill, *The Pursuit of Power: Technology, Armed Force and Power Since A.D. 1000* (Oxford: Blackwell, 1983), p. 279.

62 Wilfried Feldenkirchen, *Werner von Siemens: Inventor and International Entrepreneur* (Columbus: Ohio State University Press, 1994), p. 51.

63 Cited in Cahan, *An Institute for an Empire,* pp. 38–40.

64 Iwan Morus, *When Physics Became King* (Chicago: University of Chicago Press, 2005), p. 247.

65 For German education, see Jürgen Kocka, "Entrepreneurship," in Jürgen Kocka, ed., *Industrial Culture and Bourgeois Society: Business, Labor and Bureaucracy in Modern Germany* (New York: Berghahn, 1999), pp. 88–93. For comparisons between British and German businessmen, see H. Berghoff and R. Moller, "Tired Pioneers and Dynamic Newcomers? A Comparative Essay on English and German Entrepreneurial History, 1870–1914," *Economic History Review,* vol. 47 (1994), pp. 268–73.

66 Toni Pierenkemper and Richard Tilly, *The German Economy in the Nineteenth Century* (Oxford: Berghahn, 2004), chap. 9.

67 Jürgen Kocka, "Middle Class and Authoritarian State: Towards a History of the German 'Burgertum' in the Nineteenth Century," in Kocka, *Industrial Culture,* pp. 201–3.

68 For the "visible hand," see Alfred Chandler, *The Visible Hand: The Managerial Revolution in American Business* (Cambridge, Mass.: Harvard University Press, 1977); William Lazonick, *Business Organization and the Myth of the Market Economy* (Cambridge: Cambridge University Press, 1991), chap. 4.

69 *"Enarque"* is named after ENA—Ecoles Nationales d'Administration. For the power of this "state nobility," see Pierre Bourdieu, *The State Nobility: Elite Schools in the Field of Power* (Cambridge: Polity, 1996).

70 Fritz Ringer, *Education and Society in Modern Europe* (Bloomington: Indiana University Press, 1979), pp. 33–34.

71 For the influence of *Bildung,* the development of the *Bildungsbürgertum,* and comparisons with other European middle classes, see Jürgen Kocka, "The Middle Classes in Europe," in Kocka, *Industrial Culture,* pp. 231–54.

72 Norio Tamaki, *Yukichi Fukuzawa, 1835–1901: The Spirit of Enterprise in Modern Japan* (London: Palgrave Macmillan, 2001), p. 96.

73 Carmen Blacker, *The Japanese Enlightenment: A Study of the Writings of Fukuzawa Yukichi* (Cambridge: Cambridge University Press, 1969), pp. 129ff.

74 Predictably, there is a debate over the role of the state in Japanese development. Recent scholarship seems to be swinging back toward a slightly more "statist" interpretation. See Ian Inkster, *Japanese Industrialisation: Historical and Cultural Perspectives* (London: Routledge, 2001), chap. 5; Steven Ericson, *The Sound of the Whistle: Railroads and the State in Meiji Japan* (Cambridge, Mass.: Harvard University Press, 1996).

75 For business attitudes, see Byron Marshall, *Capitalism and Nationalism in Prewar Japan: The Ideology of the Business Elite, 1868–1941* (Stanford, Calif.: Stanford University Press, 1967), chap. 3.

76 For the comparison, see P. Windolf and J. Beyer, "Co-operative Capitalism: Corporate Networks in Germany and Britain," *British Journal of Sociology,* vol. 47 (1996), pp. 206–7.

77 This paragraph is based largely on Brian Balogh, *A Government Out of Sight: The Mystery of National Authority in Nineteenth Century America* (Cambridge: Cambridge University Press, 2009).

78 For this point, see Silberman, *Cages of Reason.*

79 David Nasaw, *Andrew Carnegie* (London: Penguin, 2007), p. 134.

80 This distinction between merchant and farmer ideologies and the analysis of developments in early-nineteenth-century America are based on Charles Sellers, *The Market*

Revolution: Jacksonian America, 1815–1849 (Oxford: Oxford University Press, 1991), especially chaps. 1–2. Balogh, *A Government Out of Sight,* chap. 2., pp. 277–84, also sees a tension between republican and Lockean, market liberal ideals and stresses the unpopularity of the central state and the dominance of merchant ideals by the 1830s. For criticisms of the Sellers thesis, see Melvyn Stokes and Stephen Conway, eds., *The Market Revolution in America: Social, Political, and Religious Expressions, 1800–1880* (Charlottesville: University Press of Virginia, 1996).

81 For these figures, see Eric Rauchway, *Blessed Among Nations: How the World Made America* (New York: Hill and Wang), pp. 16–17.

82 William Novak, "The Myth of the 'Weak' American State," *American Historical Review,* vol. 113 (2008), p. 769.

83 Nasaw, *Carnegie,* p. 348.

84 Russell Conwell, *Acres of Diamonds,* Project Gutenberg e-book, http://www.guten berg.org/files/368/368-h/368-h.htm#2H_4_0004.

85 Richard White, *Railroaded: The Transcontinentals and the Making of Modern America* (New York: Norton, 2011).

86 Lazonick, *Business Organization,* pp. 31–32; Alfred Chandler, *Scale and Scope: The Dynamics of Industrial Capitalism* (Cambridge, Mass.: Harvard University Press, 1994), part 2.

87 See Oliver Zunz, *Making America Corporate, 1870–1920* (Chicago: University of Chicago Press, 1990).

88 Oliver Zunz, *Why the American Century?* (Chicago: University of Chicago Press, 1998), chap. 1.

89 Nasaw, *Carnegie,* p. 160.

90 Chandler, *The Visible Hand,* pp. 266–69.

91 Quoted in Alan Trachtenberg, *The Incorporation of America: Culture and Society in the Gilded Age* (New York: Hill and Wang, 1982), p. 86.

92 See Alfred Chandler and Stephen Salsbury, *Pierre S. du Pont and the Making of the Modern Corporation* (New York: Harper and Row, 1971).

93 For the continuing importance of small business, see Mansell Blackford, *A History of Small Business in America* (New York: Twayne, 1991).

94 Nasaw, *Carnegie,* p. 348.

95 Jeffry Frieden, *Global Capitalism: Its Fall and Rise in the Twentieth Century* (New York: Norton, 2006), p. 59.

96 Alfred Kelly, *The German Worker: Working-Class Autobiographies from the Age of Industrialization* (Berkeley: University of California Press, 1987), pp. 167–68.

97 For the effects of Prussian corporatism and the importance of guild traditions, see Colin Crouch, *Industrial Relations and European State Relations* (Oxford: Oxford University Press, 1994), chap. 10.

98 Michael Mann, *The Sources of Social Power,* vol. 2, *The Rise of Classes and Nation-States, 1760–1914* (Cambridge: Cambridge University Press, 1993), p. 653.

99 For the reasons for American differences, see ibid., pp. 644–59.

100 For this point, see Bayly, *The Birth of the Modern World,* p. 426 and chap. 11.

101 Cain and Hopkins, *British Imperialism,* pp. 439–40, 443–44.

102 See Donald Bloxham and A. Dirk Moses, "Genocide and Ethnic Cleansing," in Don-

ald Bloxham and Robert Gerwarth, eds., *Political Violence in Twentieth-Century Europe* (Cambridge: Cambridge University Press, 2011), pp. 90–94.

103 This analysis relies on the arguments in Mark Hewitson, *Germany and the Causes of the First World War* (Oxford: Berg, 2004). He argues that there was a great deal of support for the military in Germany, though that did not necessarily involve support for war.

104 Heinrich Mann, *Man of Straw* (London: Penguin, 1984), pp. 289–90.

105 See Roger Chickering, *We Men Who Feel Most German: A Cultural Study of the Pan-German League, 1886–1914* (London: Allen and Unwin, 1984), especially chap. 4; Geoff Eley, *Reshaping the German Right: Radical Nationalism and Political Change After Bismarck* (New Haven, Conn.: Yale University Press, 1979); Marilyn Coetzee, *The German Army League: Popular Nationalism in Wilhelmine Germany* (Oxford: Oxford University Press, 1990).

106 On social Darwinism in Europe and America, see especially Mike Hawkins, *Social Darwinism in European and American Thought, 1860–1945: Nature as Model and Nature as Threat* (Cambridge: Cambridge University Press, 1997).

107 Dennis Sweeney, "Work, Race and the Transformation of Industrial Culture in Wilhelmine Germany," *Social History,* vol. 23 (1998), p. 55.

108 Mao Zedong, "A Study of Physical Education," April 1917, Maoist Documentation Project, http://www.marxists.org/reference/archive/mao/selected-works/volume-6/index.htm

109 Raghavan Iyer, ed., *The Moral and Political Writings of Mahatma Gandhi* (Oxford: Oxford University Press, 1986), vol. 25, p. 21; *Collected Works of Mahatma Gandhi* (New Delhi: Publications Division, Ministry of Information and Broadcasting, 1958–84), vol. 5, p. 353.

110 Theodore Roosevelt, *The Strenuous Life* (Stilwell, Kan.: Digireads, 2008), p. 9.

111 T. Jackson Lears, *No Place of Grace: Antimodernism and the Transformation of American Culture, 1880–1920* (New York: Pantheon, 1981), p. 116.

112 For popular views of war in Germany, see Jeffrey Verhey, *The Spirit of 1914: Militarism, Myth and Mobilization in Germany* (Cambridge: Cambridge University Press, 2000).

113 This relies on a recent contribution to the long debate over responsibility for war. See Mark Hewitson, *Germany and the Causes of the First World War* (Oxford: Berg, 2004).

114 *The Collected Poems of Rupert Brooke* (New York: John Lane, 1916), p. 113, cited in Ute Frevert, "Honor and Gender in the Outbreak of World War I," in Holger Afflerbach and David Stevenson, eds., *An Improbable War? The Outbreak of World War I and European Political Culture* (Oxford: Berghahn, 2007).

115 James Sheehan, *The Monopoly of Violence: Why Europeans Hate Going to War* (London: Faber and Faber, 2007), pp. 74–75.

116 Ford Madox Ford, *Parade's End* (London: Penguin, 1992), p. 639. On the theme of chivalry in the novel, see Parrinder, *Nation and Novel,* pp. 353–60.

117 See Erez Manela, *The Wilsonian Moment: Self-Determination and the International Origins of Anticolonial Nationalism* (Oxford: Oxford University Press, 2007).

118 Cited in Uwe Schneede, ed., *George Grosz: His Life and Work,* trans. S. Flatauer (London: G. Fraser, 1979), p. 160.

119 Cited in Robert Gerwarth, "The Central European Counter-Revolution: Paramilitary Violence in Germany, Austria and Hungary After the Great War," *Past and Present*, vol. 200 (2008), pp. 188–89.

120 David Crew, *Germans on Welfare: From Weimar to Hitler* (Oxford: Oxford University Press, 1998). On the limited development of class collaboration and corporatism, see Charles Maier, *Recasting Bourgeois Europe: Stabilization in France, Germany and Italy After World War I* (Princeton, N.J.: Princeton University Press, 1975).

121 Richard Bellamy and Darrow Schechter, *Gramsci and the Italian State* (Manchester: Manchester University Press, 1993), p. 24.

Chapter 3: Hubris and Catastrophe:
The First Merchant Age

1 Bruce Barton, *The Man Nobody Knows* (London: Constable, 1925), p. 3.

2 T. Jackson Lears, "From Salvation to Self-Realization: Advertising and the Therapeutic Roots of the Consumer Culture, 1880–1930," in R. Wightman Fox and T. Jackson Lears, eds., *The Culture of Consumption: Critical Essays in American History, 1880–1980* (New York: Pantheon, 1983), pp. 30–31.

3 For Barton's early views, see Richard Fried, *The Man Everybody Knew: Bruce Barton and the Making of Modern America* (Chicago: Ivan R. Dee, 2005), pp. 25–28.

4 Cited in ibid., p. 42.

5 Cited in Robert Murray, *The Harding Era: Warren G. Harding and His Administration* (Minneapolis: University of Minnesota Press, 1969), p. 91.

6 Gary Cross, *An All-Consuming Century: Why Commercialism Won in Modern America* (New York: Columbia University Press, 2000), pp. 24–38.

7 On "scientific management," see Samuel Haber, *Efficiency and Uplift: Scientific Management in the Progressive Era* (Chicago: University of Chicago Press, 1964); Daniel Nelson, *Frederick W. Taylor and the Rise of Scientific Management* (Madison: University of Wisconsin Press, 1980); Oliver Zunz, *Making America Corporate, 1870–1920* (Chicago: University of Chicago Press, 1995).

8 Steven Watts, *The People's Tycoon: Henry Ford and the American Century* (New York: Vintage, 2006).

9 Quoted in Cross, *An All-Consuming Century*, pp. 36–37.

10 On consumer society, see especially ibid.; Gary Cross, *Time and Money: The Making of Consumer Culture* (London: Routledge, 1993).

11 Glenna Matthews, *"Just a Housewife": The Rise and Fall of Domesticity in America* (New York: Oxford University Press, 1987).

12 Cross, *Time and Money*, pp. 166–77.

13 Victoria De Grazia, *Irresistible Empire: America's Advance Through 20th-Century Europe* (Cambridge, Mass.: Harvard University Press, 2005), p. 267; Cross, *An All-Consuming Century*, pp. 34–35.

14 For the connection between romanticism and consumerism, see C. Campbell, *The*

   Romantic Ethic and the Spirit of Modern Consumerism (Oxford: Alcuin Academics, 2005). On the creative use of material objects, see the work by anthropologist Daniel Miller, *The Comfort of Things* (Cambridge: Polity, 2008).

15 Robert Lynd and Helen Lynd, *Middletown: A Study in Contemporary American Culture* (London: Constable, 1929), pp. 82–83.

16 Edmond Goblot, *La Barrière et le Niveau* (Paris: Nouvelle Édition, 1967), p. 2.

17 Cross, *An All-Consuming Century,* p. 20.

18 See Lears, "From Salvation to Self-Realization," pp. 32–33.

19 Peter Fearon, *War, Prosperity and Depression: The U.S. Economy, 1917–45* (Deddington, U.K.: Philip Allan, 1987), p. 67.

20 Larry Bartels, *Unequal Democracy: The Political Economy of the New Gilded Age* (Princeton, N.J.: Princeton University Press, 2008), pp. 12–13.

21 Eric Rauchway, *The Great Depression and the New Deal* (Oxford: Oxford University Press, 2008); M. Olney, *Buy Now, Pay Later: Advertising, Credit, and Consumer Demand in the 1920s* (Chapel Hill: University of North Carolina Press, 1991), p. 91. See also Lendol Calder, *Financing the American Dream: A Cultural History of Consumer Credit* (Princeton, N.J.: Princeton University Press, 1999).

22 Sinclair Lewis, *Babbitt* (London: Vintage, 2006).

23 I take this analysis of Thomas Mann and the Rotary Club from Victoria De Grazia's brilliant chapter 1 in her *Irresistible Empire.*

24 E. Rosenberg, *Spreading the American Dream: American Economic and Cultural Expansion, 1890–1945* (New York: Hill and Wang, 1982), p. 111.

25 T. Wikle, "International Expansion of the American-Style Service Club," *Journal of American Culture,* vol. 22 (2004), pp. 46–47.

26 See, for instance, *The Meaning of Rotary: By a Rotarian* (London: Lund, 1927), p. 50.

27 Quoted in Rosenberg, *Spreading the American Dream,* p. 111.

28 This analysis of American policy is based on that in Patrick Cohrs, *The Unfinished Peace: America, Britain and the Stabilisation of Europe, 1919–1932* (Cambridge: Cambridge University Press, 2006), pp. 80–89, though his view of this strategy is more positive than mine. For a more critical assessment of Washington's financial-diplomatic approach, see Robert Boyce, *The Great Interwar Crisis and the Collapse of Globalization* (Basingstoke, U.K.: Macmillan, 2009).

29 Derek Aldcroft, *From Versailles to Wall Street, 1919–1929* (London: Allen Lane, 1987), pp. 47–48.

30 Ibid., p. 79.

31 For a comparison of the two systems, see Jeffry Frieden, *Global Capitalism: Its Fall and Rise in the Twentieth Century* (New York: Norton, 2006), pp. 144–45.

32 For the problems of the interwar gold standard, see B. Eichengreen, *Golden Fetters: The Gold Standard and the Great Depression* (Oxford: Oxford University Press, 1996).

33 For this critique of American policy, see Charles Kindleberger, *The World in Depression, 1929–1939* (Harmondsworth, U.K.: Penguin, 1987), pp. 11–12.

34 Herbert Hoover, *American Individualism* (London: Heinemann, 1923), p. 67.

35 For the greater involvement of the American state in imposing a market order after 1924, see Cohrs, *The Unfinished Peace,* p. 183.

36 Emily Rosenberg, *Financial Missionaries to the World: The Politics and Culture of Dollar Diplomacy* (Cambridge, Mass.: Harvard University Press, 1999), p. 151.

37 Ibid., pp. 176–83.

38 Frieden, *Global Capitalism,* p. 141.

39 David Woodruff, "The Politburo on Gold, Industrialization, and the International Economy, 1925–1926," in Paul Gregory and Norman Naimark, eds., *The Lost Politburo Transcripts: From Collective Leadership to Stalin's Dictatorship* (New Haven, Conn.: Yale University Press, 2008), p. 211.

40 Frieden, *Global Capitalism,* p. 141.

41 David Priestland, *The Red Flag: Communism and the Making of the Modern World* (London: Grove, 2009), pp. 234–49.

42 *Collected Works of Mahatma Gandhi* (New Delhi: Publications Division, Ministry of Information and Broadcasting, 1958–84), vol. 46, pp. 1–3.

43 Manoranjan Jha, *Civil Disobedience and After: American Reactions to Political Developments in India During 1930–1935* (Meerut/Delhi: Meenakshi Prakashan, 1973); Sean Scalmer, *Gandhi in the West: The Mahatma and the Rise of Radical Protest* (Cambridge: Cambridge University Press, 2011), p. 49.

44 Aldcroft, *From Versailles to Wall Street,* chap. 9.

45 For the disadvantages of the interwar gold standard, see Eichengreen, *Golden Fetters.*

46 "Says America gives earth a culture," *New York Times,* May 11, 1928, p. 5.

47 André Siegfried, *America Comes of Age: A French Analysis,* trans. H. Hemming and D. Hemming (London: J. Cape, 1927), pp. 347–53.

48 Milton Friedman and Anna Schwartz, *A Monetary History of the United States* (Princeton, N.J.: Princeton University Press, 1963).

49 For these points, made as part of a balanced analysis, see Charles Feinstein, Peter Temin, and Gianni Toniolo, *The European Economy Between the Wars* (Oxford: Oxford University Press, 1997), pp. 20–28.

50 The causes of the American collapse are the subject of a great deal of debate. At one time, analyses stressing the role of inequality in setting limits to investment and consumption and weakening the American economy were unfashionable, but they are increasingly common in historical writing. For this view, see Fearon, *War, Prosperity and Depression,* p. 67; Michael Bernstein, *The Great Depression: Delayed Recovery and Economic Change in America, 1929–1939* (Cambridge: Cambridge University Press, 1989), pp. 172–73. For the debate, see Aldcroft, *From Versailles to Wall Street,* pp. 199–200. For a recent restatement, see Robert Reich, "The Great Recession, the Great Recession and What's Ahead," http://www.irle.berkeley.edu/conference/2010/materials/reich.pdf.

51 Frieden, *Global Capitalism,* p. 176.

52 Feinstein, Temin, and Toniolo, *The European Economy,* p. 96.

53 Benjamin Lieberman, *From Recovery to Catastrophe: Municipal Stabilization and Political Crisis in Weimar Germany* (Oxford: Berghahn, 1998), pp. 46–47, 82–105.

54 Mark Blyth, *Great Transformations: Economic Ideas and Institutional Change in the Twentieth Century* (Cambridge: Cambridge University Press, 2002), p. 52.

55 Quoted in Frieden, *Global Capitalism,* p. 179.

56 Eichengreen, *Golden Fetters,* pp. 222–26.

57 William Patch, *Heinrich Bruning and the Dissolution of the Weimar Republic* (Cambridge: Cambridge University Press, 2006), p. 173.

58 Kenneth Pyle, *The Making of Modern Japan* (Lexington, Mass.: Heath, 1996), p. 188.

59 On the parties and the elites, see Gordon Berger, "Politics and Mobilization in Japan, 1931–1945," in Peter Duus, ed., *The Cambridge History of Japan,* vol. 6, *The Twentieth Century* (Cambridge: Cambridge University Press, 1995), pp. 105–18.

60 This is argued in Oscar Sanchez-Sibony, "Red Globalization: The Political Economy of Soviet Foreign Relations in the 1950s and 1960s" (PhD dissertation, University of Chicago, 2009), chap. 1. For an alternative view arguing that the policy change came earlier, in 1926–27, see Richard Day, *Leon Trotsky and the Politics of Economic Isolation* (Cambridge: Cambridge University Press, 1973), p. 175.

61 Cited in John Willett, *The Theatre of Bertolt Brecht* (London: Methuen, 1964), p. 68.

62 I. V. Stalin, *Sochineniia* (Moscow: Gosudarstvennoe Izdatel'stvo Politicheskoi Literatury, 1949), vol. 12, p. 254.

63 See Claudia Koonz, *The Nazi Conscience* (Cambridge, Mass.: Harvard University Press, 2003), p. 200. For Koonz, "Blood and race became master metaphors for the corrosive modern spirit that had almost destroyed Germany."

64 See, for instance, speech at the Nuremberg Reichsparteitag, 1937, in Adolf Hitler, *The Speeches of Adolf Hitler,* ed. Norman Baynes (London: Oxford University Press, 1942), pp. 697–99.

65 Franklin D. Roosevelt, Inaugural Address, March 4, 1933, http://millercenter.org /president/speeches/detail/3280.

66 For the increasing power of scientists and other experts in the British war machine, see David Edgerton, *Warfare State* (Cambridge: Cambridge University Press, 2006).

67 For a discussion of the recent historiography of Nazism and the Holocaust, criticizing the emphasis on scientific racism in the literature, see Dan Stone, *Histories of the Holocaust* (Oxford: Oxford University Press, 2010), chap. 4.

68 Wolfgang Koeppen, *Death in Rome,* trans. Michael Hoffman (London: Hamish Hamilton, 1992), pp. 20, 43–44.

69 Quoted in I. Kershaw, *Hitler, 1889–1936: Hubris* (London: Penguin, 2001), vol. 1, p. 187.

70 Adolf Hitler, *Mein Kampf,* vol. 2, chap. 2, http://gutenberg.net.au/ebooks02/0200601.txt.

71 See Roger Chickering, *We Men Who Feel Most German: A Cultural Study of the Pan-German League, 1886–1914* (London: George Allen and Unwin, 1984), p. 300.

72 For a recent survey of evidence on social support for the Nazis, see Michael Mann, *Fascists* (Cambridge: Cambridge University Press, 2004), pp. 147–72.

73 Adolf Hitler, Speech to the Industry Club, Düsseldorf, January 27, 1932, in Hitler, *Speeches,* pp. 777–90.

74 Hitler, *Speeches,* p. 793.

75 Hitler did not discuss *Lebensraum* in this speech, concentrating instead on Bolshevism's threat to the world economy and the need to defeat it, but it was central to his economic program. See Adam Tooze, *The Wages of Destruction: The Making and Breaking of the Nazi Economy* (London: Penguin, 2007), pp. 8–12.

76 Hitler, *Speeches,* p. 827.

77 On the ambiguities of relations between big business and the Nazis, see Tooze, *The Wages of Destruction,* chap. 4.

78 For these camps, see Peter Fritzsche, *Life and Death in the Third Reich* (Cambridge, Mass.: Harvard University Press, 2008), pp. 98–105.

79 Victor Klemperer, *The Klemperer Diaries, 1933–1945,* trans. M. Chalmers (London: Phoenix, 2000), p. 203 (February 11, 1937).

80 Fritzsche, *Life and Death in the Third Reich,* p. 102.

81 For this argument, see ibid.

82 For the Nazis' belief that Jews were a powerful threat to Germany, see A. Dirk Moses, "The Fate of Blacks and Jews: A Response to Jeffrey Herf," *Journal of Genocide Research,* vol. 10 (2008), pp. 276–81.

83 Fritzsche, *Life and Death in the Third Reich,* p. 29.

84 Bai Gao, "Arisawa Hiromi and His Theory for a Managed Economy," *Journal of Japanese Studies,* vol. 20 (1994), p. 125.

85 Thomas Havens, *Valley of Darkness: The Japanese People and World War Two* (New York: Norton, 1978), pp. 11–18; Elise Tipton, *Modern Japan: A Social and Political History* (London: Routledge, 2008), chap. 8.

86 Robert Allen, *Farm to Factory: A Reinterpretation of the Soviet Industrial Revolution* (Princeton, N.J.: Princeton University Press, 2003), p. 5.

87 Stalin, *Sochineniia,* vol. 12, p. 315.

88 See, for instance, Victor Kravchenko, *I Chose Freedom: The Personal and Political Life of a Soviet Official* (London: Robert Hale, 1947), p. 56.

89 Hiroaki Kuromiya, *Stalin's Industrial Revolution: Politics and Workers, 1928–1932* (Cambridge: Cambridge University Press, 1987), pp. 244–55.

90 John Scott, *Behind the Urals: An American Worker in Russia's City of Steel* (Bloomington: Indiana University Press, 1973), pp. 5–6.

91 For the political changes over the decade, see Priestland, *The Red Flag,* chap. 4.

92 Lewis Siegelbaum, "'Dear Comrade, You Ask What We Need': Socialist Paternalism and Soviet Rural 'Notables' in the Mid-1930s," in Sheila Fitzpatrick, ed., *Stalinism, New Directions* (London: Routledge, 2000), pp. 231–56.

93 I. V. Stalin, *Sochineniia* (Stanford, Calif.: The Hoover Institution, Stanford University, 1967), pp. 275–77. See also D. Priestland, *Stalinism and the Politics of Mobilization: Ideas, Power and Terror in Inter-war Russia* (Oxford: Oxford University Press, 2007), pp. 399–400.

94 Rossiiskii Gosudarstvennyi Arkhiv Sotsial'no-Politicheskoi Istorii [Russian State Archive of Social and Political History], 558/11/1087, 18.

95 This is convincingly and interestingly argued in relation to Stalin's views of national character in Erik Van Ree, "Heroes and Merchants: Joseph Stalin and the Nations of Europe," in Michael Wintle, ed., *Imagining Europe: Europe and European Civilization as Seen from Its Margins and by the Rest of the World in the Nineteenth and Twentieth Centuries* (Brussels: Peter Lang PIE, 2008), pp. 51–72.

96 Quoted in ibid., p. 57.

97 Ibid., p. 66.

98 I discuss this conflict between "radicalism" and "technocracy" in Priestland, *The Red Flag.*

99   For this interpretation of the Terror, see Priestland, *Stalinism and the Politics of Mobilization,* chap. 5.

100 On Stalin's view that the Soviet Union was threatened by an internal "fifth column," see Oleg Khlevniuk, "The Reasons for the 'Great Terror': The Foreign Political Aspect," in Silvio Pons and Andrea Romano, eds., *Russia in the Age of Wars, 1914–1945* (Milan: Feltrinelli, 2000), pp. 159–70.

101 For the equality and inequalities of Yan'an, see Mark Selden, *China in Revolution: The Yenan Way Revisited* (Armonk, N.Y.: M. E. Sharpe, 1995).

102 Edgar Snow, *Red Star over China* (Harmondsworth, U.K.: Penguin, 1972), pp. 153–56.

103 William Barber, *Gunnar Myrdal: An Intellectual Biography* (Basingstoke, U.K.: Palgrave Macmillan, 2008), chaps. 2–3.

104 Allan Carlson, *The Swedish Experiment in Family Politics: The Myrdals and the Interwar Population Crisis* (New Brunswick, N.J.: Transaction, 1990), pp. 47–62; K. Worpole, *Here Comes the Sun: Architecture and Public Space in Twentieth-Century European Culture* (London: Reaktion, 2000), p. 76.

105 Quoted in Worpole, *Here Comes the Sun,* p. 76.

106 Francis Sejersted and Madeleine Adams, *The Age of Social Democracy: Norway and Sweden in the Twentieth Century* (Princeton, N.J.: Princeton University Press, 2011), p. 7.

107 Quoted in Sheri Berman, *The Social Democratic Moment: Ideas and Politics in the Making of Interwar Europe* (Cambridge, Mass.: Harvard University Press, 1998), p. 157.

108 Donald Winch, "The Keynesian Revolution in Sweden," *Journal of Political Economy,* vol. 74 (1966), pp. 168–76.

109 Blyth, *Great Transformations,* p. 117.

110 Berman, *The Social Democratic Moment,* pp. 164–73.

111 J. E. Smith, *FDR* (New York: Random House, 2008), p. xii.

112 Ibid., p. 216.

113 Franklin D. Roosevelt, Inaugural Address, March 4, 1933, http://www.presidency.ucsb.edu/ws/index.php?pid=14473.

114 Alan Brinkley, *The End of Reform: New Deal Liberalism in Recession and War* (New York: Vintage, 1996), pp. 65–85; Blyth, *Great Transformations,* pp. 59–70.

115 Eric Rauchway, *The Great Depression,* p. 67.

116 For a useful survey of the nature of New Deal welfare, see ibid., pp. 98–102.

117 Patrick Renshaw, "Was There a Keynesian Economy in the United States?" *Journal of Contemporary History,* vol. 34 (1999), pp. 348–49.

118 Cited in Joshua Sanborn, *Drafting the Russian Nation: Military Conscription, Total War and Mass Politics, 1905–1925* (DeKalb: Northern Illinois University Press, 2003), p. 33.

119 Tooze, *Wages of Destruction,* p. xxiii.

120 See Mark Mazower, *Hitler's Empire: Nazi Rule in Occupied Europe* (London: Allen Lane, 2008), pp. 585–90.

121 Mikhail Gorbachev and Zdenek Mlynar, *On Perestroika, the Prague Spring, and the Crossroads of Socialism* (New York: Columbia University Press, 2002), pp. 13–14.

122 For this point, see Richard Overy, *Why the Allies Won* (London: Pimlico, 1996).

Chapter 4: The Age of Whiz

1 For a description, see Paul Hendrickson, *The Living and the Dead: Robert McNamara and Five Lives of a Lost War* (New York: Knopf, 1996), p. 21.

2 D. Shapley, *Promise and Power: The Life and Times of Robert McNamara* (Boston: Little, Brown, 1993), p. 27.

3 Ibid., pp. 28–37.

4 John Byrne, *The Whiz Kids: The Founding Fathers of American Business and the Legacy They Left Us* (New York: Doubleday, 2003), chap. 6.

5 Ibid., p. 1.

6 Quoted in Elizabeth Borgwardt, *A New Deal for the World: America's Vision for Human Rights* (Cambridge, Mass.: Harvard University Press, 2005), p. 114.

7 Ibid.

8 Robert Skidelsky, *Keynes* (Oxford: Oxford University Press, 1996), p. 101; Robert Skidelsky, *John Maynard Keynes: Fighting for Britain, 1937–1946* (London: Macmillan, 2000), p. 240.

9 James M. Boughton, "New Light on Harry Dexter White," *Journal of the History of Economic Thought*, vol. 26 (2004), pp. 179–95.

10 Robert Skidelsky notes Keynes's "Burkean side" when it came to his involvement in the governance of King's College, Cambridge. See Robert Skidelsky, *John Maynard Keynes: The Economist as Saviour, 1920–1937* (London: Macmillan, 1992), p. 8.

11 Gilles Dostaler, *Keynes and His Battles* (Cheltenham, U.K.: Edward Elgar, 2007), p. 222.

12 Skidelsky, *John Maynard Keynes: The Economist as Saviour*, p. 26.

13 Robert Skidelsky, *John Maynard Keynes: Hopes Betrayed, 1883–1920* (London: Macmillan, 1983), p. 246.

14 Jeffry Frieden, *Global Capitalism: Its Fall and Rise in the Twentieth Century* (New York: Norton, 2006), p. 262.

15 Robert Skidelsky, "Keynes, Globalisation and the Bretton Woods Institutions," *World Economics*, vol. 6 (2005), pp. 20–21.

16 Skidelsky, *Keynes*, p. 101; Skidelsky, *John Maynard Keynes: Fighting for Britain*, p. 310.

17 For the dominance of Keynesian ideas, see Peter Hall, ed., *The Political Power of Economic Ideas: Keynesianism Across Nations* (Oxford: Oxford University Press, 1989).

18 James M. Boughton, "American in the Shadows: Harry Dexter White and the Design of the International Monetary Fund" (IMF Working Paper, January 2006), pp. 15–16.

19 Melvyn Leffler, *A Preponderance of Power: National Security, the Truman Administration, and the Cold War* (Stanford, Calif.: Stanford University Press, 1992).

20 Michael Hogan, *The Marshall Plan: America, Britain and the Reconstruction of Western Europe* (Cambridge: Cambridge University Press, 1987), pp. 35–39.

21 Frieden, *Global Capitalism*, p. 268. U.S. GDP in the third quarter of 2011 was $15.181 trillion. Source: U.S. Bureau of Economic Analysis. Congress authorized the expenditure of $700 billion under the Troubled Assets Relief Program in 2008, though much less was actually spent.

22 Hogan, *The Marshall Plan*, pp. 429–36.

23 For the impact of war, see Jytte Klausen, *War and Welfare: Europe and the United States, 1945 to the Present* (Basingstoke, U.K.: Macmillan, 1998).

24 Gøsta Esping-Andersen, *The Three Worlds of Welfare Capitalism* (Cambridge: Cambridge University Press, 1990), pp. 58–61. For adjustments to Esping-Andersen's model, see Wil Arts and John Gelissen, "Three Worlds of Welfare Capitalism or More? A State-of-the-Art Report," *Journal of European Social Policy,* vol. 12 (2002), pp. 137–58. On differences in industrial relations, see Colin Crouch, *Industrial Relations and European State Traditions* (Oxford: Oxford University Press, 1994), pp. 192, 194–96.

25 Alessandro Portelli, "The Best Trash-Can Wiper in Town: The Life and Times of Valtéro Peppoloni, Worker," *Oral History Review,* vol. 16 (1988), p. 73.

26 For this model of "coordinated capitalism," see Peter Hall and David Soskice, *Varieties of Capitalism: The Institutional Advantages of Comparative Advantage* (Oxford: Oxford University Press, 2001). For links between varieties of capitalism and models of welfare state, see Torben Iversen and David Soskice, "Distribution and Redistribution: The Shadow of the Nineteenth Century," *World Politics,* vol. 61 (2009), pp. 438–86.

27 Degrees of hierarchy, however, differed. See William Lazonick, *Business Organization and the Myth of the Market Economy* (Cambridge: Cambridge University Press, 1993).

28 Edward Lincoln, "The Showa Economic Experience," in Carol Gluck and Stephen Graubard, eds., *Showa: The Japan of Hirohito* (New York: Norton, 1992), pp. 199–202; Lazonick, *Business Organization,* pp. 34–44; Mary O'Sullivan, *Contests for Corporate Control: Corporate Governance and Economic Performance in the United States and Germany* (Oxford: Oxford University Press, 2001), pp. 142–46.

29 Bo Strath, *The Organization of Labour Markets: Modernity, Culture and Governance in Germany, Sweden, Britain and Japan* (London: Routledge, 1998), pp. 141–53.

30 Though Britain's economic performance was not as poor as is sometimes thought. See Jim Tomlinson, "Thrice Denied: Declinism as a Long-Term Theme in British History in the Long Twentieth Century," *Twentieth Century British History,* vol. 20 (2009), pp. 227–51.

31 Steve Fraser, *Every Man a Speculator: A History of Wall Street in American Life* (New York: HarperCollins, 2004), p. 202.

32 Ibid., p. 201.

33 Leon Levy, *The Mind of Wall Street: A Legendary Financier on the Perils of Greed and the Mysteries of the Market* (Cambridge, Mass.: Public Affairs, 2002), p. 43.

34 G. Donaldson, "Financial Goals: Management vs. Stockholders," *Harvard Business Review,* vol. 41 (1963), p. 129, cited in Karen Ho, *Liquidated: An Ethnography of Wall Street* (Durham, N.C.: Duke University Press, 2009), pp. 203–5.

35 Cited in O'Sullivan, *Contests for Corporate Control,* p. 102.

36 On IBM, see Kenneth Flamm, *Creating the Computer: Government, Industry and High Technology* (Washington, D.C.: Brookings Institution, 1988), pp. 82–90. For the argument that Cold War science was excessively militarized, see Stuart Leslie, *The Cold War and American Science: The Military-Industrial Complex at MIT and Stanford* (New York: Columbia University Press, 1993).

37 Richard Hofstadter, quoted in Flamm, *Creating the Computer,* p. 141.

38 Raymond Aron, *The Opium of the Intellectuals* (New Brunswick, N.J.: Transaction, 2001), p. xxiii.

39 Greg Castillo, "The American 'Fat Kitchen' in Europe: Postwar Domestic Modernity and Marshall Plan Strategies of Enchantment," in Ruth Oldenziel and Karin Zach-

mann, eds., *Cold War Kitchen: Americanization, Technology and European Users* (Cambridge, Mass.: MIT Press, 2009), pp. 38–39.

40 Martina Hessler, "The Frankfurt Kitchen," in Oldenziel and Zachmann, *Cold War Kitchen,* chap. 7.

41 Annabel Wharton, *Building the Cold War: Hilton International Hotels and Modern Architecture* (Chicago: University of Chicago Press, 2001), pp. 7–8.

42 For these points, see Victoria De Grazia, *Irresistible Empire: America's Advance Through 20th-Century Europe* (Cambridge, Mass.: Harvard University Press, 2005), pp. 360–63; Francesco Alberoni, *Consumi i Società* (Bologna: Il Mulino, 1967), pp. 27–29; Henri Mandras and Alastair Cole, *Social Change in Modern France: Towards a Cultural Anthropology of the Fifth Republic* (Cambridge: Cambridge University Press, 1991), chap. 1.

43 Quoted in Richard Kuisel, *Seducing the French: The Dilemma of Americanization* (Berkeley: University of California Press, 1993), p. 38.

44 Michael Young and Peter Willmott, *Family and Kinship in East London* (London: Penguin, 2007), p. 156.

45 Quoted in Erik Van Ree, "Heroes and Merchants: Joseph Stalin and the Nations of Europe," in M. Wintle, ed., *Imagining Europe: Europe and European Civilization as Seen from Its Margins and by the Rest of the World in the Nineteenth and Twentieth Centuries* (Brussels: P.I.E. Peter Lang, 2008), pp. 58–59.

46 Jukka Gronow, *Caviar with Champagne: Common Luxury and the Ideals of the Good Life in Stalin's Russia* (Oxford: Berg, 2003).

47 Castillo, "The American 'Fat Kitchen,'" p. 41.

48 Frieden, *Global Capitalism,* p. 337.

49 Mark Frazier, *The Making of the Chinese Industrial Workplace: State, Revolution and Labour Management* (Cambridge: Cambridge University Press, 2002), p. 146.

50 Quoted in Maria Misra, *Vishnu's Crowded Temple: India Since the Great Rebellion* (London: Allen Lane, 2007), p. 263.

51 Quoted ibid., p. 265.

52 For Chandigarh and brutalism, see Kenneth Frampton, *Modern Architecture: A Critical History* (London: Thames and Hudson, 2007), pp. 229–30.

53 Quoted in Ravi Kalia Chandigarh, *The Making of an Indian City* (New Delhi: Oxford University Press, 1999), p. 133.

54 B. R. Tomlinson, *The Economy of Modern India, 1860–1970,* vol. 3 of *The New Cambridge History of India* (Cambridge: Cambridge University Press, 1993), pp. 156–213.

55 John Waterbury, "The Long Gestation and Brief Triumph of Import-Substituting Industrialization," *World Development,* vol. 27 (1999), pp. 323–41.

56 Marian Radetzki, "The Anatomy of Three Commodities Booms," *Resources Policy,* vol. 31 (2006), pp. 56–64.

57 See Sukarno, quoted in George Kahin, *The African-Asian Conference, Bandung, Indonesia, April 1955* (Port Washington, N.Y.: Kennikat Press, 1972), p. 42.

58 See Chen Jian, "China and the Bandung Conference: Changing Perceptions and Representations," in Seng Tan and Amitav Acharya, eds., *Bandung Revisited: The Legacy of the 1955 Asian-African Conference for International Order* (Singapore: University of Singapore Press, 2008), pp. 32–59.

59 Cited in Andrew Gamble, *Hayek: The Iron Cage of Liberty* (Cambridge: Polity, 1996), pp. 133–34.

60 See Robert Brenner, *The Boom and the Bubble: The US in the World Economy* (London: Verso, 2002), pp. 9–24.

61 For the trip, see Carlos Franqui, *Family Portrait with Fidel* (New York: Random House, 1984), pp. 31–32; Alan McPherson, "The Limits of Populist Diplomacy: Fidel Castro's 1959 Trip to North America," *Diplomacy and Statecraft,* vol. 18 (2007), pp. 237–68.

62 Fidel Castro, *My Life,* ed. Ignacio Ramonet (London: Allen Lane, 2007), pp. 67, 173; Volker Skierka, *Fidel Castro: A Biography* (Cambridge: Polity, 2004), pp. 19–21.

63 Cited in H. Matthews, *Castro: A Political Biography* (London: Penguin, 1969), p. 141.

64 Marifeli Pérez-Stable, *The Cuban Revolution: Origins, Course, and Legacy* (New York: Oxford University Press, 1999), chap. 1.

65 See, for instance, Amilcar Cabral, *Revolution in Guinea: An African People's Struggle* (London: Stage 1, 1974), p. 87.

66 Quoted in Frank Logevall, *Choosing War: The Lost Chance for Peace and the Escalation of War in Vietnam* (Berkeley: University of California Press, 1999), p. 393.

67 David Priestland, *The Red Flag: Communism and the Making of the Modern World* (London: Grove, 2009), pp. 470–72.

68 Cited in Joel Andreas, *Rise of the Red Engineers: The Cultural Revolution and the Rise of China's New Class* (Stanford, Calif.: Stanford University Press, 2009), p. 90.

69 Geoffrey Simons, *Libya: The Struggle for Survival* (New York: St. Martin's Press, 1998), pp. 170–72.

70 Dick Geary, *Radical Ambition: C. Wright Mills, the Left, and American Social Thought* (Berkeley: University of California Press, 2009), p. 1.

71 C. Wright Mills, *The Politics of Truth: Selected Writings of C. Wright Mills* (New York: Oxford University Press, 2008), p. 198.

72 Herbert Marcuse, *One-Dimensional Man: Studies in the Ideology of Advanced Industrial Society* (London: Routledge, 2007), pp. xx, 21.

73 Axel Schildt and Detlef Siegfried, "Youth, Consumption and Politics in the Age of Radical Change," in Axel Schildt and Detlef Siegfried, eds., *Between Marx and Coca-Cola: Youth Cultures in Changing European Societies, 1960–1980* (New York: Berghahn, 2006), pp. 1–2.

74 Ronald Fraser, *1968: A Student Generation in Revolt* (London: Chatto and Windus, 1988), p. 79.

75 Ibid., p. 58.

76 See Gerd-Rainer Horn, *The Spirit of '68: Rebellion in Western Europe and North America, 1956–1976* (Oxford: Oxford University Press, 2007), chap. 3.

77 Charles Tilly, *The Politics of Collective Violence* (Cambridge: Cambridge University Press, 2003), p. 71.

78 Robert Dallek, *Lyndon B. Johnson: Portrait of a President* (New York: Oxford University Press, 2005), chap. 13.

79 George Herring, "Tet and the Crisis of Hegemony," in Carole Fink, Philipp Gassert, and Detlef Junker, eds., *1968: The World Transformed* (Cambridge: Cambridge University Press, 1998), p. 48.

80 Diane Kunz, "The American Economic Consequences of 1968," in Fink, Gassert, and Junker, eds., *1968,* pp. 83–110.

81 For the problems of devaluation under the Bretton Woods system, see Barry Eichengreen, *Globalizing Capital: A History of the International Monetary System* (Princeton, N.J.: Princeton University Press, 2004), chap. 4, especially pp. 132–33.

82 See Eric Helleiner, "Explaining the Globalization of Financial Markets: Bringing States Back In," *Review of International Political Economy,* vol. 2 (1995), pp. 319–20. This is also argued in Dani Rodrik, *The Globalization Paradox: Why Global Markets, States and Democracy Can't Coexist* (Oxford: Oxford University Press, 2011), p. 102. See also Brenner, *The Boom and the Bubble,* pp. 28–29. Though for the practical problems of enforcing these currency controls, see Eichengreen, *Globalizing Capital,* pp. 118–22.

83 Eichengreen, *Globalizing Capital,* p. 120.

84 Cited in Frieden, *Global Capitalism,* p. 342.

85 Barry Eichengreen, *The European Economy Since 1945: Coordinated Capitalism and Beyond* (Princeton, N.J.: Princeton University Press, 2007), p. 220. For falls in investment between 1973 and 1990, see Andrew Glyn, *Capitalism Unleashed: Finance, Globalization, and Welfare* (Oxford: Oxford University Press, 2006), pp. 13–14.

86 For this point, see Eichengreen, *The European Economy,* pp. 222, 242.

87 Glyn, *Capitalism Unleashed,* p. 5.

88 For inflation rates, see Inflation.eu, "Historic Inflation Germany," http://www.inflation.eu/inflation-rates/germany/historic-inflation/cpi-inflation-germany.aspx; and "Historic Inflation Great Britain," http://www.inflation.eu/inflation-rates/great-britain/historic-inflation/cpi-inflation-great-britain.aspx.

89 Frieden, *Global Capitalism,* p. 363.

90 Glyn, *Capitalism Unleashed,* p. 15.

91 Alan Greenspan, *The Age of Turbulence: Adventures in a New World* (London: Penguin, 2008), p. 40.

92 Lisa McGirr, *Suburban Warriors: The Origins of the New American Right* (Princeton, N.J.: Princeton University Press, 2001), p. 164.

93 Jennifer Burns, "Howard Roark in New Delhi," *Foreign Policy,* November/December 2009, http://www.foreignpolicy.com/articles/2009/10/19/howard_roark_in_new_delhi.

94 On Leningrad University, see Michael David-Fox, *Revolution of the Mind: Higher Learning Among the Bolsheviks, 1918–1929* (Ithaca, N.Y.: Cornell University Press, 1997). For Rand's early years, see A. Heller, *Ayn Rand and the World She Made* (New York: Doubleday, 2009), chaps. 1–2.

95 Jennifer Burns, *Goddess of the Market: Ayn Rand and the American Right* (Oxford: Oxford University Press, 2009), p. 104.

96 Ayn Rand, *Atlas Shrugged* (London: Penguin, 1992), p. 503.

97 Ibid., p. 989.

98 For the union of these trends in Orange County, California, see McGirr, *Suburban Warriors,* pp. 163ff.

99 For these developments, see Daniel Rodgers, *Age of Fracture* (Cambridge, Mass.: Harvard University Press, 2011), chap. 2.

100   Cited in Burns, *Goddess of the Market,* p. 168.

101   For this interpretation, see Marion Fourcade-Gourinchas and Sarah Babb, "The Re-
      birth of the Liberal Creed: Paths to Neoliberalism in Four Countries," *American Jour-
      nal of Sociology,* vol. 108 (2002), pp. 533–79. For a similar analysis, see Monica Prasad,
      *The Politics of Free Markets: The Rise of Neoliberal Economic Policies in Britain, France,
      Germany and the United States* (Chicago: University of Chicago Press, 2006).

102   See Philip Mirowski and Dieter Plehwe, eds., *The Road from Mont Pélerin: The Making
      of the Neoliberal Thought Collective* (Cambridge, Mass.: Harvard University Press, 1989).

103   For popular neoliberalism, see, for instance, McGirr, *Suburban Warriors;* Mark Lassiter,
      The Silent Majority: Suburban Politics in the Sunbelt South (Princeton, N.J.: Princeton
      University Press, 2006). On intellectuals and economists, see Marion Fourcade, "The
      Construction of a Global Profession: The Transnationalization of Economics," *Ameri-
      can Journal of Sociology,* vol. 112 (2006), pp. 145–94. For the relationship between in-
      tellectual fashions and institutional change in the late 1970s and the 1980s, see Mark
      Blyth, *Great Transformations: Economic Ideas and Institutional Change in the Twentieth
      Century* (Cambridge: Cambridge University Press, 2002).

104   David Vogel, *Fluctuating Fortunes: The Power of Business in America* (New York: Basic
      Press, 1989), chap. 4; Jacob Hacker and Paul Pierson, *Winner-Take-All Politics: How
      Washington Made the Rich Richer—and Turned Its Back on the Middle Class* (New
      York: Simon and Schuster 2010), p. 118; Blyth, *Great Transformations,* p. 155.

105   Blyth, *Great Transformations,* pp. 164–65.

106   Pamela Constable and Arturo Valenzuela, *A Nation of Enemies: Chile Under Pinochet*
      (New York: Norton, 1991), p. 173.

107   For Thatcher's militaristic metaphors, see E. H. H. Green, *Thatcher* (London: Hodder
      Arnold, 2006).

108   John Major, *The Autobiography* (New York: HarperCollins, 1999), p. 169.

109   Blyth, *Great Transformations,* pp. 168–69; William Greider, *Secrets of the Temple: How
      the Federal Reserve Runs the Country* (New York: Touchstone, 1987), pp. 110–11.

110   Brenner, *The Boom and the Bubble,* pp. 27–29.

111   Frieden, *Global Capitalism,* p. 373.

112   Giovanni Arrighi, "The World Economy and the Cold War, 1970–1990," in Melvyn
      Leffler and Odd Arne Westad, eds., *The Cambridge History of the Cold War* (Cam-
      bridge: Cambridge University Press, 2010), vol 3; pp. 16, 22.

113   Rebecca Leung, "Morris: 'Reagan Still a Mystery,'" CBSNews.com, December 5,
      2007, http://www.cbsnews.com/stories/2004/06/09/60ii/main622051.shtml.

114   For Reagan's individualistic optimism and his "Emersonian" religion, see John Dig-
      gins, *Ronald Reagan: Fate, Freedom and the Making of History* (New York: Norton,
      2007).

115   Richard Wirthlin and Wynton Hall, *The Great Communicator: What Ronald Rea-
      gan Taught Me About Politics, Leadership and Life* (Hoboken, N.J.: Wiley, 2004),
      pp. 113–15.

116   Jerome Tuccille, *Alan Shrugged: The Life and Times of Alan Greenspan, the World's
      Most Powerful Banker* (Hoboken, N.J.: Wiley, 2002), pp. 131–32, 135–37.

117   Benjamin Fischer, "The Soviet-American War Scare of the 1980s," *International Jour-
      nal of Intelligence and Counterintelligence,* vol. 19:3 (Autumn 2006), pp. 480–517.

118 For these issues, see Rodgers, *Age of Fracture,* chap. 1.
119 Peggy Noonan, *What I Saw at the Revolution: A Political Life in the Reagan Era* (New York: Random House, 1990), pp. 283–84.
120 Valentin Varennikov, *Delo GKChP* (Moscow: Eksmo, 2010).
121 Donna Bahry, "Society Transformed? Rethinking the Social Roots of Perestroika," *Slavic Review,* vol. 52 (1993), p. 539.
122 For the idea of 1989 as a carnival, see Padraic Kenney, *A Carnival of Revolution: Central Europe 1989* (Princeton, N.J.: Princeton University Press, 2002).
123 Bronislaw Misztal, "Between the State and Solidarity: One State, Two Interpretations—the Orange Alternative Movement in Poland," *British Journal of Sociology,* vol. 42 (1992), pp. 55–78.
124 Lisiunia Romanienko, "Antagonism, Absurdity and the Avant-Garde: Dismantling Soviet Oppression Through the Use of Theatrical Devices by Poland's 'Orange' Solidarity Movement," *International Review of Social History,* vol. 52 (2007), p. 146.

Chapter 5: Davos Man

1 Robert Rubin with J. Weisberg, *In an Uncertain World: Tough Choices from Wall Street to Washington* (New York: Random House, 2003), p. 199.
2 Ibid., pp. 62–63.
3 Daniel Rodgers, *Age of Fracture* (Cambridge, Mass.: Harvard University Press, 2011), chap. 2.
4 For an accessible analysis of these ideas, see Justin Fox, *The Myth of the Rational Market: A History of Risk, Reward, and Delusion on Wall Street* (New York: Harper Business, 2009).
5 Ibid., p. 199.
6 On London's banks, see Philip Augar, *The Death of Gentlemanly Capitalism: The Rise and Fall of London's Investment Banks* (London: Penguin, 2001).
7 Eric Helleiner, *States and the Reemergence of Global Finance: From Bretton Woods to the 1990s* (Ithaca, N.Y.: Cornell University Press, 1994); Gérard Duménil and Dominique Levy, *The Crisis of Neoliberalism* (Cambridge, Mass.: Harvard University Press, 2011), pp. 132–34; Matthew Sherman, "A Short History of Financial Deregulation in the United States," Center for Economic and Policy Research, June 2009, pp. 5–8, http://www.cepr.net/index.php/publications/reports/a-short-history-of-financial-deregulation-in-the-united-states/.
8 Stan Clark, interview by Karen Ho, *Liquidated: An Ethnography of Wall Street* (Durham, N.C.: Duke University Press, 2009), pp. 273–74.
9 John Carlton, interview by Karen Ho, *Liquidated,* pp. 275–76.
10 *Wall Street,* directed by Oliver Stone (20th Century Fox, 1987).
11 Ho, *Liquidated,* pp. 145–46.
12 Ibid.
13 For an analysis of the performance of leveraged buyouts, see Mary O'Sullivan, *Contests for Corporate Control: Corporate Governance and Economic Performance in the United States and Germany* (Oxford: Oxford University Press, 2001), pp. 174–76.

14 Ho, *Liquidated*, pp. 137–50.

15 Matt Taibbi, "The Great American Bubble Machine," *Rolling Stone*, April 5, 2010, http://www.rollingstone.com/politics/news/the-great-american-bubble-machine -20100405#ixzz1kMYoei3L.

16 O'Sullivan, *Contests for Corporate Control*, chap. 6.

17 Ibid., p. 165.

18 Duménil and Levy, *The Crisis of Neoliberalism*, pp. 151–52.

19 For wage figures, see Andrew Glyn, *Capitalism Unleashed: Finance, Globalization, and Welfare* (Oxford: Oxford University Press, 2006), p. 117. For higher levels of profit paid to shareholders, see O'Sullivan, *Contests for Corporate Control*, pp. 192–93.

20 Luc Boltanski and Eve Chiapello, *The New Spirit of Capitalism* (London: Verso, 2007), pp. 112, 115.

21 For "digital Taylorism," see P. Brown, D. Ashton, H. Lauder, and G. Tholen, "Towards a High-Skilled, Low-Waged Workforce: A Review of Global Trends in Education, Employment and the Labour Market" (SKOPE Monograph no. 10, 2008).

22 Irena Grugulis, Ödül Bozkurt, and Jeremy Clegg, "'No Place to Hide'? The Realities of Leadership in UK Supermarkets," Skope Research Paper no. 91 (May 2010), http://www.skope.ox.ac.uk/sites/default/files/RP91.pdf, p. 8.

23 Mihir Bose, *Manchester Disunited: Trouble and Takeover at the World's Richest Football Club* (London: Aurum, 2007).

24 Dakin Campbell and Daniel Kruger, "Bond Vigilantes Push U.S. Treasuries into Bear Market," Bloomberg.com, February 10, 2009, http://www.bloomberg.com/apps/news ?pid=newsarchive&sid=adGdbnMsKTQg&refer=news.

25 Tamar Lewin, "For-Profit College Group Sued As U.S. Lays Out Wide Fraud," *New York Times*, August 8, 2011, http://www.nytimes.com/2011/08/09/education/09for profit.html.

26 Walter Isaacson, *Steve Jobs* (New York: Little, Brown, 2011), pp. 162–65.

27 Ibid., p. 15.

28 Ibid., p. 62.

29 Herbert Kitschelt, *The Transformation of European Social Democracy* (Cambridge: Cambridge University Press, 1994), chap. 1.

30 Though the current leadership of the British Liberal Democrats is more soft merchant than its membership.

31 Kitschelt, *Transformation*, chap. 1.

32 Ronald Inglehart, *Modernization and Postmodernization: Cultural, Economic and Political Change in 43 Societies* (Princeton, N.J.: Princeton University Press, 1997).

33 Herbert Kitschelt and Anthony McGann, *The Radical Right in Western Europe: A Comparative Analysis* (Ann Arbor: University of Michigan Press, 1995).

34 "Branson Beats Jesus in Role Model Poll," Opinium, February 23, 2008, http://news .opinium.co.uk/survey-results/branson-beats-jesus-role-model-poll.

35 M. Fukuo, "Japan's Lost Decade and Its Financial System," *World Economy*, vol. 26 (2003), pp. 365–84.

36 Larry Summers, "Remarks to the National Governors Association," August 4, 1998, http://www.treasury.gov/press-center/press-releases/Pages/rr2626.aspx.

37 For this process, see Gregory Chin, *China's Automotive Modernization: The Party-State and Multinational Corporations* (Basingstoke, U.K.: Palgrave, 2010).

38 Joel Andreas, *Red Engineers: The Cultural Revolution and the Rise of China's New Class* (Stanford, Calif.: Stanford University Press, 2009), p. 225.

39 Ibid., p. 231.

40 For the relative equality of this period, see Yasheng Huang, *Capitalism with Chinese Characteristics: Entrepreneurship and the State* (Cambridge: Cambridge University Press, 2008), chap. 2. However, there is disagreement over whether this was an era of pure free markets or of limited markets. For the debate, see Joel Andreas, "A Shanghai Model?" *New Left Review,* vol. 65 (2010), pp. 63–86, and the reply by Yasheng Huang, "The Politics of China's Path," pp. 87–91.

41 Suisheng Zhao, "Deng Xiaoping's Southern Tour: Elite Politics in Post-Tiananmen China," *Asian Survey,* vol. 33 (1993), pp. 739–56.

42 Andreas, *Red Engineers,* pp. 242–44.

43 Barry Naughton, "The Chinese Counter-Reformation: Rebuilding the State for a New Era," Astor Lecture, Oxford University, February 5, 2010.

44 Bruce Dickson, "Who Consents to the 'Beijing Consensus'? Crony Communism in China," http://www.cecc.gov/pages/roundtables/2009/20090522/DicksonCrony_CommunismInChina.pdf, p. 7.

45 Carl Walter and Fraser Howie, *Red Capitalism: The Fragile Foundation of China's Extraordinary Rise* (Singapore: Wiley, 2011), p. 10.

46 Edward Vickers, "Selling 'Socialism with Chinese Characteristics': 'Thought and Politics' and the Legitimisation of China's Developmental Strategy," *International Journal of Educational Development,* vol. 29 (2009), pp. 521–23.

47 For the relationship between nationalism and free-market attitudes in China, see L. Hoffman, *Patriotic Professionalism in China: Fostering Talent* (Philadelphia: Temple University Press, 2010).

48 Pranab Bardhan, *Awakening Giants, Feet of Clay: Assessing the Economic Rise of China and India* (Princeton, N.J.: Princeton University Press, 2010), p. 22.

49 For China's automobile strategy and the role of Shanghai, see Eric Thun, *Changing Lanes in China: Foreign Direct Investment, Local Governments, and Auto-Sector Development* (Cambridge: Cambridge University Press, 2006), especially chap. 4.

50 All of these details come from Karl Gerth, *As China Goes, So Goes the World: How Chinese Consumers Are Transforming Everything* (New York: Hill and Wang, 2010), pp. 27–41.

51 See Kelee Tsai, *Capitalism Without Democracy: The Private Sector in Contemporary China* (Ithaca, N.Y.: Cornell University Press, 2007).

52 Ho-fung Hung, "Rise of China and the Global Overaccumulation Crisis," *Review of International Political Eonomy,* vol. 15 (2008), pp. 161–69.

53 Ho-fung Hung, "America's Head Servant," *New Left Review,* vol. 60 (2009), p. 19.

54 Charles Duhigg and David Barboza, "Apple's iPad and Human Costs for Workers in China," *New York Times,* January 25, 2012. See also Alexandra Harney, *The China Price: The True Cost of Chinese Competitive Advantage* (New York: Penguin, 2008), chap. 8.

55 K. L. M. Walker, "Gangster Capitalism and Peasant Protest in China: The Last Twenty Years," *Journal of Peasant Studies,* vol. 33 (2006), pp. 1–33.

56 Dexter Roberts, "Using Propaganda to Stop China's Strikes," *Bloomberg Businessweek,* December 15, 2011, http://www.businessweek.com/magazine/using-propaganda-to -stop-chinas-strikes-12152011.html.

57 Chris Chan and Pun Ngai, "The Making of a New Working Class? A Study of Collective Actions of Workers in Southern China," *China Quarterly,* vol. 198 (2009), p. 300.

58 Anand Giridharidas, "Indian to the Core, and an Oligarch," *New York Times,* June 15, 2008.

59 The Marwaris and Parsis are, strictly speaking, ethnic rather than merchant caste groups, but these communities produced large numbers of merchants.

60 Bardhan, *Awakening Giants,* p. 1.

61 Maria Misra, *Vishnu's Crowded Temple: India Since the Great Rebellion* (London: Allen Lane, 2007), pp. 404–5; Lloyd Rudolph and Susanne Rudolph, "The Iconization of Chandrababu Naidu: Sharing Sovereignty in India's Federal Market Economy," *Economic and Political Weekly,* May 5, 2001.

62 Bardhan, *Awakening Giants,* chap. 7.

63 That is, "caste" in my sense, not a translation of the Hindi/Sanskrit *varna* or *jati.*

64 Vikas Bajaj, "For Wealthy Indian Family, Palatial House Is Not a Home," *New York Times,* October 19, 2011.

65 The figures are calculated using purchasing-power parity, with 1993 data as a base. See http://www.piie.com/publications/chapters_preview/348/2iie3489.pdf, p. 16.

66 For the effect of neoliberalism on "coordinated capitalist" countries, see, for instance, Vivienne Schmidt, *The Futures of Capitalism* (Oxford: Oxford University Press, 2002); Fritz Karpf and Vivienne Schmidt, eds., *Welfare and Work in the Open Economy* (2 vols.) (Oxford: Oxford University Press, 2000).

67 George Ross, *Jacques Delors and European Integration* (London: Wiley, 1995), p. 78.

68 Ibid., p. 51.

69 Neil Kinnock, quoted in Tyler Marshall, "The Odd Couple of Europe: Margaret Thatcher and Jacques Delors Are Almost Perfectly Incompatible. Their Stormy Political Relationship May Shape the Continent's Future," *Los Angeles Times,* October 22, 1989.

70 Helen Drake, *Jacques Delors: Perspectives on a European Leader* (London: Routledge, 2000), p. 27.

71 Ibid., p. 26; Ross, *Jacques Delors,* pp. 17–19.

72 For an interpretation that emphasizes the role of nation-states, rather than Delors and the European Commission, see Andrew Moravcsik, *The Choice for Europe: Social Purpose and State Power from Messina to Maastricht* (Ithaca, N.Y.: Cornell University Press 1998), chap. 5.

73 Nicholas Jabko, "In the Name of the Market: How the European Commission Paved the Way for Monetary Union," *Journal of European Public Policy,* vol. 6 (1999), pp. 475–95.

74 For this analysis, see Gil Eyal, Ivan Szelenyi, and Eleanor Townsley, *Making Capitalism Without Capitalists: The New Ruling Elites in Eastern Europe; Class Formation and Elite Struggles in Post-Communist Central Europe* (London: Verso, 1998).

75 This is the argument of Vadim Volkov in *Violent Entrepreneurs: The Use of Force in the Making of Russian Capitalism* (Ithaca, N.Y.: Cornell University Press, 2002).

76 David Hoffman, *The Oligarchs: Wealth and Power in the New Russia* (New York: Public Affairs, 2011), p. 115.

77 Ibid., pp. 111 16.

78 Ibid., p. 118.

79 Ibid., p. 116.

80 Ibid., p. 271.

81 Ibid., p. 447.

82 Cited in Peter Reddaway and Dmitri Glinski, *The Tragedy of Russia's Reforms: Market Bolshevism Against Democracy* (Washington, D.C.: United States Institute of Peace Press, 2001), pp. 239–40.

83 Quoted in Stephan Hedlund, *Russia's "Market" Economy: A Bad Case of Predatory Capitalism* (London: UCL Press, 1999), p. 112.

84 For "inverted Marxism," see Reddaway and Glinski, *The Tragedy of Russia's Reforms,* p. 239.

85 Anthony Shorrocks, "Poverty Trends in Russia During the Transition" (University of Essex, RECEP, July 2000), http://www.cepr.org/meets/wkcn/7/745/papers/shorrocks.pdf.

86 Cited in Hoffman, *The Oligarchs,* p. 326.

87 For the role of economic position and relationship to the market in voting, see Stephen Whitefield and Geoff Evans, "Class, Markets and Partisanship in Post-Soviet Russia, 1993–1996," *Electoral Studies,* vol. 18 (1999), pp. 155–78. For the role of generation in voting, see Sara Schartz, "Age Cohort Effects in the Breakdown of Single-Party Rule," *Journal of Aging Studies,* vol. 16 (2002), pp. 199–219.

88 Poiushchie Vmeste, "Takogo kak Putin," 2002.

89 VTsIOM survey, *RIA Novosti,* May 11, 2010.

90 Doug Flahaut, "My Classmate Saif Gaddafi," *Zócalo Public Square* (blog), http://zocalopublicsquare.org/thepublicsquare/2011/03/13/my-classmate-saif-qaddafi/read/nexus.

91 Alan Richards and John Waterbury, *A Political Economy of the Middle* East, 3rd ed. (Boulder, Colo.: Westview, 2008), p. 350.

92 Ibid., pp. 354–57.

93 Peter Bergen, *The Osama bin Laden I Know* (New York: Free Press, 2006), Kindle e-book, loc. 665.

94 Gilles Kepel, *Jihad: The Trail of Political Islam* (London: I. B. Tauris, 2002), pp. 67–68.

95 Ibid., p. 318.

96 Gilles Kepel and Jean-Pierre Milelli, *Al Qaeda in Its Own Words* (Cambridge, Mass.: Harvard University Press, 2008), pp. 49–50.

97 Bergen, *The Osama bin Laden I Know,* loc. 628–39.

98 Ibid., loc. 4217.

99 George W. Bush, "Address to a Joint Session of Congress and the American People," September 20, 2001, cited in Ivo Daalder and James Lindsay, *America Unbound: The Bush Revolution in Foreign Policy* (Washington, D.C.: Brookings Institution, 2003), p. 82.

100 Michael Lind, *Made in Texas: George W. Bush and the Southern Takeover of American Politics* (New York: Basic Books, 2002).

101 Cullen Murphy and Todd S. Purdum, "Farewell to All That: An Oral History of the White House," *Vanity Fair,* February 2009, http://www.vanityfair.com/politics /features/2009/02/bush-oral-history200902.

102 Daalder and Lindsay, *America Unbound,* p. 86.

103 Jonathan Powell, quoted in Lisa O'Carroll, "Tony Blair Knew Immediately That 9/11 Terror Attacks 'Changed Everything,'" *Guardian,* September 10, 2011, http://www .guardian.co.uk/world/2011/sep/10/tony-blair-knew-9-11-changed-everything.

104 Murphy and Purdum, "Farewell to All That."

105 "Background Paper on SIPRI Military Expenditure Data, 2010," SIPRI, http://www .sipri.org/research/armaments/milex/factsheet2010.

106 George W. Bush, "Remarks by the President to Airline Employees, O'Hare International Airport," September 27, 2001, http://georgewbush-whitehouse.archives.gov /news/releases/2001/09/20010927-1.html.

107 Raghuram Rajan, "The Greenspan Era: Lessons for the Future," http://www.imf.org /external/np/speeches/2005/082705.htm.

108 There seems to be disagreement among the participants whether Summers used the term "Luddite" or the less aggressive and rather more obscure "lead-eyed" (apparently taken from an F. Scott Fitzgerald poem), as the official transcript has it. Compare http://www.kansascityfed.org/publicat/sympos/2005/pdf/GD5_2005.pdf with http:// delong.typepad.com/sdj/2010/10/it-does-not-seem-to-me-that-charles-ferguson-has -gotten-it-right.html.

109 Raghuram Rajan, *Fault Lines: How Hidden Fractures Still Threaten the World Economy* (Princeton, N.J.; Princeton University Press, 2010), p. 3.

110 Edmund L. Andrews, "Fed Shrugged As Subprime Crisis Spread," http://www .nytimes.com/2007/12/18/business/18subprime.html.

111 On the fundamental weakness of the U.S. economy and the role of the consumer boom, see Glyn, *Capitalism Unleashed,* pp. 132–38.

112 Of course, the threat was denied, but a deal was done. See Jerome Tuccille, *Alan Shrugged: The Life and Times of Alan Greenspan, the World's Most Powerful Banker* (Hoboken, N.J.: Wiley, 2002), chap. 27.

113 Alan Greenspan, "The Crisis," March 2010, "Draft of Former Fed Chairman Alan Greenspan's Paper on the Financial Crisis," ProPublica, http://www.propublica.org /documents/item/draft-of-former-fed-chairman-alan-greenspan-s-paper-on-the-finan cial-crisis#p=1, pp. 43–44.

114 That is nominal consumption. Real consumption would have been 8.9 percent lower in the United Kingdom and 6.2 percent lower in the United States. For this analysis, see Graham Turner, *The Credit Crunch: Housing Bubbles, Globalisation and the Worldwide Economic Crisis* (London: Pluto Press, 2008), pp. 37–41.

115 Again in nominal terms.

116 For these issues, see Duménil and Levy, *The Crisis of Neoliberalism,* chap. 11.

117 Brian Knowlton and Michael M. Grynbaum, "Greenspan 'Shocked' That Free Markets Are Flawed," *New York Times,* October 23, 2008.

118 For the conservatism of the Obama economic team, see Ron Suskind, *Confidence Men: Wall Street, Washington, and the Education of a President* (New York: HarperCollins, 2011), part 3.

119 Nicholas Shaxson, *Treasure Islands: Tax Havens and the Men Who Stole the World* (London: Bodley Head, 2011).

120 Jacob Hacker and Paul Pierson, *Winner-Take-All Politics: How Washington Made the Rich Richer—and Turned Its Back on the Middle Class* (New York: Simon and Schuster, 2010).

121 Kitschelt, *Transformation,* pp. 15–16.

122 Avi Asher-Schapiro, "The GOP Brotherhood of Egypt," *Salon,* January 25, 2012, http://www.salon.com/2012/01/26/the_gop_brotherhood_of_egypt.

Epilogue

1 For an analysis, by two Bank of England economists, of the relationship between the dominance of finance and short-termism in British industry in recent years, see Andrew Haldane and Richard Davies, "The Short Long," 29th Société Universitaire Européene de Recherches Financières Colloquium: New Paradigms in Money and Finance? Brussels, May 2011, http://www.bankofengland.co.uk/publications/Docu ments/speeches/2011/speech495.pdf.

2 Stanley Aronowitz and William DiFazio, *The Jobless Future* (Minneapolis: University of Minnesota Press, 2010).

3 William Baumol, Robert Litan, and Carl Schramm, *Good Capitalism, Bad Capitalism, and the Economics of Growth and Prosperity* (New Haven, Conn.: Yale University Press, 2007), http://www.escholarship.org/uc/item/3zt2b504, chap. 4.

4 For a powerful statement of this argument, see Dani Rodrik, *The Globalization Paradox: Why Global Markets, States and Democracy Can't Coexist* (Oxford: Oxford University Press, 2011).

5 That is, global current account imbalances, the sum of deficits and surpluses. William Speller, Gregory Thwaites, and Michelle Wright, "The Future of International Capital Flows," Financial Stability Paper No. 12, December 2011, http://www.bankofengland .co.uk/publications/fsr/fs_paper12.pdf, p. 16.

6 Evan Osnos, "Your Cheap Sweater's Real Cost," *Chicago Tribune,* December 16, 2006.

7 For this argument, see Tim Jackson, *Prosperity Without Growth: Economics for a Finite Planet* (London: Earthscan, 2009).

8 See Robin Blackburn, "Crisis Mark Two," *New Left Review,* vol. 72 (November–December 2011), pp. 33–62.

9 This is the argument of Richard Wilkinson and Kate Pickett in *The Spirit Level: Why Equality Is Better for Everyone* (New York: Bloomsbury, 2009).

10 Jeffrey Hollender, "The Rise of Shared Ownership and the Fall of Business as Usual," *Co.Exist* (blog), http://www.fastcoexist.com/1678189/the-rise-of-shared-ownership -and-the-fall-of-business-as-usual.

11 Bonaventura de Sousa Santos, "Participatory Budgeting in Porto Alegre: Toward a Redistributive Democracy," *Politics and Society,* vol. 26 (1998), pp. 461–510.

12 Ronald Inglehart, *Modernization and Postmodernization: Cultural, Economic and Political Change in 43 Societies* (Princeton, N.J.: Princeton University Press, 1997). This research has been the subject of a great deal of controversy, and there is particular disagreement

over whether attitudinal changes are related to the greater wealth of a society, or other changes. It is likely that changes in occupational structure have an impact.

13 Lizzy Davies and Simon Rogers, "Wellbeing Index Points Way to Bliss," *Guardian,* July 25, 2012.

14 Wilkinson and Pickett, *The Spirit Level,* pp. 73–77.

15 Sarah Boseley, "Work Stress Can Raise Risk of Heart Attack by 23%, Study Finds," *Guardian,* September 14, 2012.

16 See also Richard Sennett, *The Corrosion of Character* (New York: Norton, 2000); R. Layard, *Happiness: Lessons from a New Science* (London: Penguin, 2005), p. 67.

17 For the hierarchical nature of the "new capitalism" of the post-1980s era, see Luc Boltanski and Eve Chaipello, *The New Spirit of Capitalism* (London: Verso, 2006).

18 See, for instance, the working conditions of supermarket managers and their lack of autonomy. I. Grugulis, Ö. Bozkurt, and J. Clegg, "'No Place to Hide'? The Realities of Leadership in UK Supermarkets," http://www.skope.ox.ac.uk/sites/default/files /RP91.pdf.

19 For the sociology of the Tea Party, see Theda Skocpol and Vanessa Williamson, *The Tea Party and the Remaking of Republican Conservatism* (New York: Oxford University Press, 2012), p. 29. On martial metaphors, see ibid., p. 34.

20 S. L. de Lange, "A New Winning Formula? The Pragmatic Appeal of the Radical Right," *Party Politics,* vol. 13 (2007), pp. 411–35; Jens Rydgren, "The Sociology of the Radical Right," *Annual Review of Sociology,* vol. 33 (2007), p. 249; Daniel Oesch, "Explaining Workers' Support for Right-Wing Populist Parties in Western Europe: Evidence from Austria, Belgium, France, Norway, and Switzerland," *International Political Science Review,* vol. 29 (2008), pp. 349–73.

21 "Left Behind," *Economist,* September 10, 2011, http://www.economist.com/node /21528614.

22 Jim Weill and Eric Ribellarsi, "Interview with a Young Greek Communist," *Winter Has Its End,* http://winterends.net/greece-stories/76-interview-with-a-young-greek -communist. She is a member of KOE, not the traditional Communist KKE.

23 Ernest Drucker, *A Plague of Prisons: The Epidemiology of Mass Incarceration in America* (New York: New Press, 2011)

24 Jin Baisong, "Protectionism Is Not the Answer," *China Daily,* February 17, 2012, http://www.chinadaily.com.cn/cndy/2012-02/17/content_14628884.htm.

25 Cheng Li, "China's Fifth Generation: Is Diversity a Source of Strength or Weakness?" *Asia Policy,* vol. 6 (2008), pp. 85–87.

26 Austin Ramzy, "A Chinese Leader Talks Tough to Foreigners," *Time,* February 13, 2009, http://china.blogs.time.com/2009/02/13/a-chinese-leader-talks-tough-to-for eigners/#ixzz1miRG1HwG.

27 Allan Johnston, "Chinese Middle Class Attitudes Towards International Affairs: Nascent Liberalization?" *China Quarterly,* no. 179 (2004), pp. 603–28.

28 Sarah Neville, "Survey Throws Light on Evolving National Mood," *Financial Times,* September 18, 2012.

29 Pew Research Center, "Little Change in Public's Response to 'Capitalism,' 'Socialism,'" December 28, 2011, http://www.people-press.org/2011/12/28/little-change

-in-publics-response-to-capitalism-socialism/?src=prc-headline. Americans are also sharply divided by income and political partisanship.

30 Karl Marx, *The German Ideology,* in *Karl Marx, Friedrich Engels, Collected Works* (London: Lawrence and Wishart, 1975), vol. 5, p. 46.

Appendix

1 Michael Mann, *Sources of Social Power,* vol. 1, *A History of Power from the Beginning to A.D. 1760* (Cambridge: Cambridge University Press, 1986), p. 6.

2 Karl Marx and Friedrich Engels, *The Manifesto of the Communist Party* (London: Lawrence and Wishart, 1983).

3 Mann, *Sources of Social Power,* vol. 1, chap. 1.

4 See, for instance, R. Torstendahl's discussion of "organizational power" involving cooperation. R. Torstendahl, *Bureaucratisation in Northwestern Europe, 1880–1985: Domination and Governance* (London: Routledge, 1991), pp. 11–12.

5 For this point, see Collins, "Mann's Transformation of Classic Sociological Traditions," in John A. Hall and Ralph Schroeder, eds., *An Anatomy of Power: The Social Theory of Michael Mann* (Cambridge: Cambridge University Press, 2006), pp. 20–21.

6 Charles Tilly, *Coercion, Capital, and European States, A.D. 900–1992* (London: Blackwell, 1992).

7 Mann, *Sources of Social Power,* vol. 1, pp. 17–18.

8 On *doxa,* see Pierre Bourdieu, *The Logic of Practice* (Cambridge: Polity, 1990), p. 20. On *habitus,* see Pierre Bourdieu, *Outline of a Theory of Practice* (Cambridge: Polity, 1977), p. 95. For difficulties in interpreting the idea, see R. Jenkins, *Pierre Bourdieu* (London: Routledge, 2002), p. 90.

9 Luc Boltanski and Laurent Thévenot, *On Justification: Economies of Worth* (Princeton, N.J.: Princeton University Press, 2006).

10 Robert Erikson and John Goldthorpe, *The Constant Flux: A Study of Class Mobility in Industrial Societies* (Oxford: Oxford University Press, 1992).

11 See Herbert Kitschelt, *The Transformation of European Social Democracy* (Cambridge: Cambridge University Press, 1994), pp. 12–30. For a more elaborate scheme, but one based on the same principles, see Daniel Oesch, *Redrawing the Class Map: Institutions and Stratification in Britain, Germany, Sweden and Switzerland* (Basingstoke, U.K.: Macmillan, 2006); Daniel Oesch, "Remodelling Class to Make Sense of Service Employment: Evidence for Britain and Germany" (paper presented at CREST-ENSAE Seminar of Sociology, Paris, November 20, 2008). For evidence, see Romain Lachat and Daniel Oesch, "Beyond the Traditional Economic Divide: Class Location and Political Attitudes in 21 European Countries," http://www.romain-lachat.ch/papers/lachat_oesch_2007.pdf.

FURTHER READING

One of the best introductions to "big history"—the broad sweep of the history of the world and human societies—is David Christian, *Maps of Time: An Introduction to Big History* (Berkeley: University of California Press, 2005). For the distinction between commercial and agrarian states in European history, see Charles Tilly, *Coercion, Capital, and European States, A.D. 900–1992* (Oxford: Blackwell, 1992). See also Michael Mann, *The Sources of Social Power* (2 vols.) (Cambridge: Cambridge University Press, 1986 and 1993), for an important, though less accessible, sociological approach to European and world history. For two very different views of the rise of capitalism, see Fernand Braudel, *Civilization and Capitalism, 15th–18th Century* (London: Phoenix, 2002), and the Marxist Giovanni Arrighi, *The Long Twentieth Century: Money, Power, and the Origins of Our Times* (London: Verso, 1999). For comparisons between Western and Chinese development, see R. Bin Wong, *China Transformed: Historical Change and the Limits of European Experience* (Ithaca, N.Y.: Cornell University Press, 1997). On the Indian and Islamic worlds, see André Wink, *Al-Hind: The Making of the Indo-Islamic World* (3 vols.) (Leiden: Brill, 1990–2004); C. A. Bayly, *Rulers, Townsmen and Bazaars: North Indian Society in the Age of British Expansion, 1770–1870* (Cambridge: Cambridge University Press, 1983).

On the development of Britain and British power in the eighteenth and nineteenth centuries, see S. Pincus, *1688: The First Modern Revolution* (New

Haven, Conn.: Yale University Press, 2009); John Brewer, *The Sinews of Power: War, Money and the English State, 1688–1783* (London: Routledge, 1989); and Richard Price's stimulating survey, *British Society, 1680–1880* (Cambridge: Cambridge University Press, 1999). For Britain's international economic role, see P. Cain and A. Hopkins, *British Imperialism: Innovation and Expansion, 1688–1914* (London: Longman, 1993). See especially Chris Bayly's impressively wide-ranging global history, *The Birth of the Modern World: Global Connections and Comparisons* (Oxford: Blackwell, 2004).

On the United States and the development of its form of capitalism, see the controversial C. Sellers, *The Market Revolution: Jacksonian America, 1815–1849* (New York: Oxford University Press, 1991), and a stimulating essay on American distinctiveness, Eric Rauchway, *Blessed Among Nations: How the World Made America* (New York: Hill and Wang, 2006). On America and consumerism, see Gary Cross, *An All-Consuming Century: Why Commercialism Won in Modern America* (New York: Columbia University Press, 2000). For the impact of American capitalist culture on Europe and the world, see Victoria De Grazia, *Irresistible Empire: America's Advance Through 20th-Century Europe* (Cambridge, Mass.: Harvard University Press, 2005), and Emily Rosenberg, *Spreading the American Dream: American Economic and Cultural Expansion, 1890–1945* (New York: Hill and Wang, 1982). On differences between forms of industrial organization, see William Lazonick, *Business Organization and the Myth of the Market Economy* (Cambridge: Cambridge University Press, 1991).

For the economic crisis of the interwar period, see Peter Fearon, *War, Prosperity and Depression: The US Economy, 1917–1945* (Deddington, U.K.: Philip Allan, 1987), and Charles Feinstein, Peter Temin, and Gianni Toniolo, *The European Economy Between the Wars* (Oxford: Oxford University Press, 1997). See also Jeffry Frieden's accessible history of the global economy, *Global Capitalism: Its Fall and Rise in the Twentieth Century* (New York: Norton, 2006). On alternatives to 1920s liberalism in the mid-twentieth century, see Peter Fritzsche, *Life and Death in the Third Reich* (Cambridge, Mass.: Harvard University Press, 2008); Claudia Koonz, *The Nazi Conscience* (Cambridge, Mass.: Harvard University Press, 2003); M. Barnhart, *Japan Prepares for Total War* (Ithaca, N.Y.: Cornell University Press, 1987); David Priestland, *The Red Flag: Communism and the Making of the Modern World* (London: Allen Lane, 2009); Sheri

Berman, *The Social Democratic Moment: Ideas and Politics in the Making of Interwar Europe* (Cambridge, Mass.: Harvard University Press, 1998); and Anthony Badger, *The New Deal: The Depression Years, 1933–1940* (Basingstoke; U.K.: Macmillan, 1989).

For analyses of postwar welfare states and political economies in the West, see Gøsta Esping-Andersen, *The Three Worlds of Welfare Capitalism* (Cambridge: Polity, 1990), and Peter Hall and David Soskice, *Varieties of Capitalism: The Institutional Foundations of Comparative Advantage* (Oxford: Oxford University Press, 2001). On the role of the Third World in the Cold War politics of the era, see Arne Westad, *The Global Cold War: Third World Interventions and the Making of Our Times* (Cambridge: Cambridge University Press, 2005); on 1968, see Gerd-Rainer Horn, *The Spirit of '68: Rebellion in Western Europe and North America, 1956–1976* (Oxford: Oxford University Press, 2007).

On neoliberalism and globalization, see Mark Blyth, *Great Transformations: Economic Ideas and Institutional Change in the Twentieth Century* (Cambridge: Cambridge University Press, 2002); Monica Prasad, *The Politics of Free Markets: The Rise of Neoliberal Economic Policies in Britain, France, Germany and the United States* (Chicago: University of Chicago Press, 2006); Barry Eichengreen, *Globalizing Capital: A History of the International Monetary System* (Princeton, N.J.: Princeton University Press, 2004); and Gérard Duménil and Dominique Levy, *The Crisis of Neoliberalism* (Cambridge, Mass.: Harvard University Press, 2011). On the broader culture of the 1980s and '90s in the United States, see Daniel Rodgers, *Age of Fracture* (Cambridge, Mass.: Harvard University Press, 2011). On the market in Russia after 1991, see Peter Reddaway and Dmitri Glinski, *The Tragedy of Russia's Reforms: Market Bolshevism Against Democracy* (Washington, D.C.: United States Institute of Peace Press, 2001); on Eastern Europe, see Gil Eyal, Iván Szelényi, and Eleanor Townsley, *Making Capitalism Without Capitalists: The New Ruling Elites in Eastern Europe; Class Formation and Elite Struggles in Post-Communist Central Europe* (London: Verso, 1998); on China and India, see Pranab Bardhan, *Awakening Giants, Feet of Clay: Assessing the Economic Rise of China and India* (Princeton, N.J.: Princeton University Press, 2010).

INDEX